I'VE BEEN USED

PRICE 5L $25 15

Recycle your money
Buy used books
A.S. BOOKSTORE
CSU - CHICO

Data Structures

From Arrays to Priority Queues

Wadsworth Series in Computer Information Systems

Data Structures

From Arrays to Priority Queues

Wayne Amsbury

Northwest Missouri State University

Wadsworth Publishing Company
Belmont, California
A Division of Wadsworth, Inc.

Computer Science Editor: *Frank Ruggirello*
Production: *Mary Forkner, Publication Alternatives*
Text Designer: *Michael Rogondino*
Copy Editor: *Joan Pendleton*
Technical Illustrator: *Carol Johnston*
Cover Design: *Stephen Osborn*
Signing Representative: *Myron Flemming*

© 1985 by Wadsworth, Inc. All rights reserved. No part of this book may be reproduced, stored in a retrieval system, or transcribed, in any form or by any means, electronic, mechanical, photocopying, recording, or otherwise, without the prior written permission of the publisher, Wadsworth Publishing Company, Belmont, California 94002, a division of Wadsworth, Inc.

Printed in the United States of America

1 2 3 4 5 6 7 8 9 10—89 88 87 86 85

ISBN 0-534-04590-1

Library of Congress Cataloging in Publication Data

Amsbury, Wayne, 1935–
   Data structures.

   Bibliography: p.
   Includes index.
   1. Data structures   (Computer science)   I. Title.
QA76.9.D35A47   1985   001.64′4   85-3159
ISBN 0-534-04590-1

Contents

v

Preface

Many application programs and discussions of topics in computer science are awkward without a relatively extensive acquaintance with data structures. Hence, the data structures course is moving rapidly downward in the curriculum. In the last few years it has changed from being a graduate-level course in analytical techniques to a foundation course for undergraduates and nonmajors. If it isn't already, data structures soon will be taught at four-year colleges as a prerequisite for most upper-level computer science courses and as a terminal computer science course in two-year programs and for many nonmajors. Consequently, the course is taught on a wide range of levels. The broadening of the audience requires some adjustment in the way a data structures course is taught.

Although its wide range of content and academic rigor make it suitable for use in higher-level courses, *Data Structures: From Arrays to Priority Queues* is intended to serve a broader audience. The book can function as an introduction to data structures quite early in the development of programming mastery. It is aimed at the student who has had one or more semesters of programming in a structured language and no specific college mathematics. At lower levels, a data structures course needs to develop algorithmic sophistication rather than exercise mathematical skills. Thus, this book keeps the comparison of data structures and algorithms in constant view, but it does not require a great deal of mathematical sophistication. *Data Structures* brings the reader to an awareness of the timing of algorithms, particularly at the level of the order of growth, but extensive analysis of algorithms applied to data structures is left to later courses. The intent is to foster an appreciation of the effectiveness of data structures and their associated algorithms, but in an introduction it is more important to construct a workable set of tools than to hone a smaller set. Data structures *themselves* are the primary focus, not their detailed analysis.

The topic of data structures plays much the same essential role in computer science that calculus plays in mathematics. The *apparent agenda* in a data structures course is the comparative study of alternate ways to solve and implement program solutions to problems. The *hidden agenda* is the development of an understanding of the use of abstraction in problem solving. This book focuses on the hidden agenda as a foundation for study of the apparent agenda. Skill in abstraction is developed gradually, as a natural part of problem solving with programs. Three features that explicitly address the hidden agenda are:

1. Use of Pascal-like pseudocode

2. Comparison of algorithmic and implementation variations

3. Generalized algorithms for data structure traverses

A form of pseudocode is used to present algorithms for several reasons. One reason is simply that no one language is ideal for all purposes, is used universally, or is dominant forever. A number of languages, including Algol, Pascal, ADA, and Modula-2, have common features extracted here. Another reason for presenting algorithms in pseudocode for the reader to translate into a working language is that the task requires some effort, but not too much. Translation requires a choice of parameter-passing classes for procedure variables and attention to some other details. Translating pseudocode does not, however, require the time and effort needed to *derive* an algorithm. An extensive amount of conceptual material can be presented succinctly in pseudocode. Use of pseudocode thus provides an appropriate balance between covering the maximum amount of ground and providing in-depth understanding of the details of the geography that is traversed. Use of pseudocode, plus examples in the text, also helps readers to develop skill in abstraction and understanding of shell-structuring and modularity.

The management of data structures involves pitfalls that lead to subtle bugs in programs, and such potential problems are best exposed by being viewed from several perspectives. Therefore, *Data Structures* emphasizes the variety of solutions to problems. For example, general traverse algorithms are developed for lists, binary trees, and priority queues. Such general algorithms provide a framework within which variations can be created and problems can be solved. The algorithms can be tailored to specific applications, and the exercise of doing so has merit in itself. The general algorithms are better guides to the variations needed for applications than is one specific variation that often fails to fit. General algorithms also promote the development of skill in abstraction in a relatively gentle way.

A separate collection of expansion and enrichment sections is included in Part II. The sections introduce or explore in depth topics that are related to the mainstream of the text. Some of these sections contain substantial working Pascal programs, initially developed in pseudocode, which provide examples of program development. The instructor thus has options for major examples, enrichment, and independent reading assignments, yet because the additional sections are separate, they do not distract from the main content.

To help the instructor tailor the course to students with varied backgrounds, most topics in the book can be covered at a variety of levels:

1. Pictorial discussion and general comprehension

2. Tracing of the crucial process(es) acting on a specific example

3. Pseudocode detailing of an algorithm with discussion of problems and variations

4. Program assignments based on class discussion

5. Program assignments based on reading

6. Experimentation with programs and analysis of the results

Potential assignments are separated into exercises, problems, programs, and projects, and the amount of effort required increases in that order. Possible assignments are mentioned in the text where they are appropriate, but they are grouped together at the end of the chapter so they can be found easily at any time. Summaries offer the reader an overview of material in each chapter.

The instructor's manual includes answers to the exercises and problems and a Pascal solution to a program assignment from each chapter.

The flexibility designed into this text has allowed it to be used at NWMSU for classes with students of mixed backgrounds, many of whom are second-semester freshmen. The central thrust of the course is coverage of the sections in Part One of this text that are not marked *optional*. In that course, Chapter 7 is considered remedial but is available for self-study, the timing-function portion of Chapter 1 is the only part of that chapter requiring class time, and Chapter 10 is seldom reached. Some optional sections in Part I and various sections of Part II are selected by instructors for supplementary readings, assignments, and sometimes class discussion.

Thorough coverage of the entire text requires a second semester or a very fast pace for even well-prepared students. The intent of the rich offering of Part II and the optional sections in Part I is to support flexibility through the selection of sections and levels of coverage. (Besides, students *will* explore accessible material on their own.)

The reviewers listed below made many suggestions that were incorporated into this book and improved it immeasurably. They are not, however, responsible for the remaining errors, whether inadvertant or stubborn: Cathy Dickerson, Black Hawk College; William H. Ford, University of the Pacific; Ken Friedenbach, University of Santa Clara; Judith L. Gersting, Indiana University-Purdue University; Henry Gordon, Kutztown State College; Nancy Griffeth, Georgia Institute of Technology; Greg Jones, Providence, Utah; Leonard Larsen, University of Wisconsin, Eau Claire; Louise Moyer, California State University, Hayward; Ron Peterson, Weber State College; Douglas Re, San Francisco Community College; Dean Sanders, Illinois State University.

Two groups of people aided and abetted this work in ways that must remain untold in detail but are appreciated in depth. One group is a team assembled by Wadsworth that includes: Myron Flemming, Frank Ruggirello, Serina Beauparlant, Mary Forkner, and Joan Pendleton. The other group consists of colleagues at

NWMSU: Merry McDonald, Gary McDonald, Robert Franks, Hong-Shi Yuan, Phil Heeler, and Margaret Adams.

My brother, David, put considerable effort into improving my technical writing in the early stages of this book, and I can only hope that the effect carried through the project.

Finally, this book could not have been produced if my wife, Carlene, had not taken over virtually all of the management of a busy household while working full time.

Wayne Amsbury

PART ONE

The Mainstream

Chapter 1

Algorithms and Timing Analysis

The usual way of learning to program a computer is to write programs that solve direct, simple problems. A natural result is that programs written during the learning process are quite short; they focus on some new idea or language feature. By contrast, many interesting and useful programs require greater effort than do these beginning exercises.

Some program applications are interesting or useful to many people, and good programs that deal with them are important and sometimes commercially valuable. These programs include games and simulations of competitive quality, electronic spreadsheets, accounting packages, class rollbook managers, scheduling programs, inventory control packages, and systems software that makes the use of microprocessors easier. A commercial program that takes less than a person-year of full-time effort is considered ''small.''

Because commercially available software does not always match individual needs precisely, a great deal of programming is largely redundant. The solution to this waste is to develop high-quality software designed with concern for flexibility and generality. The variety of needs in the computing community is expanding exponentially because of the increase in the number and variety of users. There will be a large demand for nontrivial software for some time to come, and someone must fill it. (Some entrepreneurs have even created a demand and filled it at the same time by writing a program that proved to be a generally useful tool.) The programming that can satisfy these demands is eased by the knowledgeable use of computing resources, and that involves the structuring of data.

1.1 Sophistication in Programming

Interesting applications call for sophisticated programs. They seldom call for programs that are merely long or for the use of the minor details of a particular programming language. This textbook is designed to help students learn to write interesting, nontrivial programs. That requires sophistication, which is based on *technique, analysis,* and *knowledge.*

■   A crucial aspect of programming *technique* is developing a logical structure that makes each program easier to read, debug, alter, and document—in short, that makes it an effective tool for communication. The technique of structured programming is a major feature of introductory programming books; this book will reinforce the reader's practice of it, in part through examples and in part through writing programs that demand (1) clean structure and (2) modularization.

■   *Analysis* is needed to determine how effectively a proposed program solves a given problem. The effectiveness of a program is determined by its use of resources—memory, computing time, and programming time. Quite often, the comparison of programs is reduced to the comparison of the problem-solving processes—the *algorithms*—upon which the programs are based. The analysis of algorithms is a major topic in itself, but it is introduced very briefly in this chapter. The ideas that are introduced are used to make comparisons throughout the book, and analysis problems are included at the end of several chapters.

■   Comparisons cannot be made without *knowledge* of more than one approach to a problem. Effective ways to arrange and manage data are not always obvious to the beginning programmer. There are applications and relationships between applications that one does not realize when first learning to program.

The intent of this book, then, is to provide a solid basis of knowledge to underlie programming sophistication while reinforcing structured programming and promoting an awareness of analysis.

The Data Structures Connection

The study of data structures is a natural link between learning a programming language and writing application programs. Data may be arranged and managed at many levels: within memory; at the programming-language level; in terms of the logical structure of an algorithm; and at the conceptual level, where a mental image of arrangements and relationships is developed. Programming tactics can differ at each of these levels, and the levels interact. For example, suppose that algorithms *Alpha* and *Beta* solve the same problem. *Alpha* is more wasteful of some resource than is *Beta,* and *Beta* is easy to implement in language A but awkward or costly in programming time to implement in language B. If programming is to be done in language A, *Beta* is the obvious choice, but if it is to be done in language B, a balance must be struck. The specific details of the application determine whether the awkwardness of *Beta* or the waste of the resource by *Alpha* is more significant.

A common example of the interaction among these levels is that the algorithms used for manipulating data in one structural arrangement are different from those used to manage data arranged in another structure. The overall plan of attack for a problem depends on a choice of data structures, which in turn may depend on features of the language to be used.

The Use of Pseudocode

The separation of a structure from any particular level of design means specifically that the structure must not be confused with a feature of some programming language, or even of such languages in general. Part of the separation is possible when algorithms are described in a form of *pseudocode.* Pseudocode is a carefully restricted set of statements that describe the logic of a program for *people* but not for computers. The restrictions promote good programming; pseudocode statements are chosen to allow easy translation into programming languages. This approach can cause problems when used in a cavalier fashion, because some "solutions" to a problem may prove difficult to implement in a working language. For example,

Unlock(door)

is a neat solution to a problem—if you have a key (that is, if the procedure *Unlock* can be rendered in a practical way). Pseudocode is used in the pages that follow, but we keep in mind that algorithms are to be translated into a working language before use, with a structured language such as Pascal, ADA, or Modula-2. Clean, logical structures are easier to translate into these languages than into others, but each language has its own foibles because each is itself the result of choices.

The conversion of a pseudocode description of an algorithm into a working language is a learning experience that focuses on the logic involved and distinguishes that logic from language features. A program or procedure given in executable form can be applied blindly and without understanding. Pseudocode requires some attention but no major effort to translate. At the same time, translating an algorithm into code is much quicker and easier than deriving the algorithm itself and thus increases the amount of material that can be applied in a limited time.

The meaning of each of the pseudocode structures used in this book is explained in the next section.

> **Note:** Part II of this book, "Expansions and Applications," includes working programs realized in Pascal. They implement some of the procedures presented in pseudocode in the main part of the text.

1.2 The Pseudocode Language SUE

If it weren't for the powerful effects of data structures and of other ideas, commands given to computers could be comfortably limited to six basic operations:

1. Copy data from one memory cell to another.

2. Perform arithmetic and logical operations.

3. Input data: place data from the outside world into memory.

4. Output data: retrieve data from memory and send it to the outside world.

5. Branch unconditionally to some command.

6. Branch on the truth of a condition to some command.

These commands are communicated to a computer from a translator (usually a compiler or assembler). The translator derives the commands from *statements* in the language being translated. Because such statements need to be explicit and unambiguous, they involve rules of syntax and conventions that are not really required to describe the logic of a program. Algorithms, which communicate program logic to people, can be reduced to simpler and more universal statements than current working languages allow.

The logical structures that follow are universal in the sense that the ideas involved can be implemented in any language. The language SUE is designed to focus attention on these logical structures, to be flexible, and to be expandable as required. All of the algorithms in this book are described in SUE.

> **Note:** The name SUE has been used for other languages, but it is difficult to avoid all short mnemonics; SUE is used here only as a useful abbreviation.

The essential constructs of SUE are

variable ← *expression*	*Assignment. The keystrokes that form the assignment operator are a matter of syntax.*
Write($v_1, v_2, \ldots, v_n$)	*Output the values of a list of variables or messages. (The distinctions between* Write *and* Writeln *in Pascal, and between the effects of commas and semicolons in* BASIC, *are features of specific languages.)*
Read($v_1, v_2, \ldots, v_n$)	*Input the values of a list of variables. This form, and* Write, *will also serve for files when* v_1 *is a file identifier.*

Read and *Write* are intended to be more general than they are in most working languages. Variables may be of *any* structural type in SUE. The format of the output of an array, record, or other variable type is provided during the translation of SUE into a working language:

if *condition*
  then S_1
  else S_2
  endif
	S_1 *and* S_2 *may be any sequence of statements. The* **else** *phrase may be missing. In a nested structure, an* **else** *phrase is taken to be part of the most recent* **if.**

For example

if $A < B$
  then if $A < C$
      then *Write(C)*
      else *Write(A)*
      endif
  endif

will, when $A = 2$, $B = 3$, and $C = 1$, display 2. By contrast, if the **else** were taken to be the alternate condition for the first **if,** there would be no output from this segment. Astute indention may resolve an **else** for the human reader, but it will not do so for a computer, and so **endif** terminates all **if** statements in the text.

Another kind of selection statement is **case,** which may appear in two forms:

case
  $cond_1$: S_1
  $cond_2$: S_2
     .
     .
     .
  $cond_n$: S_n
  else: S_e
endcase
	The conditions $cond_i$ *must be TRUE or FALSE.* S_i *can be any sequence of statements, and will be executed iff (if and only if)* $cond_i$ *is TRUE. It is the programmer's responsibility to make sure that only one condition can be TRUE; there should be no overlap. The* **else** *may be omitted, in which case if no* $cond_i$ *is TRUE, then no execution will take place in this statement.*

case of V
  $Value_1$: S_1
  $Value_2$: S_2
     .
     .
     .
  $Value_n$: S_n
  else: S_e
endcase
	Here the variable V *must take on discrete values. It is sometimes convenient to use values such as* Small, Medium, Large—*instead of, for example, 1,2,3—although many languages do not support this feature. A language that restricts* **case** *values to be ordinal (ordered discrete), may require a table lookup or other map for implementation.*

General **case** structures sometimes must be resolved in terms of nested **if . . . then . . . else** statements in a program.

    Loop structures may be classified by the location of the test for exit from the loop: at the top, at the bottom, or in the middle. They all must determine the beginning and the end of the loop; that is, what is included and what is not, as well as the exit-test position. The three essential loop forms in SUE are:

repeat
  S_1
  if *cond* **then exit endif**
  S_2
  forever
[*next statement*]
	Here S_1 *and* S_2 *may be any sequence of statements. The test for exit is in the middle, not at the top or at the bottom. The condition must be* TRUE *or* FALSE. *The exit passes control to* [next statement].

> **Note:** Not all structured languages (notably standard Pascal) provide for **exit.** An exit can be made from any loop by declaring a label and using a *GOTO* (an unconditional branch).

An example of a *GOTO* in Pascal is

Pascal	SUE
| ```
REPEAT
   Read(x);
   IF x < 0 THEN GOTO 1;
   Sum := Sum + x
UNTIL Sum > 100;
1 : Write(Sum)
``` | **repeat**<br>  *Read(x)*<br>  **if** *x < 0* **then exit endif**<br>  *Sum* ← *Sum + x*<br>  **until** *Sum > 100*<br>*Write(Sum)* |

repeat
  S
  until *cond*
	The condition cond *must be* TRUE *or* FALSE. S *is any sequence of statements. The test for exit occurs explicitly at the bottom, thus* S *will be executed at least once.* S *may include an* **exit.**

while *cond* **do**
  S
  endwhile
	The condition cond *must be* TRUE *or* FALSE. S *is any sequence of statements. The test for exit occurs explicitly at the top, thus* S *may not be executed at all.* S *may include an* **exit.**

```

A common mode of looping is the use of a control variable as a counter to keep track of the passes through a loop. This may be done in SUE with:

for v = *Init* **to** *Final* **by** *Step* **do**   S *is any sequence of statements. The* **next** v
  S   *may be replaced by* **endfor** *if convenient.*
  next v *The* **by** Step *part is omitted when the* Step
    value is 1. The use of **downto** *and a nega-*
    tive step value will run the count from high
    to low.

The **for** loop is equivalent to the following, with one disclaimer stated below:

$v \leftarrow$ *Init*   Init, Final, *and* Step *may be expressions,*
while $v \leq$ *Final* **do**   *and the control values derived from them on*
  S   *entry to the loop do not change during loop*
  $v \leftarrow v +$ *Step*   *execution. This is true even if they are vari-*
  endwhile   *ables that have assignments made to them*
    within the loop. The expression Step *may be*
    negative, in which case the test for exit
    becomes **while** $v \geq$ *Final* **do.**

The disclaimer is that—in some languages and on some machines—compiler programs apply sophisticated (increment-and-branch) instructions in the translation of the **for** loop construct. The exact translation is determined by the writer(s) of the compiler and influenced by the properties of the hardware, not by definition of the language alone. Although the **for** loop is usually implemented in programming languages as a **while,** this is not always the case. For example, the *FOR . . . NEXT* loop in at least one heavily used BASIC translator is essentially a **repeat . . . until** structure, as is the analogous FORTRAN *DO* loop. In SUE, a **for** is a specific form of **while,** and the value of v immediately upon completion of the loop is *unknown.*

1.2.1 Subprograms

Computing languages differ in the way they pass information between programs or between parts of one program. SUE simplifies the description of information-sharing as much as possible, while remaining consistent with the modularization of programs in structured languages.

A *procedure* in SUE is a segment of code that is independent in the sense that it can be invoked conveniently, it does a specified task, and it then returns control to the point immediately following its invocation. A *program* is itself a procedure that may invoke functions or other procedures, called *subprograms*. A list of parameters that provide information to or return information from a procedure may be included in the invocation and the definition. Variables not listed are considered to be global (defined and available outside of the procedure). As an example:

procedure *Main*

.

.

.

Sum ← 0

AddAbs(*x*)

Read(*y*)

AddAbs(*y*)

Write(*Sum*)

.

.

.

end {*Main*

procedure *AddAbs*(*v*)

  if *v* < 0

    then *Sum* ← *Sum* − *v*

    else *Sum* ← *Sum* + *v*

  endif

end {*AddAbs*

The variable *Sum* is global to *AddAbs*, but *v* is local. This means that the identifier *v* is redefined within *AddAbs*, and its relationship to *x* and *y* is determined at the time of individual invocations. Identifier *v* is a parameter that is related to *x* the first time, and to *y* in the second call.

The formal parameter *v* can be related to actual parameters *x* and *y* in two major ways:

1. Treat *x* (or *y*) as an expression. Its value is stored locally in *v*. No other information about the source is available to *Abs*. In this case, *v* is called a *value parameter*.

2. Treat *x* (or *y*) as an address. The address is stored in *v*, which becomes a *pointer*. Whenever an assignment is made in *Abs* to *v*, the assignment is actually to the (actual) parameter *x*. In this case, *v* is called a *variable parameter*.

The passing of parameters to subprograms is a major topic in programming languages, and no attempt to resolve or restrict it is made in SUE. A parameter in SUE may be of either type, but it is generally left unspecified. The choice may be important during implementation of an algorithm in a specific language. The best guide to making this choice is an understanding of the algorithm.

A *function* in SUE is a procedure that returns a single value. A function, therefore, may be invoked by using it anywhere that a variable can be used. The result that it calculates becomes the value of the function name. For example:

procedure *Main*
   .
   .
   .
  Sum ← 0
  Sum ← *Sum* + *Abs*(*x*)
  Read(*y*)
  Sum ← *Sum* + *Abs*(*y*)
  Write(*Sum*)
   .
   .
   .
end {*Main*

function *Abs*(*v*)
  if *v* < 0
    then *Abs* ← −*v*
    else *Abs* ← *v*
  endif
end {*Abs*

The essential distinction between *Abs* and *AddAbs* is that the identifier *Abs* is assigned a value in its definition and can be used to retrieve that value, but the identifier *AddAbs* has no assigned value—it is the name of a subprogram that performs a task.

A valuable tool for presenting the logic of some algorithms (and for implementing them when it is available) is **return.** A **return** may be used to exit immediately from a subprogram at any point. If the subprogram is a function, **return** *v* indicates that *v* is to be returned as the functional value. When it is not available as a language feature, **return** is implemented much like **exit.**

The correspondence between Pascal, for example, and SUE can be quite close:

Pascal

```
FUNCTION Min(m,n : REAL): REAL;
   LABEL    1;
   BEGIN
     IF (m < 0) AND (n < 0)
        THEN BEGIN
          Min := 0;
          GOTO 1
          END;
     IF m > n
        THEN Min := n
        ELSE Min := m;
 1 : END;
```

SUE

function *Min*(*m*,*n*)

  if *(m < 0)* AND *(n < 0)*

    then return *0*

  endif
  if *m > n*
    then return *n*
    else return *m*
  endif
end {*Min*

> **Note:** Simplifications applied in this book are the use of global variables and of multiple exits (from loops) and multiple returns (from subprograms). It is only their thoughtful use that is being endorsed here, and they may be routinely removed when algorithms are translated into a working language.

1.2.2 Records and Pointers

For the sake of completeness, records and pointers are reviewed in this section.

In a gradebook program, a name and a score may be kept in separate arrays (because they are of different types) and tied together logically by giving them the same index. An alternate storage structure for the names and scores is a *record*, perhaps declared by:

$Result$ = RECORD
    Name: STRING
    Score: INTEGER
    END   {*Result*

Result

Name
Score

A *record,* as it is used here, is a data structure in its own right, available in many languages. As a structure, however, it differs from the array structure in only two ways:

1. The cells of a record do not need to contain data of identical type.

2. The identifier of a cell (called a *field* in a record) is not an index, but a name. For a variable *Good* of type *Result, Good.Name* identifies the field of type STRING and *Good.Score* identifies the field of type INTEGER.

Some data structures are formed from records called *nodes* that are linked together in the sense that a node contains the address of one or more other nodes. Such addresses are made available as variables so they can be altered. A variable that contains the *address* of data, rather than the *value* of data in question, is called a *pointer* variable.

In a simple structure, nodes may contain single values (of some type). Each node also contains an address value, called a *link,* and so it can be declared to be:

$Nodule$ = RECORD
    Value : REAL
    Link : ↑ *Nodule* {*a pointer to records*
                {*of type* Nodule
    END {*Nodule*

Nodule

Value
Link

For a variable *xNode* of type *Nodule*, *xNode.Value* is the name of the field of type *REAL*, and *xNode.Link* is the name of the field of type ↑*Nodule*.

Suppose that *xNode* is a record of type *Nodule*. A pointer to a record like *xNode* assumes the role of a node identifier, simply because a pointer, like an identifier, is a *locator*. (Both technically determine more information than simply an address, but it is the same information as that provided by languages that allow pointer variables.) If *x* is a pointer to *xNode*, then *x* ↑ is itself an identifier *xNode*, and there may not be a need for a variable *xNode*. The value of *x* is the address of *xNode*. This is pictorially represented by:

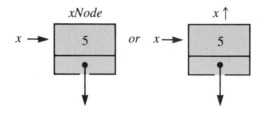

If *xNode* is of type *Nodule*, then *x* is of type ↑ *Nodule*. When *p* is a pointer of type ↑ *Nodule*, then NEW(*p*) will be assumed to have the effect

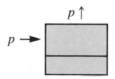

without an assumed initialization of *p* ↑ .

1.3 The Timing of Algorithms

Comparisons of algorithms are made on the basis of the management of resources, and one crucial resource is execution time. It is generally not necessary to determine exact execution times, which may be data-dependent or machine-dependent anyway and which can be seriously misleading in interactive systems. There is an important difference, however, between an algorithm that takes a minute or so to run and one that takes an hour.

The difference in execution times between two approaches to solving a problem may be small for small data sets; for large data sets, by contrast, the execution times of one approach may grow very differently from those of the other. For algorithms that are to be used many times, any difference can be significant, but generally an analysis of execution time concentrates on *how it grows* with the increasing size of data sets.

The growth of execution time as a function of the size of the problem data provides a basis for comparing ways of solving the problem.

A simple approach that is frequently adequate for our purposes can be applied to the following program segment:

[*statement 1*]
for $i = 1$ **to** n **do**
   [*statement 2*]
   [*statement 3*]
   next i

An analysis may begin by assuming that [*statement k*] takes one unit of time for $k = 1,2,3$. Then this segment requires one unit of time for [*statement 1*] followed by two units of time for each pass through the **for** loop. Therefore, the execution time is

$$T(n) = 1 + 2n$$

This can be easily generalized by assuming that [*statement i*] requires t_i units of time:

$$T(n) = t_1 + (t_2 + t_3)n$$

This equation remains true even if [*statement 2*] is itself a loop that always requires the same amount of time to execute. For example, if [*statement 2*] is

[*statement 2*]: **for** $j = 1$ **to** m **do**
       [*statement 4*]
       next j $\{t_2 = m \cdot t_4$

Complications arise, however, if the execution of [*statement 2*] depends upon i:

[*statement 2*]: **for** $j = 1$ **to** i **do**
       [*statement 4*]
       next j

Now we have, since $m = i$:

$$t_2 = i \cdot t_4$$

$$T(n) = t_1 + \sum_{i=1}^{n} [\, i \cdot t_4 + t_3 \,]$$

$$= t_1 + t_4 \times \left[\sum_{i=1}^{n} i \right] + n \cdot t_3$$

At this point, we need to document some of the properties of summations, because loop execution times are a sum of the times required for each pass through them.

(i) $\displaystyle\sum_{i=1}^{n} 1 = 1 + 1 + \cdots + 1 = n$ (n ones)

(ii) $\displaystyle\sum_{i=1}^{n} i = 1 + 2 + \cdots + n = \frac{n(n+1)}{2}$

(iii) $\displaystyle\sum_{i=1}^{n} i^2 = 1 + 2^2 + \cdots + n^2 = \frac{n(n+1)(2n+1)}{6}$

(iv) $\displaystyle\sum_{i=k}^{n} f(i) = f(k) + f(k+1) + \cdots + f(n)$

where $k < n$ and f is any function of i

(v) $\displaystyle\sum_{i=k}^{n} [a \cdot f(i) + b] = \left[a \sum_{i=k}^{n} f(i) \right] + (n - k + 1) \cdot b$

where a and b are not functions of i

From equation ii, then, the value of $T(n)$ is:

$$T(n) = t_1 + t_4 \frac{n(n+1)}{2} + n \cdot t_3$$

If it may be assumed that $t_1 = t_3 = t_4 = 1$, then:

$$T(n) = n + 1 + \frac{n(n+1)}{2} = \frac{n^2}{2} + \frac{3n}{2} + 1$$

a quadratic function on n.

As a more specific example, consider:

EP1.1 Input n numbers, and list those that follow the occurrence of the minimal entry value.

One solution is:

program *TrailMin*
  Read(Entry[1])
  Mindex ← 1
  for *i* = 2 **to** *n* **do**
    Read(Entry[i])
    if *Entry[i] < Entry[Mindex]*
      then *Mindex* ← *i*
      endif
    next *i*
  for *i* = *Mindex* + *1* **to** *n* **do**
    Write(Entry[i])
    next *i*
  end {*TrailMin*

In order to make a detailed analysis of the execution time of *TrailMin*, it would be necessary to assume some relative execution times of the *Read*, *Write*, **if,** and assignment statements and to perhaps consider the test-for-exit overhead implicit in the **for** statement. A first approximation ignores these differences and concentrates on the number of times that statements are executed. This provides a basis for an overview of the behavior of an algorithm.

With the simplifying assumption that each statement requires one unit of time, the timing function for *TrailMin* is:

$$T(n) = 2 + \sum_{i=2}^{n} 2 + \sum_{i=Mindex+1}^{n} 1$$

$$= 2 + 2[n - 2 + 1] + [n - Mindex]$$

$$T(n) = 3n - Mindex$$

Clearly, though, *Mindex* may be a function of *n* itself. In section 1.3.2 it is shown that *Mindex* can be expected to have the middle value $(n + 1)/2$, and so $T(n)$ may be taken to be $(5n/2) - \frac{1}{2}$ as a reasonable approximation. If the point of the analysis is the growth of $T(n)$ as *n* increases, then it is enough to have found that $T(n)$ is of the form: $a \cdot n + b$, a linear function of *n*.

The growth behavior of an algorithm is quite often taken to be the salient fact revealed by timing analysis, and it will be explored further in the next section. Growth behavior provides a way to choose between algorithms that are to be applied to large data sets.

Another way to characterize *Mindex* as a function of *n* arises from the recognition that the execution time of *Mindex* is partly determined by the distribution of values in the sequence of entries. Random variation plays a role in the behavior of algorithms, and thus statistics should play a role both in the comparison of algorithms and in the study of the data structures on which they are founded. (See section 1.3.2.)

The analysis of algorithms includes the study of the worst-case data set of a given size, the (statistical) average case, and the limits imposed by the problem itself. In some cases, results of importance are derived experimentally. In this text, the intent is in a rough but convenient measure that is fairly easy to recognize for common algorithms. That measure is the *order of growth.*

1.3.1 The Order of Growth

Not all timing functions are linear in the size of the data set being processed. Common timing functions include quadratics and other polynomials, logarithms (a base of 2 is used in such studies), exponential functions, and others. These functions grow with n at dramatically different rates, as Table 1.1 reveals.

Table 1.1

n	1	2	4	16	256	4096	65536
$\ln n$	0	1	2	4	8	12	16
$n \cdot \ln n$	0	2	8	64	2048	49152	1048576
n^2	1	2	16	256	65536	16777216	4.295×10^9
n^3	1	8	64	4096	16777216	6.872×10^{10}	2.815×10^{14}
2^n	2	4	16	65536	1.16×10^{77}	$>10^{1232}$	Huge

Suppose that procedure A and procedure B are both solutions to the same problem, and the timing functions for A and B are:

$$TA(n) = n \cdot \ln n \qquad TB(n) = n^2$$

Suppose further that a time unit is 1 microsecond (10^{-6} second). Then whenever $n = 1024$, $TA(n)$ is about 0.01 second, and $TB(n)$ is about 1 second. However, for $n = 65536$, $TA(n)$ is about 1 second, and $TB(n)$ is roughly 1 hour and 12 minutes. If these procedures need to be used several times to accomplish some task, then procedure B becomes impractical for large data sets. A third procedure with $T(n) = 2^n$ would require 2.81×10^{14} years to deal with just 48 data values, and that is about 20,000 times as long as the age of the universe! Clearly, algorithms with execution times that grow exponentially are to be avoided for large data sets. Unfortunately, for many very important problems, all known solutions grow exponentially. Research in the theory of algorithms is being actively pursued to study that kind of behavior and other problems.

When it is desirable to determine the growth rate of a function, it is useful to eliminate as many extraneous details as possible. As n grows large, any linear function $TL(n) - a \cdot n + b$ will be overtaken, passed, and left in the dust eventually, by any quadratic function $TQ(n) = c \cdot n^2 + d \cdot n + e$. This happens no matter what the values of a, b, c, d, and e may be. The crucial factor, for a polynomial, is the highest power of n.

Comparison of growth rates is made explicit by the following:

DEFINITION: $f(n) = O(g(n))$ **iff** (*if and only if*) *there exist constants* c *and* m *such that* $|f(n)| \leq c|g(n)|$ *for all* n $>$ m.

The term $O(g(n))$ is read "big Oh of g of n." The statement $f(n) = O(g(n))$ says, in effect, that $g(n)$ grows at least as fast as $f(n)$. An example of its formal use is $a \cdot n + b = O(n)$. A proof of this is:

$$|a \cdot n + b| \leq |a \cdot n| + |b| \leq (|a| + |b|) \cdot |n| = c \cdot |n|$$

for all $n > 1$.

We need only to extract the kernel of this approach:

$$a \cdot n + b = O(n)$$

$$a \cdot n^2 + b \cdot n + c = O(n^2)$$

$$a \cdot n^3 + b \cdot n^2 + c \cdot n + d = O(n^3)$$

$$a \cdot \ln n + b = O(\ln n) = O(\ln n)$$

$$a \cdot 2^n + b = O(2^n)$$

The most useful orders and their relative growth rates are:

$$O(\ln n) < O(n) < O(n \cdot \ln n) < O(n^2) < O(n^3) < \cdots < O(2^n)$$

Any polynomial has an order less than the order of an exponential function. The fastest growth rate dominates, and so, for example

$$\ln n + n^2 + 4 = O(n^2), \quad \text{and} \quad 2^n + P(n) = O(2^n)$$

for any polynomial $P(n)$.

Fortunately, the order of an algorithm can often be found without going through a detailed analysis. Consider:

[*statement 1*]
for $i = 1$ **to** n **do**
  [*statement 2*]
  [*statement 3*]
  next i

The order is clearly $O(n)$ as long as statements 1, 2, and 3 may be assigned unit time. If they call other procedures, however, then it may be necessary to use the analysis techniques at the beginning of section 1.3.

There are some important points to note about the analysis of algorithms:

■   If large data sets are to be handled by a procedure, then the order of its timing function is of great concern. It may be possible to recognize the order without a detailed analysis, as we will often do, and some approaches can be dismissed on that basis.

■   It is possible to place too much emphasis on the order of T. Many procedures are applied exclusively to relatively small data sets. If so, concern with $O(T(n))$ may obscure an important difference in the execution times of two algorithms.

■   The variability of data sets can profoundly affect the behavior of an algorithm. Much of statistics can be brought to bear on the study of computing processes in situations where it is useful to do so.

■   Some well-known algorithms have defied analysis, and others arise in practice that are not cost-effective to analyze in detail, even if one is prepared and able to make the analysis. It is possible, and sometimes profitable, to study procedures experimentally by varying data sets and observing the reaction of the procedures to the changes.

Exercise E1.1 and problem P1.1 are appropriate at this time.

■ 1.3.2 The Variability of Data   (optional)

When *TrailMin* (see section 1.3) is examined in terms of the order of growth, it is evident that $T(n) = O(n)$, no matter what value *Mindex* has. For a more detailed analysis, it is necessary to study the variations of *Mindex*. The statistical tool that is required is a statistical average, the *expected value*. If a variable, x, can take on values with probability $P[x]$, then the expected value is:

$$E[x] = \sum_{\text{over all } x} x \cdot P[x]$$

The possible values of *Mindex* are $1, 2, \ldots, n$. If they are all equally likely, then their probabilities are all equal to $1/n$. Hence:

$$E[Mindex] = \sum_{Mindex=1}^{n} \frac{1}{n} \cdot Mindex = \frac{1}{n} \cdot \sum_{Mindex=1}^{n} Mindex$$

$$= \frac{1}{n} \cdot \frac{n(n+1)}{2} = \frac{n+1}{2}$$

It may be known, however, that *Mindex* values tend to occur late in the sequence of entries. Suppose, for example, that the probability is q when *Mindex* = 1, $2q$ when *Mindex* = 2, and in general, kq when *Mindex* = k, for k = 1, 2, . . ., n. One of these has to be the value, so the probabilities sum to 1:

$$nq + (n - 1)q + \cdots + 2q + q = 1$$

And so

$$1 = q \sum_{k=1}^{n} k = q \ \frac{n(n + 1)}{2}$$

whence:

$$q = \frac{2}{n(n + 1)}$$

Now the expected value of *Mindex* is:

$$E[Mindex] = \sum_{Mindex=1}^{n} P[Mindex] \times Mindex$$

$$= \sum_{Mindex=1}^{n} (Mindex \cdot q) \times Mindex = q \sum_{Mindex=1}^{n} (Mindex)^2$$

$$= \frac{2}{n(n + 1)} \times \frac{n(n + 1)\,(2n + 1)}{6} = \frac{2n + 1}{3}$$

With this result, using $E[Mindex]$ to represent *Mindex:*

$$T(n) = 3n - \frac{2n + 1}{3}$$

$$= \frac{7}{3}\,n - \frac{1}{3}$$

■ 1.4 Comparison of Three Sorts   (optional)

There are many ways to sort data, and most of them have appropriate applications. The three ways that will be explored here are not suitable for large data sets, but they are relatively easy to understand and may be familiar already. The essential problem to be solved is:

EP1.2 Input n numbers, sort them, and then display them in nonincreasing order.

A whimsical solution, which is also the solemn solution of top-down programmers, is:

program *InOut*(*n*)

    Ingress(*n*)   {*Input* n *entries into array* e.
    Sort(*n*)   {*Arrange the entry values in nondecreasing order.*
    OutHaul(*n*) {*Display* e *in* (*its new*) *order.*

    end {*InOut*

The procedures *Ingress* and *OutHaul* are quickly analyzed:

procedure *Ingress*(*n*)   {$O(n)$
   for $i = 1$ **to** n **do**
     Read(*e*[*i*])
     next *i*
   end {*Ingress*

procedure *OutHaul*(*n*)   {$O(n)$
   for $i = 1$ **to** n **do**
     Write(*e*[*i*])
     next *i*
   end {*OutHaul*

Systems analysts might leave the grubby details of *Sort* to a (lower-paid) junior programmer. We would be derelict in our duty if we did this because *Sort* is the heart of procedure *InOut*. Thus, the decision about which sorting technique should be used is a major one. The splitting of *InOut* into three procedures allows us to concentrate on the kernel of the problem without distractions. The difficulties are put off and isolated, in this case by dealing with input and output external to *Sort*.

■ 1.4.1 SelectionSort   (optional)

One sorting technique begins by searching the entries for a maximal value and exchanging it with *e*[1]. The maximal value is then in *e*[1]. A repeat finds a maximal value of the other $n - 1$ entries and exchanges it with *e*[2]. Exchanges continue until $e[n-1]$ is in its proper place. When the first $n - 1$ values are arranged in nonincreasing order in this way, they are all in their proper places. Figure 1.1 is a series of snapshots of the process.

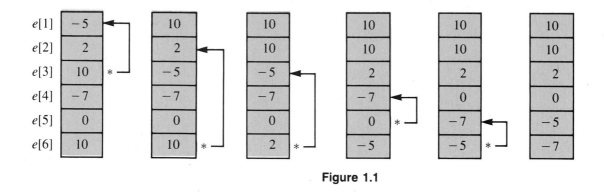

Figure 1.1

This process can be implemented by using the variable *Target* as the index of the position into which a maximal value is being exchanged. Then, for each value of *Target* from 1 to $n - 1$, a search is made for the maximal value of $e[i]$, for all $i \geq Target$. This determines an index, *Spot,* of that maximal value. The exchange is made with $e[Target]$ and $e[Spot]$.

procedure *SelectionSort(n)*
   for *Target = 1* **to** $n - 1$ **do**
     Large ← *e[Target]*
     Spot ← *Target*
     Hunt   {*For the index,* Spot, *of a maximal*
                           {*value among the remaining entries.*
     Temp ← *e[Spot]*
     e[Spot] ← *e[Target]*
     e[Target] ← *Temp*
     next *Target*
   end {*SelectionSort*

If the time required to carry out the hunt is *t,* and a unit time is required for assignment statements, then the timing function of *SelectionSort* is:

$$T(n) = \sum_{Target=1}^{n-1} (5 + t)$$

$$= 5(n - 1) + \sum_{Target=1}^{n-1} t$$

Hunt must be developed in order to resolve this further:

```
procedure Hunt
  for i = Target + 1 to n do
    if e[i] > Large
      then Spot ← i
           Large ← e[Spot]
    endif
  next i
end {Hunt
```

We see that *Hunt*, in fact, is a function of *Target*, and should properly be denoted by *Hunt(Target)*. The timing function for *Hunt*, if the statistical behavior of the **if** statement is ignored, is:

$$t = \sum_{i=Target+1}^{n} 1 = n - Target$$

If it is necessary to know the statistical behavior of the **if**, then the analysis becomes more complex. One must decide on probabilities for the condition of the **if** to be TRUE on any given pass through the **for** loop. Such a detailed analysis is generally uncalled for, because the intent is often to get a reasonable estimate of the behavior of *SelectionSort* to compare it with other sorting algorithms. Of course, if the distribution of data values is known, and the growth behaviors of the algorithms are similar, then it may be worth the effort.

With the *t* that was calculated above:

$$T(n) = 5(n - 1) + \sum_{Target=1}^{n-1} (n - Target)$$

$$= 5(n - 1) + n(n - 1) - \frac{n(n - 1)}{2} = \frac{n^2}{2} + 9\frac{n}{2} - 5$$

$$T(n) = O(n^2)$$

The $O(n^2)$ result is no surprise, since it is often produced by a loop within a loop. One would be suspicious of any other result.

Exercise E1.2 is appropriate at this point.

■ 1.4.2 BubbleSort   **(optional)**

Procedure *SelectionSort* moves the maximal value to the top of *e* in a direct way; smaller values eventually move toward the bottom. Another way to produce the same effect is to slide the smallest value to the bottom of *e*, as it is encountered on the first pass, then the second-smallest to the next-to-last position on the second pass, and so on. Because the smallest item cannot be recognized until a pass is complete, the smallest item so far slides downward during each pass. (This general technique is called a *bubble sort* here and in other places, although some programmers reserve that term for particular variations.) Large values slowly rise like a bubble in liquid, one position per pass.

Snapshots of the process that follow assume that the data in an array are originally in this order:

$$-5 \quad 2 \quad 10 \quad -7 \quad 0 \quad 10$$

BubbleSort proceeds by rearranging the data on the first pass as shown in Figure 1.2.

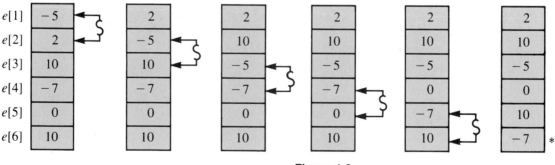

Figure 1.2

The final result of the second, third, fourth, and fifth passes is shown in Figure 1.3.

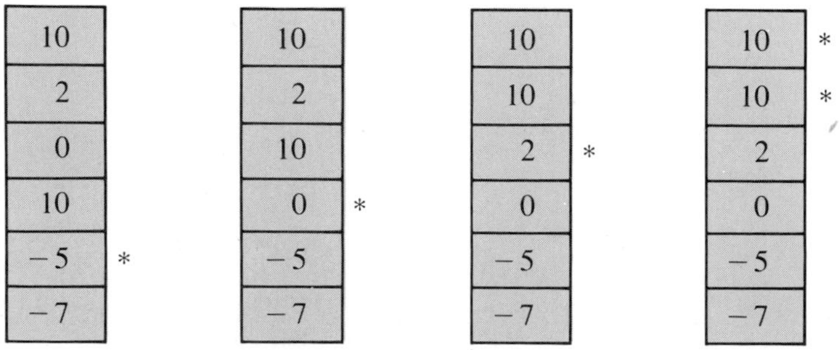

Figure 1.3

One version of the process is:

procedure *BubbleSort(n)*
  for *Target* $= n$ **downto** *2* **do**
    Slide(Target)   *{smallest-so-far into* e[Target]
    next *Target*
  end *{BubbleSort*

Clearly,

$$T(n) = \sum_{Target=2}^{n} t$$

for *BubbleSort*, where *t* is the timing function for *Slide*. "Sliding" really means "exchanging as we go," so *Slide* becomes:

procedure *Slide(Target)*
  for $i = 1$ **to** *Target* $- 1$ **do**
    if $e[i] < e[i+1]$
      then $Temp \leftarrow e[i]$
          $e[i] \leftarrow e[i+1]$
          $e[i+1] \leftarrow Temp$
    endif
    next *i*
  end *{Slide*

With the assumption that the **if** statement requires one unit of time, the timing function for *Slide* is

$$t = \sum_{i=1}^{Target-1} 1 = Target - 1$$

whence for *Slide:*

$$T(n) = \sum_{Target=2}^{n} (Target - 1) = \sum_{k=1}^{n-1} k \qquad \text{where } Target = k + 1$$

$$= \frac{n(n-1)}{2} = \frac{n^2}{2} - \frac{n}{2}$$

$$T(n) = O(n^2)$$

The surprise here is how similar the timing is for *SelectionSort* and *BubbleSort*, rather than how different. There may be a considerable difference, of course, if they are used many times on small data sets in some process. Differences in speed between algorithms with similar timing functions can be very data dependent and even reversed by some sets of data. One effect of chance is the number of exchanges actually made in *Slide*. An experimental comparison of algorithms may be in order if a critical choice is to be made between them.

A number of modifications can be made to *BubbleSort*, such as:

■ Clear a flag variable just before entering *Slide* and reset it if an exchange is made. If the flag remains cleared, then the entries are already in order, and so successive passes may be aborted.

■ Make one pass down, sliding small values; and make the next one up, sliding large values. The rationale for this is that when sliding down, a small value may move a long way, but a large value can bubble only one step up. There is then a choice between splitting *Slide* into *Slideup* and *Slidedown* or generalizing it to handle both directions.

Some modifications of *BubbleSort* are more efficient for some data sets, but not necessarily for all.

Exercise E1.3 is appropriate at this point.

■ 1.4.3 InsertionSort (optional)

Neither *SelectionSort* nor *BubbleSort* seems to be natural to card players. Most people sort cards as they are received from the dealer, one at a time. The first card is simply picked up. The second card is placed on the correct side of the first. The third goes on the outside of the first two or between them, and so on. The crux of this process is that the items input so far are always in order; thus, it is easy to search through them for the proper position of the next one. Rather than combine *Ingress* with *Sort* in procedure *InOut*, we will use the same process *in situ*: $e[1]$ is the first value, $e[2]$ is either exchanged with it or not, etc. A picture of the process in snapshots is shown in Figure 1.4.

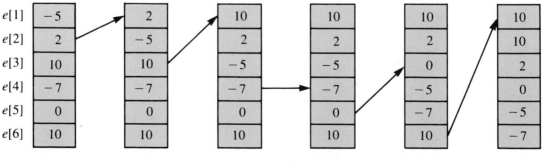

Figure 1.4

When $e[i]$ is to be (re)located, it is necessary to find the index *Target* of the position within the set $\{e[\,j\,] : 1 \leq j \leq i\}$, where $e[i]$ should be placed. If $j < i$, the values $e[\,j\,]$, $e[\,j+1]$, . . . for $k = Target$ to $(i - 1)$ need to be shifted out of the way. Finally, the old value of $e[i]$ is assigned to $e[Target]$. This becomes:

```
procedure InsertionSort(n)
  for Spot = 2 to n do
    Find(Target,Spot)
    Temp ← e[Spot]
    Shift(Target,Spot)
    e[Target] ← Temp
  next Spot
end {InsertionSort
```

The timing function of *InsertionSort* is:

$$T(n) = \sum_{Spot=2}^{n} (f + 1 + s + 1)$$

where f and s are the timing functions for *Find* and *Shift*, respectively.

The procedure *Find* is not so obvious as it may seem. The target cell can be defined as the first cell with a value smaller than that of $e[Spot]$, but what if there is no such cell? The placing of -7 in the snapshots illustrates this situation. When $e[Spot]$ is not larger than $e[\,j\,]$ for $j < Spot$, then $e[Spot]$ should be exchanged with itself or not at all—it is already in place. With this problem recognized, then:

```
procedure Find(Target,Spot)        {f = 1 + (Spot − 1)
  Target ← Spot
  for i = 1 to Spot − 1 do          {  = Spot
    if e[i] < e[Spot]
      then Target ← i
           exit
    endif
  next i
end {Find
```

Procedure *Shift* is straightforward as long as two things are recognized. First, this process will wipe out $e[Spot]$. That, however, was taken care of in *Insertion-Sort* itself (so that it would be visible to the reader and debugger). Second, the copy operation must proceed from $e[Spot]$ back to $e[Target]$ and not the other way around. (Trace it!)

procedure *Shift(Target,Spot)*
  for i = *Spot* **downto** *Target* + 1 **do**
    $e[i] \leftarrow e[i-1]$
    next i {s = *Spot* − *Target*
  end {*Shift*

Now we have:

$$T(n) = \sum_{Spot=2}^{n} (f + s + 2)$$

$$= \sum_{Spot=2}^{n} (Spot + (Spot - Target) + 2)$$

$$= \sum_{Spot=2}^{n} (2 \cdot Spot - Target + 2)$$

If it is assumed that *Target* is as likely to be one value (see section 1.3.1) in the range 1 . . *Spot* as another, then the expected value of *Target* is

$$\frac{Spot + 1}{2}$$

whence:

$$T(n) = \sum_{Spot=2}^{n} \left(\frac{3 \cdot Spot}{2} + \frac{3}{2} \right)$$

$$= \frac{3}{2} \frac{n(n-1)}{2} + \frac{3}{2} (n-1) = \frac{3}{4} n^2 + \frac{3}{4} n - \frac{3}{4}$$

$$T(n) = O(n^2)$$

It is possible to speed up the *Find* process with a search technique called *binary search,* which will be discussed in section 7.3. Binary search will not change the order of *InsertionSort,* however, because the repeated use of *Shift* forces *InsertionSort* to be an $O(n^2)$ algorithm anyway. The *Shift* operation can be avoided with a data structure, the *linked list,* which will be discussed in Chapter 3. The use of a linked list, however, precludes the use of a binary search, so the *Find* operation is relatively slow.

One might be tempted to conclude that sorting algorithms are all $O(n^2)$ or larger. The proof of statements of this type is part of the theory of algorithms. The correct statement is that sorting algorithms are at least of the order $n \cdot \ln n$. The sorting problem itself is intrinsically $O(n \cdot \ln n)$, no matter what algorithms are dreamed up to solve it. Sorting algorithms that have $O(n \cdot \ln n)$ behavior are discussed in Chapters 8 and 9.

Exercise E1.4 is appropriate at this point. Programs PGA.1 and PGA.2 and project PJA.1 (See Part II, section A of this book.) are appropriate but depend on familiarity with the material in Part II, section A.

■ 1.5 Random Processes   (optional)

Computing systems, the programs to which they are applied, and the systems that motivate creation of the programs all tend to increase in complexity as computer science matures. They frequently cannot be characterized by analytical means. One consequence is the growing realization that the behavior of these systems and of even relatively simple programs should be studied experimentally. In practice, that involves choosing from distributions with a pseudorandom number generator and applying statistical measures to results. A very brief introduction to tools that can be used for this kind of study is to be found in Part II, section A.

Summary

Programming beyond the elementary level requires *knowledge, analysis,* and *technique.* Data structures are an essential part of the knowledge, analysis at some level is needed to compare algorithms, and technique comes with practice and with the awareness of possible variations.

Pseudocode provides a language-independent medium for expressing algorithms. One form (SUE) closely tied to Pascal and similar languages is introduced here.

An introduction to the timing of algorithms leads to the determination of the order of growth by summation or inspection. The growth behavior of algorithms provides a measure of comparison for them throughout the book. The discussion in this chapter is background for understanding the assignment of orders of growth. The timing of three basic sorting algorithms provides an example of the top-down summation approach to deriving timing functions.

A brief discussion of random processes is provided in Part II, section A, as an indication of how the average-case behavior of algorithms and the experimental approach to investigating programs can be carried out. This material is optional and left to program assignments.

Exercises   immediate applications of the text material

E1.1   What are the timing functions of the following:

i	*ii*	*iii*
for i = 1 **to** n **do**	$n \leftarrow 1$	**for** i = 1 **to** a **do**
$Temp \leftarrow A[i]$	$F \leftarrow 1$	**for** j = 1 **to** b **do**
$A[i] \leftarrow A[i+1]$	**repeat**	**for** k = 1 **to** c **do**
$A[i+1] \leftarrow Temp$	$n \leftarrow F \times n$	$Write(i \times j \times k)$
next i	$n \leftarrow n + 1$	**next** k
	until $n > m$	**next** j
		next i

E1.2   Trace the action of *SelectionSort* (section 1.4.1) on the set of values:
1 10 11 5 2 7

E1.3   Trace the action of *BubbleSort* (section 1.4.2) on the set of values:
1 10 11 5 2 7

E1.4   Trace the action of *InsertionSort* (section 1.4.3) on the set of values:
1 10 11 5 2 7

Problems   not immediate, but requiring no major extensions of the text material

P1.1   What are the timing functions of the following SUE segments, if $a > b$ is
TRUE precisely one-third of the time?

i	*ii*
for i = 1 **to** n **do**	**for** i = 1 **to** n **do**
$Read(a,b)$	$Read(a,b)$
if $a > b$	**if** $a > b$
then $Temp \leftarrow a$	**then for** j = 1 **to** n **do**
$a \leftarrow b$	$a \leftarrow a + 1$
$b \leftarrow Temp$	**next** j
endif	**endif**
$Write(a,b)$	$Write(a,b)$
next i	**next** i

iii

```
for i = 1 to n do
  Read(a,b)
  if a > b
    then for j = 1 to i do
              a ← a + 1
            next j
    endif
  Write(a,b)
  next i
```

Note: There are programs and a project relevant to this chapter in Part II of this book, section A. They refer to data generated from a given distribution with the help of a pseudorandom number generator. A data file supplied by an instructor or from some other suitable source may be substituted.

The Array Structure

In most HLLs, arrays are automatically available to the programmer, but they are actually created from cells or simpler arrays. When a compiler, an operating system, or an assembler program is written, and when an HLL of limited power is used, arrays are created by the programmer. This chapter serves to isolate properties that characterize arrays as *structures* and hence organize the building of arrays, and it presents the array structure as a model data structure. A review of the role of variables and arrays in programming is included in section 2.1.

■ 2.1 Static Cell Groups   (optional)

The simplest way to manage data is to place it in a single memory cell and identify that cell with a name. To the machine, the cell identifier is a memory address or the information used to calculate one. In a high-level language, the identifier is the name of a variable. A compiler (or interpreter, or assembler) program creates the bridge from one form of identifier to the other. However the name of a cell is specified, many problems can be solved using only the simple variable as a data structure. Examples of problems natural to simple variable solutions abound in early chapters of elementary programming texts. Many of them are variations of problems like EP2.1 (Example Problem 2.1), EP2.2, EP2.3, EP2.4, and EP2.5, which follow:

EP2.1 Input 10 numbers and print the maximal value of the entries.

EP2.2 Input 10 numbers and print their mean. (The *mean* of *n* entries is defined in Part II, section A.4.

EP2.3 Calculate the *n*th Fibonacci number, $F(n)$, where $F(n) = F(n - 1) + F(n - 2)$, and $F(0) = 1 = F(1)$.

EP2.4 Given that the average topsoil in this country has a depth of six inches, that each year it is eroding at a rate of 1 percent of the depth it has that year, and that it will fail to support agriculture at depths below three inches, when does the topsoil depth fall below the critical level?

EP2.5 Input an integer, I, in the range $-32768 \leqslant I \leqslant 32767$ and display its digits separately.

Consider a familiar problem like EP2.1. Someone who lacks programming experience might well recognize that ten inputs can form a sequence $x_1, x_2, \ldots, x_{10}$ and that they can be compared with each other. The direct implementation of these ideas is expressed in such statements as:

$Read(x_1)$
$Read(x_2)$
.

.

.
$Read(x_{10})$
if $x_1 > x_2$
   then   **if** $x_1 > x_3$
               then . . .

.

.

.

This process, of course, is terribly inefficient, particularly if there are 10,000 values instead of 10. Someone with even a little programming experience will recognize that this problem can be solved simply by retaining the largest value so far. (Nearly anyone can solve this problem over a phone, but only programmers seem to recognize how they do it. It is apparently not a trivial task to make the connection between the natural selection process and the use of a single memory location.) A programmer's solution is something like this:

```
program MaxTen                                    {O(1)
    Read(Large)
    for i = 2 to 10 do
      Read(x)
      if x > Large
         then Large ← x
         endif
      next i
    Write(Large)
    end {MaxTen
```

This solution for EP2.1 can be generalized easily to find the maximal value of a sequence of any fixed length. Furthermore, modifications to *MaxTen* will allow the sequence length to be an input variable, to find out (with a counter) which entry actually determines the final value of the variable *Large,* how many entries are equal to the final value of *Large* (with another counter), how many times *Large* changes value (with a third counter), and so on.

Note that, by isolating the core of the problem, which is finding the largest-so-far value, other questions can be answered as applications of the solution. Had the problem been stated initially as a request for all of the modifications mentioned above, it might have seemed overwhelming. Much of data structures as a subject is concerned with extracting and focusing upon central ideas that can be modified and combined in order to solve specific applications.

Some problems may seem to be simply variations of EP2.1–EP2.5 but actually call for a data structure that is more complex than the simple variable. For example:

EP2.6 Input 10 numbers and display the second-largest value in the set of entry values.

EP2.7 Input 10 numbers and display them in reverse order of entry.

EP2.8 Input 10 numbers and display the negative entries, followed by the others.

EP2.9 Input 10 numbers and display them in nonincreasing order of their magnitude.

EP2.10 Input 10 numbers and count how many of them are larger than their mean.

This list could be much longer, and EP2.6 could be removed from it by clever programming, but problems like EP2.9 permeate a large portion, perhaps most, applications of programming. Example problem EP2.9 is important because data frequently have to be sorted in convenient order. (Can you imagine using a telephone directory where names are arranged according to the date on which a phone was first connected to the system?) Most government policy decisions, such as When can a drug be safely released for sale? and Which vote will mollify the most constituents? are based at some level on statistical calculations like EP2.10 and the calculation of standard deviation (see Part II, section A.4).

Problems EP2.6 –EP2.10 can be solved if all of the data are retained in memory after input, so that more than one pass through the data is possible. The collection as a whole can be identified and retained as a group of storage cells, but it is helpful to give a unique name to each memory cell in the group. A specific cell name is necessary if individual access to the cells is to be provided, but the collection of names might need to be as large as the data set. The solution to this puzzle is built into most high-level languages and is presumed to be familiar to the reader—it is the *subscripted variable,* or *array.*

> **Note:** An array with a single subscript is also called a *list* (usually indicating that it is used as one). It is not, however, a *linked list* in the sense defined in Chapter 3.

An array has an identifier for an entire group of cells, and (in the simple one-dimensional case) one other variable, the *index,* is used to select a particular cell within the group. With the usual notation for arrays, one solution to EP2.7 in SUE, with example input and output and a display of the final values of the array x, is:

program *Flip*   {*O(1)*

Data: $-5\ 2\ 1\ -7\ 0\ 0\ -3\ 4\ -1\ 10$

```
for i = 1 to 10 do
    Read(x[i])
    next i
for i = 10 downto 1 by -1 do
    Write(x[i])
    next i
end {Flip
```

	x
$x[1]$	-5
$x[2]$	2
$x[3]$	1
$x[4]$	-7
$x[5]$	0
$x[6]$	0
$x[7]$	-3
$x[8]$	4
$x[9]$	-1
$x[10]$	10

Output

$10\ -1\ \ 4\ \ -3\ \ 0\ \ 0\ \ -7\ \ 1\ \ 2\ \ -5$

2.2 The Array as a Structure

Among the reasons for studying arrays specifically as data structures, rather than just accepting them as gifts from a compiler, are these:

- In some languages, only a limited number of indices is allowed. (Limits of 2 or 7 have been used.) To get around index limitations, a programmer may construct a high-dimensional array within an array of fewer indices. To do so requires a fundamental understanding of how arrays are structured.

- It is fairly common to develop high-level, or very high-level, languages for special purposes, such as a "query language" for asking questions about the contents of a data base. Some of the structuring can be patterned after the details of array structure.

- Controlling a microprocessor, designing a compiler for a high-level language, tuning the performance of a program, or controlling the interface between a computer and the outside world, often require an understanding of assembler (and machine) languages. Assembler languages leave the formation of arrays and any controls on their misuse to the programmer. Understanding how to use the array structure provided by high-level languages is often not sufficient for assembly language programming.

- Data structures are often constructed by a programmer as superstructures imposed on arrays, although the same structures can also be implemented without arrays. Understanding these structures requires that they be distinguished from the array structure itself.

- The array is a familiar programming tool. Abstraction of its properties and the operations needed to manage it provide a model that will be applied to unfamiliar structures in this text.

With these motivations in mind, we turn to study what makes an array with a single index the creature that it is.

There is usually an advantage in thinking of an array as a geometrical sequence of adjacent cells, as depicted in Figure 2.1. For ease of discussion, such an arrangement will be called an LSC, for Linear Sequence of Cells.

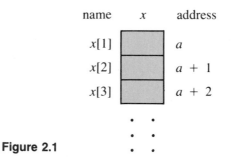

Figure 2.1

Actually, from the view of the array user, it does not matter where the memory cells of an array are located, given that the indices provide random access to them: the user must be able to access the cells in any order merely by specifying the name of the array and the correct index. That the individual cells may be jumbled or scattered in memory does not matter so long as the compiler is provided with a *map* of where the cells are and uses the index as a pointer to the correct one. Of course, cells are often arranged in storage as an LSC; but, on a magnetic drum or disk, for example, faster access may be provided by a different arrangement.

A map from an LSC to physical storage is usually provided by an *operating system,* which manages fundamental system resources. With such a map in hand, a compiler-writer can treat an array as an LSC, whether or not that is the geometry of the physical storage cells involved. The LSC becomes a logical abstraction for data-handling: a data structure.

When a multidimensional array is declared and used in an HLL, a compiler provides maps and operations that are invoked by statements in the HLL. The maps are needed to convert an array reference to a storage address. For example, suppose that an array is declared as $a[0 .. 7, -1 .. 2, 2 .. 4]$ and managed by a compiler as an LSC occupying memory cells 27, 28, ..., 122. Then $a[5,0,3]$ is *somewhere* specific in the sequence of cells, and the collection of such somewheres is a required map. Such maps are also used when programming in assembly language and other situations, and they are the subject of section 2.3.

Maps from one structure to another are invoked by operations described by program statements. In the case of arrays and LSCs, the operations are relatively simple, but they are general enough to apply to the declaration and use of any array that is legitimate in the language being translated. They are even more general than that: the operations CREATE, STORE, and RETRIEVE are needed whenever arrays are used. Their *implementation* differs from one application to another and is intimately tied to storage maps. The operations essential for array management are derived below as the kernel of a set of general management features that apply to other data structures as well: activation, viability, assignment, retrieval, and location.

Activation

Arrays do not spring into existence simply because they are mentioned (although BASIC allows them to do so to a limited extent). Storage must be allocated for them, and in most languages the amount allocated never changes. (SNOBOL provides an exception.) Array allocation is *static*—once done, it cannot be changed by the program. Activation of those arrays that are supported by a language is done, for example, with a *DIM* statement in BASIC and a *VAR* declaration in Pascal. These creation statements also provide information needed to access individual cells of the array—given the location of $a[0]$, where is $a[3]$? Sometimes, activation must be programmed because the required array features are missing (more indices in BASIC; any array in an assembler language).

The general activation operation is called CREATE, and so is the analogous operation for other data structures. (The first example in the book of a CREATE operation that is not simply a language declaration is based on arrays and is found in section 2.5.)

Viability

Activation of an array does not necessarily imply that it has been initialized to a standard value (although it may be in some languages). Strict control of operations can be provided by making retrieval from an uninitialized memory cell illegal. Usually, programs are allowed to retrieve unchecked garbage instead, because the overhead required to make such checks is considered to be too high.

Assignment

The ability to copy information into the cell of index i of array a is commonly provided in at least two forms:

$a[i] \leftarrow x$
$Read(a[i])$

The general operation will be written STORE(a,i,x) or simply STORE(i,x). Hence STORE($Grade,3,85$) has the effect of

$Grade[3] \leftarrow 85$.

Retrieval

The ability to copy information from the cell of index i is provided in at least two forms:

$x \leftarrow a[i]$
$Write(a[i])$

The general operation will be written RETRIEVE(a,i) or simply RETRIEVE(i). Hence RETRIEVE($Grade,3$) immediately after the STORE example above will retrieve the value 85.

Location

Retrieval and assignment operations depend upon the ability to locate a specified cell within the array structure. The array index provides *direct access* to the cell because it determines an absolute memory address. How it does so will be explained in section 2.3. The location of a cell within other structures is not always so direct.

In summary:

■ An instance of the structure ARRAY is operated on by CREATE, STORE, and RETRIEVE.

■ Any cell in an array can be accessed by STORE and RETRIEVE through the use of its index.

■   An array is static in the sense that no cells can be inserted or deleted from it by an operation.

■   There is usually no check on validity of the values in an array.

Finally, note that CREATE, STORE, and RETRIEVE are implicit rather than explicit in high-level languages, but their service *is* provided.

2.3 Array Addresses

STORE and RETRIEVE: it is the mapping of an index to a unique memory location for each possible in-bounds index. This map is needed to build multidimensional arrays from those with fewer dimensions. Even in the one-dimensional case a map is required, because the address of an array cell and its index are not identical—they are just in one-to-one correspondence. In many languages, array indices may lie in a range that does not begin with zero or one: $a[L . . U]$ is to mean that storage is allocated for $a[L], a[L+1], . . ., a[U]$. There are $U - L + 1$ legal (in-bounds) indices in this case.

> **Note:** In some languages, such as Pascal, memory cells in an array may be specified by any values that form an ordinal sequence. For example, $a[Red . . Violet]$ may mean that *Red, Orange, Yellow, Green, Blue,* and *Violet* follow in order, as indices. In effect, they represent indices 0,1,2,3,4, and 5. An auxiliary map is used by the compiler to preprocess the names of colors in order to bring about this effect, but the essential correspondence is still the map of [0 . . 5] onto six memory addresses.

Suppose that the absolute address of $a[L]$ is α, and in general, the address of $a[L+i]$ is $\alpha + i$. This linear storage scheme conforms to the standard geometrical picture of an array. With it, the map from index i to its corresponding address is simply:

$$address \leftarrow \alpha + i - L$$

(The address α will be treated as a variable, *Alpha,* so that we may discuss its computation.)

However, this map itself provides no check for an out-of-bounds address. To make such a check requires a procedure or perhaps some variation of the following:

procedure *Main*

.

.

.

err ← FALSE	**function** *Map(i)*
address ← *Map(i)*	**if** $i < L$ OR $i > U$
if *err* **then** ...	**then** *err* ← TRUE
.	**endif**
.	**return** *Alpha* + i + L
.	**end** {Map

end {*Main*

With the use of this function, if the declaration is $a[1 .. 10]$ and the storage is linear, then $a[7]$ has the address *Alpha* + 6, and $a[-1]$ is out of bounds. If the declaration is $a[-5 .. 4]$, then (the same) 10 memory cells are allocated, but $a[7]$ is out of bounds, and $a[-1]$ has the address:

$$Alpha + (-1) - (-5) = Alpha + 4$$

If two indices are allowed, then the structure may be thought of as a table, arranged in rows and columns, such as in Figure 2.2.

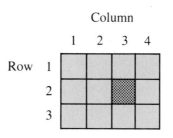

Figure 2.2

Each pair of indices specifies a row and a column. Usually $a[2,3]$ is thought of as the cross-hatched square in Figure 2.2—row 2, column 3. However, as long as a program is consistent about storing and retrieving from a table, the choice makes no difference at the program level. The picture is merely an aid to the programmer. In some languages, however, a table can be manipulated as a unit, even for input and output. Then it matters whether or not *Read(a)* is expecting the input in the order $row_1, row_2, \ldots$ or in the order $column_1, column_2, \ldots$. That is still a programming issue. The structural issue is how to arrange the data in successive addresses *Alpha*, *Alpha* + 1, ... so that the two indices specify a unique memory cell. The two common arrangements are shown in Figure 2.3.

a	address	a
$a[1,1]$	Alpha	$a[1,1]$
$a[1,2]$	Alpha + 1	$a[2,1]$
$a[1,3]$	Alpha + 2	$a[3,1]$
$a[1,4]$	Alpha + 3	$a[1,2]$
$a[2,1]$	Alpha + 4	$a[2,2]$
$a[2,2]$	Alpha + 5	$a[3,2]$
. .	.	. .
. .	.	. .
. .	.	. .
$a[3,4]$	Alpha + 11	$a[3,4]$

Figure 2.3   Row-Major   Column-Major

Note: Most versions of BASIC use the row-major scheme, and FORTRAN uses column-major storage.

When a table is to be arranged in a linear pattern as is Figure 2.3 (or in a one-dimensional array), the map from an index-pair to an address (or to a single index) is designed to work for only one of these schemes. Figure 2.4 depicts the two common storage arrangements.

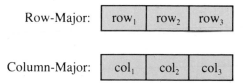

Row-Major: | row_1 | row_2 | row_3 |

Column-Major: | col_1 | col_2 | col_3 |

Figure 2.4

Consider the declaration $a[1 .. 3, 1 .. 4]$, and assume that a is stored in row-major order. To get to $a[2,3]$, for example, it is necessary to count past row 1 and then choose the third item in row 2. Since there are four items in row 1, the address of $a[2,3]$ is:

$$Alpha + 4 + 2 = Alpha + 4(i - 1) + (j - 1)$$
$$= Alpha + 6$$

Note that the factor of *4* comes from the number of *columns* in each row.

More generally, for $a[1 .. U_1, 1 .. U_2]$, the row-major address of $a[i,j]$ would be:

$$Alpha + U_2(i - 1) + (j - 1)$$

Generalizing further, for $a[L_1 .. U_1, L_2 .. U_2]$, the address of $a[i,j]$ would be:

$$Alpha + (U_2 - L_2 + 1)(i - L_1) + (j - L_2)$$

Similar calculations for the column-major scheme are left to the exercises.

The general row-major storage scheme for a table is pictured in Figure 2.5.

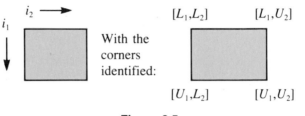

Figure 2.5

In order to picture the storage layout for three indices i_1, i_2, and i_3 in row-major (or in column-major order), it is necessary to generalize the meaning of "row-major" (or of "column-major"). Row-major storage of an array is normally taken to mean the following if the array is stored linearly:

■   As addresses increase from the initial value *Alpha* toward the last address, the first index changes most slowly, and the last index changes most rapidly.

For the declaration: $a[1 .. U_1, 1 .. U_2, 1 .. U_3]$, the indices change like this:

$$a[1,1,1], a[1,1,2], ..., a[1,1,U_3], a[1,2,1], ..., a[1,U_2,U_3], a[2,1,1], ...$$

As a consequence, the last two indices define a table, one selected by the first index, as shown in Figure 2.6.

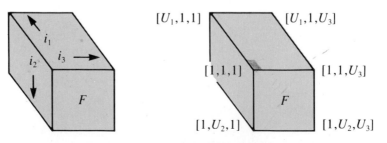

Figure 2.6

The front face F is simply the table defined by i_2 and i_3 when i_1 is fixed at 1.

For the most general declaration of a three-dimensional array a, lower bounds L_i replace 1, and the address calculation for $a[i_1,i_2,i_3]$ involves counting past $(i_1 - L_1)$ tables and then locating a spot within table $(i_1 - L_1)$. There are $(U_2 - L_2 + 1)(U_3 - L_3 + 1)$ cells in each table that is passed, hence:

$$address \leftarrow Alpha + (U_2 - L_2 + 1)(U_3 - L_3 + 1)(i_1 - L_1) + \\ (U_3 - L_3 + 1)(i_2 - L_2) + (i_3 - L_3)$$

For the n-dimensional case, let $s_k = U_k - L_k + 1$, the number of indices in the range of i_k. Then:

$$address = Alpha + s_2 \cdot s_3 \cdots s_n(i_1 - L_1) + s_3 \cdots s_n(i_2 - L_2) + \cdots + (i_n - L_n)$$

Suppose, for example, that we wish to find the address of $a[0,0,0,0]$ in an array declared as: $a[-4 .. 3, 0 .. 4, -5 .. 5, -2 .. 6]$. Then $s_1 = 8$, $s_2 = 5$, $s_3 = 11$, and $s_4 = 9$. The resulting address is:

$$Alpha + 5 \times 11 \times 9(4) + 11 \times 9(0) + 9(5) + 2 \\ = Alpha + 1980 + 0 + 45 + 2 \\ = Alpha + 2027$$

Section 2.6 contains an application of the unfolding of many dimensions into one.

Exercises E2.1–E2.5 are appropriate at this point.

2.4 A Sparse and Static Table

Jon Bentley's column "Programming Pearls" in the May 1984 ACM *Communications* contains an array storage scheme that differs from the usual one for a good reason—it saves a valuable resource. Saved is the storage space that can be wasted when a table is *sparse*—meaning that most of the entries are the same, usually zero. From the standpoint of information retrieval, only two things are necessary: storing the table entries that are *not* zero (nonstandard) and detecting a zero entry in some way. The structure developed in this section that does these two things follows Bentley's solution to storing a table in less space than is required by the maps of section 2.3.

Suppose that a map is contained in a grid of NR by NC points that include some fixed number, NI, of items of interest—it is *static*. The items of interest might be the number of finches in the bird sanctuaries on a state grid, or nuclear reactors on a world grid, or sections containing wheat-rust on a satellite image. There are $NR \times NC$ grid points and NI may be much less than that. (In Bentley's problem, *NI* was 2000, *NR* was 150, *NC* was 200, and hence *NR* × *NC* was 30,000.) By comparison, there are about 200,000 controlled points on a television screen, and over half a million in the input-output table that describes the United States economy. The resolution provided by the human eye would allow even more points of interest on a large road map of Nevada—but they aren't there. Clearly, storage of *all* points in a table can be very wasteful of space, and the space may not even be available. In examples of this sort, the data that are likely to be provided for the location of a value are two coordinates—row and column.

The core of this problem is twofold:

1. Many fewer than *NR* × *NC* items occupy that much storage in the standard row-major (or column-major) map of an array, and the number of items does not change.

2. The row-and-column format is natural to the problem and provided as the input data for the search for a value in the structure.

The core of a solution is to provide maps from row-and-column data into a compact memory space so that it appears to a user to be a standard table. This approach saves the storage resource and preserves ease-of-use. The user's time, effort, and comfort are themselves important resources.

One scheme for packing the nonzero entries of a table *T* (illustrated in Figure 2.7) is to store *only* the nonzero entries and associate them with their row index. Figure 2.7 can be reduced to Figure 2.8. In Figure 2.9 the entries and their rows are stacked together in arrays *Value* and *Row*, and a map *FirstInCol*[1 .. *NC* + 1] provides the index in *Row* of the first nonzero row in each column of *T*. The extra column, 6, and its value *NI* + 1 = 9 is added to provide a sentinel for *Retrieve*. The resulting structure is SST (for Sparse and Static Table).

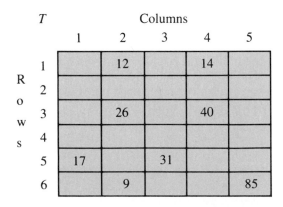

T		Columns		
1	2	3	4	5
	12		14	
	26		40	
17		31		
	9			85

Figure 2.7

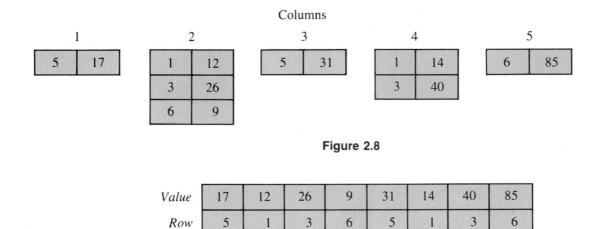

Figure 2.8

Figure 2.9

If it is assumed that the values and the indices require one word of storage each, conventional table storage requires $NR \times NC$ words of storage. The conventional RETRIEVE operation is $O(1)$, and initialization of the structure requires NI STORE operations. A crucial point to be noticed is that NI can be *changed* with $O(1)$ STORE operations in the conventional scheme.

Part of the price of the compactness of SST is that assignment of a zero to a cell in the structure or insertion of a nonzero value to a cell not represented in the structure would amount to deletion or insertion of a cell. SST just does not provide for this flexibility.

With the same assumptions, SST requires NI words for *Value*, NI words for *Row*, and $NC + 1$ words for *FirstInCol*, a total of $2 \times NI + NC + 1$ words instead of $NR \times NC$ words. The RETRIEVE operation becomes:

```
function Retrieve(i,j)                          {O(NI)}
    for k ← FirstInCol[ j] to FirstInCol[ j+1] − 1 do
        if Row[k] = i
            then return Value[k]
            endif
        next k
    return 0
    end {Retrieve
```

This is an $O(NI)$ operation because most of the entries *could* be in a single column and the **for**-loop would then iterate up to NI times. If table entries are randomly located, the expected number of entries to be searched is NI/NC. (See section 1.3.2.) The search for the row index could be speeded up by using a binary search as discussed in section 8.3 in the sense of making the search for the row an $O(\ln NI)$ operation. This apparent speedup is misleading, however, because the overhead required to set up and carry out the search is more than would be needed in the linear search above for the small number of row indices expected per column.

This back-of-the-envelope analysis shows that SST may save a great deal of storage space at the cost of some processing time. It is probably not suitable unless the table is sparse with the entries shared fairly evenly by the columns. The trade of processing time for storage is not uncommon, and sometimes the search for either compactness or efficiency will improve both because it promotes thoughtful analysis.

An HLL program that includes SST would create the arrays *Value, Row,* and *FirstInCol* simply by declaration. That does not perform CREATE for SST, however, because SST is a data structure that is shaped by its values and reasonably includes those pairs of indices $[i,j]$ that denote nonzero entries. Hence CREATE should include initialization of the supporting arrays.

Suppose that the information for SST is available as a sequence of triplets (i,j,v) representing row i, column j, and value v, and is sorted by column and by row within each column. Then CREATE is both supporting-array declarations and the assignment of values to them.

The initialization procedure illustrates a theme that occurs for other data structures: the care needed to deal with special cases. In the general case, when a row i, column j, and value v are retrieved from an input file, a suitable procedure response is, for the right *Dexi:*

S_1: $Row[Dexi] \leftarrow i$
       $Value[Dexi] \leftarrow v$
       $Dexi \leftarrow Dexi + 1$

However, column j of the input triplet may be the one that follows the column of the previous entry triplet, in which case the above is preceded by (for the right *Dexj*):

S_2: $FirstInCol[Dexj] \leftarrow Dexi$
       $Dexj \leftarrow Dexj + 1$

What, however, must be done about missing columns? Examination of *Retrieve* reveals that if S_2 is repeated until $j = Dexj$, the interplay between the two procedures will generally work. In particular, though, what if the *first* few or the *last* few columns are empty? Initialization of *Dexj* to 0 takes care of an empty leading column and a loop similar to S_2 takes care of an empty trailing column.

Finally, the sentinel column $NC + 1$ can be initialized by simply treating it as the empty last column. The result is:

procedure *CreateSST* $\{O(NI + NC)$
    Dexi ← 1
    Dexj ← 0
    for k ← 1 **to** *NI* **do**
      Read(i,j,v)
      while $j > Dexj$ **do**   *{skip empty columns*
        Dexj ← *Dexj* + 1
        FirstInCol[Dexj] ← *Dexi*
      endwhile
      Row[Dexi] ← *i*
      Value[Dexi] ← *v*
      Dexi ← *Dexi* + 1
      next k
    while $Dexj \leq NC$ **do**   *{skip empty columns*
      Dexj ← *Dexj* + 1
      FirstInCol[Dexj] ← *Dexi*
    endwhile
    FirstInCol[NC + 1] ← *NI* + 1
    end *{CreateSST*

(The indication $O(NI + NC)$ is one way to point out that this algorithm is either $O(NI)$ or $O(NC)$, whichever is larger.)

The interaction of a data structure and its implementation are illustrated with SST by the fact that if the entry triplets were available sorted by row, then column, the roles of rows and columns would switch: *Row* and *FirstInCol* would be replaced by *Col* and *FirstInRow*. The structure of SST would not change in any meaningful sense by storing the entries one row at a time—SST is an idea imposed on the underlying arrays by the programmer.

For an application where the number of entries in a table makes it sparse, but that number is not static, there are structures more suitable than SST. They include forms of the *sparse matrix* of sections 6.4 and 6.5 and Part II, section N, as well as the *adjacency list* applied in Chapter 10. (But they are less suitable than SST for a static table that is simply to be searched often once it is created.)

The discussion of SST given in this section assumes that the values in the structure are the values of interest. Such a structure is *endogenous*. It is also possible for the entries in *Value* to be pointers—indirect references to data external to the structure itself. Such a structure is *exogenous*. The data structure and the operations on it are little affected by such a change, but the leverage available is large. The data accessed through *Value* may be bulky and sorted on disk or some other external storage medium in any order. When used as an exogenous structure, SST becomes part of a map or *directory* to a file of records.

Finally, note that SST is an example of *information hiding*—the details of the implementation are not important at a user level. A user (program) that acquires a value in row *i*, column *j* with *Retrieve(i,j)* is indifferent to the choice between SST and the standard two-dimensional table format referenced by a particular form of *Retrieve*. The trade-off between compactness and efficiency and the details of implementation are isolated from functional behavior. At the user level, it is the functional behavior of a structure that needs to be considered in order to use the structure as a tool. The details of its design are distractions at that level. In telegraphic form: SST STILL AN ARRAY.

Exercise E2.6, problem P2.1, and program PG2.1 are appropriate at this point.

■ 2.5 Hash Tables   (optional)

It is not always the case that array indices are natural identifiers for items that are to be stored, accessed directly one at a time, and retrieved. Consider the following items:

beef	bellpepper	blackpepper	dillweed
onion	potato	olive	salt
cumin	carrot	mushroom	tomatopaste

These items could be maintained in lexicographic order, in which case *potato* would be item number 10 after all items were placed in the list. With standard algorithms, the RETRIEVE operation would be $O(\ln n)$ and the STORE operation $O(n)$ if order were maintained as the items were entered. While it is true that STORE and RETRIEVE are $O(1)$ operations for arrays, that is only so if the indices are *known* and the value in the target of a STORE can be *discarded*. Without a complete set in hand it cannot be known that *potato* has index 10 in the sorted list of items.

Because an index integer is not known on the entry of one of the items, it would be helpful if the item *itself* could be used as a key to index the cell where it will be stored. If, for example, the data-space (the set of all possible data values) were the set of all possible recipe ingredients, the required array would be large, and most of it would be wasted as storage for any one recipe.

A solution would be to convert the keys (the list items, here) into unique integers and use them as array indices. A function that does so is called a *hash function*, the conversion process is called *hashing*, and the storage structure is called a *hash table* or *scatter-storage*. One such function (not commonly used) is to simply associate integers 1–26 with letters A–Z and add the integers corresponding to the letters of an item together. With this function, HF_1, the hashed indices are:

Item	$HF_1(Item)$	Item	$HF_1(Item)$
beef	18	carrot	75
onion	67	salt	52
cumin	60	blackpepper	105
dillweed	74	olive	63
bellpepper	107	tomatopaste	145
potato	87	mushroom	122

Here is an apparent solution, although an array of 145 cells is needed to store these 12 items. For an arbitrary recipe, 20 or 25 items is quite a lot. With this function, there are 27^{10} possible keys of no more than 10 characters, and the maximum value of HF_1 is only 260. The number of possible ingredients, named in English, is several thousand, many of which will have the same HF_1 values.

Schemes to restrict the range of the function, like using HF_1 (*Item*) MOD 25, creates the same problem that arises when just one more item is added to this list: broth. $HF_1(broth) = 63 = HF_1(olive)$. This is called a *collision*, and collisions are inevitable if a hash table is to be reasonably space-efficient.

Computer scientists have spent much time exploring how to deal with collisions and juggle the space and time efficiency of hash tables because the utility of hashing is not confined to storing recipe ingredients. Hashing should be considered when any large collection of items is to be stored and retrieved efficiently from a small space.

A discussion of hash tables, confined to the use of array support for them, is to be found in Part II, section B. A supplement to the discussion there is found in Part II, section L, and may be read after other support structures have been introduced.

■ 2.6 Unfolding Indices   (optional)

Many things have a natural dimensionality; they are most easily associated with one or two or some number of indices. However, they do not have to be modeled according to their natural dimensionality. Two-dimensional slices can be used to describe three-dimensional objects. Cross-sections of the atmosphere in a weather model or of a person in a CAT-scan can be used to store essentially three-dimensional information. Sometimes three dimensions can be usefully projected into a single pair of dimensions, as in a contour map.

In the other direction, an indexed set of essentially planar structures can be managed with three indices, forming a three-dimensional data structure. Examples include a sequence of board configurations for almost any board game, an item-count table for each of a family of warehouses, or a set of crossword puzzles.

The success of these dimension changes, however, lies in the fact that they are *reversible*—it is possible to devise a picture of natural dimension from the data format. On balance, if a programmer thinks most easily and clearly about a problem when it is portrayed as three-dimensional (or two-dimensional or five-dimensional), then it should be programmed in its natural form. This is not simply information-hiding, but information-packaging.

In this section, a game is used as the model of a system that has a natural dimensionality. Games, it should be noted, serve as models for many things because they can be designed to eliminate extraneous concerns.

Suppose that a program is written to monitor (or to play) three-dimensional tic-tac-toe. The rules of the game and its interaction with users are important parts of the program design, but so is the management of a three-dimensional array. Assume that the language L in which the program is written does not allow three indices, and so the board array, *B*, needs to be unfolded into a one-dimensional array, *Stretch*. Suppose that the natural three-dimensional array would be declared as

$$B[1 .. 3, 1 .. 3, 1 .. 3],$$

in a language which allowed such a thing. The array *B* can be used to think about the design of the program, but the program will actually be implemented with *Stretch*[1 .. 27].

One way to organize the unfolding of *B* into *Stretch* is to develop procedures *Create*, *Store*, and *Retrieve*, which handle the index map from three indices to one, and then rely on the language *L* for the versions of the CREATE, STORE, and RETRIEVE operations that manage the array *Stretch*. *Create*, *Store*, and *Retrieve* can then be called upon by the rest of the program, much as though the language L *did* implement three-dimensional arrays. A clean treatment of that management allows the programmer to focus on aspects of the program other than index calculations.

In most languages, *Create* must be handled by the programmer, in the sense that *Stretch* must be declared with sufficient storage to hold *B*. The array *Stretch* probably should not be declared with any extra cells, simply as a debugging safeguard.

If *Retrieve* is implemented as a function with three parameters, then

$$x \leftarrow y - Retrieve[i,j,k] \quad \text{or} \quad Write(Retrieve[i,j,k])$$

may be used naturally in place of:

$$x \leftarrow y - B[i,j,k] \quad \text{or} \quad Write(B[i,j,k])$$

A simple version of *Retrieve* that does no out-of-bounds checks of i, j, and k is:

function *Retrieve(i,j,k)* $\qquad\qquad\qquad\qquad$ {*O(1)*
$\quad$ *Index* ← $9 \times (i-1) + 3 \times (j-1) + (k-1) + 1$
$\quad$ *Retrieve* ← *Stretch[Index]*
end {*Retrieve*

This can be easily generalized with the help of section 2.5, but a caution is in order: there are illegal combinations of i, j, and k that are not out of bounds in *Stretch* itself. An example is [1,5,5], which this version of *Retrieve* maps blithely into *Stretch*[17], but which should not exist in the array B at all. This problem can be avoided if the bounds for B are checked individually as they are unfolded, in which case the bounds for *Stretch* will not be violated either. Furthermore, [1,1,1] corresponds to *Index* = 1 and not to the address *Alpha* of [1,3,2]. In terms of absolute addresses:

$$\text{Index} - 1 \leftarrow 9(i-1) + 3(j-1) + (k-1)$$

An equally stripped version of *Store* is:

procedure *Store(Value,i,j,k)* $\qquad\qquad\qquad$ {*O(1)*
$\quad$ *Index* ← $9 \times (i-1) + 3 \times (j-1) + (k-1) + 1$
$\quad$ *Stretch[Index]* ← *Value*
end {*Store*

Store can be used in situations like this

Store(Value,i,j,k) $\qquad$ and $\qquad$ *Read(Value)*
$\qquad\qquad\qquad\qquad\qquad\qquad\qquad\qquad$ *Store(Value,i,j,k)*

in place of:

B[i,j,k] ← *Value* $\qquad$ and $\qquad$ *Read(B[i,j,k])*

$\quad$ Clearly, the bodies of the stripped versions of *Store* and *Retrieve* could be simply incorporated as needed in the program, but when index bounds on i, j, and k are included, separating them as procedures removes a lot of clutter and simplifies debugging. Note that the array B exists only in the programmer's mind and perhaps in the documentation.

> **Note:** In this example, it was assumed that *Store* and *Retrieve* were to operate on only one array, *Stretch*. They can be modified by including an array name in the argument list in order to generalize them to deal with an arbitrary one. In that case, the bounds may also need to be generalized. They may be passed as an array of bounds or be stored in an array that is global and hence accessible to both procedures. Such generalization should be used with common sense, when it enhances more than it obscures.

Problems P2.2–P2.6, and programs PG2.2–PG2.5 are appropriate at this point.

Summary

Even a simple variable, supported by memory cells, is a structure. As a structure, the simple variable is not adequate to handle some common computing problems. For those, the array is needed.

The structure ARRAY provides some contrast with the structures discussed in later chapters. It is static in that it does not grow and shrink with the insertion or removal of information. An array is *created* (generally by including a variable declaration or dimensioning statement in a program). It can be accessed by two operations, STORE and RETRIEVE, which allow direct access to any cell of the array with the use of indices. These operations really characterize an array.

Array access via the indices requires a map that can be put in general form. This map is explored enough so that arrays can be constructed from arrays of fewer dimensions.

A specialized form of array, the SST (for Sparse and Static Table), illustrates four common features of data structures:

- It is explicitly a structure built out of supporting structures by programming.

- It is not a language feature.

- It is an example of information-packaging.

- It is used for a specific application as a conscious choice between competing structures.

A large collection of keys may be mapped into a few indices that then provide many of the benefits of array access. Such a map into a *hash table* is frequently used in applications. The hash tables introduced in section 2.5 are the subject of Part II, sections B and L.

In Chapters 6 and 10, arrays are supported with structures quite different from the linear string of memory cells assumed in this chapter, and the number of competing choices for such applications is increased.

Further Reading

The "Programming Pearls" column written by Jon Bentley for ACM *Communications* is a delight. It is nearly entirely accessible to anyone in the throes of a data structures course and surely totally accessible to anyone who has completed one. A common theme in "Pearls" is the wise choice of data structures, frequently based on problems that confronted professionals while they were practicing the craft of programming. (The first "Pearls" column appeared in the August 1983 issue.)

Exercises   immediate applications of the text material

E2.1 How many memory cells are required by $A[0 .. 5]$? by $B[-1 .. 4, 5 .. 10]$? by $C[-5 .. -2, 2 .. 5, -2 .. 2]$?

E2.2 Assume that the arrays A, B, and C of E2.1 are stored linearly in row-major order, beginning in addresses α, β, and γ, respectively. What are the indices for the cells with addresses $\alpha + 2$, $\beta + 12$, $\beta + 17$, $\gamma + 7$, $\gamma + 16$, $\gamma + 37$?

E2.3 What is the address of $A[0,0,0]$ in an array stored linearly in row-major order beginning in address α if it is declared as
$A[-5 .. 0, -2 .. 3, -2 .. 0]$?
as $A[-1 .. 5, -2 .. 2, 0 .. 3]$?

E2.4 Suppose that the array B is stored linearly in column-major order, beginning in address β.

If B is declared as $B[1 .. 3, 1 .. 4]$, then what is the address of $B[2,3]$?

If B is declared as $B[1 .. U_1, 1 .. U_2]$, then what is the address of $B[i,j]$?

If B is declared as $B[1 .. U_1, L_2 .. U_2]$, then what is the address of $B[i,j]$?

If B is declared as $B[L_1 .. U_1, L_2 .. U_2]$, then what is the address of $B[i,j]$?

If B is declared as $B[L_1 .. U_1, L_2 .. U_2, L_3 .. U_3]$, then what is the address of $B[i,j,k]$?

If B is declared as $B[-4 .. 3, 0 .. 4, -5 .. 5, -2 .. 6]$, then what is the address of $B[0,0,0,0]$?

E2.5 Using $s_k = U_k - L_k + 1$, what is the general form for the address of an n-dimensional array B, stored linearly in column-major order beginning in address β?

E2.6 Cells of a 12-by-12 table contain either zero or the sum of their row and column indices. The cell value is zero except when *both* indices are prime: 2,3,5,7,11. Diagram the SST structure (of section 2.4) for this table.

Problems not immediate, but requiring no major extensions of the text material

P2.1 Redesign SST, *Retrieve,* and *CreateSST* with the roles of rows and columns interchanged.

P2.2 Most computing languages do not check to make sure that a memory cell has had a value assigned to it (that it is initialized), before retrieval from it is allowed. Simulate this type of checking for a one-dimensional array *A,* in the following way: develop (in SUE, perhaps) procedures *CreateBF, StoreBF,* and *RetrieveBF. CreateBF(A,n)* will initialize an array *BF* of *n* Boolean flags to *FALSE,* essentially to indicate that no cell in the array *A* has yet been initialized. *StoreBF(A,i,x)* will set the flag $BF[i]$ to *TRUE* and then perform $A[i] \leftarrow x$. *RetrieveBF(A,j)* will check $BF[j]$, and if $A[j]$ has not been initialized, then it will return an error signal, otherwise it will perform *RetrieveBF* $\leftarrow A[j]$.

PG2.2 asks for a program that implements this map.

P2.3 In language L, arrays can be indexed only by integers. It is desirable to extend L within the confines of a large program to allow an array, *Redletday,* to have rows indexed by the letters *'A'* through *'D',* and columns indexed by *'V'* through *'Z'.* After invoking *CreateL* to create an appropriate index map, a programmer should be able to use *Store('B','X',Value)* in place of *Redletday*[3,2] *Value.* Design the routines *CreateL, StoreL,* and *RetrieveL* in SUE.

PG2.3 asks for a program that implements this map.

P2.4 Suppose that language L allows only one-dimensional arrays. Programmer Z is in the habit of declaring an array *Dump*[1 .. 64], and unfolding multidimensional arrays with index ranges of the form 1 .. 2, or 1 .. 4, or 1 .. 8, and so forth, into this array in every possible way. The number of possibilities when all 64 cells are used is surprisingly small. How many are there?

P2.5 Referring to P2.4, Programmer Z normally chooses arrays of dimension 1,2,3,4, or 5. Z uses a nondecreasing sequence of maximum indices for the range, but does not necessarily use the entire array *Dump.* For example, with 3 dimensions, the index ranges might be [1 .. 2,1 .. 2,1 .. 4]. Z has developed general procedures *Cfold, Sfold,* and *Rfold* that do the following:

Cfold(n_1,n_2,n_3,n_4,n_5) initializes an array, *Unfold*[1 .. 5], which can be used to map into *Dump* from the multidimensional array

$$Origami[1 .. n_1, 1 .. n_2]$$

or perhaps *Origami*[$1 .. n_1, 1 .. n_2, 1 .. n_3$]. The array *Origami* exists only in Z's mind, of course, since it cannot exist in language *L*. The number of dimensions in *Origami* are determined by the number of n_i's greater than 1.

Storage into *Origami* is carried out by *Sfold*, and retrieval from it by *Rfold*. Both use *Unfold* in order to manage their operations.

Design *Cfold, Sfold,* and *Rfold*.

PG2.4 explores this map, and PG2.5 asks for a program that implements the routines *Cfold, Sfold,* and *Rfold*.

P2.6   Design a procedure that copies array *A*[1 .. 5, 0 .. 5], stored in row-major order, into array *B*[1 .. 10, 1 .. 3], stored in column-major order. (Just such a transformation is required to transfer array *A* as created by a Pascal program into array *B* to be used by a FORTRAN program.)

Programs   for trying it out yourself. A program, when written for an interactive system, should display instructions that explain to the user what it does and how to use it. It should provide a graceful way for the user to quit.

PG2.1   Write a program that accepts no more than 100 (i,j,v) triplets, counts them, creates an appropriate SST structure for storing them, and displays the resulting structure. The number of rows *NR* and the number of columns *NC* are input data. Test your program with the example data, that data less column 1, less column 2, and less column 5.

PG2.2   The solutions to problem P2.2 are procedures that check to make sure that the individual cells of an array *A* have been initialized before retrieval from them is allowed. Write a program to test procedures of this type. The program should allow a user to make entries into, and retrievals from, an array *A*[−5 .. 10] in any sequence. If retrieval is attempted from *A*[*i*], and there has been no store into *A*[*i*], then a message to the user should be generated.

Comment: In a language such as Pascal, the Boolean arrays must be declared in advance of the call to *CreateBF* and may as well be tailored to their use. A declaration *BF*[−5 .. 10] would be appropriate here.

PG2.3   Write a program that emulates the addition of alphabetic indices to the language L of P2.3, with *CreateL, StoreL,* and *RetrieveL*. The user should be able to provide any sequence of letter-pairs and values in order to effect storage into *Redletday,* and to request the correct value of an entry in *Redletday* by specifying a pair of letters. Out-of-bounds pairs should prompt a message to that effect.

Please note that *CreateL, StoreL,* and *RetrieveL* assume *INTEGER* indices only.

PG2.4 Write a program that will accept one to five integers $n_1, \ldots, n_5$ and display the map of *Origami* into the array *Dump* as it is developed in problem P2.5. For example, if 2, 4, 0, 0, 0 are entered, then one form of the map is:

Origami indices		*Dump* index
1	1	1
	2	2
	3	3
	4	4
2	1	5
	2	6
	3	7
	4	8

PG2.5 Emulate the implementation of the *Cfold, Sfold,* and *Rfold* discussed in P2.5 with a program that will accept $n_1, \ldots, n_5$, which in turn define the virtual array *Origami,* and then any sequence of indices (and values). The program should make out-of-bounds checks and allow apparent storage into and retrieval from *Origami,* while actually maintaining only *Dump* as an array.

Projects   for fun; for serious students

PJ2.1 An attendant at a parking lot must keep track of the position of cars as they are parked in any available spot as well as their license numbers. When customers leave, they request their cars by license number, and one more parking slot becomes free. Help the attendant by writing a program that admits up to 16 cars into this (very small) lot and responds to an arbitrary sequence of requests for parking space, car retrieval, and display of the current status of the parking spaces. Arrays are to be used as data structures, and the design of the lot is your lot.

Chapter 3

List Processing

One common way to preserve a sequence of items is to make a list of them. The shopping list in a kitchen, for example, grows as family members notice the need for additional items. Items may be added at the bottom, but such a list differs from a simple sequence because of the other operations applied to it. Occasionally an item will be scratched off the list when a supply of it is rediscovered, and certainly items will be removed at each stop of a shopping tour. A shopping tour may (or may not) reduce the list to nothing. A different list, perhaps developed as a party is planned, may be appended to the current list. Duplicate items may be noted and removed from one of the lists. When an item is to be added, the list will be searched to see if it is already there; but the list is not likely to be alphabetized in order to make the search easier. Occasionally a family member will update an entry by, for example, specifying a particular breakfast cereal in place of a general entry, "cereal." The list may be partitioned at shopping time into lists appropriate for different stops on a shopping tour. These list operations appear in a large variety of other applications as well.

The list is a commonly used data structure and can certainly be incorporated into programming. Lists are so general, common, and useful that even restricted forms of lists are major topics and are the basis for the two chapters that follow this one.

3.1 The List as a Structure

A data structure is many things, including an abstraction. In particular, it is a combination of allocated storage with a set of operations performed on it. The feature that best characterizes structure LIST is that its cells are linked together. Some idea of the nature of structure LIST can be gained by contrasting it with data structure ARRAY. The contrast is related to operations performed on instances of both structures.

The operations applied to lists differ significantly from those applied to arrays.

Activation

The list that forms a class roll usually exists, even if there are *no* names on it, which is true before registration or if everyone drops the course. It defines the roll, empty or not. A list is normally created empty, with no storage occupied by list entries. It may be necessary to allocate space for the list to grow into, just as a piece of paper is reserved for a shopping list; but it may also be possible to avoid the allocation of space before it is needed. In either case, the list itself is initially *null* (empty), as opposed to an array that is not yet initialized but consists of cells that contain *some* value.

Viability

A list is not only created null, it can become null through the removal of its entries. A list of chores, for example, is *supposed* to become null eventually. The attempt to remove an entry from a null list is usually treated as an error in a removal operation, and so the emptiness of a list is an often-checked property of it. (An alternate view is that removal of a specified item from a null list cannot fail—the item is no longer there after the attempt.)

Attachment

A list grows when an entry is attached to it. In many implementations, it is not simply a value that is attached, but rather a package containing at least one, but perhaps many, values. A common example is an entry in a list of personnel records. Placement of an entry into a sequence of entries in such a list is quite distinct from the assignment of values to the entry itself. No general restriction forces attachment to be made only to the "tail" of a list. Carefully chosen insertion positions can be used to maintain a list in some order.

Assignment

The assignment of values to entries, before or after the entries are attached to a list, is the only form of assignment for lists. Assignment does not really affect the list structure itself, which takes its form from its entries and their relationships, not from their values. For example, a revision of the job description in an entry of a list of available jobs does not change the number of jobs and probably will not change their order in the sequence.

Partitioning

It is convenient to be able to divide a list into sublists. For example, the list of tasks required to construct a building is often divided into separate lists for subcontractors. The essential partition divides a list into just *two* sublists. A list maintained in some order needs to be partitioned so that a new entry can be inserted at a specified position. An entry can be removed by partitioning a list into three pieces and rejoining a pair of them. (There are also analogs of a "scratch" operation in list processing, in which an entry is marked "inactive," but not removed.) Partitioning is usually a transparent—implicit rather than explicit—part of other operations.

Retrieval

The return of a value from a list requires the location of the entry that contains it and then retrieval of the value from the entry itself. The entries may be simply values (as in a shopping list), or the entry may instead be a structure (as in a list of personnel records). Retrieval must be supported by location of the correct entry —a search.

Lists are an extremely general data structure, so general that it seems wise to form a composite view of them by focusing on several particular restrictions and forms of lists. One form of list is the *linear linked list* of the next section, in which entries contain both sequencing information and values.

The (linear) linked list serves as the general model of a list. Recognize, however, that a singly subscripted variable can be a list of a particular and restricted sort. The cells $a[1]$, $a[2]$, . . . , $a[n]$ of a variable $a[1 . . Max]$ can form a linear list of array cells, or support *some other data structure*. In particular, the use of a subscripted variable for list support as it is discussed in section 3.5 is quite different from this simple meaning of "list."

A data structure such as a linked list may serve as a *directory* to data. If all of the data of interest is contained in its nodes, it is *endogenous*. If its nodes contain addresses of data stored elsewhere, it is *exogenous*. The auxiliary data may be on a disk or in some other form of secondary memory—or simply in another structure. This book generally deals with endogenous examples, and the reader should recognize that the node "value" may only be a key to more data.

Linked lists are:

1. *Dynamic*. They can grow and shrink to suit the need of the moment, and usually their occupancy of storage space does too.

2. *Blind*. It is not necessary to know in advance how large or small they will actually become as they are used.

3. *Sparse*. The potential data space may be much larger than the set of data in the list at any given time.

When a problem echoes these characteristics, linked lists are likely to be helpful in its solution.

3.2 Linked Lists

A linked list is a set of *nodes*. Each node contains a value and at least one *link*, which tells where to find another node. The format of a node may be a structure such as a record or an array. The crucial idea is that each node in a linked list contains information about how to find the next in a sequence of nodes. Immediate access to *every* node is not necessary, for one node will lead to another, just as stepping stones lead from one side of a creek to another.

In the simplest arrangement, shown in Figure 3.1, the links are linear: the address of *Node* 1 is stored in variable *Head*, a link to node 2 is stored in node 1, and so forth. The last link points to a special node, *NIL*, which is recognizably not the address of any node.

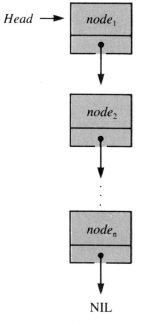

Figure 3.1

The links have a specialized role to play. They are *pointers*, which point to nodes of some type; and specialized notation is used for them. The notation $p \uparrow$ (*p-Target*) is used as the name of the node pointed to by the pointer p. The value of p itself is the memory address of $p \uparrow$.

Note: The node pointer *NIL* has no target. If p = NIL, $p \uparrow .Value$ is an error that will crash a program in most systems.

It can be convenient in some applications for the last link in a list to point to a special node that is the same for all lists in a program—the *universal sentinel node* u. The choice is a matter of personal taste, but it can affect the simplicity of a procedure. In particular, u acts much like sentinel values commonly used to signal the end of an input stream. Sentinel lists will be used in some examples in the book, in the polynomial lists of section 3.8 for example, but *NIL*-end lists are the usual choice.

A sequence of nodes linked together in a (sentinel) list may be identified by their values or keys as is the list in Figure 3.2, but there is no intended implication that the nodes contain *only* the keys.

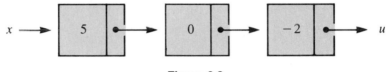

Figure 3.2

An operation must be provided to acquire storage space for a new node and to identify it. (In some implementations, this may be done by simply updating a variable that serves as an index to an array.) When p is a pointer of type $\uparrow Nodule$, then NEW(p) has the effect shown in Figure 3.3 without an assumed initialization of $p \uparrow$.

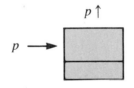

Figure 3.3

As long as *NEW* can acquire storage space for a new node in some manner, nodes can be added to a list. They can also be deleted or updated, and the list can be searched for given values. Nodes can be inserted and deleted at the beginning, at the end, or at any point in the list.

When a node is deleted, the removed node still exists in memory, but not in the list structure. It generally cannot be relocated by a program—it is wasted space. In most languages which support pointer variables, there is an operation DISPOSE(p) that returns the memory occupied by $p \uparrow$ to available space. In small programs for small applications, *DISPOSE* may not be needed. It will not be explicitly indicated in all the in-text algorithms where it might be useful for some applications.

Restrictions placed on where insertions or deletions are allowed to occur in the list are used to define the important data structures STACK and QUEUE, which are the subjects of Chapters 4 and 5. Some list operations are common to queues, stacks, and other applications of list processing. They receive a general definition in the sections that follow.

3.3 Common List Operations

Like all data structures, lists must be created; and so some operation CREATE is needed. This operation is dependent on the implementation and the support provided by the language involved. It can simply be the declaration of *aList,* for example, as a pointer to objects with the type that the *aList* nodes will have, and usually an initialization:

aList ← NIL

However, it is very convenient for some applications to have *two* pointers to the nodes of the list, usually called *Head* and *Tail,* as depicted in Figure 3.4. (Much of what follows can be simplified if the tail pointer is not used.)

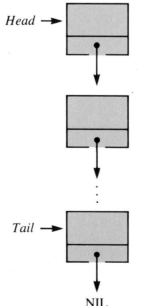

Figure 3.4   NIL

In this book, we will frequently take advantage of this convenience in the list processing by creating the identifying node of a linear linked list as a record containing a pair of pointers. Thus, the result of CREATE(*aList*) is:

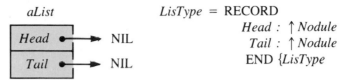

A nonempty list then takes the form shown in Figure 3.5.

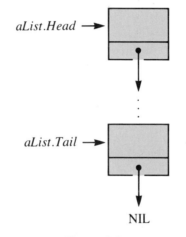

Figure 3.5

This form creates an entity accessed through a single identifier, *aList,* but it does make names longer. For convenience, we sometimes assume in this book that the body of a procedure operates under the blanket of

with *aList* **do**

.
.
.

endwith

within which *aList.Head* and *Head* are equivalent, as are *aList.Tail* and *Tail.* Alternate approaches are to assume that *Head* and *Tail* are global or to pass both variables to a procedure as arguments. The logic of an algorithm is not affected by the ·choice, although an implementing program can be affected. All three approaches are illustrated in this book.

Because lists are dynamic their management is not simply a matter of updating cells accessed directly. There may not even *be* cells in a list. The head node of a list is manipulated easily, interior nodes require a search to locate, and the tail node lies between these extremes. One result of the dynamic nature of lists is that they are extremely *flexible* choices for problem solving. As a consequence of flexibility, there are many variations of structure within lists and of operations to apply to them. Fortunately, there are commonalities (such as procedure *LT* of section 3.3.2) that reduce the apparent complexities to real convenience.

Some of the sections that follow present several versions of a process where one would do. The intent is to encourage the reader to develop a personal style, rather than to copy one.

3.3.1 The Empty List

As nodes are inserted and deleted, a list grows and shrinks. It is impossible to delete a node from an empty list, so a test for an empty list is a useful operation. Formally, the test is a function, EMPTY, of a list identifier and it returns either *TRUE* or *FALSE*. When applied to an empty list (one with no nodes), EMPTY returns the value *TRUE*. It is easily written as:

{*NIL*-end list}
function Empty(aList)   {O(1)}
  if Head = *NIL*
    then return *TRUE*
    else return *FALSE*
  endif
end {Empty

{sentinel list}
function Empty(aList)
  if Head = u
    then return *TRUE*
    else return *FALSE*
  endif
end {Empty

3.3.2 List Traversal

A great deal of list processing can be done with a *traverse*—a systematic visit to every node with one or more processes applied during the visitation.

As an example of a traverse, a list is easily displayed with the help of a routine *NodeOut*, which writes out the (possibly structured) value of a given node:

procedure *DisplayList(aList)*   {O(*number of nodes*)
  p ← Head
  while *p* ≠ NIL **do**
    NodeOut(p)
    p ← p ↑ .Link
  endwhile
end {*DisplayList*

The general form of this procedure provides a framework on which a large part of list processing can be draped:

```
procedure LT(aList)                                    LT
    PROCESS0
    while CONDITION do
        PROCESS1
        p ← p ↑ .Link
        endwhile
    PROCESS2
    end {LT
```

Note: Because lists are such a general structure, there are many variations of any list process and it is well to keep procedure *LT* in mind when designing algorithms. *LT* is the basis of most algorithms that make a list-walk (search a list).

DisplayList is an example of *LT* (List Traverse) described by:

CONDITION : $p \neq$ NIL
PROCESS0 : $p \leftarrow Head$
PROCESS1 : $NodeOut(p)$
PROCESS2 : NULL

There are useful variations of the **while** condition used to test for exit, such as:

CONDITION : $p \uparrow .Link \neq$ NIL
CONDITION : $p \neq u$
CONDITION : $p \uparrow .Link \neq u$
CONDITION : $p \neq Tail$
CONDITION : $p \uparrow .Link \neq Tail$

Similarly, *Head* may be replaced by some other value in the initialization assignment.

PROCESS2 is particularly useful if *LT* is configured as a function: it then is used to return a value.

The time required to traverse a list of *n* nodes with *LT* is:

$$T(n) = t_0 + n \times t_1 + t_2,$$

where t_i is the time required for *PROCESSi*. This may need to be modified if there is an **exit** or **return** in *PROCESS1*.

Suppose that p is the pointer to a node, created perhaps by NEW(p), and then assigned a value, by, for example: $p\uparrow.Value \leftarrow x$. The two natural places to insert into a list like *aList* are at the head and at the tail as shown in Figure 3.6. These operations are created by changing links one at a time, in a sequence that will not destroy necessary information:

procedure *InsertHead(aList,p)*   {$O(1)$
   if *Empty(aList)*   **then** *Tail* $\leftarrow p$ **endif**
   $p\uparrow.Link \leftarrow Head$
   Head $\leftarrow p$
   end {*InsertHead*

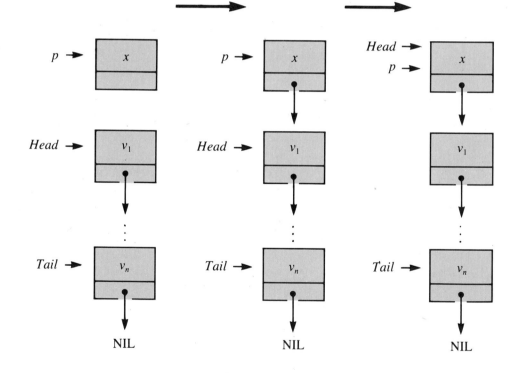

3.3.3 Insertion

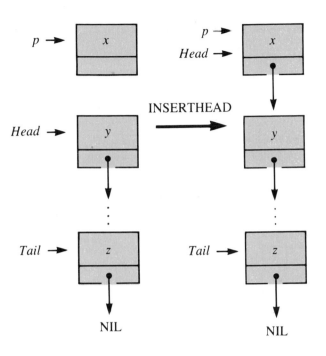

INSERTHEAD

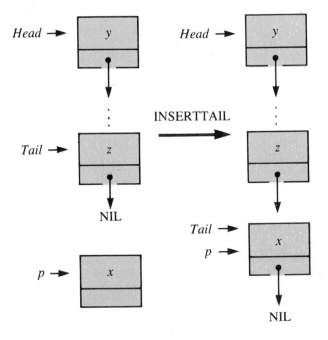

INSERTTAIL

Figure 3.6

procedure *InsertTail(aList,p)*   {*O(1)*
    if *Empty(aList)*
        then *Head ← p*
              Tail ← p
    endif
    Tail ↑ .Link ← p
    p ↑ .Link ← NIL
    Tail ← p
    end   {*InsertTail*

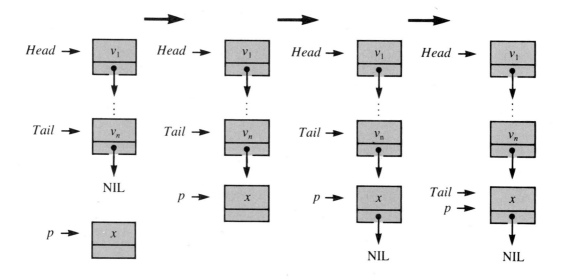

Note that the last assignment cannot precede the first assignment (after the **if**)
in either *InsertHead* or *InsertTail*.

If the tail pointer is not used, *InsertTail* involves an *O(n)* traverse to find the
tail node.

Exercises E3.1 and E3.2 are appropriate at this point.

3.3.4 Deletion

Deletion is done most easily at the node pointed to by *Head*. Deletion at the tail
position requires a traverse to locate the predecessor of the node pointed to by *Tail*.
At both positions, care must be taken to avoid trying to delete from an empty list.
The two options are shown schematically in Figures 3.7 and 3.8.

Deletion at the head position is simply:

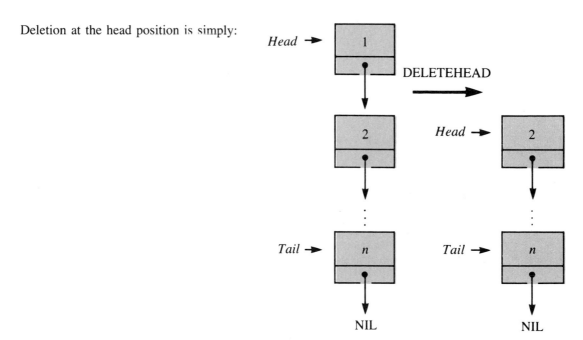

Figure 3.7

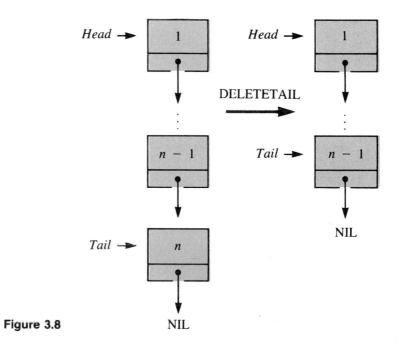

Figure 3.8

```
procedure DeleteHead(aList)                    {O(1)
    if Empty(aList)
        then {deal with this error
        else p ← Head
             Head ← Head ↑ .Link
             DISPOSE( p)
    endif
end {DeleteHead
```

Without disposal of the head node, the **else** clause reduces to:

else *Head ← Head ↑ .Link*

Deletion at the tail position presents an apparent problem and a real problem. If the final node of a list is deleted, *Tail* (if used) still points to it. However, as it is implemented, *Empty* is indifferent to *Tail,* and *no* operation is affected, because operations are carefully designed with *Empty* in mind. Besides, the deleted node is disposed.

Deletion at the tail position requires a pointer to the next-to-last node in order to delete the last one. Hence a search must be made for it by starting at *Head* and working down to detect *Tail* one step ahead. A variable *q,* which trails one node behind *p* and "remembers" the previous node, is introduced. It eventually points to the new *Tail.* Figure 3.9 depicts the final configuration.

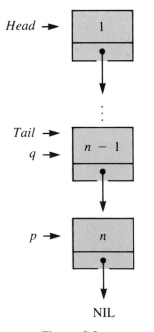

Figure 3.9

Once q is known, deletion is simply:

$q \uparrow .Link \leftarrow p \uparrow .Link$ {*since* p $\uparrow$ .Link *may be* u
$Tail \leftarrow q$
DISPOSE(p)

The relinking works even if *Tail* is not known for the list. Last-node deletion can be done with the help of *LT*, using it to find the last node q and to reset the links. A version that assumes that *Tail* is available is

procedure *DeleteTail(aList)*   {*O(LT)*
  if *Empty(Head)*
    then {*deal with this error*
    else if *Head = Tail*
        then *Head ← Tail* $\uparrow$ *.Link*
            DISPOSE *(Tail)*
        else *LT*
        endif
    endif
  end {*DeleteTail*

where *LT* uses:

CONDITION : $p \neq Tail$
  PROCESS*0* : $q \leftarrow Head$
          $p \leftarrow q \uparrow .Link$
  PROCESS*1* : $q \leftarrow p$
  PROCESS2 : $q \uparrow .Link \leftarrow Tail \uparrow .Link$
      DISPOSE*(Tail)*
      $Tail \leftarrow q$

When these processes are assembled into one structure, the result is:

procedure *DeleteTail(Head,Tail)*   {*O(n)*

   if *Empty(Head)*
     then {*deal with this error*
     else if *Head = Tail*
          then *Head ← Tail ↑ .Link*
              DISPOSE(*Tail*)
          else *q ← Head*
              p ← q ↑ .Link
              while *p ≠ Tail* **do**
                 q ← p
                 p ← p ↑ .Link
              endwhile
              q ↑ .Link ← Tail ↑ .Link
              DISPOSE(*Tail*)
              Tail ← q
          endif
     endif
   end {*DeleteTail*

Note: These and all list-processing routines should be checked for correctness with empty, singleton, and general lists. Treatment of the first and last node as well as a general node should be checked whenever pertinent.

The search for the pointer *q* to the next-to-last node provides some contrast in programming styles: using or not using *Tail*, using sentinel or *NIL*-end lists, and using nested **if**s or **return**s. In the version given, for instance, *Tail ↑ .Link* may be either *NIL* or *u*. Some possibilities for *DeleteTail* follow.

One variation of *DeleteTail* is to replace both **else** clauses with:

  return
endif

Another is to pass only *Head* to *DeleteTail*. The search loop for a *NIL*-end list then becomes:

$q \leftarrow Head$ {PROCESS*0*

$p \leftarrow q \uparrow .Link$ {PROCESS*0*

if p = NIL   {PROCESS*0*

  then DISPOSE(q)

      $Head \leftarrow$ NIL

      return

  endif

while $p \uparrow .Link \neq$ NIL **do**   {CONDITION

  $q \leftarrow p$ {PROCESS*1*

  $p \leftarrow p \uparrow .Link$

  endwhile

$q \uparrow .Link \leftarrow p \uparrow .Link$ {PROCESS2

DISPOSE(p)   {PROCESS2

$Tail \leftarrow q$ {PROCESS2

There are two ways to look at this variation: *Tail* is not needed, or *Tail* is generated for free and may as well be retained.

    It is possible to bury the test for a singleton, at the expense of making a subtle change: the roles of p and q are initially reversed in the algorithm below, in order to avoid the expression "$p \uparrow .Link$" when p = NIL.

procedure *DeleteTail(aList)*   {*standard* DeleteTail

  if *Empty(aList)*   {$O(n)$

    then {*deal with this error*

    else $p \leftarrow Head$

      $q \leftarrow p \uparrow .Link$ {q *will be and stay* NIL iff aList *is a singleton*

     while $p \uparrow .Link \neq$ NIL **do**

      $q \leftarrow p$

      $p \leftarrow p \uparrow .Link$

     endwhile

     if q = NIL

      then $Head \leftarrow$ NIL

      else $q \uparrow .Link \leftarrow p \uparrow .Link$

        $Tail \leftarrow q$

     endif

     DISPOSE(p)

  endif

  end {*DeleteTail*

Formally, the **if** nested in the outer **else** is *PROCESS2*.

    Finally, a sentinel version that simply ignores the attempt to delete from an empty list has a rather different flavor.

```
procedure DeleteTail(Head)                    {O(n)
    q ← Head                                  {PROCESS0
    p ← Head ↑ .Link                          {PROCESS0
    while p ↑ .Link ≠ u do                    {CONDITION
        q ← p                                 {PROCESS1
        p ← p ↑ .Link
    endwhile
    if p ≠ u                                  {PROCESS2
        then DISPOSE( p)
            q ↑ .Link ← u                          .
        else Head ← u                              .
            if q ≠ u then DISPOSE (q) endif        .
    endif                                     {PROCESS2
end {DeleteTail
```

The choice between these variations and others is largely a matter of programming style, tempered by the application and features of the language used to implement them.

The deletion of tail nodes has been used here to illustrate how much even a simple data structure operation may vary and how much care must be taken with linked structures. However, if deletion of tail nodes is common in an application, the doubly-linked list structure of section 6.1 may be preferred. (The additional complexity of that structure does exact a price that must be taken into account; it is an option, not a clear improvement.)

Exercises E3.3–E3.6 and project PJ3.1 are appropriate at this point.

With *DeleteHead* and *InsertHead* it is easy to insert into or delete from the head of a list. A structure formally restricted to these moves is called a STACK. It is also relatively easy to insert into the tail of a list (with *InsertTail*) and delete from the head of it. A structure formally restricted to this pair of moves is called a QUEUE.

3.3.5 Search and Copy

Procedure *LT* can be structured as a search operation that returns a pointer to that node in a linear linked list that contains a given value, or return *NIL* if the value is not in the list:

```
function Hunt(aList,x)                    {O(n)
    p ← Head                             {PROCESS0
    while p ≠ NIL do                     {CONDITION
      if p↑.Value = x                    {PROCESS1
        then return p endif
      p ← p↑.Link
      endwhile
    return NIL                           {PROCESS2
    end {Hunt
```

For n nodes in *aList* and the assumption that *PROCESS1* takes a unit of time, the timing function of *Hunt* is as given: $T(n) = O(n)$. A closer estimate of the timing of *Hunt* is that if the *expected value* (section 1.3.2) of the index of the node returned is k, then $T(n)$ is approximately k. Briefly, $T(n) \sim E[Hunt]$.

Problems P3.1 and P3.2 are appropriate at this point.

Of particular interest for some applications of linked lists is the operation that returns a copy of a list. It, too, is an adaptation of *LT:*

```
function Copy(aList)
    NEW(bList)                           {O(n)
    if Empty(aList)                      {creates a list header, not a list value node.
      then bList.Head ← NIL              {this is not equivalent to: {return aList.
            bList.Tail ← NIL
          return bList
      endif
    NEW(r)
    bList.Head ← r
    p ← aList.Head
    while p ≠ NIL do
      q ← r
      q↑ ← p↑
      NEW(r)                             {create one node ahead
      q↑.Link ← r
      p ← p↑.Link
      endwhile
    q↑.Link ← NIL
    bList.Tail ← q
    DISPOSE(r)
    return bList
    end {Copy
```

Copy can be written without the extra node r, as indicated in one of the problems.

Exercise E3.7 and problems P3.3 and P3.4 are appropriate at this point.

■ 3.4 The Upper Crust at Ballyhoo U   (optional)

Suppose that J. F. Joy of Ballyhoo U decides to teach a short course called *"Voila!"* toward the end of this semester. She enters a proclamation in her public account describing the course content and the time and place of course meetings. In this account is room for two lists of names: IN, limited to 25 entries, and WANTIN, of unlimited length. Entrance to the list IN is provided on a first-come-first-served basis *for juniors and seniors*. Other students and latecomers must sign the WANTIN list. Those who are on the IN list and find that they will not be able to attend are asked to remove their entry.

One week before the first course meeting, those on the IN list must personally confirm with Dr. Joy that they will be able to attend; otherwise, they are scratched, and their place taken by the leading entries of the WANTIN list. Let us see how the lists IN and WANTIN are managed.

A simple way to manage the lists is by writing a "driver" program that accepts a limited set of commands from a user and executes them. A suitable set is:

`"IN"`	: Add my entry to the IN list.
`"WANTIN"`	: Add my entry to the WANTIN list.
`"SCRATCH"`	: Remove my entry from the IN list, or if it is not there, from the WANTIN list.
`"INLIST"`	: Display the entries of the IN list.
`"WANTLIST"`	: Display the entries of the WANTIN list.
`"QUIT"`	: Thanks, but I must go now.

The commands "IN" and "WANTIN" call on a common function, *WhoAreYou,* which prompts the user to enter his or her student number (for checking upper-class status). Function *WhoAreYou* packages the information it receives into a node suitable for entry into the lists IN and WANTIN. The resulting node is the functional value of *WhoAreYou*. This procedure maintains a counter, *InCount,* of the number of entries in IN. If *InCount* is 25, new entries are added to WANTIN.

Both "INLIST" and "WANTLIST" simply use the procedure *LT* of section 3.3.2, specialized for listing as *ListOut*.

The "SCRATCH" command involves a search through IN, and perhaps WANTIN, which can be done with *Hunt*. The search is followed, if successful, by the removal of a node from the appropriate list with a procedure *Scratch*.

A driver that behaves as a command-shell is outlined as:

```
program JoinUp
    Write {instructions to the user.
    repeat
        Read(Command)
        case of Command
                "IN":    if InCount < 25
                            then me ← WhoAreYou
                                 InsertTail(IN,me)
                                 InCount ← InCount + 1
                            else Write {explanation
                                 me ← WhoAreYou
                                 InsertTail(WANTIN,me)
                         endif
            "WANTIN":    me ← WhoAreYou
                         InsertTail(WANTIN,me)
           "SCRATCH":    me ← WhoAreYou
                         p ← Hunt(IN,me)
                         if p ≠ NIL
                            then Scratch(IN,p)
                            else p ← Hunt(WANTIN,me)
                                 if p ≠ NIL
                                    then Scratch(WANTIN,p)
                                    else {report failure to find me
                                 endif
                         endif
            "INLIST":    ListOut(IN)
          "WANTLIST":    ListOut(WANTIN)
              "QUIT":    exit
                else:    {Provide the user with a list
                         {of legitimate commands.
        endcase
    forever
end {JoinUp
```

Function *WhoAreYou* is not specifically list processing and is left to the reader.

Procedure *Scratch* does not need to be a general deletion routine. When it is invoked, the pointer *p* provided by *Hunt* is known to be non-*NIL*. The deletion operation, though, needs the *predecessor* of *p*, which is to become linked to the *successor* of *p*, *p* ↑ *.Link*, instead of *p:*

```
procedure Scratch(aList,p)                          {O(n)
  if p = Head
    then DeleteHead(aList)
    else q ← Head
      while q ↑ .Link ≠ p do
        q ← q ↑ .Link
      endwhile
      q ↑ .Link ← p ↑ .Link
      DISPOSE(p)
  endif
end {Scratch
```

InCount is not decremented by *Scratch*, and so an upper-class student who is forced to enter WANTIN is not kept there by a latecomer who follows a withdrawal.

Searching through the list twice is a waste, and so *Hunt* and *Scratch* may be combined.

Program PG3.1 is appropriate at this point.

Professor Joy can use *JoinUp* to easily remove "no-shows" from IN; but, since *JoinUp* does not increment *InCount*, a routine is needed to do so. On most academic systems, this routine can be proprietary—unavailable to the student. The transfer of *m* nodes from WANTIN to IN with *JoinUp* will use *WhoAreYou m* times, even after adding a routine to readjust *InCount*. A short program can be written to do the same thing by either transferring nodes from WANTIN to IN or copying them. The copying procedure is:

```
program Floodgate                                   {O(n)
  m ← 25 − InCount
  for i = 1 to m do
    NEW(p)
    p ↑ ← WANTIN.Head ↑
    DeleteHead(WANTIN)
    InsertTail(IN,p)
    InCount ← InCount + 1
  next i
end {Floodgate
```

Note: The command-shell format of *Joinup* can be adapted to the management of a variety of resources. In this case the resource is a pair of lists, and the commands are the only contact the user needs with them. Details of the algorithms and implementation of the lists are deliberately transparent to the user (not visible).

3.5 Array Support for Linked Lists

A linked list may be implemented with values and links stored in arrays. One way to do this is to store single node values in array *Value*[1 .. Max], and their corresponding links in array *Link*[0 .. Max]. In effect, *Value*[i] and *Link*[i] together form the *i*th node of the list. Helpful conventions are: *Link*[0] points to the first node; *Link*[i] = 0 is equivalent to the *NIL* link used with pointer variables. Essentially, the correspondences between a pointer-linked list and an index-linked list are:

$Head \longleftrightarrow Link[0]$
$p \longleftrightarrow i$
$p \uparrow .Value \longleftrightarrow Value[i]$
$p \uparrow .Link \longleftrightarrow Link [i]$

Figure 3.10 depicts a specific example, with some of the links indicated.

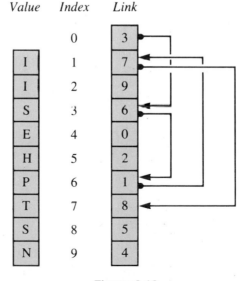

Figure 3.10

A display routine for such a list, based on the general traverse of it, *ALT* (Array-List Traverse), by substituting a *Write* for *PROCESS1*, an initialization for *PROCESS0*, and leaving *PROCESS2* null:

```
                                                              ALT
    procedure ALT(Value,Link)      {O(n)
        Next ← Link[0]             {PROCESS0
        while Next ≠ 0 do          {CONDITION
            PROCESS1(Next)
            Next ← Link[Next]
        endwhile
        PROCESS2
    end {ALT
```

The result is an orderly "SPITSHINE".

With the data in front of us, we easily see that this word can be hyphenated with the insertion of the new value " − " in the list:

Value[10] ← " − "
Link[10] ← *Link*[7]
Link[7] ← 10

The number of characters in the list, its *Length*, can be determined by the substitutions:

PROCESS0 : *Length* ← 0
                Next ← *Link*[0]
PROCESS1 : *Length* ← *Length* + 1

If two pointers are used, which is a great convenience for some applications, then a declaration of *Link*[0 . . *Max* + 1] can be helpful, allowing *Link*[*Max* + 1] to serve as the tail pointer.

A feel for the effect of array support can be gained by rewriting some of the procedures discussed in conjunction with pointer variables in this new context. If it is assumed that *Value* and *Link* are global variables, deletion of the head node is accomplished as follows and in Figure 3.11.

```
procedure DeleteHead                          {O(1)
    if Link[0] = 0
        then {deal with this error
        else Link[0] ← Link[Link[0]]
    endif
end {DeleteHead
```

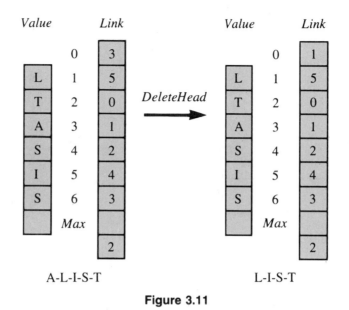

A-L-I-S-T   L-I-S-T

Figure 3.11

If k is the index of a node to be added to the tail of the list, a version of *InsertTail* is needed:

```
procedure InsertTail(k)                    {O(1)
    if Link[0] = 0
        then Link[0] ← k
    endif
    Link[Link[Max + 1]] ← k
    Link[Max + 1] ← k
    Link[k] ← 0
end {InsertTail
```

The result of adding "S" to the tail of the preceding list is depicted in Figure 3.12.

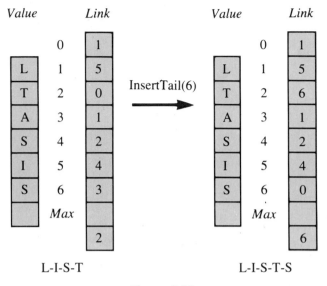

Figure 3.12

The rewriting of other list-processing procedures for array support is explored in the exercises.

Exercises E3.8–3.10 and project PJ3.1 are appropriate at this point.

If a value input or generated within the program is to be inserted, index k must be located. The program must keep track of storage available within the array *Value*, even after arbitrary deletions.

Note: The programmer must provide for the possibility that there will *be* no available storage within the value array.

To insert a value, say x, at the tail of an array-supported list generally requires two moves:

GetSpace(k)
InsertTail(k)

Unhappily, *GetSpace* may not be simple. It can be kept simple if insertions are made into *Value*[1 . . *n*] for $n \leq Max$, and the space occupied by deleted values is just ignored.

Memory is essentially an array of cells, so consideration of storage allocation will eventually come to the programmer's attention even if pointer-variables and built-in *NEW* operations are available in the programming language being used. These language features cause details of the allocation and retrieval of storage to be transparent (invisible) to the user. Transparency is not the same as nonexistence.

The problem of the use and release of storage during program execution is called *dynamic memory allocation*. Approaches commonly taken to solve this problem use material that is discussed in several later chapters. Chapter 6 deals with this topic again.

3.6 Ordered Lists

The list of people who have contributed to the Planetary Society or to a politician's campaign or who have had contact with a known disease carrier may grow to be large or remain small. Information about these people needs to be maintained in order, usually as determined by their full name used as a key to a record of pertinent data. Several factors form the core of the problem of maintaining the list and affect the choice of data structure used to solve it: the list is of indeterminate size, it changes size, it is sparse in the data-space of possible full names, and it must be *ordered* so that searching it is convenient. The core of a data structure that mirrors such problem domains is an *ordered list,* a list of nodes sorted by value (or key). Such a list may be either endogenous or exogenous, depending on the role played by node values in a particular application.

Figure 3.13 is an example of an ordered list where the node values are chosen for convenience to be simply integers serving as keys.

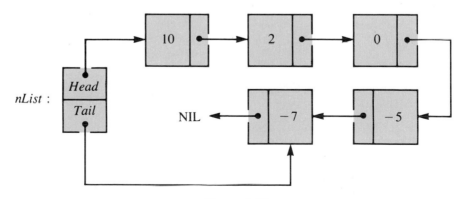

Figure 3.13

Nodes in *nList* have a natural type:

NumNode = RECORD
                Value : INTEGER
                Link   : ↑ *NumNode*
                END {*NumNode*

Search-and-display routines for a list like *nList* are variations of procedure *LT* (section 3.3.2). Deletions at either end could be taken care of by *DeleteHead* and *DeleteTail* (both discussed in section 3.3.2). The management of *nList* as an *ordered* list requires that deletions take place from *any* position and that additions can be made so that the node values retain their numeric order.

The first requirement for insertion of a new value into *nList* is to encase it into a node:

{*determine x*
NEW(*xNode*)
xNode ↑ .*Value* ← *x*

The next requirement is to locate the position in which *xNode* should appear. It is convenient to make "position" mean a pointer to the *proper* predecessor of *xNode:* the node which should precede *xNode* when the new ordered list is formed by the incorporation of *xNode*.

A parameter *Spot* is added for convenience so that *IntoList* inserts *xNode* if it should precede the node *Spot*. When *Spot* ← NIL, the entire list is available to define an insertion position.

The proper interior position can be found between *Head* and *Spot* (possibly *NIL*) with a version of *LT, using:*

CONDITION : p ↑ .*Link* ≠ *Spot*
 PROCESS0 : p ← *Head*
 PROCESS1 : *Next* ← p ↑ .*Link*
                if x ≥ *Next* ↑ .*Value* **then exit endif**

Insertion is then:

PROCESS2 : *xNode* ↑ .*Link* ← p ↑ .*Link*
           p ↑ .*Link* ← *xNode*

However, if x = 15 were to be included in the example list, then there would *be* no proper predecessor for it. A FIND operation would need to return information specifying that fact as well as to return the proper predecessor in the general case.

Here modularity can be overdone, and it is easier to find and insert in a single operation:

```
procedure IntoList(nList,xNode,Spot)                    {O(n)
    if Empty(nList)
        then Head ← xNode
             Tail ← xNode
             xNode ↑ .Link ← NIL
             return
    endif
    x ← xNode ↑ .Value
    if (x ≥ Head ↑ .Value) OR (Spot = Head)
        then xNode ↑ .Link ← Head                       {new Head node
             Head ← xNode
        else p ← Head                                   {LT
            while p ↑ .Link ≠ Spot do
                Next ← p ↑ .Link
                if x ≥ Next ↑ .Value then exit endif
                p ← p ↑ .Link
            endwhile
            xNode ↑ .Link ← p ↑ .Link
            p ↑ .Link ← xNode
    endif
end {IntoList
```

Exercise E3.11 is appropriate at this point.

Procedure *IntoList* can be readily adapted to the sorting of a stream of input values into a linked list.

Problem P3.5 is appropriate at this point.

A more difficult task is an analog of *InsertionSort* (section 1.4.3) that sorts a linear linked list that already exists, rather than building it by steps so that it is sorted at each stage of its construction. The relinking involved can be studied by considering the stages of an example. In Figures 3.14–3.18, the links generated at each stage are dashed.

In Figure 3.14, the second node is to be inserted before the first. Figure 3.15 shows the third node inserted before the (new) first. The fourth node remains in place in Figure 3.16. In Figure 3.17, the fifth node is inserted between the second and third. Figure 3.18 shows that the sixth node is then inserted before the first.

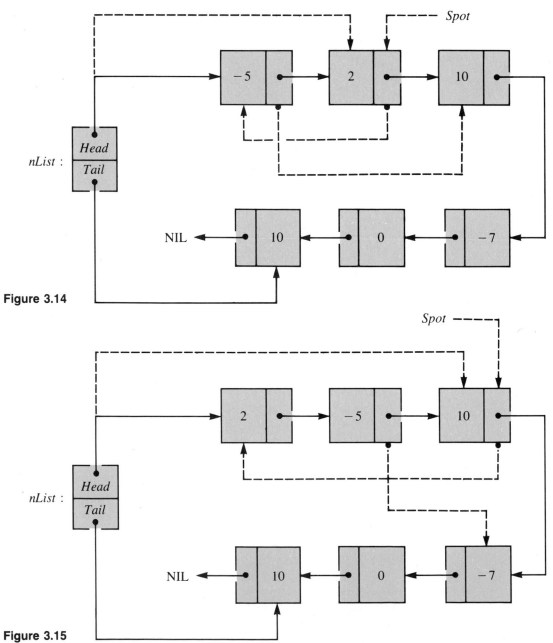

Figure 3.14

Figure 3.15

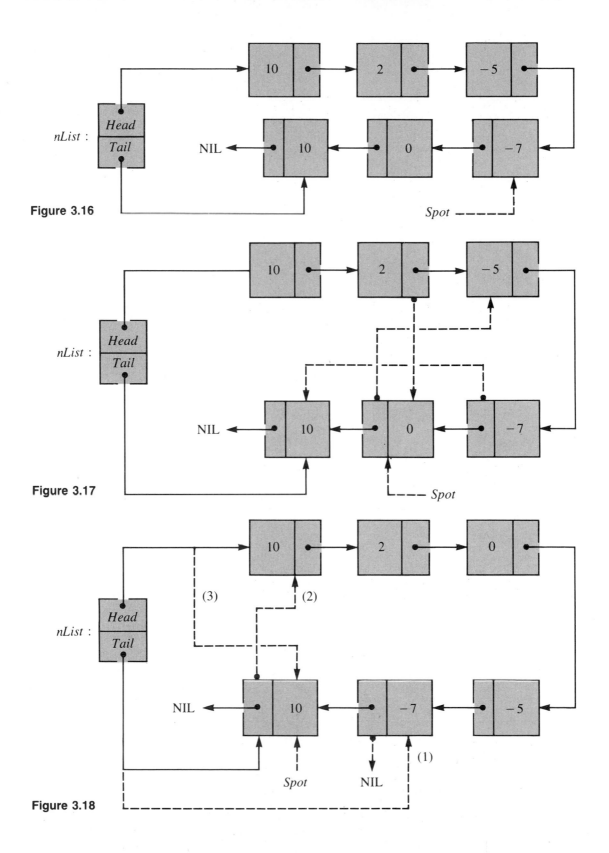

Figure 3.16

Figure 3.17

Figure 3.18

An examination of the pointer moves required to insert the node designated by *Spot* shows that moves 2 and 3 (Figures 3.15 and 3.16) are essentially the action of *IntoList(nList,Spot,Spot ↑ .Link)* after *Spot* is excised from the list. Hence the sorting procedure becomes:

procedure *LinearSort(nList)*   {*O(n²)*}

    if *Empty(nList)*
        then {*deal with this error*
        else *Spot* ← *Head* ↑ *.Link*
                if *Spot* = NIL **then return endif**
                Prior ← *Head*
                while *Spot* ↑ *.Link* ≠ NIL **do**
                    SpotLink ← *Spot* ↑ *.Link*
                    Prior ↑ *.Link* ← *SpotLink*
                    IntoList(nList,Spot,SpotLink)
                    if *Prior* ↑ *.Link* ≠ *SpotLink*
                        then *Prior* ← *Spot*
                      endif
                    Spot ← *SpotLink*
                endwhile
                Prior ↑ *.Link* ← NIL
                *IntoList(nList,Spot,*NIL)
                if *Tail* ↑ *.Link* ≠ NIL
                    then *Tail* ← *Prior*
                  endif
        endif
    end {*LinearSort*

Exercise E3.12, problems P3.6–P3.9, and programs PG3.2–PG3.4 are appropriate at this point.

3.7 Circular Lists

The tail node of a linear list can point back to the head node, forming a cyclic structure called a *circular list,* illustrated in Figure 3.19.

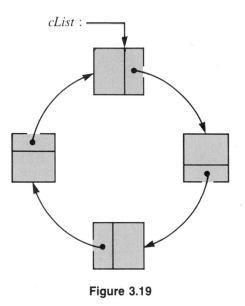

Figure 3.19

Circular lists find their place as a programming convenience in some applications because of two different effects of circularity on a sequence of searches:

1. An exhaustive search of a circular list returns to the first node searched. The list may be one of several in a combination of lists connecting common nodes, as is the case for the sparse matrix structure of section 6.3. Return to the initial node then brings a traverse to a point from which it may branch onto another substructure.

2. If a pointer to the last node of a circular list traverse is retained to become the first node of the next walk, a *sequence* of searches is distributed over the list. Even-handed attention can be useful in applications such as the dynamic storage allocation model of section 6.4.

> **Note:** Insertion, deletion, and walking in circular lists differ little from the same operations applied to linear lists. The needed algorithms are to be found in Part II, section C, or derived by analogy.

■ 3.8 Polynomial Arithmetic   (optional)

Polynomials like those below are prime examples of objects that should be managed as linked lists:

$$P_1: \quad 31x^{17} - x^{11} + 5x^4 + 10x^3 - 3$$
$$P_2: \quad 7x^{17} + 4x^6 - 2x^2 + 8$$
$$P_3: \quad x^{11} - 5x^4 + x^2 + 3$$

P_1 is a polynomial of degree 17, because 17 is the largest exponent of its nonzero terms. Only the coefficient-exponent (CE) pairs $(31,17)$, $(-1,11)$, $(5,4)$, $(10,3)$, and $(-3,0)$ are needed to describe P_1, since terms specified by $(0,16)$, $(0,15)$, . . . all have zero coefficients.

Given only that the largest exponent allowed for polynomials in a collection of them is n, a collection-manager is *blind* in the sense that the number of CE pairs needed to store one or the whole collection is not determined by n.

Polynomials such as P_1, P_2, and P_3 are intrinsically *sparse:* a polynomial of degree 17 could take as many as 18 CE pairs to describe, but the examples clearly do not.

In a system where arithmetic is done on polynomials, they are *dynamic.* $P_1 + P_3 = P_4$ is $31x^{17} + 10x^3 + x^2$, described by CE pairs $(31,17)$, $(10,3)$, and $(1,2)$. The assignment $P_1 \leftarrow P_1 + P_3$ changes the number of CE pairs needed to describe P_1.

An ordered linked sentinel list is a natural structure for polynomials. For P_3 such a list has the form shown in Figure 3.20 where nodes are of the type:

PolyNode = RECORD
             exp : INTEGER
             Coef : REAL
             Link : ↑ *PolyNode*
             END {*PolyNode*

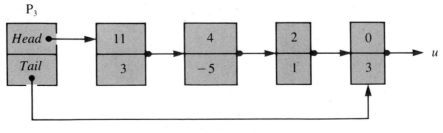

Figure 3.20

A system that deals with polynomial lists of this sort can create them with the help of *IntoList* (section 3.6), and a display routine is easily devised. Writing a program that performs polynomial arithmetic, which has a very algebraic flavor, then becomes a reasonable project (PJ3.2, in fact). Most of the effort required to devise polynomial arithmetic routines depends on understanding polynomials, rather than difficulties in procedure design, and that is typical of much programming. As an example of polynomial arithmetic on linked lists, here is a function that returns the sum of linked-list polynomials P and Q:

function *PolyAdd(P,Q)*
  PAQ ← *u*
  while $P \neq u$ AND $Q \neq u$ **do**
    NEW(*R*)
    case
      $P \uparrow .exp > Q \uparrow .exp$: $R \uparrow \leftarrow P \uparrow$
                        $P \leftarrow P \uparrow .Link$
                        InsertTail (*PAQ,R*)
      $P \uparrow .exp = Q \uparrow .exp$: $R \uparrow .exp \leftarrow P \uparrow .exp$
                        $R \uparrow .Coef \leftarrow P \uparrow .Coef + Q \uparrow .Coef$
                        $P \leftarrow P \uparrow .Link$
                        $Q \leftarrow Q \uparrow .Link$
                        if $R \uparrow .Coef \neq 0$
                            then *InsertTail(PAQ,R)*
                        endif
      $P \uparrow .exp < Q \uparrow .exp$: $R \uparrow \leftarrow Q \uparrow$
                        $Q \leftarrow Q \uparrow .Link$
                        InsertTail(PAQ,R)
    endcase
    endwhile
  if $P = u$
    then *Rest* ← *Q*
    else *Rest* ← *P*
    endif
  while $Rest \neq u$ **do**
    NEW(*R*)
    $R \uparrow \leftarrow Rest \uparrow$
    InsertTail(PAQ,R)
    $Rest \leftarrow Rest \uparrow .Link$
    endwhile
  return *PAQ*
  end {*PolyAdd*

Exercise E3.13, problem P3.10, program PG3.5, and project PJ3.2 are appropriate at this point.

■ 3.9 Arithmetic of Unbounded Precision (optional)

The federal deficit of the United States in 1983 was a number of approximately this size:

$197,800,400,650.23

Such a number is difficult to store in most programs. Only *approximations* to it can be stored as either an integer or a real number because it has too many significant digits. (Even when the number of digits of interest is small, the number base in most computers is 2, not 10, which causes some decimal values to be approximate.) The *precision* of a number is the number of significant digits in it, and a budget number surely needs to be precise to the penny.

The approximate forms available to the programmer as types *INTEGER* and *REAL*, double-precision or not, are a compromise between the time-and-space efficiency suitable for most programs and the need for precision in some. In most applications, 1.978×10^{11} would be an adequate representation of the number above.

Unbounded precision in arithmetic can be gained by retaining *every* digit generated in any arithmetic calculation. A suitable data structure for such arithmetic would need to grow and shrink during execution (be dynamic) and be open-ended (blind to the eventual size of a number). One solution is to use a linked list for the storage structure of an unbounded number, as was done for the polynomials of section 3.8. In fact, a value such as 743.1 *is* a polynomial in powers of the number base 10:

$$743.1 = 7 \times 10^2 + 4 \times 10^1 + 3 \times 10^0 + 1 \times 10^{-1}$$

Figure 3.21 shows this value stored as a linked list.

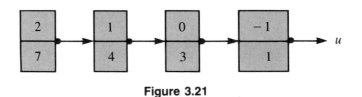

Figure 3.21

Given that there is a data structure suitable for values of unbounded precision, it is possible to write a program (which could be used as a procedure within a larger program) that acts as a calculator for such numbers. In Part II, section D, a Pascal program acting as a calculator is given a command-shell form that supports commands to add, subtract, multiply, and divide integer values in a way that provides precision bounded only by the storage capacity of the Pascal system on which it is executed. The restriction to integer values simplifies both the supporting list structure and the arithmetic routines and allows the focus of the program to be a simulation of the response of a hand calculator to a sequence of keystrokes.

Summary

The LIST is such a general structure that lists with restricted access are the basis for later chapters and sections of the book. The linked list is the structure of choice for some applications because it is *dynamic, sparse,* and *blind.* It may serve as a directory for data and hence be *exogenous,* or it may contain the data of interest and be *endogenous.* (The data structures of following chapters are also used in these two ways.)

A list may be supported as a programming structure in several ways. The list model most used in this book is based on records linked by pointers. The final pointer may be *NIL* or a universal sentinel node, u. Array support is also possible and sometimes convenient.

The information in the nodes of a list is accessible via the head node and a sequence of links, but not directly, in contrast to the array structure. The head node is easily reached, the interior nodes require a list-walk to reach, and the reachability of the tail node depends on implementation.

Common list operations include a test for an empty list from which an attempt to delete usually represents an error. (Later in the book it is sometimes useful to assume that deletion from an empty list is an operation that cannot fail.)

Insertion at the head and tail of a list and deletion at the head are $O(1)$ operations. These operations provide one definition of structures STACK and QUEUE to follow in later chapters. Deletion at the tail involves a search for its predecessor and so is $O(n)$.

List operations (and operations on other structures) should be tested for their treatment of empty and singleton lists and behavior at the head, tail, and interior nodes.

Many list algorithms are modeled after one—the list-traverse (or list-walk) from head to tail. Procedures *Search* and *Copy* are examples of such algorithms. The general walk *LT* of section 3.3.2 has an array-support form *ALT* described in section 3.5.

Ordered lists and circular lists provide specialized variations that have a number of applications, some treated in later chapters.

Two list-management paradigms (that lead to exploratory assignments) are a sign-up list *JoinUp* (example in section 3.4) and polynomial arithmetic (introduced in section 3.8). Both *JoinUp* and the arithmetic of unbounded precision that was introduced in section 3.9 and is programmed in Pascal in Part II, section D, provide examples of *command-shells* that hide extraneous information from the user.

Exercises immediate applications of the text material

E3.1 Show, with a diagram, the result of switching the two assignments after the **if** in *InsertHead* of section 3.3.3. What is the effect of moving the **if** statement below one or both assignments?

E3.2 In *InsertTail* of section 3.3.3, why aren't the two assignments of *p* to *Tail* redundant? Why must the **if** statement be executed before the assignments? Can the order of the assignments be altered in any way?

E3.3 A deletion (or insertion) procedure should be checked for performance on these lists:

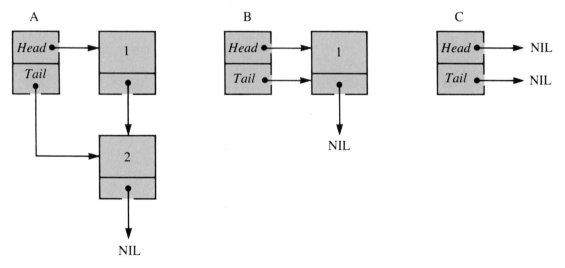

Trace the action of both *DeleteHead* of section 3.3.4 and *DeleteTail* of section 3.3.4 on lists A, B, and C.

E3.4 Trace the action of the standard *DeleteTail* of section 3.3.4 on lists A, B, and C of E3.3 when ($q \leftarrow p \uparrow .Link$) is omitted. What is the result?

E3.5 Trace the action of the standard *DeleteTail* of section 3.3.4 on lists A, B, and C of E3.3 when (**if** $q = $ NIL . . .) is replaced by just the **else** phase. What is the result?

E3.6 Trace the action of the standard *DeleteTail* of section 3.3.4 on lists A, B, and C of E2.3 when the **while** condition is changed to: ($p \neq $ NIL). What is the result?

E3.7 Trace the action of *Copy* of section 3.3.5 on lists A, B, and C of E3.3. Is it possible to change the sequence of assignments in the body of the **while?**

E3.8 Rewrite *InsertHead* of section 3.3.3 for explicit array support.

E3.9 Rewrite *DeleteTail* of section 3.3.4 for explicit array support.

E3.10 Rewrite *Hunt* of section 3.3.5 for explicit array support.

E3.11 Trace the action of *IntoList* of section 3.6 with insertion of values 10, 3, and -10.

E3.12 Trace the action of *LinearSort* of section 3.6 on the example of section 3.6 by keeping track of all pointer variables during placement of the first and last node.

E3.13 For polynomials P_2 and P_3 of section 3.8, find: $P_2 + P_3$, $P_2 - P_3$, $P_2 \times P_3$, and both the quotient Q and remainder R of P_2 / P_3.

Problems   not immediate, but requiring no major extensions of the text material

P3.1 If the nodes of a list are numbered from 1 at *Head* to N at *Tail*, then there is an expected value, $1 \le ex \le N$ for the number of the node located by *Hunt* of section 3.3.5. Assume that every node is equally likely to contain the searched-for value x and that there is only a 50 percent chance that x is a node value at all. Determine $T(N)$ for *Hunt*, as a function of ex.

P3.2 Continue the analysis of P3.1 with the assumption that x tends to be found near the head of the list. In particular, assume that finding x at $node_k$ is twice as likely as finding it at $node_{k+1}$ for $1 \le k \le N - 1$. In effect, find ex.

P3.3 Diagram the behavior of the alteration of *Copy* of section 3.3.5 shown below, for the lists A, B, and C of E3.3.

```
NEW(q)
bList. Head ← q
p ← aList.Head
while p ≠ NIL do
   q↑ ← p↑
   NEW(r)
   q↑.Link ← r
   q ← r
   p ← p↑.Link
   endwhile
q↑.Link ← NIL
return bList
```

P3.4   Diagram the behavior of the altered *Copy* of P3.3 for the lists A, B, and C of E3.3 if the **while** condition is changed to: ($p \uparrow .Link \neq$ NIL).

P3.5   Write a procedure *InputSort,* which inputs a stream of values, encases them in nodes, and inserts them with *IntoList* of section 3.6 as they are entered into an ordered list. See PG3.2.

P3.6   Determine the timing function for *LinearSort* of section 3.6.

P3.7   Rewrite *LinearSort* of section 3.6 so that the **while** condition is: ($Spot \neq$ NIL).

P3.8   Rewrite *SelectionSort* of section 1.4.1 to sort a linked list, using pointer variables, and determine its timing function. See PG3.3.

P3.9   Rewrite *BubbleSort* of section 1.4.2 to sort a linked list, using pointer variables, and determine its timing function. See PG3.4.

P3.10   Write a procedure that multiplies two linked-list polynomials.

Programs   for trying it out yourself

PG3.1   Write and run program *JoinUp* of section 3.4.

PG3.2   Turn the procedure *InputSort* of P3.5 into a program that inputs a stream of values and sorts them by insertion into a linked list, then displays the values in order.

PG3.3   Turn the procedure of P3.8 into a program that inputs a stream of values, places them in a linked list, sorts them by exchange, and displays the values in order.

PG3.4   Turn P3.9 into a program that inputs a stream of values, places them into a linked list, sorts them as *BubbleSort* of section 1.4.2 does, and displays the values in order.

PG3.5   Write a program to accept two polynomials (supplied as coefficient-exponent pairs) and display their product.

Projects   for fun; for serious students

PJ3.1   Rewrite PJ2.1, using linked lists to track available space and in-lot cars. (The lot may be enlarged, although checking the ''lot-full'' test then becomes a bore.)

PJ3.2   Write a program that will manage a collection of linked-list polynomials and perform arithmetic on them as requested. The operations to be provided are addition, subtraction, multiplication, and division.

Chapter 4

Stacks

A wide variety of processes exhibit a pattern similar to the movement of trays in a cafeteria, in and out of a spring-loaded pile. Trays are added to the top of the pile and also removed from the top of the pile. As a result, the last tray in is the first tray out. Common terminology for a list of items that grows and shrinks in this way is a *LIFO* (Last-In-First-Out) *list* or *stack*. The same pattern appears in discussions of the strategies available for inventory control of items on local grocery store shelves and in large warehouses. Stacks are used to unravel the flow of control when one computing procedure calls another, which calls another, etc. They are sometimes used as essential design features of computing hardware, of language translation, and of computing languages. The stack structure even imposes itself on the precious junk in a storeroom of a private dwelling, not always with happy effect.

Stacks can be implemented in arrays without the use of link indices, but linked lists are also a natural way to discuss stacks. Consider the linked list in Figure 4.1.

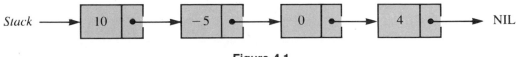

Figure 4.1

If two deletions are made from the top (the head) of this list, and the value 2 is added at the top, the effect is to carry out the operations:

DELETE
DELETE
INSERT 2

The resulting snapshots of the list are shown in Figure 4.2.

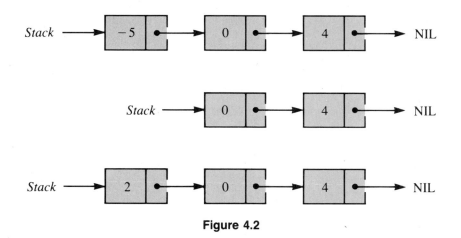

Figure 4.2

In terms of the list-processing routines of Chapter 3, a linked-list structure is a stack iff insertion is restricted to *InsertHead* and deletion is restricted to *DeleteHead*.

4.1 The Stack Structure

Stacks need to be created, like any other structure, but insertion and deletion both occur at the top (the head), so no tail pointer or index is required. The formal operation that gives birth to a stack is CREATE.

Activation of a stack is usually accompanied by initializing the top pointer to *NIL* (or *u*). A stack may grow and then decrease until it is again empty, as though freshly activated. The formal (Boolean) operation that checks the viability of a stack is EMPTY.

A stack grows iff a single node is inserted into its top position. No way of assigning values directly to stack nodes is available in a pure stack. The formal operation that inserts a node into a stack is PUSH.

The only value of a stack accessible to its environment is the value of its top node.

The *only* retrievable value of a stack is that of its top node. The formal operation that returns the value of the top node is TOP.

The top node must be removed from a stack before the values of other nodes can be retrieved. The formal operation that removes the top node from a stack is DELETE.

The behavior of a stack is entirely described, however it may be implemented, by CREATE, EMPTY, INSERT, DELETE, and TOP, and their interactions. TOP followed by DELETE, implemented as one operation, is called POP.

However a stack is stored, it can be used to alter a sequence of values. For example, the input stream of characters S-T-A-C-K can be arranged in reverse order by stacking them and then unstacking them, as depicted in Figure 4.3.

Pushes:

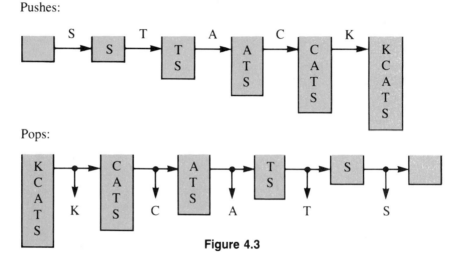

Pops:

Figure 4.3

The output produced by the pops is: K-C-A-T-S.

Figure 4.4 shows that the consonants can be moved after the vowel A by stacking them as encountered. The output produced by the pops is: A-K-C-T-S.

Pushes:

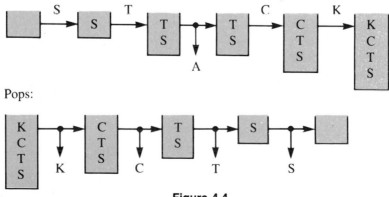

Pops:

Figure 4.4

This process is easily generalized into the separation of two classes of items in a stream into leading and trailing segments in $O(n)$ time.

Railroad cars are separated on siding tracks in just this way, although more than one siding (stack) may be needed for more than one category of car.

With the aid of more than one stack, shuffling can become more sophisticated. Suppose the letters I-N-P-U-T-S-T-R-E-A-M are placed in stack S_1 in nondecreasing order, and the others shunted to stack S_2 as in Figure 4.5.

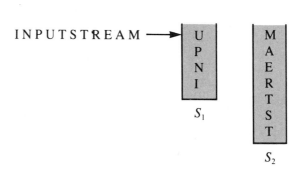

Figure 4.5

Unstacking of S_1 followed by unstacking of S_2 forms a new stream: U-P-N-I-M-A-E-R-T-S-T. Now this stream may be reversed (by stacking it, for example) to form: T-S-T-R-E-A-M-I-N-P-U. Apply the process in Figure 4.5 to the new stream, depicted in Figure 4.6.

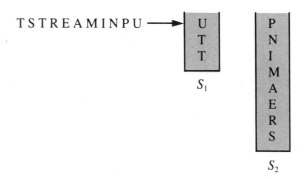

Figure 4.6

If S_1 and S_2 are unloaded with the help of a third stack as before, the resulting stream is: S-R-E-A-M-I-N-P-T-T-U.

Surprising as it may seem, six more repetitions of this process will produce the sorted stream: A-E-I-M-N-P-R-S-T-T-U. Try it!

Devising a sorting routine from this process is project PJ4.1.

Project PJ4.1 is appropriate at this point.

4.1.1 Stack Implementation and Management

Two natural implementations are a list structure, which uses pointer variables, and an array-management scheme. If the list is called *liStack* and the array is called *aStack,* then the same data set takes two schematic forms, shown in Figure 4.7.

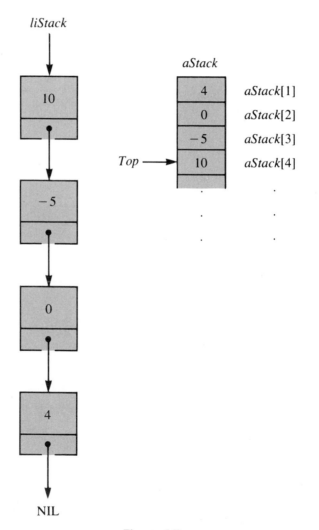

Figure 4.7

There is also a hybrid form, in which a stack is implemented as a linked-list structure, which in turn is supported in arrays:

Hybrid Stack

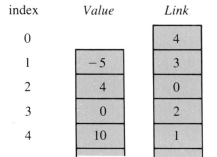

index	*Value*	*Link*
0		4
1	−5	3
2	4	0
3	0	2
4	10	1

{*Items in* Value *are stored*
{*at random, rather than in*
{*order-of-entry, to emphasize*
{*the role of* Link. *The top*
{*node is* Link[0], *and the*
{*last one has* Link[*] = 0.

This form is seldom used and will not be pursued.

Any stack supported in an array must be programmed with some concern for the maximum possible index, *Max.* A variable, *Top,* is required to locate the top item in *aStack.* Table 4.1 allows comparison between the two major treatments by examining the stack operations in parallel. For comparison, the linked-list form of *Push* accepts values instead of nodes. Note that all of the stack management routines are fast: $O(l)$. This intrinsic efficiency promotes the use of stacks in applications.

The programming that manages a stack with an input file (such as a sequence of keyboard entries) is straightforward. For example, a sequence of commands of the form: *I* (for INSERT), and *D* (for DELETE) can be processed by this loop:

```
repeat
    Read(Command)
    case of Command
        "I"  : Read(Item)
                Push(Stack,Item)
        "D" : Delete(Stack)
        "E" : exit      {E stands for End-Of-File
        else  : {deal with this error
        endcase
    forever
```

Commands to invoke TOP or the display of the complete stack are easily added to the preceding command loop. Difficulties (challenges) arise from exception handling (dealing with errors) and from the quirks of individual applications.

A command loop like the one above is thought of as a *shell* that surrounds the machinery of resource management. It forms an interface with the user, who sees it as a *virtual machine.* The user supplies commands that evoke a response. From the user's view, the loop is a machine that does whatever the commands say to do.

Table 4.1

	liStack	CREATE	*aStack*	
	liStack ← NIL	*{O(1)*	*Top* ← 0	*{O(1)*
EMPTY				
	function *Empty(liStack)*	*{O(1)*	**function** *Empty(aStack)*	*{O(1)*
	if *liStack* = NIL		**if** *Top* = *0*	
	then return TRUE		**then return** TRUE	
	else return FALSE		**else return** FALSE	
	endif		**endif**	
	end {*Empty*		**end** {*Empty*	
INSERT				
	procedure *Push(liStack,i)*	*{O(1)*	**procedure** *Push(Stack,i)*	*{O(1)*
	New(*iNode*)		**if** *Top* > *Max*	
	iNode ↑ .*Value* ← *i*		**then** {*deal with this error*	
	iNode ↑ .*Link* ← *liStack*		**else** *Top* ← *Top* + *1*	
	liStack ← *iNode*		*aStack[Top]* ← *i*	
	end {*Push*		**endif**	
			end {*Push*	
DELETE				
	procedure *Delete(liStack)*	*{O(1)*	**procedure** *Delete(aStack)*	*{O(1)*
	if *Empty(liStack)*		**if** *Empty(aStack)*	
	then {*deal with this error*		**then** {*deal with this error*	
	else *liStack* ← *liStack* ↑ .*Link*		**else** *Top* ← *Top* − *1*	
	endif		**endif**	
	end {*Delete*		**end** {*Delete*	
TOP				
	function *TopValue(liStack)*	*{O(1)*	**function** *TopValue(aStack)*	*{O(1)*
	if *Empty(liStack)*		**if** *Empty(aStack)*	
	then {*deal with this error*		**then** {*deal with this error*	
	else return *liStack* ↑ .*Value*		**else return** *aStack[top]*	
	endif		**endif**	
	end {*TopValue*		**end** {*TopValue*	

The details of how the response gets done internally are of no concern at the command level. This kind of deliberate information-hiding is also present in the use of a data structure, and the concept of a virtual machine is a major guiding philosophy in the design of a modern operating system.

The shell format that professionals use to deal with complexity is well worth imitating.

Note: A realization in Pascal of the loop above as a "stack machine" is found in Part II, section E.

The display of a stack can be carried out by standard list procedures but only if the stack is treated as a *list,* not a stack. As an instance of STACK, display of the contents proceeds the same way as the display of the contents of a crowded closet or a full deep-freezer: items are popped off the stack, displayed, and then pushed onto an auxiliary stack. Restoration is a reverse of this process, without the display. It is more reasonable and common practice to forgo rigid formality and use a list-walk to display the contents of a stack.

> **Note:** STACK is a structure that *does not require a traverse* in most applications. There is no direct access to interior nodes. For other data structures in the book, with the exception of QUEUE, the traverse is a fundamental skeleton for constructing algorithms.

4.1.2 On the Use of Stacks

Stacks are sometimes chosen as a data structure simply because they model *behavior* that occurs in the system to be modeled (as would be the case in a cafeteria simulation). Actually, modeling natural stack behavior may not even require a stack, as indicated in section 4.5. Stacks may also be chosen to deliberately shape a computing scheme.

Stacks are dynamic—growing and shrinking at will—but that fact is *hidden* from the user who sees only the top item. Stacks are blind because it is not necessary to know their potential size when they are created. Stacks can be sparse because *no interior item in a stack occupies a special place in it* — only the sequence of PUSH and POP operations determines where in a stack an item is to be found. Furthermore, it does not matter except to determine when an item reaches the top. All of these features indicate that a linked list is a natural support for a stack.

Stacks provide $O(1)$ direct access, although only to one item at a time, and the direct access moves from one item in the stack to another. That indicates the utility of an array as a natural support for a stack.

Neither support system captures the nature of the stack in and of itself, which arises from two major attributes:

1. A stack can *resequence* a stream of entries.

2. A stack is *immediate*. Entry and exit from a stack are $O(1)$ operations. What you get is what you see on top; there is no *apparent* depth or size or structure to a stack. In some sense, a stack is a point-like structure.

Above all, a stack is so very easy to use, if what you want from it is the last thing put into it.

■ 4.1.3 The Calculation Game   (optional)

The game described below comes from Nancy Griffith of Georgia Institute of Technology. It is introduced here to serve as an example of the use of multiple stacks and as a source of assignments.

A deck of cards can be represented by 52 symbols, four each of: A, 2, 3, . . . , 9, 10, J, Q, K. They may be regarded as the numbers 1 . . . 13. Suppose one card at a time is dealt from the deck and placed onto one of four *foundations* so that cards in the foundations F_1 . . . F_4 are in the order:

F_1: A 2 3 4 . . . F_2: 2 4 6 8 . . .
F_3: 3 6 9 Q 2 5 8 . . . F_4: 4 8 Q 3 7 J . . .

This is not possible for most shufflings of the deck, of course, but it can be done with the help of four waste piles, W_1 . . . W_4. The top of any waste pile can be used as a source for a card to be moved to a foundation at any time.

One of the possible strategies for the use of the waste piles is to deal from the deck onto them in the order W_1, W_2, W_3, W_4, W_1, . . . but to move a card from a waste pile to a foundation whenever possible. A program can be written to accomplish these moves and verify the result.

A shuffle can always be produced from a real deck of cards; the order produced in the real world can be used as an input stream. The professional approach is to use a random number generator (see Part II, section A). With each of the 52 card symbols $S[i]$ arranged in some standard order, associate a pseudorandom number $RN[i]$, as shown in Figure 4.8. Now sort S, using the values in RN as a key. The symbols of S will be distributed as randomly *after* the sort as the values in RN were *before* the sort.

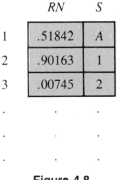

Figure 4.8

This is a valuable exercise to do with all three variations of stack support in order to compare them and develop a feel for their commonalities and differences.

Program PG4.1 is appropriate at this point.

4.2 Stacks in Language

Stacks are associated with programming languages, their translation, and their execution in a variety of ways at several levels. Some applications of stacks in computer languages are explored in the remainder of this chapter, and others are mentioned in passing.

When one procedure invokes another, the programmer must provide some means to return control to the point of invocation. The central problem is that procedures are written to be invoked as needed and cannot include a fixed point to which they return. A simple model (that has been put in practice) of a return mechanism is:

- Each time one procedure invokes another, the address to which control is to be returned after execution of the invoked procedure is placed on a stack.

- A **return** is executed by transfer of control to the address popped off of the return stack.

This process may be depicted by snapshots of a return stack, *rStack,* depicted in Figure 4.9. In practice, more than an address is stacked. The processing unit executing a calling procedure includes information needed to carry out the program it is executing. Crucial information is kept in *registers* that act as memory cells internal to the processor. These registers are used by the invoked procedure also, and that destroys information needed on return. As a consequence, the *state* of the processor, as embodied in its registers, is usually stacked for recall upon return.

A similar but more elaborate use of stacks is required for languages that support recursive procedures (see Chapter 7).

Stacks and their management are designed into both hardware and software in a number of overlapping ways that are difficult to separate. Some uses of stacks in language are:

1. A compiler for a high-level language may reorganize arithmetic (and logical) expressions that are in the *infix* form (such as $A + B * C$) into a *postfix* form, or R.P.N.—Reverse Polish Notation (such as $A\ B\ C\ *\ +$). In this form, operators can be applied immediately when encountered in a left-to-right pass through the expression. The postfix expression that results from the conversion can then be translated into machine code a *token* at a time, sequentially, with the aid of a stack. (In the example, the tokens are: ''A'',''B'',''C'',''*'', and '' + ''.) Both the high-level statement and the instructions of the target machine may have *nothing* explicit to do with a stack. In its pure form, this is a translation device.

2. A compiler for a high-level language may translate *all* statements into an *intermediate code,* which in turn can be readily translated into instructions for a particular machine. The result is enhanced *portability*—the intermediate

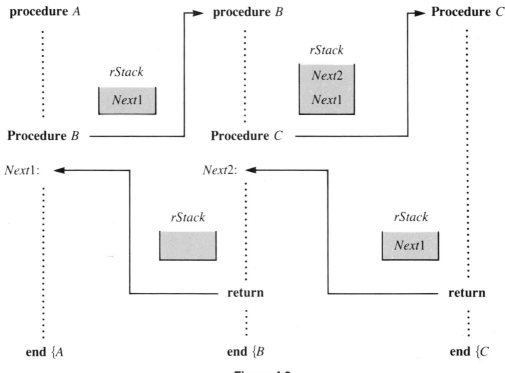

Figure 4.9

code is the same for all machines; programs written and tested on one machine will tend to work on one of different design, because only the final translation step needs to be customized. One of the most accessible examples of intermediate code is the p-code created by some Pascal compilers: p-code is a stack-manipulation language, and stacks can be managed on any machine. Some machines have been designed to execute p-code directly—the *hardware* is a "p-code machine," but most p-code is executed after further translation. When further translation is required, the first phase of the translation process is for a *virtual* p-code machine, treated as though the target machine *did* execute p-code directly.

3. A language may be *designed* as a stack-manipulation language. *All* operations of the language combine or otherwise affect or use the top item(s) of a stack and leave results on the stack. One such language is FORTH, discussed in section 4.3. Hardware can be designed to carry out stack operations directly as machine instructions, or the operations can be translated into quite different machine instructions that have the same effect.

4. A machine, either hardware (actual) or software (virtual), can execute a stream of tokens like *A B C* * + sequentially, using a stack. The ALU (for Arithmetic and Logic Unit) hardware can be designed to execute postfix

expressions this way. The input stream must be provided in the appropriate postfix form for this to work properly. Some hand calculators require the *user* to formulate the expression correctly. Most high-level computer languages translate from a form more comfortable to the user. The execution of postfix expressions is treated in section 4.2.1, and the translation from infix to postfix is discussed in section 4.2.2.

5. The designs of microprocessors (and other processors) commonly provide facilities for the manipulation of one or more stacks located in memory. In effect, a portion of memory is treated as an array structured as a stack. The microprocessor contains a register, called a *stack-pointer,* which in effect contains the value that would be returned by TOP. The INSERT and DELETE operations are provided as machine instructions. Generally, the possibility that a stack will grow out of bounds is left as a programming challenge. Manipulation of the built-in stack(s) requires careful planning at the machine language (or assembler language) level. This planning is taken care of by the compiler of a high-level language for the same microprocessor. The power to manipulate a memory stack easily is an added feature, distinct from arithmetic execution on a stack top as discussed in item 3. Arithmetic instructions in a microprocessor with a stack-pointer usually involve fetching operands from memory (not necessarily the stack) and leaving the result in a designated place other than the stack.

6. The design of some machines focuses to a large extent on stack manipulation. In some designs the instruction set consists solely of operations involving a stack. They are then said to possess a stack *architecture* (roughly, the machine design as seen by a machine-language programmer). A CPU (Central Processing Unit) which directly executes Pascal p-code would be such a machine. (The May 1977 issue of the IEEE Computer Society journal *Computer* is devoted to stack machines.)

Some of the uses of stacks in language are pursued more fully in the next several sections.

4.2.1 Postfix Execution

Consider a specific expression of the form *A B C* ∗ +, such as: 5 3 2 ∗ +. The five tokens involved are "5", "3", "2", "∗", and "+". To evaluate this expression by a "postfix machine" so that it is equivalent to the usual meaning of *5 + 3 ∗ 2*, it is only necessary to:

■ Read tokens left to right.

■ As they are encountered, place operands, such as "5", on a stack, *ValueStack.*

- As they are encountered, operations pop (retrieve and delete) their operand(s) from the stack, perform their function, and then push the result back on *ValueStack*.

It is convenient to add a special symbol that terminates an expression. With "&" as the terminator, snapshots of the operation of *ValueStack* during the evaluation of the expression "5 3 2 * + &" form the sequence in Figure 4.10.

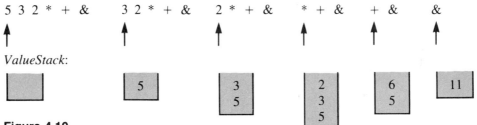

Figure 4.10

It is more common to manipulate variables, rather than explicit values, and to do so it is only necessary to stack *addresses*, represented by identifiers, instead of the values themselves. Figure 4.11 depicts the equivalent process.

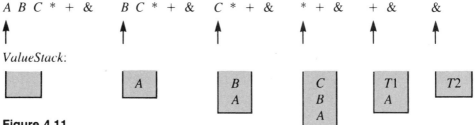

Figure 4.11

$T1$ is a temporary location where the result $B * C$ is stored, and $T2$ is the temporary location where the result $T1 + A$ is stored.

Unary operations (one operand) may also be included in postfix expressions but need to be distinct from any related binary operations. For example, in $-A * B - C$, the first " − " is *not* subtraction, it is unary minus. Let "~" be the symbol for the unary minus operation. Then this expression becomes:

A ~ B * C − &

In particular, 3 ~ 5 * 6 − & is evaluated (directly) as shown in Figure 4.12.

ValueStack:

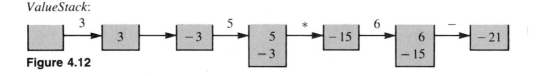

Figure 4.12

If a machine is to operate with $\sim$, $*$, $/$, $+$, $-$, and & and access the next token by *Next(Token)*, then a suitable emulation of the machine operating with the stack *Post* is:

```
function DoPostFix                          procedure Binary(i)
    Next(Token)                                 v ← Top(Post)
    while Token ≠ "&" do                         Delete(Post)
      case of Token                             case of i
        "~" : begin                               1 : v ← Top(Post) * v
                Value ← Top(Post)                 2 : v ← Top(Post) + v
                Delete(Post)                      3 : v ← Top(Post) − v
                Push(Post, − Value)               4 : v ← Top(Post) / v
              end                               endcase
        "*" : Binary(1)                         Delete(Post)
        "+" : Binary(2)                         Push(Post,v)
        "−" : Binary(3)                       end {Binary
        "/" : Binary(4)
        else : Push(Post, Token)    {Token must be an operand
      endcase
      Next(Token)
    endwhile
    return Top(Post)
end {DoPostFix
```

Exercise E4.1 and program PG4.2 are appropriate at this point.

4.2.2 Conversion of Infix to Postfix

Conversion of infix expressions to postfix form depends upon the precedence of operations. To know that multiplication is done before addition in the expression $A + B * C$ requires a "look-ahead" process, because the addition may or may not be applied immediately to the operands A and B that bracket it. It is true, in contrast, that $A + B - C$ is equivalent to $(A + B) - C$ in most languages.

In order to process a postfix expression left-to-right in the manner indicated, the tokens in the expression must be sequenced so that the operations occur in the order in which they are to be performed. With a little practice, one can spot the appropriate order. For example, the equivalent infix and postfix forms of several expressions are:

Infix Expression	*Postfix Expression*
$a * b + c$	$a\ b * c +$
$a + b * c$	$a\ b\ c * +$
$a * (b + c)$	$a\ b\ c + *$
$(a + b) * c$	$a\ b + c *$

A stack may be used to provide the same effect.

Parentheses complicate the conversion because they override the precedence and must be dealt with in some manner.

As a simple example, suppose that operators are restricted to:

$\sim$, $*$, $/$, $+$, $-$ {*and parentheses*

A common assignment of precedence would be:

level 3: $\sim$

level 2: $*$, $/$

level 1: $+$, $-$

A further assumption is that operators on the same level of precedence are to be evaluated left-to-right.

By examining the four variations of the example expression we can see that:

- When an operator is encountered, it is not put in the postfix list *PostX* until its operands have been acquired. It may be retained on a stack, *OpStack,* until its proper postfix position is reached. This position is determined by the processing of a sentinel value, a right paren, or an operator with precedence at least as low.

- If an operator that has been retained is of precedence higher than or equal to an incoming one, then it is unstacked and added to the list. The sentinel value has the lowest possible effective precedence.

- A left paren—"("—is placed on *OpStack.* A right paren—")"— causes the transfer of *OpStack* items to *PostX* down to a left paren. Both parens are discarded.

The behavior of the stack and the list for $a * b + c$ & is depicted in Figures 4.13 – 4.15. The resulting list is quickly retrieved.

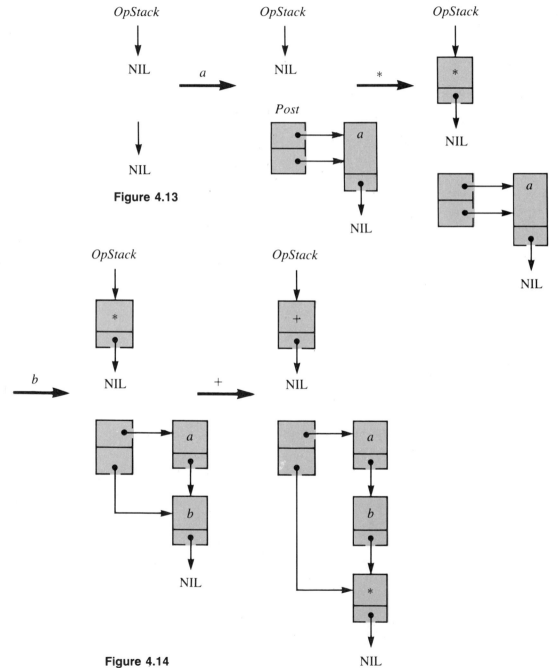

Figure 4.13

Figure 4.14

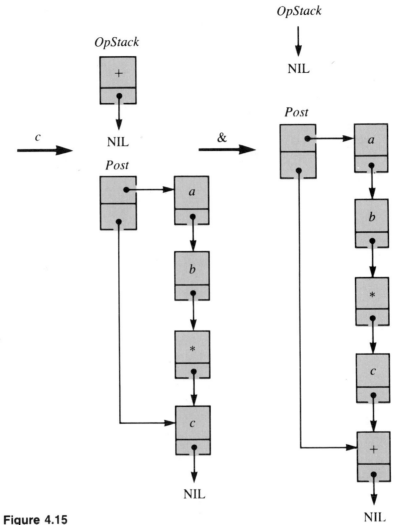

Figure 4.15

With a function *Level* that returns the level of an operator, the infix-to-postfix conversion becomes:

```
procedure IntoPostfix
  Next(Token)
  while Token ≠ "&" do
    case of Token
      {operand} : InsertTail(PostX,Token)
      ")" : begin
                while NOT Empty(OpStack)
                  Op ← Top(OpStack)
                  Delete(OpStack)
                  if Op ≠ "("
                    then InsertTail(PostX,Op)
                    else exit
                    endif
                  endwhile
                end
      "(" : Push(OpStack,Token)
      else : begin {new operator
                Op ← Top(OpStack)
                while Level(Op) ≥ Level(Token) do
                  Delete(OpStack)
                  InsertTail(PostX,Op)
                  if Empty(OpStack)
                    then exit
                    else Op ← Top(OpStack)
                    endif
                  endwhile
                Push(OpStack,Token)
                end
    endcase
    Next(Token)
  endwhile
  while NOT Empty(OpStack) do
    Op ← Top(OpStack)
    Delete(OpStack)
    InsertTail(PostX,Op)
    endwhile
  end {IntoPostfix
```

Exercise E4.1, problem P4.1, and program PG4.3 are appropriate at this point.

■ 4.2.3 Postfix Lists in Translation   (optional)

Conversion of infix expressions to postfix lists is not followed immediately by *execution* of the postfix list in most computing systems. The conversion normally occurs in a compiler, followed by *translation* of the list into instructions for a machine that may or may not provide stack operations directly. Nevertheless, the translation is driven by a process very similar to the execution of a postfix list. Schematically for $A\ B\ C * + \&$ in a postfix stack, the execution might proceed as in Figure 4.16.

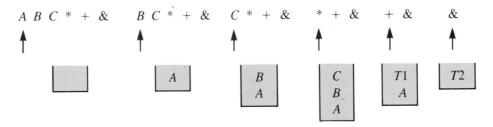

Figure 4.16

Here "*" causes the generation of the machine instructions to multiply the values of the top two addresses on the stack, place the result in $T1$ and push the address $T1$ onto the stack. The translation algorithm then places $T1$ on its postfix stack, but the translated result of the encounter with "*" is simply the set of instructions equivalent to "multiply B and C and place the result in $T1$." The actual multiplication occurs at execution time, not compilation time, in a manner dependent on the machine architecture and details of translation. The postfix list and stack are used simply to organize the sequence of machine operations. A compiler is developed to translate a language into the instructions of a particular target machine. Several features of the design of the target machine might be used to make the resulting translation more efficient, but the essence of the stacking scheme is likely to remain in the design of the translation process.

Compilers are very complex programs, but much about them is general, if not universal; and the details of a specific target machine are only involved in parts of their design. Much of their generality and much of that machine isolation follow from the informed use of data structures.

■ 4.3 Stacks in the Language FORTH   (optional)

Charles H. Moore invented a language, FORTH, which is now in use in many varied applications. It is difficult to determine how much of the power of available versions of FORTH is due to the central role of stacks in the design of the language, but stack ideas certainly give it much of its character. FORTH has a unique combination of properties, as it is commonly implemented and used.

Two aspects of FORTH are of particular interest in the context of this chapter:

1. Statement syntax is intrinsically postfix in form.

2. Statement semantics are based on stack manipulation.

These are independent properties, although they form a natural partnership. Partly because of this combination, the modularity of FORTH programs has a different flavor and genesis than that of, say, Pascal programs.

A very brief introduction to elementary FORTH is found in Part II, section F. It is included as an interesting example of stack management made explicit in a computer language.

■ 4.4 The p-Machine (optional)

When Pascal is translated into the intermediate code, *p-code,* the semantics of Pascal statements are translated into actions of a machine, the *p-Machine.* P-code statements are designed to invoke the possible actions of the p-Machine. For the translation of Pascal into p-code, it does not matter whether p-code will be executed directly in hardware. If p-code is further translated into machine instructions of a machine that is not a p-Machine, then the p-Machine that is the target of the translation is a *virtual* machine. The apparent operation of a virtual machine is the same as that of a hardware version, so an understanding of the p-Machine is still a guide for correct translation. To understand the p-Machine is to understand an elegant application of stack ideas.

A discussion of the p-Machine that is sufficient to program in p-code or to serve as the basis for a discussion of some of the aspects of HLL (High Level Language) translation is found in Part II, section G.

■ 4.5 The Use of Stacks in Simulations (optional)

A stack may appear in a variety of guises—as a (physical or geometrical) model, as a formal data structure, as a programming technique, and in general as an idea. A program written to emulate the behavior of some process that apparently involves a stack may not actually use the data structure STACK.

Suppose a program models the conceptual behavior of the stock of canned flan on a grocery shelf. (Flan is custard in intimate contact with carmelized sugar.) A simple model is a stack of cans on the shelf. The public's desire for flan is sporadic, but it may be modeled either by a distribution derived algebraically from a uniform variate or by one derived from an experimentally measured PDF (Probability Distribution Function—see Part II, section A). In either case, a number of strategies for restocking the shelf are possible, each having costs associated with it.

If there is more than one stack of cans, the withdrawal, distribution, and restocking strategy between them determine such values as the mean number of cans on the shelf (in the stack or stacks). Pursuit of the many options is left to the exercises. Deeper questions of verification and the validity of a program model for the restocking problem are left to a course in simulations and models.

If the goal of the simulation is to determine the mean stack depth, the "stack" can be modeled simply with a counter. Each withdrawal decreases the count by one; restocking increases it by the number "added to the stack." Statistics may be gathered in several ways during the process to collect measurements of the stack depth.

Instead of mean depth, the desired information may be mean length of time that a can of flan spends on the shelf. (The carmel may crystallize after some length of time, causing rejection or dissatisfaction—flan has an estimated shelf life.) To determine mean shelf-time, a stack of can-records may be used, each marked with the (simulation) time at which they were stocked. Time passage statistics may be recorded when a can is withdrawn. A meaningful comparison study of "front-loading" and "rear-loading" restocking strategies may then be made from mean shelf-times. (Note that "rear-loading" defines a nonstack, a *queue* in fact—a structure studied in Chapter 5.)

Program PG4.5 is appropriate at this point.

■ 4.6 Backtracking with Stacks   (optional)

Inexperienced cave explorers sometimes play out string as they trace out the twists, turns, branches, and interconnections of a cave. The string allows them to *backtrack*—to return to a previous branch point by gathering in the string and hence retracing their path backwards. The **call . . . return** model of subprogram invocation (as well as its more sophisticated variates), is an example of backtracking that uses a stack rather than string for a temporary memory.

Stacks can be used to backtrack during traverses of some of the structures yet to be introduced, in particular the *binary tree* of Chapter 8. Carefully structured traverses of data structures play a role in artificial intelligence, and some of them use backtracking. A very simple model of an "intelligent" behavior requires no background except ARRAY and STACK: this model of how to explore a maze with the aid of a backtracking stack is found in Part II, section H.

Summary

Stack behavior is that of a LIFO (Last-In-First-Out) collection. Formally STACK is a structure in which only the top, last-entered item is accessible. Like a list, it is dynamic, growing with insertions and shrinking with deletions. Unlike a list, interior items can only be reached by repeated removal of the top item. A stack does not require a traverse.

In all its forms, a stack is managed by CREATE, PUSH (insert), DELETE, and TOP (value return). All of these are $O(1)$ operations, and so wherever a stack is appropriate it is highly efficient.

STACK may be chosen as a data structure because it models common behavior. When chosen as a deliberate design basis, it is used to *resequence* a stream of items or because it is an *immediate* structure that is very easy and efficient to use.

Stacks can be supported as lists restricted to insertion and deletion at the head only. The nodes can be linked records, linked with pointer variables or indices. A direct form of array support that is attractive and common because of its simplicity does not involve links, only an index *Top*. It does, however, have the universal limitation of array-supported structures: it can be asked to grow out of its array.

The stack structure has had a profound influence on computing; in the theory of computing; and in the design of language translators, processors, and computing languages. Processors and languages not only incorporate the concept of a stack as a tool, but some have also made it a central feature of their design.

Applications of stacks that are treated in the chapter include a stack-directed sorting scheme, the game *Calculations,* reverse Polish notation, the language FORTH, the p-Machine used by some versions of Pascal, and the use of stacks in simulations. Extended discussions of FORTH and the p-Machine are found in Part II, sections F and G.

Stacks appear in most of the later chapters. In section 7.2 stacks play a central role in describing variations of the programming solutions of a problem. In a number of places they are used to help rearrange a sequence of items.

A realization of a stack manager (in Pascal) is found in Part II, section E.

Exercises   immediate applications of the text material

E4.1   Trace the growth and decay of the stack *Post* managed by function *DoPostFix* of section 4.2.1 for the following token streams:

3 5 * 6 + &

3 5 6 * + &

3 5 6 + * &

3 5 + 6 * &

E4.2 Trace the behavior of the stack *OpStack* and the list *PostX* as determined by procedure *IntoPostFix* of section 4.2.2 on the following:

$a * b + c$ $(a + b) * c$ &

$a + b * c$ $3 + ((a + b) * c) + d$ &

$a * (b + c)$ & $\sim (a + b) * (c + d)$ &

Problems not immediate, but requiring no major extensions of the text

P4.1 The precedence of operations is not the same for all languages. Find three infix expressions (possibly including Boolean operators) that are legal in both of two languages but have distinct postfix forms. (BASIC and Pascal are worth examining in this context.)

Programs for trying it yourself

PG4.1 Write a program to play the game *Calculation* of section 4.1.3, using stacks implemented in one of the following ways:

(a) pointer-linked records,

(b) an array, or

(c) an array-based linked list.

This is intended to be used for up to three program assignments.

PG4.2 Write a program that uses the function *DoPostFix* of section 4.2.1 to evaluate a sequence of postfix expressions.

PG4.3 Encase procedure *IntoPostFix* of section 4.2.2 in a program that accepts infix expressions and displays their postfix equivalent. (Note that this program may be combined with PG4.1 to evaluate infix expressions.)

PG4.5 Write a program that simulates a flan-can row of a grocery shelf that holds 15 cans. Withdrawals are to be generated at random times with any of the distributions discussed in section 1.5. Restock at the front (top) when there are fewer than three cans on the shelf, and determine the mean-age-since-stocking of the cans on the shelf after 100 cans have been withdrawn. Run again with restocking at regular intervals.

Projects for fun; for serious students

PJ4.1 Write a program that uses two or more stacks to sort an input stream of up to 50 integers.

Chapter 5

Queues

Waiting lines of people often form at banks and ticket booths, and lines of cars form at freeway exits. Waiting lines occur, in fact, whenever and wherever the number of demands on a resource in some time span exceed the capacity of that resource. A cashier serves only one customer at a time, and the number of lanes in an exit ramp limits the number of cars that can pass a given point at the same time. The pattern of entrance to and exit from a waiting line is that *entities* (such as people or cars) are served in the order in which they arrive. A waiting line with this pattern of entry and exit from it is said to be a *queue,* a FIFO list. FIFO, (First-In-First-Out) is in contrast to a LIFO, (Last-In-First-Out) list, a stack.

The effect of a waiting line at a resource is to smooth out an *arrival sequence,* the times of arrival of entities. Items remain in the queue until the server (the resource) can process them. Items arrive at the *rear* and leave at the *front,* rather than arriving and leaving at the top as they do in a stack.

Suppose that jobs tagged by letters W-A-I-T-S arrive at a milling machine from other stations in a machine shop at irregular intervals, but the milling process takes three minutes for each job. If the times of arrival from start-up are 5, 6, 8, 9, and 13, then a queue would form. Figure 5.1 shows snapshots of the queue contents at arrivals and departures.

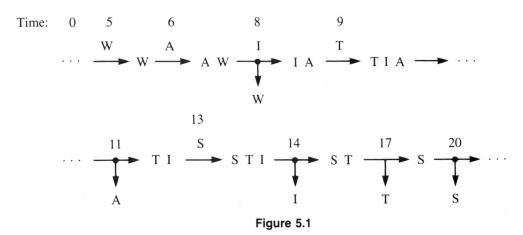

Figure 5.1

Arrival times of 5, 8, 11, 12, and 14 produce output at the same times, but the arrival sequence 5, 8, 12, 13, and 14 does not do so because the server is idle part of the time.

Now suppose that the service times are 2, 1, 5, 5, and 2. Figure 5.2 shows the new snapshots. The distribution of arrival times and the distribution of service times both affect the queue length and the amount of time that an entity spends in a queue. This is *queueing behavior,* a basic model from which the idea of a queue is derived. Such behavior is central to simulations and other applications, and is treated in more detail in section 5.1. Waiting lines *will* occur, and some feel for where and when they do is an aid in the design of programs.

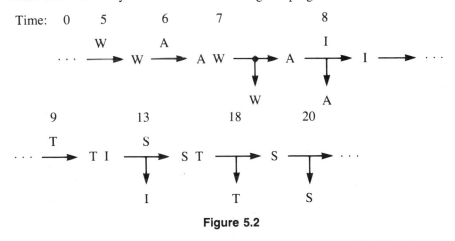

Figure 5.2

A queue can be stored and managed as a data structure QUEUE. Like AR-RAY and STACK, QUEUE is not concerned with the complexities of the flow of a sequence of items through it, but only with access to cells. Queueing behavior is to be distinguished from the data structure QUEUE, which is simpler to deal with than the behavior it models.

5.1 Queueing Behavior

In a program, items seldom wait for a specific time to arrive, but they *do* wait for some process to complete (as do drivers at a traffic-light controlled by pedestrians). An input routine waits for a user to hit one or more keys, perhaps saving a string of keyed characters until they form a recognized token before allowing some other process to be initiated. On the other hand, processing of one input token may take longer than the entry of the next one. Systems that queue inputs and those that sometimes treat the keyboard as a nonentity have differing psychological impacts on the user.

Examples of queueing abound in the operating systems and in the hardware of computing systems. For instance, in a time-sharing system some jobs wait for service from a disk drive or a printer while another job is being processed by the CPU (Central Processing System). The common use, however, is simply to store items, *in order,* for later processing.

Queueing is fundamental to some of the applications of stacks in Chapter 4. The conversion of an infix expression to a postfix expression in section 4.2.2, for example, creates a queue called *PostX*—the postfix expression itself. The token stream *PostX* is a queue because tokens are both inserted to it and removed from it in the order in which they are encountered during execution of a program or during translation in a compiler.

From the viewpoint of processing tokens, stacks and queues are used in conjunction in a stack machine only to save a token and temporarily delay the processing of operands encountered in sequence in the token stream. In FORTH, the programmer creates the token queue. In Pascal, a compiler that translates to p-code creates the queue. In both these languages, the preparation of a queue is crucial to the successful operation of a stack. The stack eliminates the necessity to look ahead an arbitrary (and varying) number of predetermined tokens to decide when to insert the current token into the processing queue. Use of a stack allows the rest of the processing applied to the token stream to be done sequentially.

Queueing behavior is common in machine shops (and other manufacturing facilities), where jobs tend to back up somewhere: at a lathe, at a milling machine, at any work station where job requests arrive at a rate faster than the throughput determined by the mean service time of the work station for such jobs. Queueing behavior also occurs in the flow of goods from manufacturers to customers.

Machine shops, marketing systems, and computing systems are examples of *networks* where jobs (or other entities) flow from one server to another and where jobs may spend more time waiting than being served. Service is *distributed* in such systems, as it is in service networks of all kinds. Where service occurs in a network through which requests for service flow, so does queueing behavior. Analysis of queueing networks, done both analytically and operationally, is based on the behavior of an isolated queue, and that behavior is the pattern for the data structure QUEUE.

5.1.1 The Queue Structure

A data structure that models queueing behavior must do so through general data structure operations tailored to that behavior:

- Queues need to be created with access (by pointer or index) to both a head (front) and a tail (rear), because insertions take place at the rear and deletions at the front. The formal operation which gives birth to a queue is CREATE.

- A queue becomes empty at any time when there have been as many departures as arrivals. The formal (Boolean) operation that checks the viability of a queue is EMPTY.

- A queue grows iff a single item is inserted into its rear position. No way of assigning values directly to queue items is available in a pure queue. The formal operation that inserts a value into a queue is INSERT.

- The only retrievable value of a queue is the value of its front item. The formal operation that returns the value of the front item is FRONT.

- The front item must be removed from a queue if the values of the other items are to be retrieved. The formal operation that removes the front item from a queue is DELETE.

- The behavior of a queue (as a data structure) is entirely described, however it may be implemented, by CREATE, EMPTY, INSERT, DELETE, and FRONT.

- A queue changes size with insertions and deletions and so is dynamic. It is created without knowledge of its future size and so is blind. It is sparse because the collection of potential entries is generally much larger than its actual entries at any given time. All of these things make the pointer-linked list of records a natural support structure for the queue.

- A queue provides direct access, although only at the front and rear, and that access should be efficient. Hence, if the maximum size of a queue is predictable, an array is a natural structure for queue support.

5.2 Queue Implementation and Management

A formal structure QUEUE defines a data management policy, independent of implementation. Implementation, however, affects program writing. To contrast the two natural implementations, suppose that two queues are to be managed by a program: Q_1, implemented with a linked list, *LinearQ,* and Q_2, implemented with an array, *aQueue*. Figure 5.3 depicts the two queues.

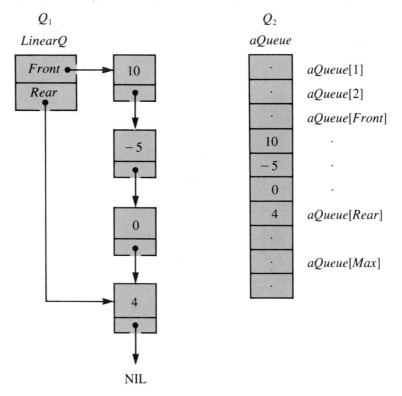

Figure 5.3

The scheme depicted in Figure 5.3 for the implementation of a queue in an array has a peculiarity: the index *Front* is one less than the actual index of the front value. The neatness of this scheme becomes apparent when queue operations are developed as procedures.

As two items are deleted from *LinearQ* and a node of value 2 is inserted, snapshots of Q_1 would look like those in Figures 5.4 and 5.5. (The terms *Head* and *Tail* have been replaced by *Front* and *Rear* as a reminder of the waiting-line model of queueing behavior.) A queue is a list structure for which insertion is always done with *InsertTail* and deletion with *DeleteHead*. In contrast, when the list of Figure 5.3 is treated as a stack, insertions are made with *InsertHead*. For this example, the difference would be the placement of the value-2 node at the front of the list, rather than at the rear. This difference is significant; queueing behavior is quite distinct from stack behavior.

Exercise E5.1 is appropriate at this point.

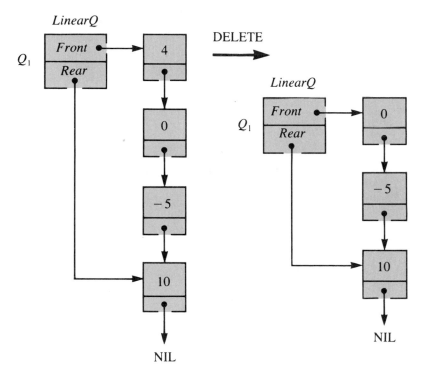

Figure 5.4

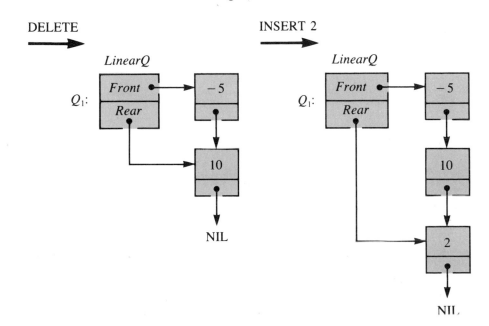

Figure 5.5

When this same set of operations is applied to Q_2, a quirk of the array implementation of a queue becomes apparent: deletions and insertions move a queue along in its substrate array: they have an *inchworm effect*. The effect on Q_2 of DELETE, DELETE, INSERT 2 is shown in Figure 5.6. No new insertions can be made to Q_2 (in this implementation, with the value of *Max* as shown) without shifting the entire queue Q_2 within the substrate array *aQueue*. The array index *Rear* has reached its limit *Max*, but the array *aQueue* is not filled by Q_2. It is convenient to develop a procedure, *ShiftQ*, to deal with the shift.

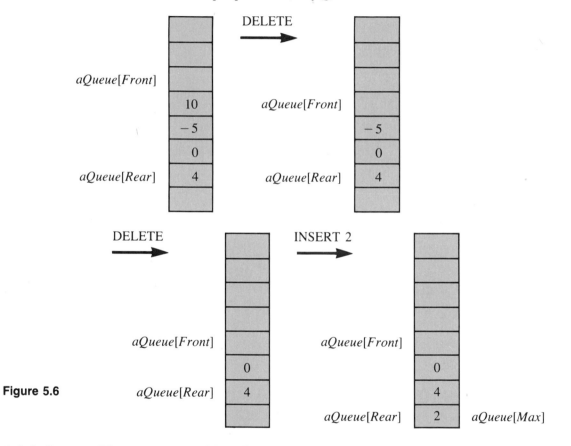

Figure 5.6

5.2.1 Queue Management Algorithms

A comparison between the management routines for Q_1 and Q_2 can now be made. (An assumption is made that **with** *LinearQ* **do** . . . is in effect where it is convenient for Q_1. The identifiers *InsertRear* and *DeleteFront* replace *InsertTail* and *DeleteHead* to emphasize the specific application to queues.) For comparison, the list form of *InsertRear* in Table 5.1 accepts values instead of nodes.

Values rather than nodes are inserted into *LinearQ* to emphasize similarities with routines applied to *aQueue*. Sentinel lists, convenient for some applications, require little change in the procedures.

Table 5.1

Q1		Q2	
		CREATE	
declarations $\{O(1)$		*declarations* $\{O(1)$	
LinearQ.Front ← NIL		*Front* ← 0	
		Rear ← 0	

		EMPTY	
function *Empty(LinearQ)* $\{O(1)$		**function** *Empty(aQueue)* $\{O(1)$	
if *Front* = NIL		**if** *Rear* = 0	
then return TRUE		**then return** TRUE	
else return FALSE		**else return** FALSE	
endif		**endif**	
end {*Empty*		**end** {*Empty*	

INSERT

```
procedure InsertRear(aQueue,i)        {O(O(ShiftQ))
  if Rear = Max
    then ShiftQ(aQueue)
  endif
  if Rear = Max {still
    then {deal with a full-array error
    else Rear ← Rear + 1
         aQueue[Rear] ← i
  endif
end {InsertRear
```

```
procedure InsertRear(LinearQ,i)    {O(1)
  NEW(iNode)
  iNode↑.Value ← i
  iNode↑.Link ← NIL
  if Empty(LinearQ)
    then Front ← iNode
    else Rear↑.Link ← iNode
  endif
  Rear ← iNode
end {InsertRear
```

```
procedure ShiftQ(aQueue)              {O(Max)
  if Front > 0
    then for k = 1 to Rear − Front do
           aQueue[k] ← aQueue[Front + k]
         next k
         Rear ← Rear − Front
         Front ← 0
  endif
end {ShiftQ
```

DELETE

```
procedure DeleteFront(LinearQ)    {O(1)
  if Empty(LinearQ)
    then {deal with this error
    else p ← Front
         Front ← Front↑.Link
  endif
  DISPOSE(p)
end {DeleteFront
```

```
procedure DeleteFront(aQueue)       {O(1)
  if Empty(aQueue)
    then {deal with this error
    else Front ← Front + 1
         if Front = Rear
           then Front ← 0
                Rear ← 0
         endif
  endif
end {DeleteFront
```

FRONT

```
function FrontView(LinearQ)    {O(1)
  if Empty(LinearQ)
    then {deal with this error
    else return Front↑.Value
  endif
end {FrontView
```

```
function FrontView(aQueue)       {O(1)
  if Empty(aQueue)
    then {deal with this error
    else return aQueue[Front+1]
  endif
end {FrontView
```

Exercises E5.2 and E5.3, problem P5.1, and programs PG5.1 and PG5.2 are appropriate at this point.

A sequence of *I* (insert) and *D* (delete) commands that manage an input file as a queue are processed in essentially the same way as they were for a stack at the end of section 4.1.1.

Note: A realization in Pascal of the command loop as a "queue machine" is to be found in Part II, section I.

A queue can be displayed as a *list* by a simple variation of *LT* in section 3.3.2; but, *as a queue,* there is no access to internal nodes. One way to list a queue is to display the front node, delete it, and insert it back into the queue:

```
procedure ListQ(q)                      {O(n)
   if Empty(q) then return endif
   Start ← q
   repeat
      DISPLAY(Front(q))
      Node ← q
      Delete(q)                         {Delete should not include DISPOSE
      Insert(Node)
   until Node = Start
end {ListQ
```

5.2.2 On the Use of Queues

Queues are sometimes chosen to model a pervasive natural system, the *waiting line*. In many systems waiting lines are unavoidable. The effects of waiting on a time sequence of entities passed through a queue can be complex, but the data structure QUEUE is relatively simple. It does, however, take more care than does STACK. In pointer-linked record form, access to the tail node (the *rear* node) must be provided to make INSERT an $O(1)$ operation. When supported by an array, not only is the maximum number of entries limited, but the *inchworm effect* can also occasionally force an $O(n)$ shift operation of the queue within its array. (This problem can be alleviated with the use of circular lists as a support structure, as described in section 5.3.) The queue is more complex to manage, as a data structure, than is the stack.

The queue is a dynamic, immediate structure, and it can make efficient use of time and space. Above all, a queue is a *retainer*—it retains the order in which items enter it and produces them as needed.

Note that the word "queue" is commonly used to refer to structures more general than QUEUE. Generalizations of QUEUE are outlined in section 5.4, introduced in section 8.5.2, and applied in Chapter 10. One use of QUEUE is to provide a basis for its own generalizations.

5.3 Circular-Track Queues

Nodes linked into a cycle, like the list in Figure 5.7, were introduced in section 3.7:

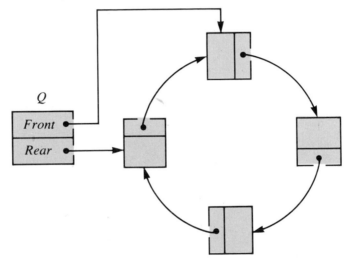

Figure 5.7

A circular list may be maintained as a queue by the proper choice of INSERT and DELETE operations: *InsertAfter* and *DeleteBack*, both discussed in section 3.7. The result is a queue supported by a circular list, but it is commonly called a *circular queue*. A queue is said to be a linear structure, but it is actually a *point structure,* because only two points of a queue exist for the outside world, whatever its implementation. (If the queue is a two-point structure, then the stack is a one-point structure.)

In a queue maintained in an array, circularity can be transferred to index-management in the substrate array. An awkwardness inherent in the implementation of a queue with an array is that the queue array may not be full even though the cell of maximum index is in use—hence, the procedure *ShiftQ* in section 5.2. This inefficiency can be resolved in an array dimensioned $a[0 . . Max - 1]$ with the help of modular arithmetic. In that case

(1) $k \leftarrow (k + 1)$ MOD *Max*

calculates a remainder upon division by *Max*, and so has the same effect as:

if $k = Max - 1$
   then $k \leftarrow 0$
   else $k \leftarrow k + 1$
endif

The effect is to bend the array itself into a (virtual) ring, shown in Figure 5.8.

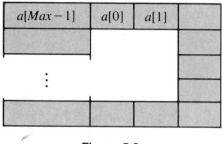

Figure 5.8

The assignment (1) is a clockwise index shift, no matter what the value of k, $0 \leq k \leq Max - 1$. This scheme forms a circular *array* without regard to the structure it supports, but it is normally used in support of a queue.

Now *Front* and *Rear* can both be moved clockwise when a deletion or addition is made, as shown in Figure 5.9.

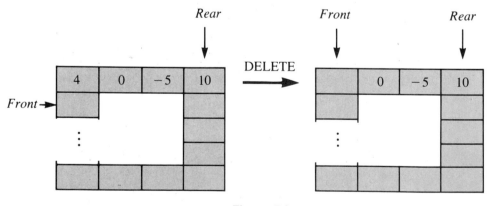

Figure 5.9

If no more than $Max - 1$ items are allowed into the queue, then ($Front = Rear$) signals that the *queue* is empty; and, after ($Rear \leftarrow (Rear + 1)$ MOD Max), ($Front = Rear$) also signals that the *array* is full. If Max items are allowed into the queue, an additional flag needs to be carried in order to distinguish between the empty and full conditions. One approach (of several) is to use the flag *Some*, reset *TRUE* during insertion, and set *FALSE* when deletion produces an empty queue.

The queue operations become:

function *Empty*   {*O(1)*

  if (NOT *Some*) AND (*Front* = *Rear*)

    then return TRUE

    else return FALSE

    endif

  end {*Empty*

procedure *InsertCQ(x)*   {*O(1)*

  if (*Front* = *Rear*) AND *Some*

    then {*report full array*

    else *Rear* ← (*Rear* + *1*) MOD *Max*

      a[Rear] ← *x*

      Some ← TRUE

    endif

  end {*InsertCQ*

procedure *DeleteCQ*   {*O(1)*

  if *Empty*

    then {*deal with this error*

    else *Front* ← (*Front* + *1*) MOD *Max*

      if *Front* = *Rear*

        then *Some* ← FALSE

      endif

    endif

  end {*DeleteCQ*

Problem P5.2 is appropriate at this point.

5.4 Generalized Queues

Queueing behavior is exhibited in structures that are not queues in the strict sense. One of these is called DEQUE (double-ended-queue). This structure allows both entry and exit at either end, but nowhere else. Why it is not called a double stack is a mystery, since that is at least as accurate a description. If two nodes are inserted at one end and removed from the other, they will exit in queue order. If they are both removed from the entry end, then they exit in stack order. If they are removed from opposite ends, then their exit order is whimsical.

A queueing generalization of much greater utility than the deque is the *priority queue*. A priority queue is a structure in which nodes have a *priority*. This may be the key or other value, and it may even be possible to update the priority of a node. Retrieval from a priority queue is of the *node with highest priority* and no other. In that sense, there is one "front" node. At retrieval time, the entry order *per se* is of no significance.

Note: It is not uncommon for the term "queue" to refer to a structure that proves to be a priority queue on close examination. This meaning may even be more common in the general literature than that of pure queue.

A priority queue may be supported in many ways. One such is simply a sorted list, and the highest priority item in the queue is the head node. Another priority queue is an instance of QUEUE in which priority is the negative of the entry order (or the inverse of it). Another priority queue is an instance of STACK in which priority is given to the most-recently entered item (the entry order itself is the priority measure). There are many other ways to support priority queues.

One application of priority queues is as a retainer for events that have been scheduled to happen. Discrete-event simulations are those that move from action to action, and in such a simulation, this holding structure is called an *event queue*. An example of an event-queue application is the doctors'-waiting-room model treated in section 5.7.

Note: A Pascal program that simulates an airport customs process is to be found in Part II, section K. The heart of the simulation is the management of an event queue.

A common way to support a priority queue so that insertion and retrieval are efficient when entry order does not determine the priority is a *heap*, discussed in Chapter 8. A major application of priority queues is made in the treatment of graphs in Chapter 10.

In some sense, this book is a bridge between the array of introductory programming and variations of priority queues used in practice.

■ 5.5 Queues in Hardware   (optional)

A buffer containing data to be written on a printer or a disk is usually generated at a different rate than it is serviced. As a consequence, either these jobs are retained in a queue, or some process must become idle until another is complete. Such queues may be managed by either software or hardware, since both can perform the same essential logical operations.

Some queueing within computing systems is normally the domain of hardware, rather than software. Instructions in a machine are fetched, then executed, in an endless cycle. Both the execution phase and the fetch phase can exhibit *overlap* in which two or more instructions are being processed in some way at the same time. Specifically, these two overlap modes are *pipelining* and the use of *cache memory*. They are both associated with queueing behavior.

> **Note:** Discussions of pipelining and cache memories are to be found in Part II, section J.

■ 5.6 On the Simulation of a Doctors' Waiting Room (optional)

Many physical processes are expensive or impractical to observe directly, and certainly they can only be observed in operation during conditions that actually exist. Almost any industrial process, almost any natural biological, physical, or social environment, and almost any large computing system is quite complex. For example, building a large chemical plant based on a newly discovered sequence of reactions without knowing that it will work on a large scale much as it does in the laboratory would not be wise. In such a case it is worthwhile to model such processes and to study the model extensively, with the assumption that the behavior of the model is a valid surrogate for the behavior of the process itself.

If suitable approximations to a process behavior can be constructed mathematically, it is often cost-effective to use mathematical software to study that behavior. An alternative, sometimes the only one, is the development of a simulation of the process. A *simulation* is a program that *imitates* the behavior of a process, in contrast to an analytical *model,* which *describes* it.

When simulating a system involving queues it is not necessary to use queues as a data structure in the simulation program. It is natural, however, and may be efficient in several ways. Queueing behavior may also be effected with structures that are not strictly of type QUEUE, such as a generalized (priority) queue. On the other hand, queues are often involved in simulations that do not themselves emulate queues, as a scheduling structure, the *event queue*. In practice, the "event queue" is usually a priority queue.

The conjunction of these ideas can be illustrated with a model of a doctors' office that does not explicitly involve a queue, but does use queueing ideas, and that is programmed with an event queue. Some familiarity with statistical ideas is helpful (see Part II, section A).

The office is serviced by five doctors and several support staff. Patients arrive in some distribution during an eight-hour day, are treated after a while, and leave. The treatment-with-wait generates a mean-service-time, *mst*, as a whole, shown schematically in Figure 5.10.

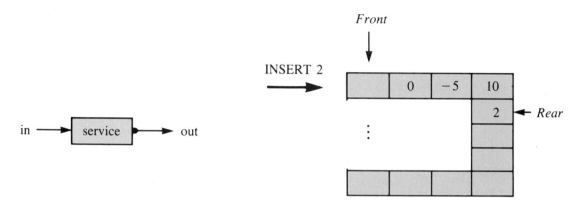

Figure 5.10

At random intervals one of the doctors is called away and returns after a random length of time. The number of services can vary from 0 to 5. One question that can be asked is: how many chairs are needed in the waiting room?

Four distributions are involved in this model:

- *ia,* the *interarrival time,* or time between patient arrivals. (This would generally be modeled as an exponential distribution: $ia \leftarrow -(1/\lambda) \cdot \ln(Rand)$.

- *fixup,* the mean service time for one doctor to treat one patient (possibly exponential again)

- *out,* the time between doctor exits (possibly uniform, *Rand*)

- *back,* the length of time a doctor will be gone when called away (perhaps a normal distribution)

These distributions can be generated either as needed or as four sequential files, to be stored and retrieved as needed. They are, in effect, queues. At any given moment, the next event might be a patient arrival, a patient exit, a doctor exit, or a doctor arrival. Each event can be described by a procedure that is simple or elaborate, depending upon how much detail is defined by the model and how much information is to be gathered for statistical analysis.

The event procedures need to be *scheduled.* One reasonable approach is to take care of the next (in time) event next.

Simulation programs often deal with event scheduling by having each event-procedure determine when the next event of its type is to occur, by generating it or reading it from a file and then generating a record to be added to the *event queue*. This record is called an *event*. The event-record contains the time at which it is to take place and other attributes of interest. Above all, it can produce the *next event*—the one scheduled to happen soonest— considered to be the event with the *highest priority*. In terms of the structures studied so far, the event queue can be maintained as an ordered list. Event-procedures process event-records, selected for processing by their position on the event list and their attributes.

It is necessary to resolve *collisions,* times occupied by more than one event, as well as other aspects of the program that affect the validity of the model. (The *validity* of a model is how well its behavior conforms to that of the system being modeled.) For example, is it valid to allow a doctor to leave while treating a patient, or must the service be completed? (Are there any emergencies?) Should patient arrivals be handled before doctor arrivals in collision with them? (This affects the number waiting and hence the statistics generated by the program.) Since collisions can occur, the priority used to sort events to determine their order of processing cannot be simply their scheduled event time.

Suppose that in a program *Infuse,* which simulates the doctors' office, the event list is named *eList* and contains records of the form:

eListype = RECORD
        Time : INTEGER
        Tag : INTEGER { *patient ID*
        Type : ARRAY[*1 . . 8*] OF CHAR
        Info : {*a record of attribute information*
        Link : ↑ *Listype*
        END {*eListype*

Types of events would reasonably include but not necessarily be confined to, *SadSack* (a patient arrival), *CoolOff* (a patient moves to an examination room), *Aok* (a patient departure), *StatOut* (a doctor departure *now*), *AgainSam* (a doctor arrival). The time might represent minutes from the start of the day. An integer *Avail* might be used to keep track of the number of doctors currently available, and *Waiter* the number being served.

Suppose that the current event list is of the form shown in Figure 5.11. When the next record of *eList* is retrieved, it is found to be at (simulation) time 106. When it is removed for examination the result is the list of Figure 5.12:

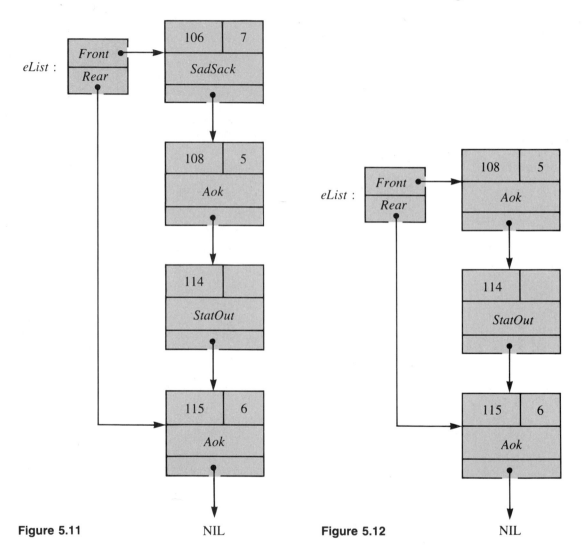

Figure 5.11

Figure 5.12

When the retrieved record is examined, it is found to be a patient arrival (*SadSack*). As part of the execution of the procedure that handles patient arrivals, at least one new record will be scheduled:

- The next *SadSack* record is scheduled at the time determined by the next *ia* value.

If patient arrivals have precedence over patient departures, but not doctor departures, then various values of *ia* that produce collisions would instead yield the snapshots shown in Figure 5.13.

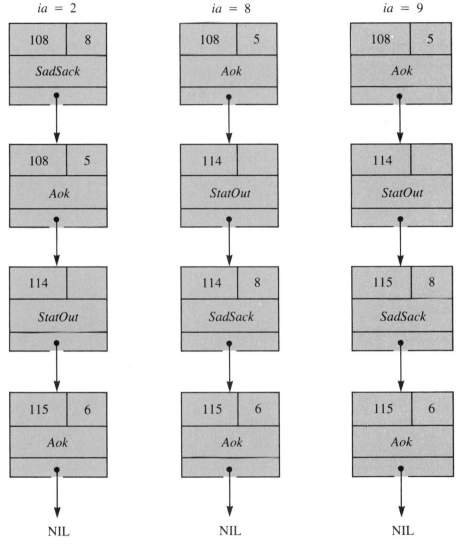

Figure 5.13

The patient who arrived at time 106 does not disappear — even though the arrival *event* disappears. The arrival procedure increments a counter representing the "queue" of patients in the waiting room. If individual patients are to be tracked through the process, then the waiting room may become a true queue structure, and a record is added to the rear of that queue when *SadSack* events are processed. Patient attributes such as illness type might be chosen at that point, if they are to affect the simulation. If so, service times must be split into categories.

A simulation program having a reasonable degree of validity involves many decisions, some hidden deep in the coding. Writing a simulation program is time-consuming and hence expensive; worse, it is very difficult to establish validity. Nevertheless, simulations are sometimes the most cost-effective approach to exploring a problem, but mathematical analysis should be tried first. For this reason, a great deal of effort is expended on *approximate* solutions to problems that are unsolved (or intractable). An alternate approach, available at major installations, is the use of *simulation languages*—languages written especially for this purpose. A discussion of the pros and cons of their use lies outside the bounds of this book.

Project PJ5.1 is appropriate at this point.

Note: A realization in Pascal of a simulation of the customs system at an airport is to be found in Part II, section K. It is based on the use of a priority queue.

Simulation begins to be accessible with a knowledge of queues, but the crux of a simulation is the thoughtful analysis of the results. That requires a background in statistics. The simulation language SIMULA is perhaps the easiest for the user of languages related to pseudocode to learn. There are introductory texts for SIMULA, but compilers are not common.

Summary

Queueing behavior is that of a FIFO (First-In-First-Out) collection. It is to be found wherever there are waiting lines, and waiting lines occur wherever an arrival sequence and a servicing process are not synchronized, a common pattern. The time-sequencing effects of queueing can be complex, but the data structure used to model it is relatively simple. A queue has the effect of storing items until they are needed. It is a *retainer*.

Formally, QUEUE is a structure in which only the oldest (earliest-entry) item in the collection is accessible for viewing by FRONT or for removal by DELETE. An interior node can be accessed only by deleting the items in front of it. Like lists and stacks and unlike arrays, queues are dynamic, growing with insertions and shrinking with deletions, but they are point-like objects that hide their internal dynamism from the user.

Queues can be supported as lists to which insertion is applied at the rear (tail) and deletion at the front (head). A queue can also be supported in a direct way in a single array, using two indices *Front* and *Rear*.

The array-supported queue can reach the last cell in its array in two senses— by position and by total number of entries. The shifting required to resolve the position problem causes insertion to be $O(n)$ in the worst case, although it is typically an $O(1)$ operation like deletion.

The position problem for an array-supported queue can be eliminated by using circular queues, but then an extra flag is required to resolve empty and full conditions.

The queue has generalizations, one of which is the *priority queue,* to be explored in later chapters. Many applications of programmed queues involve the generalized forms, but pure queues have uses such as the pipelining of instructions and simulations of waiting lines.

A realization in Pascal of a "queue machine" is to be found in Part II, section I, and a Pascal program that simulates an airport customs system is to be found in Part II, section K.

Exercises   immediate applications of the text material

E5.1   What would the final list be if the sequence: 4   0   − 5   10 were treated as a stack with operations DELETE, DELETE, INSERT 2?

E5.2   Trace the behavior of the queue: 4   0   − 5   10, implemented with pointer variables, with the operations: DELETE, INSERT 2, DELETE, DELETE, INSERT 3, DELETE.

E5.3.   Trace the behavior of the queue: 4   0   − 5   10, implemented as an array, with the operations: DELETE, INSERT 2, DELETE, DELETE, INSERT 3, DELETE. Assume that the value 10 is initially in *aQueue* [*Max* − 1].

Problems   not immediate, but requiring no major extensions of the text material

P5.1   Redesign the procedures for an array implementation of queues in section 5.2, using *Front* as the index of the front value itself.

P5.2   Modify the queue operations of section 5.3 so that up to (*Max* − 1) items may be kept in a *circular* queue implemented as an array, and *Some* is not required.

Programs for trying it yourself

PG5.1 At the beginning of this chapter, an input stream of characters was associated with both an entry time into a waiting line and a service time. Together these times determined the contents of a queue.

Write a program that accepts a sequence of triplets—for example, $(W,5,2)$, $(A,6,1)$, $(I,8,5)$, $(T,9,5)$, and $(S,13,2)$ —and produces a snapshot of the queue each time there is a change in it. The triples are to be (identifier, arrival time, service time) and the time at which a change in the queue occurs should be displayed with its contents.

It is not a bad idea to produce two versions of this program, one using pointer-linked records, and the other using array support for the queue. Obviously, only a few procedures should change from one version to the other.

PG5.2 A buffer B holds N blocks of data to be displayed by output device P. Programs generate blocks of output at random intervals with a mean of 11 seconds, and they are queued in B. P removes a block from B at regular intervals, every 10 seconds when there is one to remove.

Suppose that, because of overhead and storage limitations, each increment of N above 1 costs an average of $1 for each storage of a block into B. Each time a program finds the buffer full, it must be rerun, at a cost of $100. Clearly, if there is no variation in the production of blocks, $N = 1$ is optimal. If there *is* variation, blocks are sometimes generated close together, and $N = 1$ will exact a cost of $100.

The problem here is to write a program that experimentally determines the optimum value of N for clearly stated conditions of spread (dispersion) in the generation of blocks. A simple variation is to use a pseudorandom number generator to generate times between blocks that vary uniformly in the interval [i .. j] (for example, in [7 .. 15]). The material in Part II, section A, will allow a much more sophisticated experiment to be designed with little additional programming.

Projects   for fun; for serious students

PJ5.1 Write and run the simulation of the doctors' office discussed in section 5.7.

PJ5.2 A small popular restaurant has six tables that seat 4, two that seat 2, and one table that seats 8. It has room for only 15 people in its lobby.

The input stream consists of parties of 1 to 8 people. A party that arrives at a time when there is not enough space in the lobby (or at the tables) for the entire party is turned away at the door. Naturally, the headwaiter has some strategy for either seating parties at tables that would hold more people or saving a table for later.

Write a command-shell program that manages the seating at the restaurant. Commands should provide for parties to arrive at the door, parties to complete their dinner and leave, and display of the contents of both the dining room and the waiting room.

The lobby is to be managed as one or more queues.

The input stream of commands can be interactive, generated from statistical distributions (see Part II, section A) or provided by the instructor.

General Lists: Multiple Access Paths

Structures STACK, QUEUE, and DEQUE are fundamentally simple in design. They provide immediate access to their nodes only at the ends of the list. Access to interior nodes is not part of their structure but can be gained by following a sequence of links from an end node—by making a list-walk.

For some problems it is natural to develop a solution that uses a more complex structure having multiple access paths to an interior node. The multiplicity of paths is created by a multiplicity of links leading from each node; any given node generally has more than one successor and more than one predecessor.

One class of multiply linked structures is the *binary tree* and its variations. The classes of tree-like structures are themes of Chapters 8 and 9. Trees are a special case of the *graph,* described and traversed in Chapter 10. However, some multiply linked structures can be managed with a combination of the structures discussed in previous chapters.

Several sections of Chapter 6 give different examples of multiply linked structures or applications of them. Doubly linked lists are introduced in section 6.1. Linkage patterns of interwoven lists called *n-braids* are introduced in section 6.2. The adjacency matrix and graph models that form much of the basis for design and analysis of general data structures are introduced in section 6.3. A survey of sparse matrix structures in section 6.4 provides the background for discussion of two structures for them: Main Diagonal Circulation in Part II, section N, and Orthogonal Lists in section 6.5. Both models use circular 2-braids. The doubly linked lists of section 6.1 are used in the sparse-matrix model and in modeling dynamic memory allocation in section 6.5.

Relatively simple combinations of list structures can be used to construct alternates to the hash table structure of Part II, section B. These combinations are discussed in Part II, section L.

Most of the algorithms that walk a general list structure use stacks, either implicitly (to support *recursion*—see Chapter 7) or explicitly, in analogy with the maze-walk of Part II, section H. An algorithm that walks a general list without using stacks is introduced in section 7.7 and discussed in Part II, section M.

6.1 Doubly Linked Lists

Linearly linked lists can be altered by fast operations when the INSERT and DELETE operations are proscribed, as they are in the STACK and QUEUE structures. In contrast, if additions and deletions are to be made at arbitrary positions within a list, then the fundamental operations become $O(n)$ instead of $O(1)$ because a search is required to locate an interior node.

When a node to be deleted from a linearly linked list has been located, its removal requires a pointer to both of its immediate neighbors in the list—its predecessor as well as its successor. The same requirement makes some operations, such as the *DeleteTail* procedure of section 3.3.4, awkward. In an operation on a linear list where the predecessor of a node is required, the predecessor must be located with a search. One way to enhance access to neighboring nodes within a list is to weave two linked lists together to form a doubly linked list, as shown in Figure 6.1:

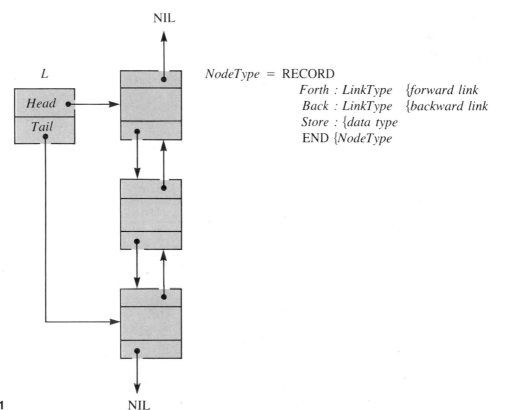

$NodeType = \text{RECORD}$
  $Forth : LinkType$ {*forward link*
  $Back : LinkType$ {*backward link*
  $Store : \{data\ type$
  $\text{END} \{NodeType$

Figure 6.1   NIL

Procedures *DeleteHead*, *InsertHead*, and *InsertTail* are straightforward adaptations of single-linked list routines. With a simple return as a response to an empty list, *DeleteTail* is:

procedure *DeleteTail(dList)*   {*O(1)*
  if *Empty* **then return endif**
  e ← *Tail* ↑ .*Forth*   {NIL *or* u
  Up ← *Tail* ↑ .*Back*
  if *Up* = *e*
    then *Head* ← *e*   {*singleton response*
    else *Up* ↑ .*Forth* ← *e*
  endif
  DISPOSE(*Tail*)
  Tail ← *Up*
  end {*DeleteTail*

The deletion of a node from the middle of such a list is relatively straightforward. To remove an already located *p*, the deletion procedure might follow the schema in Figure 6.2.

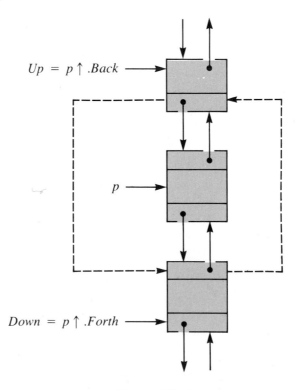

$Up = p \uparrow .Back$

p

$Down = p \uparrow .Forth$

Figure 6.2

The relinking can be done with:

procedure *UnDouble(dList,p)*   {*O(1)*
  if *Empty* **then return endif**
  Up ← *p* ↑ *.Back*
  Down ← *p* ↑ *.Forth*
  e ← *Tail* ↑ *.Forth*   {NIL *or u*
  if *Down* = *e*
    then DeleteTail(*dList*)
      return
    endif
  if *Up* = *e*
    then DeleteHead(*dList*)
      return
    endif
  Up ↑ *.Forth* ← *Down*
  Down ↑ *.Back* ← *Up*
  DISPOSE(*p*)
  end {*UnDouble*

An assumption made in *UnDouble* is a necessary condition for a list to be *doubly linked;* for any interior node (not *Head* or *Tail*):

$$p = p \uparrow .Forth \uparrow .Back = p \uparrow .Back \uparrow .Forth$$

Program PG6.1 is appropriate at this point.

Double links are especially efficient in circular lists, such as that in Figure 6.3. There is no distinguishable *position* in such a list, although Q is the distinguished *node*. It can be convenient to let Q float from node to node in a sequence of "search and process" operations, pointing to the last (distinguished) node associated with an operation. Because such a ring has no natural head or tail, treating it as a stack or queue requires care.

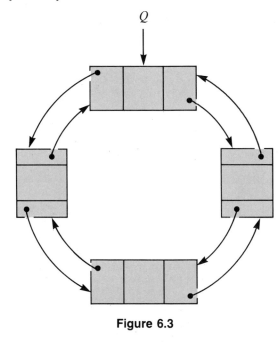

Figure 6.3

Exercises E6.1 and E6.2 are appropriate at this point.

6.2 *n*-braids

The doubly linked assumption can be relaxed for more general linked lists, as shown in Figure 6.4. The *Forth* list defines the sequence 1,2,3,4. The *Back* list defines the sequence 4,2,3,1. The independence of the *Back* and *Forth* linearly linked lists reintroduces the need to search for predecessors. The structure in Figure 6.4 is fundamentally two *interwoven* lists, a *2-braid*, not a doubly linked list. A 2-braid can be used to simultaneously sequence one set of nodes in two ways. In general, an interweaving of n linear lists on one set of nodes (an *n-braid*) can be used to sequence the nodes in n ways without duplicating the nodes.

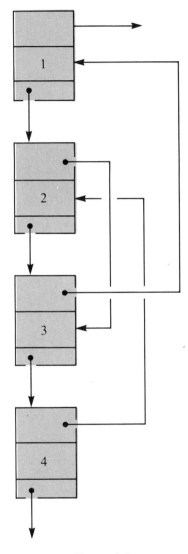

Figure 6.4

The nodes of an n-braid contain link fields associated with more than one list. Procedures to be applied to such nodes must either be written to process a specific braid or be generalized in some way. One way to generalize such procedures is to use an array of link-fields: *Braid*[1 . . *n*]. Then an index k is used to specify the braid link and hence to select braid k to be processed. It then requires very little alteration of standard list procedures to construct general braid procedures. In this chapter, we will assume that the following are available:

■ *RingIn(b,p,q)* inserts node *p* as the successor to node *q* into braid *b*, shown in Figure 6.5.

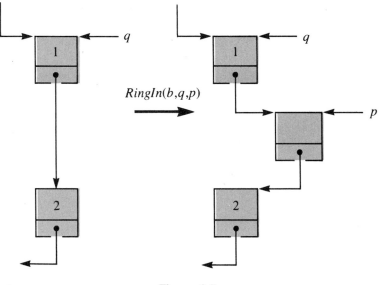

Figure 6.5

■ *RingOut(b,q)* deletes the successor of node *q* from braid *b*, shown in Figure 6.6.

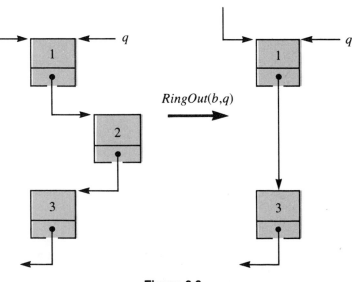

Figure 6.6

The search for q in both *RingIn* and *RingOut* may depend on the structure within which a braid lies and the starting point of the search.

> **Note:** Insertion into and deletion from an n-braid involves location of the node in *each braid*. Disposal of a node must be delayed until it is deleted from all its braids.

Problem P6.1 is appropriate at this point.

6.3 Matrices and Graph Adjacency

The systems to which combinations of data structures can be applied are sometimes complex. Two models that are powerful simplifiers and organizers are commonly applied to such systems to make them accessible to analysis and design. These two models are the *matrix* and the *graph*. They are introduced very briefly here as necessary background for discussions in later parts of the book.

When the arithmetic operations ADDITION and MULTIPLICATION and their interactions are defined for tables, the tables become *matrices*. There is a strong analogy between the definition of such mathematical structures and computing structures such as ARRAY, STACK, and QUEUE. The operations of the structure MATRIX can even be defined algorithmically, in which case the mathematical structure and the data structure correspond very closely to each other.

The algorithmic definitions of the matrix operations ADDITION and MULTIPLICATION are:

■ For two $n \times m$ tables, $A[1 .. n, 1 .. m]$ and $B[1 .. n, 1 .. m]$, added to form $C[1 .. n, 1 .. m]$, ADDITION is defined by:

```
function AddMatrix(A,B)                    {O(n²)
  for i = 1 to n
    for j = 1 to m
      C[i,j] ← A[i,j] + B[i,j]
      next j
    next i
  return C
  end {AddMatrix
```

■   For $A[1 .. n, 1 .. p]$ and $B[1 .. p, 1 .. m]$, multiplied to form the product $C[1 .. n, 1 .. m]$, MULTIPLICATION is defined by:

```
function MultiMatrix(A,B)                 {O(n³)
    for i = 1 to n
        for j = 1 to m                    {C[i,j] = Σ A[i,p] × B[p,j]
            Sum ← 0
            for k = 1 to p
                Sum ← Sum + A[i,k] * B[k,j]
            next k
            C[i,j] ← Sum
        next j
    next i
    return C
end {MultiMatrix
```

Tables can be used to describe many systems, physical and conceptual. It is uncanny and satisfying that matrix operations often model the *behavior* of such systems. As an example, many systems can be modeled geometrically as a *graph:* informally, a collection of nodes joined by edges, as in Figure 6.7.

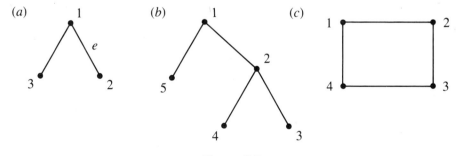

Figure 6.7

Graphs participated in the genesis of topology, may be involved in the demise of some management schemes, and certainly picture all networks, including those used to approximate topographies in models of agricultural regions.

Graphs depict the connections called *edges* between entities called *vertices;* that information may also be tabulated. The table associated with a graph is called its *adjacency matrix*. To tabulate a graph:

■   Number the nodes (as done in Figure 6.7) and associate both a row and a column of table G with each node.

■   If there is an edge connecting node i with node j, then $G[i,j] \leftarrow 1$, otherwise $G[i,j] \leftarrow 0$.

Figure 6.8 shows the graphs from Figure 6.7 in tabulated form.

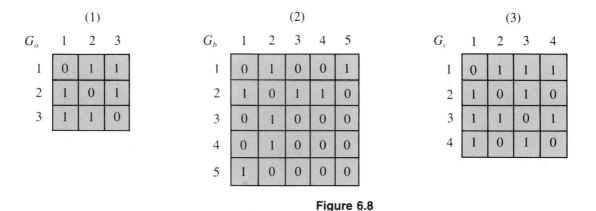

(1)

G_a	1	2	3
1	0	1	1
2	1	0	1
3	1	1	0

(2)

G_b	1	2	3	4	5
1	0	1	0	0	1
2	1	0	1	1	0
3	0	1	0	0	0
4	0	1	0	0	0
5	1	0	0	0	0

(3)

G_c	1	2	3	4
1	0	1	1	1
2	1	0	1	0
3	1	1	0	1
4	1	0	1	0

Figure 6.8

One way to interpret these tables is that they select the pairs of nodes connected by a one-step path. A *chain* in a graph is a sequence of edges that lead from one node to another. Technically, if an edge is defined by the pair of nodes it connects, like $\{1,2\}$ for the edge e in (a), then a chain is a sequence $\{N_1,N_2\}$, $\{N_2,N_3\}$, . . . , $\{N_{n-1},N_n\}$ that joins node N_1 with node N_n. The charming effectiveness of mathematics appears when the graph tables are treated as matrices and raised to powers as G_c^2 is in Figure 6.9.

G_c^2	1	2	3	4
1	3	1	2	1
2	1	2	1	2
3	2	1	3	1
4	1	2	1	2

Figure 6.9

An entry $G_c^2[i,j]$ is *the number of chains of precisely two steps* that joins Node i to Node j. Similarly, G_c^3 tabulates the number of paths of length 3 that join pairs of nodes in the graph of example (c). Hence the powers of a graph matrix provide valuable information about the system modeled by the graph. This is not the only connection between matrices and graphs, but merely an illustration of the ubiquity of matrix operations.

Chapter 10 deals with graph representations as data structures. In this chapter, it is the mathematical nature of a matrix that determines the structure used to represent it; and that structure differs from those used in Chapter 10.

Exercise E6.3, problem P6.2, and program PG6.2 are appropriate at this point.

6.3.1 Directed Graphs

There is no need to restrict the linkage patterns of data elements to linear structures or even to combinations of linear structures. For example, four nodes may be linked as in Figure 6.10.

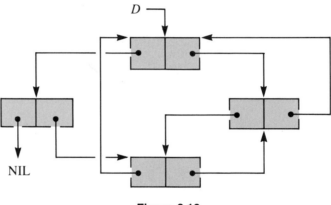

Figure 6.10

A simpler geometrical model for this pattern is a *digraph* (directed graph), which differs from a graph precisely because the edges possess direction, as shown in Figure 6.11.

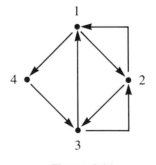

Figure 6.11

Like a graph, a digraph model has an adjacency matrix, although a digraph matrix is not symmetric about the main diagonal ($M[i,i]$, $1 \leq i \leq Max$) in contrast to the adjacency matrix of a graph. An entry of 1 in $M[i,j]$ for a digraph signifies a *directed* arc (an *edge*) from node *i* to node *j*. An edge is thus an *ordered* pair, (i,j). For the example above, the adjacency matrix *M* is shown in Figure 6.12.

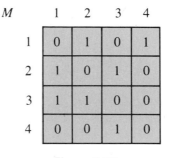

M

	1	2	3	4
1	0	1	0	1
2	1	0	1	0
3	1	1	0	0
4	0	0	1	0

Figure 6.12

Since edges in a digraph are directional, so are sequences that follow them from one vertex to another. The analog of a graph chain is a digraph *path*. It is still true that $M^k[i,j]$ is the number of *k*-step paths from [*i*] to [*j*], as shown for this example in Figure 6.13.

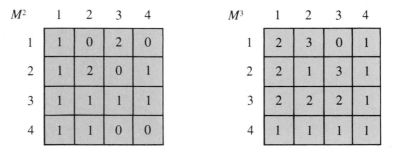

M^2

	1	2	3	4
1	1	0	2	0
2	1	2	0	1
3	1	1	1	1
4	1	1	0	0

M^3

	1	2	3	4
1	2	3	0	1
2	2	1	3	1
3	2	2	2	1
4	1	1	1	1

Figure 6.13

Digraphs arise as models of such diverse systems as dominance relations in sociology and management, communication networks, and relations between data elements in the flight and ticket information of an airline. Data can be structured as a collection of nodes linked in the same pattern as the natural digraph model. Such a node structure is called a *digraph list,* also a *general list*.

Note: It is the *digraph* rather than the graph that corresponds most closely to data structures formed with pointers, because they are directional. In data structures that model graphs, *two* links represent each edge, one for each direction.

The design of fundamental operations like INSERT and DELETE become very application-dependent and sometimes difficult in a general list. A search through a digraph structure appears to be forbidding; nevertheless, it is required in some applications. Hence there *are* algorithms for visiting each node of a general list, and a node may be processed in any desired way during the visit. One such algorithm is to be found in Part II, section M. A different visitation algorithm for general lists is the subject of section 7.7, where it serves as an example of a recursive algorithm. The traverse of a (restructured) general list can also be patterned very closely after the treatment of graphs in Chapter 10.

6.4 Sparse Matrix Representation

In many applications of graphs modeled by matrices and in other applications involving matrices, *most* of the entries are zero. Such a matrix is called a *sparse matrix*. A workable pair of definitions is that an N by N matrix is sparse if it contains $O(N)$ nonzero entries and *dense* if it contains $O(N^2)$ nonzero entries.

The value of the nonzero entries in a sparse matrix as well as their location by row and column can be important, and a listing of the nonzero entries defines the zero entries by default if it is known to be complete. Any structure to which matrix operations are applied needs a row and column organization. It is nevertheless possible to trade simplicity and the independent access to a large and sparsely used storage space for complexity of structure coupled with more efficient use of storage. The trade of fast access for efficient storage is frequently made for problems that involve sparse matrices.

A number of data structures can be used to represent a sparse matrix:

1. SST (Sparse and Static Table). This structure is intrinsically static; not only is its storage allocation fixed, but it is also designed for a specific subset of the cells of the large (virtual) matrix it represents. It is excellent for some sparse table storage, as indicated in section 2.4, but difficult at best to adapt to the general situation of a changing (but still sparse) matrix.

2. MDC (Main Diagonal Circulation). The backbone of this structure is a collection of nodes, each representing a header for two circular lists: a row list and a column list. Each nonzero cell is represented by a node braided into one row list and one column list. This structure is detailed in Part II, section N.

3. AM (Adjacency Matrix) and AL (Adjacency List). These are the structures of choice for supporting a graph traverse, and they are explored in Chapter 10.

4. HT (Hash Table). The indices of a cell in a large table can be used to form a hashed address in a smaller table. This approach depends on the discussions of hashing in Part II, sections B and L. It is the basis of PJ6.1.

5. OL (Orthogonal Lists). A circular list of row headers and a circular list of column headers form the framework of row and column (circular) lists. Each cell in the array is braided into one row and one column list. This approach is discussed in section 6.5.

For all of these structures, the user is generally a procedure that accesses the matrix as a table, as would those of section 6.3 when applied to sparse matrices. The desired service is provided by STORE(i,j,x) and RETRIEVE(i,j).

> **Note:** It may be possible to rewrite procedures that access a sparse matrix to make them "more efficient," but *don't*. The result tends to be logical spaghetti, which is hard to debug. Leave it for another course.

In all of these structures, deletion is awkward, and deletion can occur as the result of STORE. When an assignment is made to sparse matrix M, as done by $M[i,j] \leftarrow x$, several possibilities must be distinguished:

- An existing node is to be updated:

  $M[i,j] \neq 0$ and $x \neq 0$

- A new node is to be inserted into M:

  $M[i,j] = 0$ and $x \neq 0$

- A node is to be deleted from M:

  $M[i,j] \neq 0$ and $x = 0$

In the case of MDC and OL, deletion and insertion are made into both row and column braids with the *RingIn* and *RingOut* procedures of section 6.2.

■ 6.5 The Orthogonal List   (optional)

An example of a very small but relatively sparse matrix is:

M	1	2	3	4
1	7	0	0	0
2	5	9	0	6
3	0	8	0	0
4	7	0	0	0

n by n
for
$n = 4$

This matrix may be represented by an interwoven collection of circular lists in which there are $(2n+1)$ header nodes and precisely as many cell nodes as needed for nonzero entries. Every node is braided into a row braid and a column braid, and the headers are distinguished by having either a row or a column index that is illegal, as in Figure 6.14, where 0 is the illegal index.

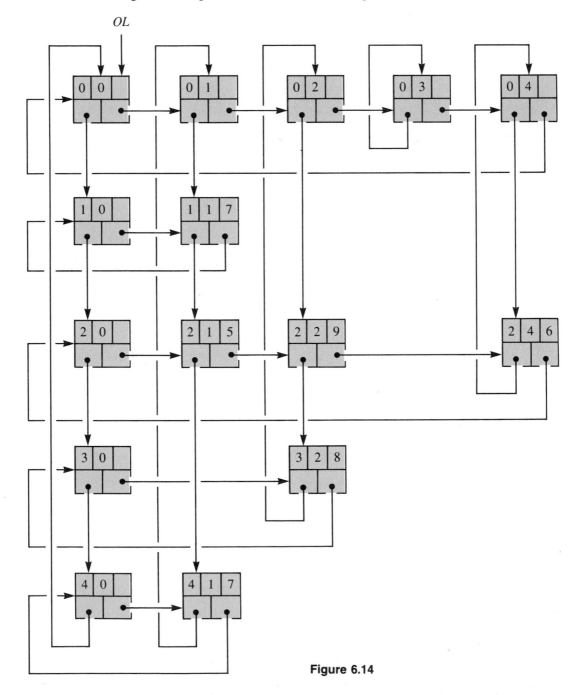

Figure 6.14

Exercise E6.4 is appropriate at this point.

General procedures such as *RingIn* and *RingOut* (section 6.2) are applicable to the OL structure if node records use indexed braid pointers and dimension identifiers (for row and column):

row	column	data
Braid[1]	*Braid*[2]	*Value*
Dim[1]	*Dim*[2]	

$$NodeType \; = \; \text{RECORD}$$
$$Braid[1 \, . \, . \, 2] \; : \; \uparrow NodeType$$
$$Dim[1 \, . \, . \, 2] \; : \; \text{INTEGER}$$
$$Value \; : \; \{data \; type$$
$$\text{END}$$

Both STORE and RETRIEVE involve finding the correct header, then the predecessor of the node to be accessed. Header location for row or column *dex* is an adaptation of *LT* (section 3.3.2):

function *FindBraid(Other,dex)*   {*O*(*n*)
   b ← (*Other* MOD 2) + *1*
   Head ← *OL* ↑ .*Braid*[*Other*]
   while *Head* ≠ *OL* **do**
     if *Head* ↑ .*Dim*[*b*] = *dex*
       then exit endif
     Head ← *Head* ↑ .*Braid*[*Other*]
     endwhile
   return *Head*
   end {*FindBraid*

The appropriate row and column can then be located by:

Row ← *FindBraid*(2,*i*)
Col ← *FindBraid*(1,*j*)

A very similar routine locates the predecessor of the node with a given index in the other direction, within a given braid:

function *FindPred(Head,b,dex)* {*O(n)*

  Pred ← *Head*

  s ← *Head* ↑ *.Braid*[*b*]

  Other ← (*b* MOD 2) + *1*

  while *s* ≠ *Head* **do**

    if *s* ↑ *.Dim*[*Other*] ≥ *dex*

      then exit endif

    Pred ← *s*

    s ← *s* ↑ *.Braid*[*b*]

  endwhile

  return *Pred*

end {*FindPred*

With these tools available, RETRIEVE is straightforward: the node in the position where *M*[*i,j*] is expected is located as *p*. If *M*[*i,j*] is not present, *p* ↑ *.Braid*[1] will not have the correct column index:

function *Retrieve(i,j)* {*O(n)*

  Row ← *FindBraid(2,i)*

  RowPred ← *FindPred(Row,1,j)*

  p ← *RowPred* ↑ *.Braid*[*1*]

  if *p* ↑ *.Dim*[2] ≠ *j*

    then return *0*

    else return *p* ↑ *.Value*

    endif

end {*Retrieve*

STORE is more complex, since it may involve inserting or deleting a node. One version, tuned for clarity but not for efficiency, is:

```
procedure Store(i,j,x)                              {O(n)
    Row ← FindBraid(2,i)
    Col ← FindBraid(1,j)
    RowPred ← FindPred(Row,1,j)
    ColPred ← FindPred(Col,2,i)
    p ← RowPred↑.Braid[1]
    if x = 0
        then if p↑.Dim[2] = j                       {M[i,j] is in the matrix
                then RingOut(1,RowPred)
                     RingOut(2,ColPred)
                     DISPOSE(p)
             endif
        else if p↑.Dim[2] = j                       {M[i,j] is in the matrix
                then p↑.Value ← x
                else NEW(n)
                     n↑.Value ← x
                     n↑.Dim[1] ← i
                     n↑.Dim[2] ← j
                     RingIn(1,RowPred,n)
                     RingIn(2,ColPred,n)
             endif
    endif
end {Store
```

Program PG6.3 is appropriate at this point.

■ 6.6 A Dynamic Storage Allocation Model   (optional)

At the lowest level, the main store of a computing system is a large array, part of it preempted by housekeeping procedures necessary for interface of the system to the outside world and to working programs. The operating system, called on by compiler-generated instructions, is asked to provide storage on demand from the main store each time a program is activated and each time a utility routine such as *NEW* is executed.

The main store array has a maximum address, like other arrays. If memory is *partitioned* among several users, each user has a segment available which—to that user—appears to be the entire store. No other user has access to this segment of memory at the same time.

If memory is *shared*, then its management becomes delicate, because a user may change values in memory cells accessed by other users. Memory is not actually increased in size by sharing, even though its utilization may be greater during a given span of time it would be for unshared memory. The issues involved with shared memory are dealt with in the study of operating systems.

In this section we assume that a single user—while active—has command of a store of fixed size. With that assumption, a program that manages a block of memory by allocating subblocks of fixed size behaves like the memory-management process of an operating system.

Consider a time-sharing system that has a finite number of *active* programs resident in memory, each waiting for or using a slice of processor time. A program is allocated storage space when it is activated. The amount to be allocated is specified when it is compiled, and no more space becomes available during execution. An apparent limitation of this scheme is that dynamic allocation of memory for pointer variables is not allowed. In some implementations the space allotted to a program may be large enough to allow some dynamic allocation during execution, but the allocation cannot exceed a set maximum.

A request for the allocation of memory for a new program comes from a scheduling process, the *scheduler*, to the memory management program, *Mem*. If memory is available, it is provided by *Mem*, and the program is activated. From time to time, a program completes its execution and becomes *passive*. When this happens *Mem* is informed and the storage occupied by the formerly active program is released; it is *free* and may be used for activation of new programs.

> **Note:** The management scheme presented here is a model, based on data structures that have been described in previous sections. More sophisticated structures are applied in practice.

In practice, memory is soon broken into segments occupied by active programs, separated by segments of free storage. The blocks of free storage are linked together by *Mem* in a circular list called *Avail*, like the one in Figure 6.15. The release of each of the active blocks 1,3,5,6, and 7 differs somewhat from the release of the others.

The guiding principle for release is that when a block is freed, it is to be joined with any contiguous free blocks, enlarging them. The newly freed block is not to be joined to free blocks separated from it by active programs. This is one of several possible strategies, one that allows "quick release."

The catch to this strategy is that "contiguous" means adjoining, in *absolute location*, to blocks that are not on the *Avail* list. Blocks are adjoining on the availability list because of the sequence of entries into and exits from *Avail*, not because of their absolute location.

The property of being contiguous is bidirectional in memory, and so a natural way to link together all blocks, free and active, is as a doubly linked list, *Store*, illustrated in Figure 6.16. *Mem* is exogenous; it uses nodes that are records that point to memory blocks, although an operating system could store the linkage and other information in the blocks themselves (because it has the use of machine instructions that access any cell in any available way).

Memory

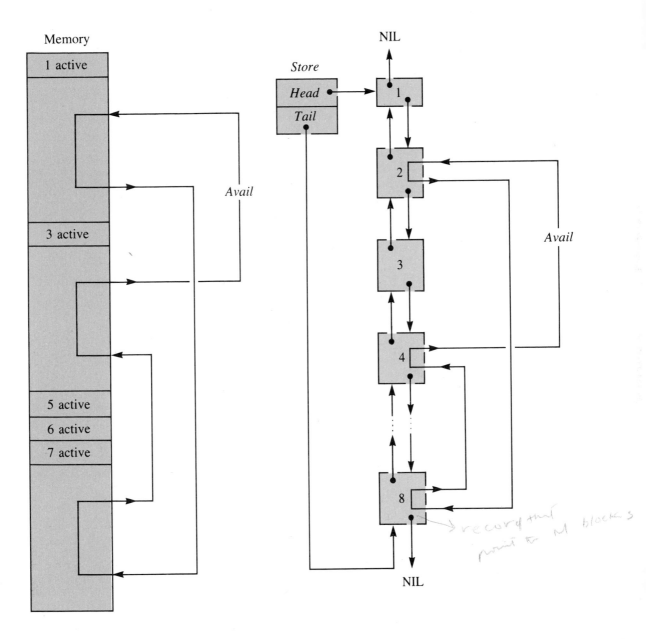

Figure 6.15

Figure 6.16

If block 3 is deactivated, then blocks 2,3, and 4 are collapsed into one block, say block 2, and the resulting structure is depicted in Figure 6.17.

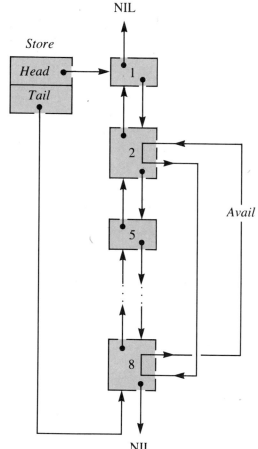

Figure 6.17

The information required in a block node is an identifier (for active programs), three pointers (two for *Store* and one for *Avail*), the absolute starting address, and the size of the block:

```
BlockType = RECORD
              id : ARRAY[1 .. 20] OF CHAR
            Back : ↑BlockType      {Store
           Forth : ↑BlockType      {Store
            Next : ↑BlockType      {Avail
           Start : INTEGER
            Size : INTEGER
            END {BlockType
```

The two major operations are the release of active blocks and the activation of a program. Both are nontrivial.

Both doubly linked lists and circular lists were used without introducing much complexity in previous chapters, and so it might seem that their action in concert would not be complicated. In fact, combined structures can present a much more complex management task.

■ 6.6.1 The Release of an Active Block   (optional)

Given a node p that is to be deactivated, several possibilities must be distinguished in the procedure *UnLeash* that frees it. With the use of

$Up \leftarrow p \uparrow .Back$
$Down \leftarrow p \uparrow .Forth$

the possibilities are delineated in Table 6.1. A straightforward implementation of this organization will produce a nest of **if . . . then . . . else** constructs. An alternative way to orchestrate the release operation is to define simpler subtasks and then structure the way they work together to solve the overall task.

Table 6.1

Up = NIL	$Down$ = NIL	Avail *was empty and now is to contain a single node,* p.	
	$Down \neq$ NIL	$Down \uparrow .next$ = NIL	Down *is active; it cannot be joined to* p, *and so* p *is added as a new node to* Avail.
		$Down \uparrow .Next \neq$ NIL	Down *is free; it is already in* Avail, *and so it can be updated to engulf* p.
$Up \neq$ NIL	$Down$ = NIL	$Up \uparrow .Next$ = NIL	Up *is active; it cannot be joined to* p, *and so* p *is added as a new node to* Avail.
		$Up \uparrow .Next \neq$ NIL	Up *is free; it is already in* Avail, *and so it can be updated to engulf* p.
	$Down \neq$ NIL	$Up \uparrow .Next$ = NIL	Up *is active; it cannot be joined to* p. *However,* Down *may be either free or active, and two cases result.*
		$Up \uparrow .Next \neq$ NIL	Up *is free; it is already in* Avail, *and so it can be updated to engulf* p. *However,* Down *may be either free or active, and two cases result.*

If *Up* is free, then *p* and *Up* may be joined to form a single free block. From the perspective of *Up*, it is simply extended to engulf *p*. Hence, a natural operation is the joining of a lower block to an upper block, say *Join(dList,q)*, where *q* points to the upper block in a doubly linked list, *dList*. Then *Join(dList,Up)* can be followed by deletion of the lower block from *dList* with a standard DELETE operation, *UnDouble(dList,p)*. (In this example, the specific list involved will be called *Store*.) If *p* is not absorbed by *Up* it is inserted into *Avail* with *Free(p)*. If *Up* engulfs *p* the combined block is renamed *p*.

If *Down* is free, then *p* and *Down* may be joined; their joining can be considered an engulfment of *p* by *Down*. When *p* and *Down* are combined with *Bind(Down)* block *p* must be deleted from *Avail* as well as from *Store*. This deletion from *Avail* is simply a DELETE operation of a node from a circular list.

When the special cases are taken care of, *UnLeash* becomes:

procedure *UnLeash(p)*
  Up ← *p* ↑ .*Back*
  Down ← *p* ↑ .*Forth*
  if *Up* ≠ NIL
    then if *Up* ↑ .*Next* ≠ NIL
        then *Join(Store,p)*   *{join* p *to* Up
            UnDouble(Store,p)
              p ← *Up*
        else *Free(p)*
        endif
    else *Free(p)*
    endif
  if *Down* ≠ NIL
    then if *Down* ↑ .*Next* ≠ NIL   *{join (new)* p *to* Down
        then *Bind(Down)*
            UnDouble(Store,p)
        endif
    endif
  end {*UnLeash*

The details of *Join*, *Free*, and *Bind* are left to the problems.

Problems P6.3 and P6.4 are appropriate at this point.

■ 6.6.2 The Activation of a Program   (optional)

When a request (by one part of the operating system to the activation routine) is made to activate a program of size s, several possibilities must be distinguished:

1. There is a block p in *Avail* for which $p \uparrow .Size = s$.

2. There are blocks in *Avail* with size at least as large as s (but not necessarily an exact fit).

3. There is no single block in *Avail* large enough to contain the program, but if active programs are shifted in absolute location, several blocks in *Avail* can be joined to form a block larger than s.

4. The total of the sizes of the blocks in *Avail* is less than s, and so the request cannot be granted at all.

The shifting-and-collapsing operation implied in possibility 3 is called *garbage collection*. It is not always clear just when garbage collection should be done and how. Automatic garbage collection can be incorporated into the release operation so that, on release, all programs are shifted: only one free block ever exists. Analysis reveals that this is a wasteful overhead in most systems. The assumption here is that it is to be done if no single block is of size s or greater, but the sum of all free sizes is greater than s.

Possibility 2 includes possibility 1; several strategies have been devised to deal with it, and there are various implementations of them. In general, some piece of the free block is left over when there is no exact fit. A large number of activation-deactivation cycles can leave many blocks on the *Avail* list too small to be useful for active programs. One way to alleviate this problem is to allocate an *entire block* if it is a "close fit." The effectiveness of this technique is naturally dependent on the statistics of an application. Strategies for allocating blocks as large as s to a program include:

■　　*first-fit:* Work around *Avail* until a free block is located as p, for which $p \uparrow .Size \geq s$, and then return p.

■　　*best-fit:* Search all of *Avail*, and return p, where $(p \uparrow .Size - s) \geq 0$ is minimal.

■　　*worst-fit:* Search all of *Avail*, and return p, where $p \uparrow .Size - s$ is maximal and at least 0.

Allocation for any of these strategies involves transferring the program to p and unlinking p from *Avail*. They are not particularly difficult to program, and they are left to the problems.

It is convenient to move an active program into the bottom of a free block so that, if the excess forms a free block, it is already linked into *Avail,* although its size has changed.

The ideas of first-fit, best-fit, and worst-fit are used as strategies for solving other problems (such as bin-packing, the solution to which is related to the solution of a huge collection of important problems).

Problems P6.5–P6.7 are appropriate at this point.

Garbage collection in practice involves difficulties outside the scope of this book. For one thing, *programs* are moved, and they must execute after being moved. If the active blocks are treated as though they can be moved simply by updating the fields of their records, then garbage collection is a relatively straight-forward shifting operation. It is convenient to shift active blocks upward in memory, leaving a single free block at the bottom of storage. Hence *Avail* can be ignored during the shift and then reinitialized as a single node.

Writing a simulation of memory management that explores the effect of activation strategies and the effect of the distributions of program size and execution times is a substantial project as a class assignment. It is, however, a minor task compared to writing an operating system.

Projects PJ6.1–PJ6.3 are appropriate at this point.

Summary

Control traffic flows over links in one direction only, and so it is sometimes useful to trade space for the convenience of multiple-link paths. The most straightforward multiple-path structure is the doubly linked list, but lists may be interwoven in almost any pattern to form *n-braids*. Deletion and insertion in interwoven lists requires more care than in singly linked lists; the doubly linked list is intermediate in this respect.

The *adjacency matrix,* the *graph,* and the *digraph* are models with great power to simplify, synthesize, and organize. All three correspond to data structures of wide application and provide background for understanding them.

Matrices (and other tables) commonly waste space because many cells contain a standard value (such as zero). A number of structures are available for dealing with this situation and are treated in section 2.7; Part II, sections B, L, and N; section 6.4; Chapter 10; and PJ6.1. The *Orthogonal List* structure is detailed in section 6.4. This structure and the one detailed in Part II, section N, represent cells of the matrix as nodes braided into circular lists.

One (simplified) model of the dynamic allocation of memory in a computing system is a doubly linked list of blocks that contain either active programs or available storage. The available storage blocks are also on an interwoven circular list. Activating and deactivating programs presents a number of interesting problems not restricted to management of the structures themselves.

Exercises   immediate applications of the text material

E6.1   Write an insertion procedure for a doubly linked list, as discussed in section 6.1.

E6.2   Write the procedures for both insertion and deletion in a doubly linked *circular* list.

E6.3   Determine the number of two-step and the number of three-step paths for graphs (*a*) and (*b*) of section 6.3, and verify by calculating the products G_a^2, G_a^3, G_b^2, and G_b^3.

E6.4   Draw the graphs (*a*) and (*b*) of section 6.3 as sparse matrix lists.

Problems   not immediate, but requiring no major extensions of the text material

P6.1   Write procedures *RingIn* and *RingOut* of section 6.2 for nodes in an *n*-braid.

P6.2   Determine the timing functions of *AddMatrix* and *MultiMatrix* of section 6.3.

P6.3   Write the procedure *Join* of section 6.6.1.

P6.4   Write the procedure *UnDouble* of section 6.6.1.

P6.5   Write a first-fit strategy procedure *Firstfit* for locating storage in *Avail* as described in section 6.6.2. Return *NIL* if no free block is large enough.

P6.6   Write a best-fit strategy procedure *Bestfit* for locating storage in *Avail* as described in section 6.6.2. Return *NIL* if no free block is large enough.

P6.7   Write a worst-fit strategy procedure *WorstFit* for locating storage in *Avail* as described in section 6.6.2. Return *NIL* if no free block is large enough.

Programs   for trying it yourself

PG6.1   Write a program that inputs a sequence of paired names and test scores and puts them together in a two-link record. The records are to be linked so that they are in order alphabetically by one sequence of links, and in order by score in another sequence of links. Display the records in alphabetic order, on a line with their score successor, and then vice versa.

PG6.2 Write a program that will accept a sequence of edges (pairs of nodes), and calculate the number of k-fold paths from node i to node j for any specified i, j, and k.

PG6.3 Write a program designed around an entry loop that allows a user to insert and retrieve values from an $n \times n$ Orthogonal List form of a sparse matrix (as described in section 6.5).

Projects   for fun; for serious students

PJ6.1 (Assumes knowledge of Part II, sections B and L.) Investigate the hashing of a table $T[1 .. 30, 1 .. 30]$ into $HT[1 .. 10, 1 .. 10]$. The values in T are all to be either 0 or 1. Start with a loading of HT of 20 percent and determine the mean number of collisions generated by random retrievals and by random assignments, half of which are zero. Determine the loading after 20, 40, . . . , 100 assignments. Repeat this experiment for greater initial loading of HT.

PJ6.2 Write an emulation of memory management as described in section 6.6. The user should be able to activate or deactivate programs by name on command.

PJ6.3 Write a simulation of memory management as described in section 6.6. The user should be able to specify several control parameters and the mean and standard deviations for program sizes. Control parameters should include the number of activations and deletions, fitting strategy, and the ''closeness'' factor.

Chapter 7

Recursion

Recursion is an idea, and it is a programming technique. Calculations and definitions in and out of mathematics both involve recursion, and so it appears in computing as a natural expression of such definitions and calculations.

7.1 A Recursion Sampler

As others have pointed out [LEDGARD, 1981], a natural and effective definition of the word *descendant* is:

DEFINITION: *A* descendant *of a person is*
an offspring or
the descendant *of an offspring of the person.*

This definition is said to be recursive because it is in terms of *itself*. Two properties common to recursive definitions make it possible to search a statement to test whether or not a candidate satisfies the requirements for being recursive:

■ an escape clause (''an offspring'') that allows a search to terminate, and

■ a refresh clause (''the descendant . . . '') that continues the search at a new point if escape is not invoked.

If Lottie has child Leonard has child David, then the check to test Leonard as a descendant of Lottie terminates at the first stage through the escape clause. The check for David as a descendant of Lottie must be refreshed once, continuing the search from Leonard.

Many natural-language words are defined by *indirect* recursion because they are defined in terms of each other. Some, like the word *descendant,* may be defined by direct recursion, in terms of themselves. Dictionaries are usually not so courageous.

Mathematical forms and functions can be recursive:

DEFINITION: $N! = 1$ for $N = 0$
$$= N \times [(N - 1)!] \text{ for } N > 0$$

DEFINITION: $X^k = 1$ for $k = 0$
$$= X \times X^{k-1} \text{ for } k > 0$$

Both of these (and most similar examples) are closely tied to one of the pervading ideas of mathematical sciences—*Mathematical Induction, MI* for short. MI is ubiquitous because it is one of the defining properties of the counting numbers $1,2,3. \ldots$ For the sake of completeness, here is a description of MI:

■   Suppose that $S(n)$ is a statement that involves the positive integer n:

If *1.* $S(1)$ is true, and
  2. $S(k)$ is true whenever
    $S(1), S(2), \ldots , S(k-1)$ are true
then $S(n)$ is true for all positive integers n.

The *statement* of MI leads naturally to iteration: prove $S(1)$, then $S(2)$ from it, then $S(3)$ from $S(1)$ and $S(2). \ldots$

The *proof* that $S(n)$ is true for all n for some statement S has the flavor of *recursion:* to prove $S(k)$, reduce it to statements about $S(k-1)$ and perhaps $S(k-2), \ldots , S(1)$ and by repetition of this, chase the truth of the supporting statements back to $S(1)$. The chain of reasoning is then reversed for the flow of results, building back up to $S(k)$.

A full discussion of MI is outside the scope of this book, but some of it would resemble the discussion of recursion to follow.

The simplest applications of recursion in programming are statements that act as alternates to simple iterations. For example, to find the pointer to the bottom node of a nonempty stack, pointed to by the pointer p, either an iterative or a recursive routine will do:

```
function ChaseTail(p)                              {iterative
    q ← p
    while q↑.Link ≠ NIL do
      q ← q↑.Link
    endwhile
    return q
    end {ChaseTail
```

```
function UnderDog( p)                          {recursive
    if p ↑ .Link = NIL
      then return p
      else UnderDog( p ↑ .Link)
    endif
  end {UnderDog
```

UnderDog is logically valid because it repeatedly calls itself at a new point until the escape clause is invoked, and the escape clause is bound to occur. *UnderDog* can be implemented because a compiler that allows recursion will translate it into an iterative procedure. Very briefly, for languages in which recursion is legal, the translator of *UnderDog* would build a stack of pointers p, $p ↑ .Link$, $p ↑ .Link ↑ .Link$, . . . and then return the last one when the nest of invocations is unraveled. *Underdog* may be slower than *ChaseTail*, the iterated form of the operation, but both are $O(n)$ for a stack of depth n.

Recursion can be applied at a more abstract level as it is in the English language to *define* data structures. For example:

DEFINITION: *A linear linked list is* NIL, *or it is*
                 a node linked to a linear linked list.

This definition describes a process by which a candidate may be searched for conformation, but it does not describe an algorithm. It does not force the process of refinement to terminate after a finite number of steps.

Figure 7.1 shows how the process described by the definition may be depicted.

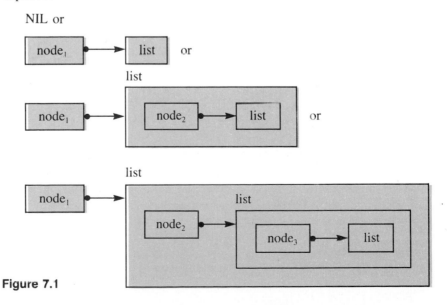

Figure 7.1

A more specific form of the linear list definition is:

DEFINITION: *A linear linked list,* LinearList, *is either*
　　　　　　NIL *or*
　　　　　　a node, HeadNode, *linked to a linear linked list,* TaiList.

With this specification at hand, a formal structure LINLIST can be defined as any linked list that satisfies it. Given a formal data structure, there are natural operations on it, although they are not part of the definition. Examples that use a right arrow to denote ''produces'' are:

■　　HEAD(*LinearList*) → *HeadNode* and TAIL(*LinearList*) → *TaiList,* or, more abstractly:

■　　HEAD(*LinearList*) → *node* and TAIL(*LinearList*) → *LinearList,* where *node* is an item of class NODE, and *LinearList* is an item of class LINLIST.

These can be implemented as (rather abstract) functions:

function Head(LinearList)	**function** Tail(LinearList)
if LinearList $=$ *NIL*	**if** LinearList $=$ *NIL*
then return *NIL*	**then return** *NIL*
else return HeadNode	**else return** TaiList
endif	**endif**
end {Head	**end** {Tail

Neither of these functions is recursive, although the structure on which they act was defined recursively.

No part of the topic *data structures* is exclusively the domain of either recursion or iteration—they are both universal tools.

Problems P7.1–P7.7 are appropriate at this point.

■ 7.1.1 From Front to Rear　　　　　　　　　　　　　(optional)

The structure STACK of Chapter 4 was defined nonrecursively in terms of operations, yet *UnderDog* is a recursive operation that may be carried out on it. In fact, finding the bottom of a stack, or the last node of an instance of LINLIST, is inherently an operation requiring a repeated search. (The search may be described iteratively or recursively, but it cannot be escaped.) Essentially the same operation appears *recursively* in one description of the interaction between FRONT and IN-SERT in the structure QUEUE, as:

$FRONT(INSERT(Q,i)) \leftarrow$ **if** $Empty(Q)$
        then i
        else $FRONT(Q)$
        endif

It is difficult to describe the relationship succinctly any other way, and the interaction between FRONT and INSERT is independent of implementation.

The trace of this interaction for a particular example demonstrates how recursion can be unraveled. After $INSERT(Q,10)$ is applied in Figure 7.2, then $FRONT(INSERT(Q,10))$ is also $FRONT(Q)$. $FRONT(Q)$ is $FRONT(Q')$, where Q' is the queue to which $INSERT(Q',-5)$ is applied to construct Q, as in Figure 7.3.

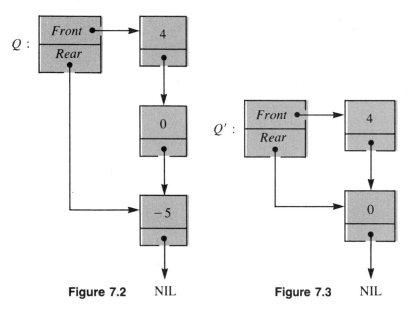

Figure 7.2 NIL   **Figure 7.3** NIL

Q', in turn, is not empty, hence $FRONT(Q') = FRONT(Q'')$, where, as in Figure 7.4, $Q' = INSERT(Q'',0)$.

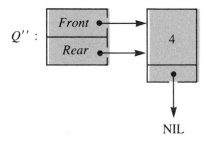

NIL

Figure 7.4

But Q'' is not empty, and FRONT(Q'') is FRONT(INSERT(Q''',4)), where Q''' is empty. The value added to an empty queue is finally the front of the queue resulting from an INSERT operation, hence:

$$4 = \text{FRONT}(Q'') = \text{FRONT}(Q') = \text{FRONT}(Q)$$

In general, FRONT(Q) is the first value not yet deleted; it can be found by tracing back through all of the insertions made since it was inserted into Q. This process of determining FRONT(Q) by applying FRONT itself as part of the process is recursive. It is a natural basis of a formal, operational definition of FRONT.

An alternate way to define a structure such as STACK, QUEUE, and LIN-LIST is to make the definition *functional*— expressed in terms of the operators that act on it and the relationships between them. The description of the FRONT and INSERT interaction given above serves as part of such a definition of QUEUE.

Formal definitions of the kind indicated by this section are the subject of current development and research on computer science, under the title of *abstract data structures*.

7.2 The Fibonacci Connection

Any sequence may be described by a function of the positive integers. The ideal function of this kind describes a simple rule by which the nth value is to be calculated. For some sequences such as 1,2,4,9,16, . . . , a description as a function of the positive integers can be very direct: $f(n) = n^2$.

The sequence of integers 1,1,2,3,5,8, . . . , the Fibonacci Sequence, can be taken to be $f(1) = 1, f(2) = 1, f(3) = 2, f(4) = 3, f(5) = 5, f(6) = 8, \ldots$, but no simple description of this function is apparent. The advantage of modeling a sequence as a function is that the function may describe the sequence more succinctly than does a (partial) listing or it may provide insight into its behavior. There is such a function for the Fibonacci Sequence.

A pattern that describes the Fibonacci Sequence 1,1,2,3,5,8, . . . relates each value to the previous values: $1 + 1 = 2, 1 + 2 = 3, 2 + 3 = 5, 3 + 5 = 8$, and so on. The rule that describes the nth value as a function of the previous values is:

$$f(1) = 1 \qquad f(2) = 1$$

$$f(n) = f(n - 2) + f(n - 1) \text{ for } n = 3,4,5, \ldots$$

This function may be used as a description of how to *derive* the nth value. For example:

$$f(5) = \quad f(3) \quad + \quad f(4)$$

$$= [f(1) + f(2)] + [f(2) + f(3)]$$

$$= [\,1 \quad + \quad 1\,] + [\,1 \quad + [f(1) + f(2)]\,]$$

$$= \qquad 2 \qquad + [\,1 \quad + [\,1 \quad + \quad 1\,]\,]$$

$$= \qquad 2 \qquad + [\,1 \quad + \qquad 2 \qquad]$$

$$= \qquad 2 \quad + \qquad 3$$

$$= \qquad \qquad 5$$

This search for the nth value involves only f itself—and f *invokes* itself.

Self-invocation is relatively common. It appears, for example, in solving algebraic equations such as

$$2h(n) = h(n) - 3n + 1$$

This definition of h is in terms of itself, and the solution is $h(n) = 1 - 3n$, so $h(1),h(2),h(3), \ldots$ is the sequence $-2, -5, -8. \ldots$. A major difference between h and f is in the methods of solution that can be effectively applied to them.

The solution techniques for f that are relevant here are the algorithmic ones. For example:

```
function Fibo1(n)                        {O(2ⁿ)    TRANSPARENT STACK
    if n = 1 then return 1 endif
    if n = 2 then return 1 endif
    return Fibo1(n−2) + Fibo1(n−1)
    end {Fibo1
```

This is a recursive procedure because it invokes itself. It exhibits *direct recursion;* if, however, procedure A invokes procedure B, which itself invokes procedure A, *indirect recursion* is at work.

Procedure *Fibo1* is a neat expression of the *mathematical* model of the Fibonacci function, but it will not work properly in a language that does not support recursion. Not all languages will support the recursive use of routines, since omitting recursion usually simplifies program compilation and speeds up the execution of programs.

If a recursive procedure is allowed in a language, then it must be possible to restructure it as an iterative procedure, or else it could not be executed on a machine that does one thing at a time. The use of recursion in programming languages can be allowed because the conversion from recursive algorithms to iterative executions is always possible and can be programmed in general into a compiler. As a direct consequence, problems having a natural expression in terms of recursion can be written that way by a programmer. The programmer can assume that the conversion to an iterative form is made correctly in translation.

The two main approaches to iterative calculations such as those needed for the Fibonacci sequence may be thought of as *bottom-up iteration* and *top-down iteration*.

Bottom-up Fibonacci Iteration

Bottom-up iteration starts with known or easily found values and builds up to the desired value. A bottom-up Fibonacci calculation is:

function *UpFibo*(n)   {*O(n)*   NO STACK
  Fibo ← *1*
  OneBack ← *1*
  for *i* = *3* **to** *n* **do**
    TwoBack ← *OneBack*
    OneBack ← *Fibo*
    Fibo ← *TwoBack* + *OneBack*
    next *i*
  return *Fibo*
  end {*UpFibo*

A bottom-up Fibonacci calculation can also be done with the help of a stack in which the top values play the role of *TwoBack, OneBack,* and *Fibo*. For simplicity, assume that a particular stack is accessed by PUSH, POP, DELETE, and TOP without explicitly naming the stack. This *implicit* stack is similar to the stack of the FORTH machine of Part II, section F. The procedure to be developed has the flavor of the FORTH language itself, in which the standard set of stack operations is augmented with others (that can be defined in terms of the standard set). Stack operations DUP (duplicate the top value), ROT (rotate the top three values so the third comes to the top), and SUM (sum the top two values) operate as shown in Figure 7.5.

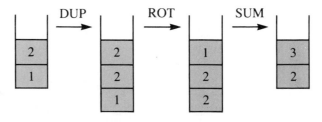

Figure 7.5

A procedure for finding $f(n)$ with these operations is:

function *UpStack(n)*   {$O(n)$ IMPLICIT STACK
  Push(1)
  DUP
  for $i = 3$ **to** n **do**
    DUP
    ROT
    SUM
    next i
  return *Top*
  end {*UpStack*

Top-down Fibonacci Iteration

In order to calculate $f(5)$ in the top-down fashion it is first necessary to calculate $f(3)$ and $f(4)$ upon which it depends, neither of which can be directly evaluated. In order to calculate $f(4)$, $f(3)$ is needed again. In one case, $f(3)$ is "requested" by $f(4)$, and in the other by $f(5)$. Evaluation records can be constructed as an integer k, a value f (set to zero if not yet known), and a link back to the requesting record, shown in Figure 7.6.

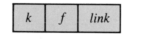

Figure 7.6

Figure 7.7 pictures the calculation of $f(5)$.

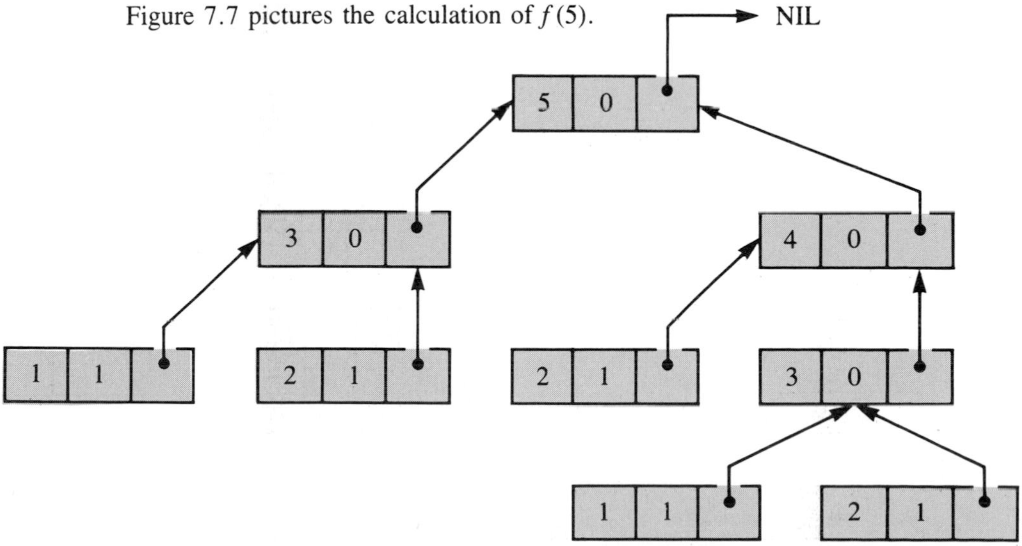

Figure 7.7

With the requests reduced to this form, the values of higher nodes can be determined from lower nodes, as shown in Figure 7.8, and finally reaching the calculation in Figure 7.9.

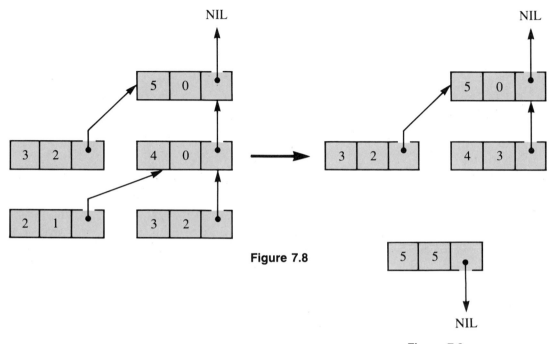

Figure 7.8

Figure 7.9

A direct expression of this scheme as a data structure must be deferred to Chapter 8; but, with the help of a stack, the evaluation records can be saved as they are generated and discarded as they are used. Using levels in the stack as links, $f(n)$ can be calculated by repeating:

1. If the f-value of the top record is not zero and the level is 1, then return that value.

2. If the f-value of the top record is zero, then generate two new records (for $k-1$ and $k-2$) and stack them, linking them back to the record that led to their generation.

3. If the f-value is not zero for the top value but is zero for the next-to-top value, then generate two new records from the latter.

4. If the f-value is not zero for the top two values, then sum them and add the sum to the value to which they are linked. (It happens that they *will* be linked to the same source of their generation because records are generated in pairs.)

A trace of this process for $f(5)$ is shown in Figure 7.10.

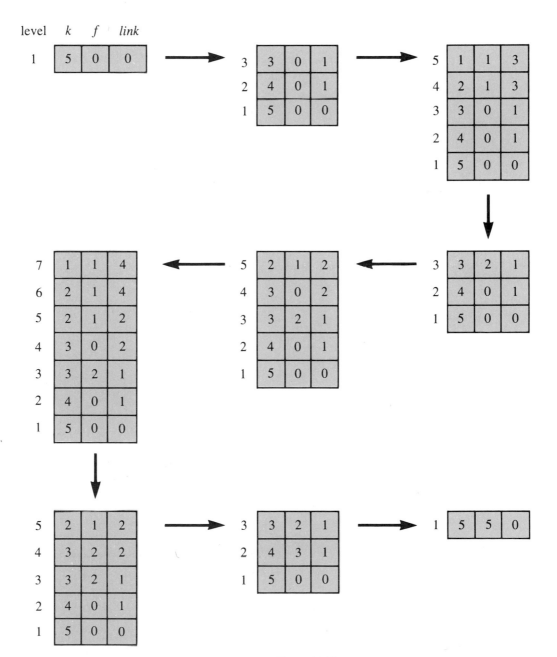

Figure 7.10

This picture of the stack is reflected in an array implementation of the records where array indices act as the level for both the values and the links. A new record that is linked to the record with index *Level* and has a given *kValue* may be placed on the stack by:

procedure *NewRecord* (*kValue*,*Level*)
  Top ← *Top* + *1*
  if *kValue* < *3*
    then $f[Top] ← 1$
    else $f[Top] ← 0$
    endif
  $k[Top] ← kValue$
  $Link[Top] ← Level$
  end {*NewRecord*

A record at index *level* can be split to produce two new records on top of the stack by:

procedure *Split*(*Level*)
  kValue ← *k*[*Level*]
  NewRecord(*kValue* − *1*,*Level*)
  NewRecord(*kValue* − *2*,*Level*)
  end {*Split*

With these operations defined, a top-down iterative calculation of the *n*th Fibonacci number is:

function *DownStack*(*n*)   {$0(2^n)$ **EXPLICIT STACK**
  if *n* ≤ *3* **then return** *1* **endif**
  Top ← *0*
  NewRecord(*n*,*0*)
  repeat
    if $f[Top] = 0$
      then *Level* ← *Top*   {*split top record*
         Split(*Level*)
      else if $f[Top-1] = 0$
         then *Level* ← *Top* − *1*   {*split next-to-top record*
            Split(*Level*)
         else *Level* ← *Link*[*Top*]   {*sum top values*
            Sum ← $f[Top] + f[Top-1]$
            $f[Level] ← Sum$
            Top ← *Top* − *2*
         endif
      endif
    until *Top* = *1*
  return $f[1]$
  end {*DownStack*

A compiler that translates the recursive function subprogram *Fibo1* would generate *activation records* for each call—activation records that would resemble the evaluation records of *DownStack*. Note that the "*n*" in the definition of *Fibo1* keeps changing with each invocation. If the records of *DownStack* are taken to be the actual activation records, the second stack snapshot depicts three values of *n:* $n = 3,4$, and 5 stored in $k[Level]$ for *Level* $= 3,2$, and 1.

The availability of some language features, however, may complicate the activation records (and their generation). Even the relatively simple PL/0 compiler that generates p-code (section 4.4) must take into account the block structure of the language. Specifically, an identifier may be redefined within a subprogram, where use of the identifier has a limited scope. It is not the same variable as one named identically elsewhere. The linkage patterns within the activation stack must trace variable references back to the location of their values within the stack. That location is determined by the sequence of procedure calls during execution, in conjunction with the effects of identifier scope.

The complex problems associated with the implementation of recursive routines like *Fibo1* can be left to language design and compiler writing. What is not to be left to them is: How can recursion be used as a design tool? When *should* it be used as a program design?

There is no definite answer to these questions, but—as a rule of thumb —if recursion is a natural expression of a problem solution and execution-time is not crucial, then use it.

7.3 Search in an Ordered List

The search through an ordered list for an arbitrary element is a common operation in computing. If output is ordered, then a search through it is efficient—the justification for sorting in the first place. The output of a program ultimately is ordered for the convenience of a search by a human or another program that accepts it as input. Sorting is justified by searching, and searching is made cost-effective by sorting.

The collection of objects to be searched in this section is essentially a file, a collection of records. The records may simply be numeric or character or string data stored in an array or list structure, or they may be more complex records. Records are assumed to contain a *key*, an item by which the looked-for record can be uniquely identified, and by which the file has been sorted. The sorting can be indirect through a map, but the crucial factor is whether there is *independent* (random) access to the key.

The problem addressed in a *search,* as the term is used here, is to locate an arbitrary key, *Lost,* somewhere in an ordered file of keys or determine that it is not there.

Two natural assumptions that can be made in casting about for efficient search techniques are (1) the file to be searched is ordered and (2) it allows independent access to keys. The simplest model of such a structure is an array containing key values that may be compared to *Lost*. The essential logic of the search is unchanged if the keys are not the only record values of interest or if they must be accessed through a memory map. It will be assumed here that the keys are the entries in array *Key*, and *Lost* is to be found in *Key*[1 . . *Max*].

7.3.1 Sequential Searches

A general (unordered) linked list, *aList*, with only two accessible entries (*aList.Head* and *aList.Tail*), supports only an exhaustive, linear search. (To determine that *Lost* is not present, every node must be checked.) The ordering of such a list structure provides for ordered output but still supports only sequential searching. The only advantage offered by ordering such a list for a linear search is that the search may be terminated as soon as the values become too large (or too small) for an absent search value to be found in the remainder of the list.

One not very efficient sequential search is LSD (for Linear Search—Dumb):

function *LSD(Key,Max,Lost)*   {*O(n)*
   Here ← 0
  for *k ← 1* **to** *Max* **do**
   if *Key[k] = Lost*
    then *Here ← k*
   endif
  next *k*
 return *Here*
 end {*LSD*

LSD has the fault that it just keeps floating along, even after finding *Lost*. It could be fixed in appearance by replacing *Here ← k* with **return** *k,* but in some HLL languages it cannot be implemented that way.

The **for** loop contains a test for the end of the search, which is what the *body* of the loop also contains. Only *one* test would suffice if it were always the case that *Lost* would be found. If *Key* is large enough, this becomes LSE (Linear Search—Extended):

function *LSE(Key,Max,Lost)*   {*O(n)*
   Key[Max + 1] ← Lost
   k ← 1
  while *Key[k] ≠ Lost*
   k ← k + 1
  endwhile
 return *k*
 end {*LSE*

This is an example of *code-tuning*. It can save 20–30 percent of the execution time in a long search. That is still slow, compared to the search discussed in the next section, but LSE is advantageous because it can be applied to linked lists and even unsorted lists.

7.3.2 Binary Searches

A natural and recursive way to look for *Lost* among the values in *Key*[1 .. *Max*] stored in nondecreasing order is:

■   If *Lost* is the middle value, then quit looking. If it is smaller, then search the lower half of *Key*, otherwise the upper half of *Key*, this same way.

Each iteration of this search has roughly half as many objects to search through. If $Max = 2^k$, then the first iteration is searching within 2^k objects, the second 2^{k-1}, and so on until there is only one value, *Key*[*i*], to compare with *Lost*. No more than $(k + 1) = (\ln Max) + 1$ comparisons need to be made. In general, *Max* may not be a power of 2, and the search may terminate at any stage, and so a careful analysis must consider these factors. The result is of the same order, however, and the algorithmic expression of a binary search proves to be $O(\ln n)$. For large data sets this is a *major* difference from the $O(n)$ needed for a linear search. (For $n = 1,048,576$, $\ln n$ is 20.)

Given that the essential *idea* of a binary search is recursive, there is still a choice between an iterative and a recursive algorithm for carrying it out. The iterative version that returns the index of the found value, or zero if it is *not* found, is:

```
function IBS(Key,Max,Lost)          {O(ln n)      ITERATIVE BINARY
    Lower ← 1                                      SEARCH
    Upper ← Max
    while Lower ≤ Upper do
      Mid ← (Lower + Upper) DIV 2
      case
        Lost > Key[Mid] : Lower ← Mid + 1
        Lost = Key[Mid] : return Mid
        Lost < Key[Mid] : Upper ← Mid − 1
      endcase
    endwhile
  return 0
  end {IBS
```

It is worthwhile to trace this algorithm on a simple example.

Exercise E7.1 is appropriate at this point.

The recursive version of binary search needs to have *Lower* and *Upper* passed to it, since it operates on a *segment* of an array, not on an entire array. This is a fairly common effect of the change from an iterative to a recursive routine. Some local variables become parameters because they must change with each invocation of the routine. One version, initially invoked as *RBS(Key,1,Max,Lost)*, is:

```
function RBS(Key,Lower,Upper,Lost)    {O(ln n)        RECURSIVE BINARY
    if Lower ≤ Upper                                  SEARCH
      then Mid ← (Lower + Upper) DIV 2
          case
              Lost > Key[Mid] : RBS(Key,Mid+1,Upper,Lost)
              Lost = Key[Mid] : return Mid
              Lost < Key[Mid] : RBS(Key,Lower,Mid−1,Lost)
          endcase
      else return 0
      endif
  end {RBS
```

In one sense, *RBS* is more restrictive than *IBS* because it involves more parameters in the initial call. In another sense, *RBS* is less restrictive because it can be used to search *any segment* of an array, whereas *IBS* must search an initial segment. The latter can be easily generalized to do the same thing and both provide the same service.

More run-time overhead can be expected for *RBS* than for *IBS* because of the stacking of activation records, but both are still $O(\ln n)$ algorithms. Otherwise, for large n, *RBS* may use a great deal of space on the stack.

The *idea* of binary search is recursive, but the implementation does not have to be. The idea of dividing a data set into segments and dealing with each of them recursively has been generalized to an entire class of algorithms—the general technique is called *Divide-and-Conquer* (D-and-C). Among the D-and-C algorithms are sorting algorithms, one of which is the subject of section 7.5.

Exercise E7.2 is appropriate at this point.

■ 7.4 The Towers of Hanoi (optional)

A rich variety of stories have been formed about an apparently ancient puzzle:

- There are three pegs, *a*, *b*, and *c*, and a stack of disks on peg *a*. The disks are all of different sizes and stacked so that this condition holds: *no disk rests on a smaller disk*. How can they be shifted to peg *b* (using all three pegs) so that the condition never fails on any peg during the process?

It is told that the Tibetan lamas know the solution, have been shifting 64 golden disks on three golden pegs by hand for centuries (with centuries more to go); if they succeed in some future millenium—the legend goes—the universe will end.

From the common name of the puzzle it must be known in Indochina. From its occurrence in this text, the puzzle has a role in computer science. That role is to be an example of the power of recursion.

To (legally) shift *n* disks from *a* to *b*, simply shift the top $n - 1$ disks to *c*, move the bottom disk from *a* to *b*, and then shift the disks on *c* to *b*. The second shift requires a change of role for the pegs, and so the information passed to the solution procedure is the number of disks to be moved, the source peg, the target peg, and the helper peg. The recursive solution is then:

procedure *Towers(n,Source,Target,Helper)*
  if $n = 0$ **then return endif**
  Towers(n − 1,Source,Helper,Target)
  MoveOne(Source,Target)
  Towers(n − 1,Helper,Target,Source)
  end {*Towers*

If the pegs are represented by stacks, *MoveOne* simply pops the top value of *Source*, and pushes it onto *Target*.

Exercise E7.3, problems P7.1–P7.7, and program PG7.1 are appropriate at this point.

■ 7.5 QuickSort (optional)

A number of sorting techniques involve exchanging one value (or node) for another. An obvious source of inefficiency with exchanges is that elements of a file to be sorted are exchanged more than once during the sorting process. If it were possible to exchange an element directly into its proper position (ignoring the chaos in the rest of the file at that point), then *n* such operations would sort the file. It would be an $O(n)$ process.

It is not possible to make a direct exchange of an element to its correct (sorted) position because that position is not known. The correct position of an element is not even detectable without a check of the entire file for the property of being sorted. The sorted position of any element is a *global* property of the file.

One way to develop sorting techniques is to examine weaker properties—those that are possessed by a sorted file but do not imply that it is necessarily sorted. A combination of such properties or the repeated establishment of one can lead to a sorted file.

Consider an array $Key[1 .. Max]$. If Key is sorted then for any index k, $1 \leq k \leq Max$, the following property holds:

Property $P(k)$:

$Key[i] \leq Key[k]$ for $1 \leq i \leq k$

$Key[k] \leq Key[j]$ for $k \leq j \leq Max$

Property $P(k)$ for some k can be true with otherwise arbitrary order, and so provide a subgoal on the way to the sorting of Key. For example, Figure 7.11 has $P(4)$, but not $P(k)$ for other values of k, and this sequence is not sorted.

15	05	10	20	30	25	40	35

Figure 7.11

However:

■   If $P(k)$ is true for *every* k, $1 \leq k \leq Max$, then Key is necessarily sorted.

A recursive sort called *QuickSort* can be developed by repeatedly establishing $P(k)$ within the subrange $Key[i] .. Key[j]$. The details of *QuickSort* are to be found in Part II, Section O, where it is developed and implemented in Pascal.

■ 7.6 The Eight-Queens Problem   (optional)

Simply because of aesthetics some problems have become part of the repertoire of nearly everyone who is acquainted with computer science beyond an elementary programming course. Either the problem itself or its solution is elegant. One such problem is:

■   Place eight chess queens on a chess board so that they do not threaten each other.

A chess queen can capture another piece by moving any number of squares along one of the eight rows or eight columns or any 45-degree diagonal. Eight queens is an upper bound because no two queens can occupy the same column (or row). A solution places the *n*th queen in column *n* of the board and determines the row, *Queen*[*n*], of the *n*th queen so that it controls a row and diagonals distinct from those on which the other queens lie. It is possible to do this iteratively [WIRTH, 1971]. The solution presented here is recursive.

Suppose that procedure *Remainder* is designed so that *Remainder(n)* places the queens from the *n*th one through the eighth one to solve the problem, if possible, and also sets *TruePath* to *TRUE* if it succeeds and to *FALSE* otherwise. In particular, if *TruePath* is set *TRUE* by *Remainder*(1), the problem is solved. A solution is:

```
program EightQueens
  SetUp
  Remainder(1)
  if TruePath
    then DisplayBoard
    else "No solution was found."
  endif
end {EightQueens
```

If the procedure call *Remainder(n)* is made with $n > 8$, then eight queens have been successfully placed, and it returns with *TruePath* = TRUE. When entered with $n \leq 8$, *Remainder* makes a procedure call *NextRow(i,j)* that searches for an available row beginning at row *i*. Initially *NextRow* is called with $i = 0$ and $j = n$ and looks for the available row of lowest index, then documents the placing of queen *n* on that row and column *n*. To check the ultimate suitability of that choice, *Remainder(n + 1)* is called, which of course makes *Remainder* recursive. If it fails (*TruePath* = FALSE), then the row chosen by the call *NextRow(i,n)* is canceled (with procedure *Cancel*) and a row of greater index is attempted:

```
procedure Remainder(n)
  TruePath ← FALSE
  if n > 8
    then TruePath ← TRUE
         return
  endif
  Row ← NextRow(0,n)
  while (Row ≤ 8) AND (NOT TruePath) do
    Remainder(n + 1)
    if NOT TruePath
      then Cancel(Row,n)
           Row ← NextRow(Row,n)
    endif
  endwhile
end {Remainder
```

The function called *NextRow(i,j)* simply steps through the rows *i*, *i*+1, . . . , *j* and checks to see if they are safe, meaning unoccupied, with a function *Safe:*

function *NextRow(Row,Column)*
   repeat
     Row ← Row + 1
     until *Safe*
   if *Row* ≤ 8 **then** *Document* **endif**
   return *Row*
   end {*NextRow*

> **Note:** Cancellation is a form of *backtracking*—a retraction of a partially developed solution in order to try another direction. Backtracking is a general approach to solving problems often applied to binary trees and to trees, discussed in Chapters 8 and 9.

At this point in the development of *EightQueens,* it is no longer possible to avoid the details of how to mark and detect the presence of a queen in the rows and diagonals controlled by it.

A queen in row *i*, column *j*, also controls two diagonals, one tilting 45 degrees to the right from vertical, and one tilting 45 degrees to the left. From the view of placing another queen, it does not matter *which* position in a row, column, or diagonal is occupied by another queen. Rows and columns are characterized by their index. The fifteen distinct diagonals that tilt to the right are characterized by positions for which $i + j$ is constant and has one of the values: 2,3, . . . ,16. (A move of one step up and to the right on a right-tilted diagonal decreases the row by one and increases the column by one.) Similarly, the fifteen diagonals that tilt left are characterized by $i - j$ (in the set -7, . . . , 7).

Figure 7.12 shows the row, column, and diagonals controlled by a queen at row 5, column 6. No information about the occupation of columns is needed since columns are possessed in sequence. Controlled rows and columns are marked in Boolean variables *RowMark, TiltRight,* and *TiltLeft,* all initialized to *FALSE* to indicate that they are not controlled by any queen. Documentation of an occupation is performed by setting the appropriate cells to *TRUE,* cancellation by resetting them to *FALSE,* and checking for safety by insuring that the appropriate row and diagonals are all *FALSE:*

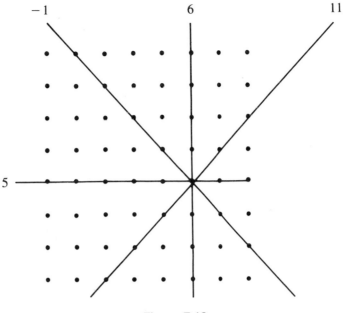

Figure 7.12

```
function Safe
   if Row > 8
      then return TRUE
      else return NOT (        RowMark[Row]
                        OR TiltRight[Column + Row]
                        OR TiltLeft[Column − Row] )
      endif
   end {Safe

procedure Document
   Queen[Column] ← Row
   RowMark[Row] ← TRUE
   TiltRight[Column + Row] ← TRUE
   TiltLeft[Column − Row] ← TRUE
   end {Document

procedure Cancel(Row, Column)
   RowMark[Row] ← FALSE
   TiltRight[Column + Row] ← FALSE
   TiltLeft[Column − Row] ← FALSE
   end {Cancel
```

Program PG7.2 and project PJ7.1 are appropriate at this point.

■ 7.7 A General-List Visitation Algorithm (optional)

The records of a general list (graph) structure may contain any number of link-fields, and the links may form a tangle of great complexity. With just two link-fields a small number of nodes may form a pattern that is not any structure studied in the previous chapters—for example the pattern in Figure 7.13.

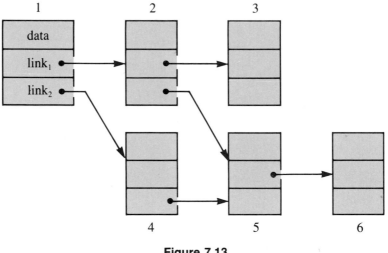

Figure 7.13

It is necessary to visit every node in such a structure to search within it, or copy it, or process the data field(s) in any way. Ways to traverse graphs based on the data structures of Chapters 8 and 9 are treated in Chapter 10. In this section, the structure is modeled by its own form.

A general record format that will serve for such a structure is:

aNode = RECORD
 Data : DataType
 Link : ARRAY[1 . . Max] OF ↑ aNode
 END {*aNode*

A recursive process that visits every node of a structure and processes it is:

```
procedure Rvisit0( p)                    {Recursive Visit 0
  if p ≠ NIL
    then Process( p)
        for i = 1 to Max do
            Rvisit0(Link[i])
            next i
    endif
  end {Rvisit0
```

When *Rvisit0* is applied to this example with *p* initially pointing to node 1, it will process nodes 1, 2, 3, 5, 6, 4, 5, 6. The multiple processing of nodes (such as 5 and 6 in this example) can cause severe problems for a user as well as inefficiency. A more serious problem is that if a link-field of node 6 pointed to node 1, it would put *Rvisit0* into an infinite loop. One remedy for both problems is to introduce a *Mark* field set to *TRUE* for a node not yet processed and *FALSE* otherwise:

```
Node = RECORD
            Data : datatype
            Mark : BOOLEAN
            Link  : ARRAY[1 .. Max] OF ↑Node
            END {Node
```

With this change, a recursive visit algorithm that processes each node only once is:

```
procedure Rvisit( p)                      {Recursive Visit
  if ( p ≠NIL) AND ( p ↑ .Mark)
    then Process( p)
        p ↑ .Mark ← FALSE
        for i = 1 to Max do
            Rvisit(Link[i])
            next i
    endif
  end {Rvisit
```

The advantage of recursive algorithms such as *Rvisit* is that they tend to be much simpler and more easily developed than equivalent iterative algorithms. Nevertheless, they do have shortcomings.

One problem with *Rvisit* itself is that if the mark-fields are all initially *TRUE*, then after one execution of *Rvisit*, they are all *FALSE;* and it cannot be reapplied. A separate (and similar) routine is required to complement the values of the *Mark* field, or *Rvisit* must be changed to allow p ↑ .mark to be compared to a Boolean argument that can then be alternated between *TRUE* and *FALSE*.

A more severe problem with *Rvisit* and other recursive routines is that if a large number of nodes are involved, the run-time stack may become quite large, for it contains a copy of the information needed to continue the process for each currently unresolved link.

It is possible to derive an equivalent iterative algorithm from any recursive algorithm, but it is an awkward process and the result often benefits from rewriting. More importantly, the translation is essentially the building of *explicit* stacks to replace the *implicit* stacks that allow recursion to work.

An alternative to *Rvisit* that is not recursive or the explicit-stack translation of a recursive routine was discovered by Deutsch, Schorr, and Waite. A structured version, *Visit,* is presented in Part II, section M.

Project PJ7.2 is appropriate at this point.

■ 7.8 LISP: Lists and Recursion (optional)

A language used extensively in the field of artificial intelligence, and hence of increasing importance, is LISP. It is a working language becoming more widely available; a number of introductory books treat LISP programming. (One such is [TOURETSKY, 1983].) LISP combines a number of views about computation that give it a quality drastically different from Algol-derivations (Pascal-like languages). These include the central importance of applying functions and the use of predicates—statements with Boolean values. This section is only intended to point out how LISP is related to two themes of importance in this book: linked lists and recursion.

The central objects in a LISP program are lists, including functions that operate on them and the definitions of the functions. In the usual syntax, lists are enclosed in parentheses, and each pair of parentheses forms a list:

■ ITEM is not a list, but an *atom*.

■ (ITEM) is a list and has the effective structure shown in Figure 7.14.

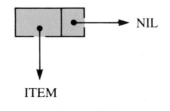

ITEM

Figure 7.14

■   Similarly, (TWO ITEMS) has the structure shown in Figure 7.15.

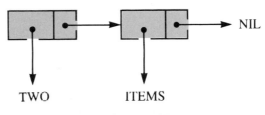

TWO   ITEMS

Figure 7.15

■   The structure of ((TWO ITEMS)) is depicted in Figure 7.16.

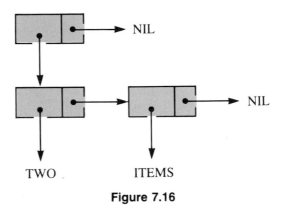

TWO .   ITEMS

Figure 7.16

■   And (((TWO ITEMS))) has the structure shown in Figure 7.17.

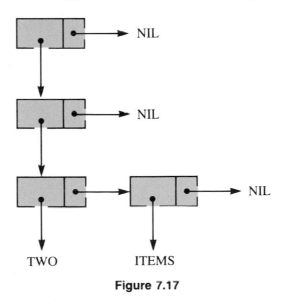

TWO   ITEMS

Figure 7.17

Storage efficiency is gained by saving atoms only once, as illustrated in Figure 7.18.

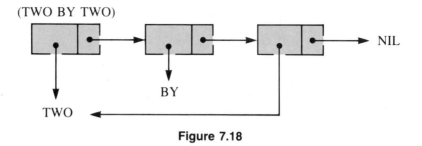

(TWO BY TWO)

Figure 7.18

One list may be the atom of another, shown in Figure 7.19.

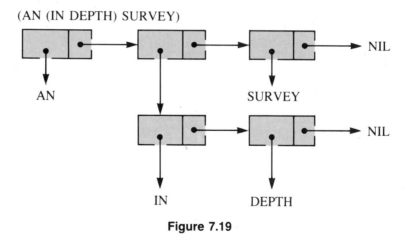

(AN (IN DEPTH) SURVEY)

Figure 7.19

The recursive nature of LISP is evident in the four primitive functions below from which other functions are built. They are all designed to be used most naturally in recursive ways:

- CAR returns the first atom of a list.

- CDR returns the tail of a list—all but the first atom.

- CONS returns a list constructed from an atom and a list.

- LIST returns a list constructed from atoms.

The action of these are illustrated in Figure 7.20.

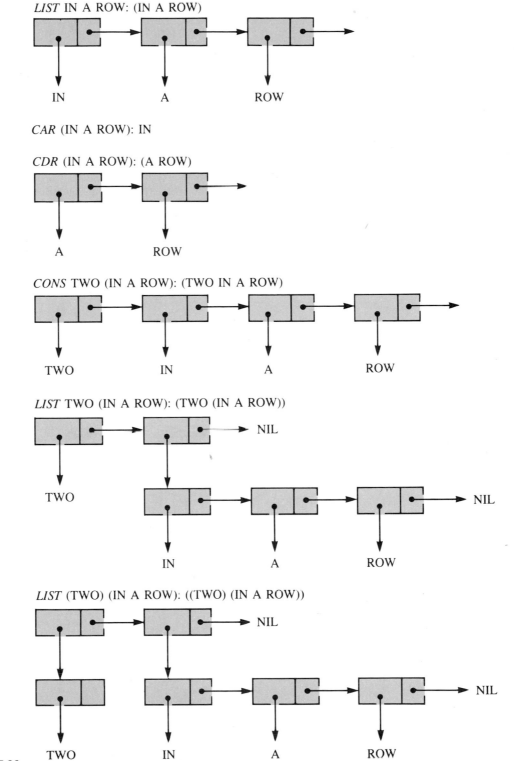

Figure 7.20

One way to retrieve an interior atom from a list is to recursively apply CDR until it is the first atom of the list, then apply CAR. That process is typical of the way LISP is written.

> **Note:** CAR is derived from: "Contents of Address portion of Register," CDR from "Contents of Decrement portion of Register." The terms have apparently been retained for the love of the arcane found in cults.

Further pursuit of LISP itself requires a more extensive treatment than belongs in this book, but the effect of CDR, CAR, CONS, and LIST can be programmed in any language.

Project PJ7.3 is appropriate at this point.

Summary

Recursion is a fundamental way to express some relationships. When available, it can be a very convenient and delightfully succinct form for the expression of procedures.

The foundation on which language translators build recursion is a stack of activation records. Activation records are linked together on the "stack" in (possibly) interwoven lists that trace the value determinations of variables to their appropriate sources. (The p-Machine of section 4.4 and Part II, section G, is a relatively simple example of how this can be done.)

Recursion can be a marvelously easy form within which to structure an algorithm. It can also be wasteful of time and space, as illustrated by various ways to calculate the Fibonacci sequence.

The values of recursion are convenience, saving of programming time, and the development of an understanding of a problem. These may be traded for execution efficiency at the cost of the time and care required to develop an iterative solution.

Some examples in which recursion is generally deemed to be worth the run-time cost are: binary search, the Towers of Hanoi, *QuickSort,* and the Eight-Queens problem. (Other ways to traverse a general list are to be found in Chapter 10 and Part II, section M.)

QuickSort is frequently the sorting method of choice in applications because its average-case behavior is $O(n \ln n)$. *QuickSort* is an example of a recursive algorithm that tends to execute more efficiently than most iterative rivals.

The Eight-Queens solution is an example of *backtracking*, a programming technique of general utility.

LISP is a language that incorporates recursion and list processing into the mold of thought that it promotes in programmers.

Above all, recursion is a choice for problem solving that should be available to any programmer.

Exercises   immediate applications of the text material

E7.1   Trace the procedure calls *IBS*(*Key*,6,8) and *IBS*(*Key*,6,5) when *Key* contains these values: *Key*[1] = 1, *Key*[2] = 3, *Key*[3] = 4, *Key*[4] = 6, *Key*[5] = 8, *Key*[6] = 10.

E7.2   Trace the calls of procedure *RBS*(*Key*,1,6,8), *RBS*(*Key*,1,6,5), and *RBS*(*Key*,3,6,5) with the values of *Key* given in E7.1.

E7.3   Trace the stacks representing the pegs in procedure *Towers* of section 7.4 for *n* = 4. (PG7.1 asks for a program that does this.)

Problems   not immediate, but requiring no major extensions of the text material

Write recursive versions of problems P7.1–P7.4:

P7.1   Search a singly linked list for a given node value.

P7.2   Search a circularly linked list for a given node value.

P7.3   Calculate *N*-factorial.

P7.4   Calculate the sum of the first *N* integers.

P7.5   (Difficult) Develop an iterative version of the Towers of Hanoi solution given in section 7.4.

P7.6   Find the GCD (Greatest Common Denominator) of two values *N* and *M* as GCD(*N*,*M*), calculated as either of them if *M* = *N*, otherwise the GCD of the smallest of them and their difference. (Use a recursive procedure.)

P7.7   Find the determinant of an *N* by *N* matrix. The determinant of *A* can be calculated as *A*[1,1] for *N* = 1 and the sum from *j* = 1 to *N* of ($(-1)^{i+j}$ times *A*[*i*,*j*] times the determinant of the *ij*-cofactor of *A*). The *ij*-cofactor of *A* is the matrix formed by deleting the *i*th row and the *j*th column of *A*. (Use a recursive procedure.)

Programs for trying it yourself

PG7.1 Implement procedure *Towers* of section 7.4 with a trace of the stacks. Run it for $n = 4,5$, and 6.

PG7.2 Implement the Eight-Queens solution of section 7.6 with a display routine that forms a board representation with queen markers in place.

Projects for fun and for serious students

PJ7.1 Write a program to find *all* solutions to the Eight-Queens puzzle.

PJ7.2 Implement *Rvisit* of section 7.7.

PJ7.3 Write a command-shell program to evoke functions CAR, CDR, CONS, LIST, DISPLAY, INSERT, and DELETE. The last two commands allow insertion and deletion at *any* depth in a list. The program is to implement DISPLAY, INSERT, and DELETE internally with the *other* command functions.

Comment: You may wish to implement the one-cell-per-token rule as a separate project.

Chapter *8*

Binary Trees

Program logic involves branches where there is more than one possible next action: two for an **if** statement, two or more for a **case** statement. People have zero or more children who may in turn have zero or more children who. . . . People have two immediate ancestors who in turn have ancestors. One-to-(some number) relationships are involved in these situations and in many others. A graphical structure that describes such relationships is a (directed) *tree*—mathematically, a (directed) graph without cycles.

As an example, if Faye has children Alia, March, and Ralph, two of whom have children, their family relationship may be described by Figure 8.1. The notation associated with such structures is fairly comfortable for anyone conversant with both families and botany. Faye is the *root node* of a tree, Faye's Family. The tree rooted at Faye has three branches, and they are called *subtrees*. The subtree rooted at Alia has two branches, at Ralph one, and at March none. Wrye, Jan, March, and Will are *leaf nodes* of Faye's Family and of its subtrees. All other nodes are *interior* nodes. Alia and Faye are both *ancestors* of Wrye and Jan.

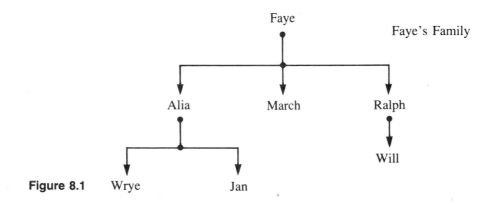

Figure 8.1

In the literature, Faye is commonly called the *father* of March, Alia, and Ralph, and these three are the *sons* of Faye. (It is perfectly acceptable to use *mother* and *daughter,* as is done for cells in biology.) Wrye and Jan are *siblings,* often called *brothers.* Faye is the *grandfather* of Jan.

A single node with *NIL* (or *u*) children is a tree, and so is the empty tree. Faye's Family is specifically a tree within the more general category *graph.* The crucial feature making it a graph is that the subtrees (subgraphs) reachable from any pair of nodes are *disjoint.* To generalize, the *i*th child of a node is the root of a tree itself. It is the *ith subtree* of the tree rooted at *n*. This is abbreviated to "the *i*th subtree of *n*."

Faye's Family can be modeled by a data structure with links representing the directed access from a node to its children. The many applications for general tree structures are limited by their own generality: the nodes of a general tree might need to have any number of links. In some applications, such as representations of family trees, it may not always be possible to foretell how many links are enough. Even if a maximum is imposed, most of the links of most nodes may be unused.

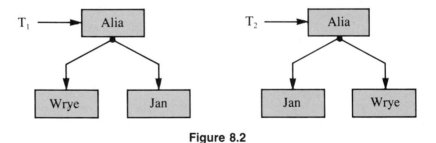

Figure 8.2

A useful compromise that contains a one-to-many relationship and yet controls the proliferation of children is the *binary tree.* A binary tree may have a *left child* and a *right child,* which is not the same as having two children. The trees in Figure 8.2 are equivalent as trees, but not equivalent as binary trees. As binary trees $T_1 \neq T_2$ because their left children (and redundantly their right children) differ. Will may be implemented as either the left child or the right child of Ralph, giving rise to two distinct binary trees, shown in Figure 8.3.

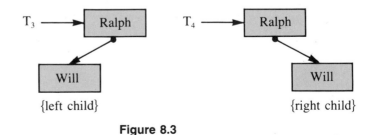

Figure 8.3

General trees with more than two children per node can be transformed into binary trees by the rule:

- Order the children of a node N of tree T to obtain children $c_1, c_2, \ldots, c_k$. Then c_1 becomes the left child of N. If N is the $(i - 1)$st child of a node P and there is an ith child of P, then that ith child of P becomes the right child of N.

The tree structure rooted at Faye becomes a binary tree in Figure 8.4.

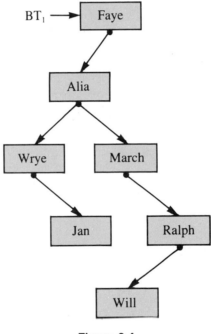

Figure 8.4

Note: The distinction between binary trees and trees is important to recognize, but it is common to ignore the distinction in situations where it is not significant.

One advantage that tree-like structures have over linear linked lists is that, on the average, fewer links need to be processed to get from one node to another (assuming, of course, that the choice of *which* branch to take can be determined). The binary tree BT_1 in Figure 8.4 has given up some of the advantage inherent in the original tree because there are more links between the root and some leaves than there were. That advantage can be regained by *balancing* the binary tree so that the distances from root to leaves tend to be as near the minimum as the application allows. In this particular case, rearranging the binary tree would lose the information modeled by it; for some applications, however, balancing is an advantage.

We will return to the issue of balancing in section 8.7—after examining general features of binary trees in 8.1, their implementation in section 8.2, finding our way around them in sections 8.3 and 8.4, ordering them in section 8.5, and applying them in section 8.6. Section 8.8 exhibits one more way to walk around a tree.

Exercises E8.1 and E8.2 are appropriate at this point.

8.1 General Features of Binary Trees

Binary trees, like the data structures introduced in previous chapters, are defined by the operators applied to them. In contrast to the previous structures, binary trees have *shape;* and shape is determined by the number of nodes at various distances from each other. The efficiency of management algorithms is affected by the shape of binary trees. Insertion and deletion algorithms themselves *change* the shape of a tree. If no operations that change shape or size are applied to a binary tree, then it is *static;* otherwise it is *dynamic.*

The efficiency of algorithms that provide access to trees is *amortized* by averaging over a sequence of operations. For many applications, restrictions are applied in the form of *structural parameters* that control shape. For static trees, these restrictions only affect the cost of searching; but, for dynamic trees subject to many insertions and deletions, shape *changes* are controlled by constraints defined by parameters. Shape control is introduced in the interest of increasing the amortized efficiency at the cost of more overhead during individual uses of the algorithms.

8.1.1 Operations

The nature of the structure BINARY TREE is determined by the operations applied to it. Binary trees can be empty, and they remain empty until a node is added to them; and so their locator, *root,* has an appropriate initial value: *NIL* or *u* (or zero for array implementations). The genesis of a binary tree is an operation formally called CREATE.

Deletions from a binary tree can remove all of its nodes, and so *root* may be dynamically set to *NIL* or *u* (or zero for an array implementation). The formal name of the operation that checks the viability of a binary tree is EMPTY.

A node may be inserted into a binary tree at any link that is *NIL*. Such a node (any node!) is itself the root node of a binary tree. If the attached binary tree is a singleton, it becomes a leaf node. The formal operation involved is INSERT, but the question of *where* to insert depends heavily on the application. INSERT can be universal only if it inserts a subtree as a given child of a given node, replacing whatever was there.

The left child or right child of a given node may be set to *NIL,* which detaches the binary tree rooted at that child and hence *partitions* the binary tree into two binary trees. Note that—like attachment—partitioning deals with a subtree, not necessarily a single node. Deletion of a single node, like insertion of a single node, is application-dependent and of considerable interest in the management of binary trees.

In distinction from stacks and queues, *all* nodes of a binary tree are accessible by following links from the root node. The ways a binary tree can be systematically traversed to visit every node are treated in sections 8.3 and 8.4. In many applications information is available to make a choice at each node; there is a guide to following a link to the left or to the right. When this is possible, the process of locating a node can be much faster than for a general traverse. The efficiency of this guided branching is one major advantage of trees over both linear structures and more general structures (such as graphs).

Because every node in a binary tree can be located, values can be retrieved from and assigned to every node. These operations do not change the structure, they *update* it.

8.1.2 Node Levels and Counts

In practice, a procedure that manages a binary tree revolves about *location,* whether for attachment and detachment of nodes or for retrieval and assignment of values. Location, in turn, is tied to the concept of the *level* of the nodes in a binary tree. Briefly:

- The root of a binary tree is at level zero and a child of a node is at the next higher level. The *depth* of a binary tree is the maximum level of any node.

For example, in BT_1,

- Faye is at level 0.

- Alia is at level 1.

- Wrye and March are at level 2.

- Jan and Ralph are at level 3.

- Will is at level 4.

The particular binary tree BT_1 is structured to retain the family relationships of Faye's Family; but, if that is disregarded, the same names may be rearranged in a binary tree in a more compact shape, as shown in Figure 8.5.

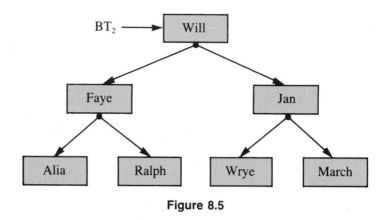

Figure 8.5

The maximum number of nodes at level 0 in a binary tree is 1, at level 1 is 2, at level 2 is $2 \times 2 = 4$, and so on. In general:

- There are no more than 2^L nodes at level L in a binary tree.

- There are no more than $2^{d+1} - 1$ nodes in a binary tree of depth d.

(Both results can be proved by easy induction arguments.)

When the empty (*NIL* or u) nodes of a binary tree are included, it becomes an *extended* binary tree; the nonempty nodes are called *internal* nodes, and the empty nodes are called *external* nodes. The binary tree in Figure 8.6 uses u for empty, and hence external, nodes.

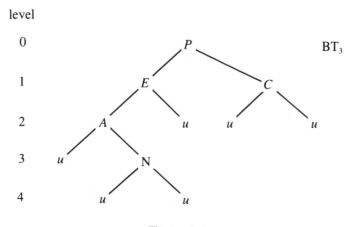

Figure 8.6

Note: N is an *internal* node of BT_3; but, if the external nodes are removed, N is *not* an *interior* node—it is a leaf node.

Every time a new internal node replaces an external node, it increases both the number of internal nodes and the number of external nodes by 1. Hence, by induction, a binary tree with n internal nodes has $n + 1$ external nodes.

The *internal path length,* IPL, of a binary tree is the sum of the levels of all of the internal nodes: IPL(BT_3) = 7, and could be minimized to 6 by moving "N" to level 2.

The *external path length* (EPL) of a binary tree is the sum of the levels of all of the external nodes: EPL(BT_3) = 17. If "N" were moved up to level 2, EPL(BT_3) would decrease to 16.

The *averages* of the internal and external path lengths provide a measure of the average number of links needed to reach nodes during searches from the root. For BT_3 these are:

$$\frac{\text{IPL}(BT_3)}{n} = \frac{7}{5} \qquad \frac{\text{EPL}(BT_3)}{n + 1} = \frac{17}{6}$$

A binary tree is *full* if, when it is extended, each internal node is either a leaf or has *two* internal descendents, not *one*. A binary tree is *complete* if all leaf nodes lie on the lowest levels and those on the bottom level are as far left as possible. Figure 8.7 shows an example of each. A complete binary tree has minimal depth for the number of nodes it contains.

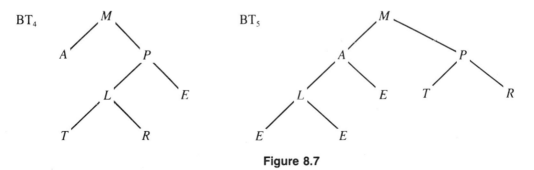

Figure 8.7

Binary tree BT_4 is full but not complete, and BT_5 is complete.

If there are N nodes in a binary tree of *minimal* depth, then the path from the root to a leaf has no more than INT(ln N) links. The potential minimal cost of a search for a node is that of a binary search. In practice, the information required to know which way to branch at a node during a search is incorporated into the shape of the binary tree and tends to increase its depth.

Exercise E8.3 and problem P8.1 are appropriate at this point.

8.1.3 Shape

The two binary trees in Figure 8.8 are both constructed so that their node values can be retrieved in nondecreasing order with the same standard algorithm (*InOrder;* see section 8.3):

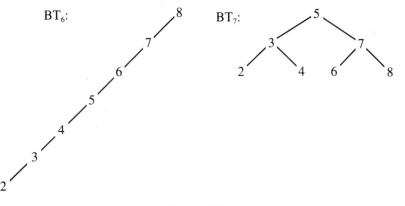

Figure 8.8

The location of the value 2 by a standard search algorithm (BSTT; see section 8.5.1) applied to BT_7 takes a third as many link-hops as it does for BT_6. If the values in these trees were arranged at random, the expected number of hops would be intermediate between these extremes. An insertion algorithm guaranteed to produce a more efficient binary tree form is itself less efficient than one that simply builds a tree suitable for searching. The compromise between forcing the shape of a binary tree and losing the speed of location within it is a central issue in section 8.7.

8.1.4 On the Use of Binary Trees

Trees are a naturally occurring pattern that can be modeled closely by data structures. Their fundamental feature is *branching*. Branching is an essential part of language and thought— of any conceptual framework that involves choices. The binary tree reduces branching to its most elementary form, two-way branching. Each branch that is taken in a binary tree also represents a branch that is *not* taken and sharpens the focus of attention. A sequence of branches sharpens exponentially, much like binary search.

The data structure BINARY TREE is a *decision* tool, a *separator* of subsets. Ways to exhaustively traverse a binary tree are useful and sometimes necessary, but in many major applications nodes are reached by relatively short sequences of branches. BINARY TREE provides *guided access* to an arbitrary node in the structure. It is the data structure of choice when such guidance can be built into the structure.

8.2 Implementations of Binary Trees

When binary trees are implemented with pointer-linked nodes, the nodes are constructed with three fields:

TreeNode = RECORD
               Value : {*value type*
               Left   : ↑ *TreeNode*
               Right : ↑ *TreeNode*
               END {*TreeNode*

Value	
Left	Right

The *Value* field can, of course, be complex and include pointers to more data of interest. It is not uncommon for binary trees to be exogenous—to be used as *directories* to information stored elsewhere. This approach is particularly useful when the directory is small enough to place in the main memory of a computing system, but the data is not and resides on a disk or other peripheral storage. Sometimes the value of interior nodes are used simply to locate an appropriate leaf node that is a guide to the information of interest.

A binary tree rooted at node *btLeft* is linked as the left child of a node *bt* simply by *bt* ↑ .*Left* ← *btLeft,* shown in Figure 8.9. Linking to a right child is similar.

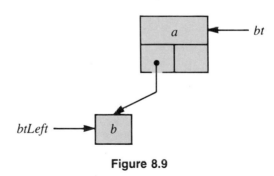

Figure 8.9

8.2.1 Array Support and the Heapform

A binary tree can be supported with arrays in several ways. One way is to use two separate arrays for links and one for values. The 0th cell of one of the link-arrays can be used as a pointer to the root. The link array *Left* is used for this purpose in Figure 8.10.

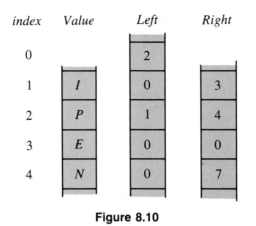

Figure 8.10

A binary tree may be implemented in a single array $A[0 .. Max]$ in such a way that no explicit links are needed:

- The left child of node $A[i]$ is $A[2i]$.

- The right child of node $A[i]$ is $A[2i+1]$.

With this scheme, called *heapform*, the example above is stored as:

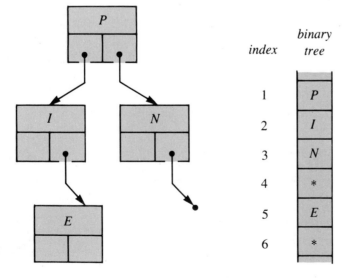

Note that *Max* must allow enough room for the rightmost leaf of the structure.

When a *complete* binary tree of *n* nodes is stored in an array in heapform, it occupies the span $[1 \ . \ . \ n]$, a very compact, convenient, and efficient arrangement.

When an order condition is imposed on the placement of values within the binary tree, the result is a *heap,* a structure that merits a separate discussion in section 8.6.

Exercise E8.4 and problem P8.2 are appropriate at this point.

8.3 Recursive Binary Tree Traverses

Three kinds of operations are required to visit and process the nodes of a binary tree:

- a move to the left child
- a move to the right child
- processing a node in some manner

It can be advantageous to process a node when:

- It is first reached.
- Its left child (subtree) has been processed.
- Its right child (subtree) has been processed.

It is possible to mix these six things in a number of ways, but two conventions are used to reduce the number of possibilities:

- The left subtree of a node is visited before its right subtree.
- A node is processed only once during a traverse.

Three standard traverses remain when these conventions are applied. In recursive form, they are:

procedure *PreOrder*(*bt*) OR   **procedure** *PreOrder*(*bt*) {*O*(*n*)
  if *bt* = NIL   **if** *bt* ≠ NIL
    then return endif   **then** PROCESS*1*(*bt*)
  PROCESS*1*(*bt*)   *PreOrder*(*bt* ↑ .*Left*)
  PreOrder(*bt* ↑ .*Left*)   *PreOrder*(*bt* ↑ .*Right*)
  PreOrder(*bt* ↑ .*Right*)   **endif**
  end {*PreOrder*   **end** {*PreOrder*

procedure *InOrder*(*bt*)   {*O*(*n*)
  if *bt* = NIL **then return endif**
  InOrder(*bt* ↑ .*Left*)
  PROCESS*2*(*bt*)
  InOrder(*bt* ↑ .*Right*)
  end {*InOrder*

procedure *PostOrder*(*bt*)   {*O*(*n*)
  if *bt* = NIL **then return endif**
  PostOrder(*bt* ↑ .*Left*)
  PostOrder(*bt* ↑ .*Right*)
  PROCESS*3*(*bt*)
  end {*PostOrder*

These may be combined into one:

```
                                                          RBTT

procedure RBTT(bt)              {O(n)
  if bt = NIL then return endif
  PROCESS1(bt)
  RBTT(bt ↑ .Left)                  {Recursive Binary Tree Traverse
  PROCESS2(bt)
  RBTT(bt ↑ .Right)
  PROCESS3(bt)
  end {RBTT
```

Consider the binary tree shown in Figure 8.11. Any traverse visits *A* (and processes it or not), then *B* (and processes it or not), then *C*, then *B* again, and so on. Each node is visited three times and processed on (at least) one of its visits.

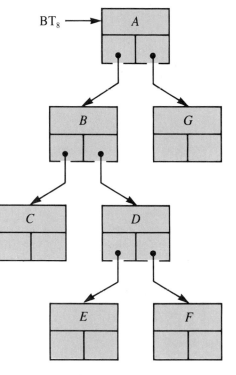

Figure 8.11

The *visitation sequence* of example BT_8 is:

A B C C B D E E E D F F F D B A G G G A

1 1 1 2 3 2 1 1 2 3 2 1 2 3 3 3 2 1 2 3 3

The three standard traverses select the first, second, or third visit to a node in the visitation sequence for processing. Suppose, for example, that *PROCESSi* is simply a display of the node value. Then traverses of BT_8 produce:

```
Preorder: A  B  C  D  E  F  G
Inorder: C  B  E  D  F  A  G
Postorder: C  E  F  D  B  G  A
```

Program PG8.1 is appropriate at this point.

8.3.1 A Recursive Tree Display

The display of a binary tree presents a fundamental problem: one of any great size will not fit comfortably within a screen or print-page. That problem can be resolved by the recursive nature of trees: display a tree of modest size where the leaf nodes identify subtrees, then display the subtrees separately.

Whether to display levels on separate lines or turn the tree sideways so that levels run right to left is a design decision. For a binary tree formed from B-I-G-S-H-A-D-E, the two options, without frills, are shown in Figure 8.12.

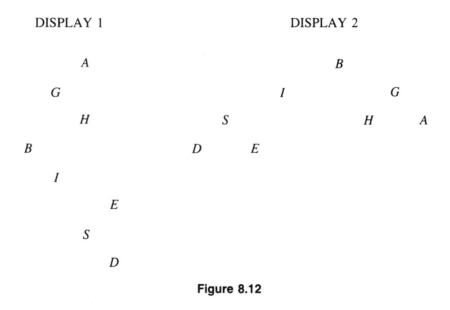

Figure 8.12

Display 2 is an application of the "breadth-first" traverse of section 8.4.3. (The values are displaced from the center of the display-line by an amount determined by their depth. There must be enough spread to accommodate the bottom line, which may have 2^d items in a tree of depth d.)

Display 1 can be done with a recursive traverse that violates the left-first rule. The version that follows prints a string that includes the node value and prints blank spaces or the node value at each level. It is initially called with $d = 0$:

```
procedure SideView(d,bt)                              {O(n)
    if bt ≠ NIL
        then SideView(d + 1,bt ↑ .Right)
             Writeln({d blank strings},bt ↑ .Value)
             SideView(d + 1,bt ↑ .Left)
        endif
    end {SideView
```

8.3.2 Traversals of Arithmetic-Expression Trees

As indicated by their names, the standard traverses are related to the common forms of display for arithmetic expressions.

If the interior nodes of a binary tree correspond to binary operations and the leaf nodes to their operands, it is an *arithmetic-expression tree*. For example, suppose that *A, B,* and *D* in BT_8 (section 8.3) are replaced by /, *, and +, respectively, as shown in Figure 8.13.

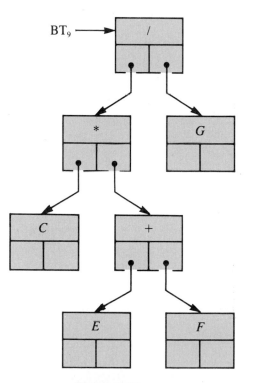

Figure 8.13

The postorder traverse of BT_9 produces

$$C\ E\ F\ +\ *\ G\ /$$

which, when the usual precedence is applied, represents the postfix form of the infix expression:

$$C * (E + F) / G$$

A compiler often reverses this process, although the binary tree may not be explicitly constructed [AHO, 1977].

The preorder traverse produces:

$$/\ *\ C\ +\ E\ F\ G$$

the prefix form of the same expression. If we think of an operation as adding left and right parentheses around its results, the inorder traverse of BT_9 produces:

$$((C * (E + F)) / G)$$

To be sure, producing an expression with correct precedence requires either additional processing or additional (parenthesis) nodes, but the *order* of the tokens is that of the infix expression. The parenthesized expression can be generated by processing an operation node three times: on contact, display "("; on return from the left subchild, display the operation; and on return from the right child, display ")".

Exercise E8.5 and problem P8.3 are appropriate at this point.

■ 8.3.3 A Copy Procedure   (optional)

One fundamental tool that can be applied to a binary tree is a procedure to make a copy of it. The recursive version is particularly apt, because it only requires that a copy be made of both the left and right subtrees and that they be joined:

```
function TreeCopy(bt)
    if bt = NIL then return NIL endif
    NEW( p)
    p ↑ ← bt ↑
    p ↑ .Left ← TreeCopy(bt ↑ .Left)
    p ↑ .Right ← TreeCopy(bt ↑ .Right)
    return p
    end {TreeCopy
```

8.4 Iterative Tree Walks

The recursive forms of tree walks (traverses) are quite elegant, but they can be costly to use because extensive stacks are formed when they are executed. Recursive traversal obscures a salient fact: the links of a binary tree are directional. When a traverse is at node p, the links of p lead to its children, but *not* to its parent. Some way is needed to backtrack to previously visited nodes while an iterative traverse is in progress.

Explicit backtracking is usually done by stacking node pointers (indices in an array implementation) and then unstacking them to make a return. Explicitly programmed stacks contain only the necessary pointers, whereas a recursive routine is compiled so that the entire routine can be reentered. Additional information is stacked to make that possible.

A binary tree can be traversed by stacking each node when it is first encountered, and then again just prior to traversing each of its subtrees. Each node is then stacked and unstacked three times. The order of stacking is arranged so that when a subtree traverse is complete, the parent node will be unstacked next. Some way is needed to distinguish between three encounters with a node during the traverse: the initial contact and two subtree returns. Processing at these three encounters corresponds precisely to preorder, inorder, and postorder processing. All three processing modes can be combined in one algorithm, or done with walks tuned for them individually.

8.4.1 A General Binary Tree Walk: BTT

For the algorithm that follows, nodes of a tree structure are assumed to contain an integer field, *Visit*, which counts the encounters of the walk with the node:

```
VisitNode = RECORD
              Value : {value type
              Left  : ↑ VisitNode
              Right : ↑ VisitNode
              Visit : INTEGER
            END
```

The *Visit* field of each node is assumed to contain 1 at the beginning of the walk and is left that way on exit. An explicit stack, *NodeStack*, replaces the implicit stack of the recursive procedures. *NodeStack* is a stack in which the *Key* field of a node contains a pointer to a tree node. *NodeStack* may be implemented with records, but it is less obtrusive to think of it as array-based so that *Pop* and *Push* take tree node pointers as arguments without the need to encase those pointers in stack nodes.

BTT

```
procedure BTT(bt)                           {O(n)
    if bt = NIL then return endif
    Push(bt)
    while NOT Empty(NodeStack) do            {Binary Tree Traverse
        Pop(p)
        case of p ↑ .Visit

            1 : PROCESS1(p)                  {Prefix processing
                p ↑ .Visit ← 2
                Push(p)
                if p ↑ .Left ≠ NIL then Push(p ↑ .Left) endif

            2 : PROCESS2(p)                  {Infix processing
                p ↑ .Visit ← 3
                Push(p)
                if p ↑ .Right ≠ NIL then Push(p ↑ .Right) endif

            3 : PROCESS3(p)                  {Postfix processing
                p ↑ .Visit ← 1

        endcase
    endwhile
end {BTT
```

BTT can be used as a preorder listing procedure by setting processes 2 and 3 to *NULL* and using *PROCESS*1 as a display. The operation of the stack during such a walk can be traced by indicating a snapshot of it each time **endcase** is reached. For a preorder treewalk on BT_8:

stack				*output*
A	B			A
A	B	C		B
A	B	C		C
A	B	C		
A	B			
A	B	D		
A	B	D	E	D
A	B	D	E	E
A	B	D	E	
A	B	D		
A	B	D	F	
A	B	D	F	F
A	B	D	F	
A	B	D		
A	B			
A				
A	G			
A	G			G
A	G			
A				

This causes more stack activity than would a tree-walk algorithm with a planned restriction to preorder processing.

Problems P8.4 and P8.5 and program PG8.2 are appropriate at this point.

■ 8.4.2 Individualized Iterative Tree Walks (optional)

BTT works the stack heavily: every node is popped from it three times. A quite different approach is based on the statement:

■   A tree walk is made by stepping left as far as possible, then taking a step to the right.

For the preorder display, the form is:

procedure *PreStack(bt)*   {*O(n)*
  if *bt* = NIL **then return endif**
  p ← *bt*
  repeat
    while *p* ≠ NIL **do**
      PROCESS*1*(*p*)
      Push(*p*)
      p ← *p* ↑ .*Left*
    endwhile
    if *Empty*(*NodeStack*)
    then return   .
    else *Pop*(*p*)
        p ← *p* ↑ .*Right*
    endif
  forever
  end {*PreStack*

The corresponding inorder walk is derived from *PreStack* simply by moving the processing position. The adaptation of this kind of walk to postorder processing involves reintroducing a *Visit*, although only two values are required. Because only two values are required for *Visit*, in an array implementation the (integer) pointers may simply be negated to indicate a previously visited node.

procedure *PostStack(bt)*   {*O(n)*
  if *bt* = NIL **then return endif**
  p ← *bt*
  repeat
    while *p* ≠ NIL **do**
      Push(*p*)
      p ← *p* ↑ .*Left*
    endwhile
    Pop(*p*)
    while *p* ↑ .*Visit* = *3* **do**
      PROCESS*3*(*p*)
      p ↑ .*Visit* ← *1*
      if *Empty*(*NodeStack*) **then return endif**
      Pop(*p*)
    endwhile
    p ↑ .*Visit* ← *3*
    Push(*p*)
    p ← *p* ↑ .*Right*
  forever
  end {*PostStack*

Exercises E8.6 and E8.7 are appropriate at this point.

■ 8.4.3 A Breadth-First Traverse (optional)

The binary tree traverses of sections 8.3, 8.4.1, and 8.4.2 all move from the root of a tree first to the deepest level of the leftmost path or the rightmost path (in *SideView*), then move to siblings on the same level. This is called *depth-first* traversal. An alternate class of traverses that may be applied to trees in general as well as binary trees is a *breadth-first* traversal.

With the help of a queue, *Q,* and the queue operations applicable to it, *InsertRear* and *DeleteFront,* it is possible to process nodes in the order of their levels, left-to-right within each level.

A node *p* of *Q* consists of a pointer *p* ↑ *.ptr* to a tree node, and a queue-link field. The insertion of a tree node *t* into *Q* in bare outline is:

procedure *Insert(Q,t)* {*O(1)*
  NEW(*p*)
  p ↑ *.ptr* ← *t*
  InsertRear(Q,p)
  end {*Insert*

The level order traverse is then:

procedure *LevelOrder(BinaryTree,Q)* {*O(n)*
  Insert(Q,BinaryTree)
  while NOT *Empty(Q)* **do**
    p ← *Front(Q)*
    t ← *p* ↑ *.ptr*
    DeleteFront(Q)
    PROCESS(*t*)
    if *t* ↑ *.Left* ≠ NIL
      then *Insert(Q,t* ↑ *.Left)*
      endif
    if *t* ↑ *.Right* ≠ NIL
      then *Insert(Q,t* ↑ *.Right)*
      endif
    endwhile
  end {*LevelOrder*

When *PROCESS(t)* is a display routine, *LevelOrder* is the basis of a top-down display of a binary tree, in contrast to the sideways display of *SideView* (section 8.3.1). A display of this kind requires that the queue nodes contain information about both horizontal and vertical positioning. It is an interesting but reasonable challenge to adapt *LevelOrder* to that task.

Program PG8.3 is appropriate at this time.

The traversal of *LevelOrder* technique is generalized to use a priority queue and applied to graph structures in Chapter 10.

8.5 Ordered Binary Trees

A given subtree, *st*, may easily be inserted as the left or right subtree of a given node, *p*, if the old subtree can be dispensed with:

$$p \uparrow .Left \leftarrow st \qquad \text{or} \qquad p \uparrow .Right \leftarrow st$$

Applying these statements with *st* = NIL removes a subtree without regard to what it contains. Thus, the fundamental issue in most applications is what to do with the other nodes of a subtree when a *single* node *p* is added or deleted at its root. Both subtrees of *p* cannot be used as direct replacements for *p* when it is deleted, and so decisions about what to do with a subtree involve the relationship of the subtree nodes to the rest of the structure. Such relationships generally exhibit some *structural parameter*, a restriction on the placement of nodes in the binary tree. In particular, binary trees may be *ordered*.

A binary tree *bt* may be constructed so that it has property *order:*

■ If *p* is any node of *bt*, no node in the left subtree (rooted at $p \uparrow .Left$) has a value that is as large as $p \uparrow .Value$, and no node in the right subtree (rooted at $p \uparrow .Right$) has a value that is as small as $p \uparrow .Value$. This imposes the restriction that no value be duplicated.

DEFINITION: A binary tree with property *order* is a *binary search tree* (BST).

8.5.1 A Binary Search Tree Traverse: BSTT

BT_{10} in Figure 8.14 is a BST but would not be one if the value 15 were replaced by 25 because the defining condition would be violated for the root node.

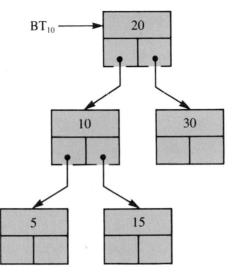

Figure 8.14

Note that an inorder traverse of BT_{10} returns the values in the defining order. (This statement can be used as a definition of a BST.) The creation of a BST is thus a sorting method. Without control of the depth of the tree, it is an $O(n^2)$ procedure.

The values of a BST do not, of course, need to be numeric. Any operator that has the mathematical property of *transitivity* ($A.op.B$ and $B.op.C$ implies $A.op.C$), together with the values on which it operates, will do for the formation of a BST.)

The traverse of a BST is greatly simplified because *no* backtracking is required—the order property guides a search directly to the appropriate node (which may be external). It is:

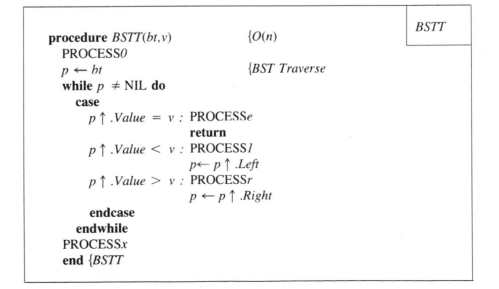

8.5.2 Insertion and Deletion in a BST

In a BST, the insertion and deletion of nodes must be done in a way that maintains the structural parameter *order*. Insertion replaces an external node of the extended tree and only involves finding the appropriate parent and which child of the parent the inserted node is to become. Deletion may be of an interior node and involve shifting subtrees. The first task of either is to determine where in the binary tree a node belongs and if that spot is occupied.

Three possibilities need to be determined:

- The value is already in the BST.
- The value is (or would become) the left child of node *Pred* (if inserted).
- The value is (or would become) the right child of a node *Pred* (if inserted).

The procedure given here finds the value v in the binary search tree bt. It returns pointer p to the node in bt with value v, the predecessor *Pred* of p, and a signal *Trio*. *Trio* is zero or negative if v was found to be the value of an internal node, and positive if it was not found. Zero values of *Trio* can occur in two ways: when bt = NIL or when v was found to be the value of the root node. For a non-*NIL* bt, |*Trio*| is 1 if p is the left child of *Pred*, and 2 if it is the right child. This value is derived from BSTT by:

PROCESS0 : *Trio* ← 0
             Pred ← NIL
PROCESSe : *Trio* ← −*Trio*
PROCESS1 : *Trio* ← 1
             Pred ← p
PROCESSr : *Trio* ← 2
             Pred ← p
PROCESSx : NULL

The resulting procedure is:

```
procedure NodeSpot(bt,v,Trio,p,Pred)  {O(depth)
  Pred ← NIL
  Trio ← 0
  p ← bt
  while p ≠ NIL do
    if v = p ↑ .Value                  {v is an internal value and
      then Trio ← − Trio               {Trio will not be positive
           return
      endif
    Pred ← p
    if v < p ↑ .Value
      then Trio ← 1
           p ← p ↑ .Left
      else Trio ← 2
           p ← p ↑ .Right
      endif
  endwhile
end {NodeSpot
```

NodeSpot is O(depth) for a binary tree of n nodes because it does not need to traverse the structure. The order property allows the algorithm to dispense with backtracking.

The insertion of a non-*NIL* node n with *NIL* child links into a BST *bt* is then done by first invoking *NodeSpot(bt,n ↑ .Value,Trio,p,Pred)*, followed by:

```
procedure InsertNode(bt,n,Pred,Trio)   {0(1)
  if bt = NIL                          {create a new BST from n
    then bt ← n
         return
    endif
  if Trio ≤ 0                          {v is already present. This
    then return endif                  {could be treated as an error.
  if Trio = 1
    then Pred ↑ .Left ← n
    else Pred ↑ .Right ← n             {Trio = 2
    endif
end {InsertNode
```

For some applications, it is convenient to allow the insertion of duplicate values into an ordered tree. Insertion of duplicate values is not so straightforward as *InsertNode*, and deletion is much more complex. For example, equal values may be inserted either randomly or consistently to the left or right, but deleting *all* occurrences of a value presents a problem. In any case, the resulting tree is *partially ordered*, not *ordered*.

A deletion procedure must deal with a number of cases. Problem P8.6 asks the reader to try to display all of the cases graphically. It is worthwhile to do so before reading the algorithm given here.

Problem P8.6 is appropriate at this point.

The deletion procedure reads:

procedure *CutValue(bt,v)*   {*O(depth)*
  if *bt* = NIL
    then {*deal with this error.*
    endif
  NodeSpot(bt,v,Trio,p,Pred)
  if *Trio > 0*   {v *was not found in* bt.
    then {*deal with this error.*
    endif
  TackOn ← p ↑ .Right   {TackOn *is the subtree that is*
                                       {*to replace* p *as a* Pred *child.*

  if *p ↑ .Left* ≠ NIL
    then *TackOn ← p ↑ .Left*
      if *p ↑ .Right* ≠ NIL
        then *NodeSpot(p ↑ .Left,p ↑ .Right ↑ .Value,Top3,s,sp)*
            InsertNode(p ↑ .Left,p ↑ .Right,sp,Top3)
      endif
  endif
  if *Pred* = NIL   {*the root node must go.*
    then *bt ← TackOn*
    else *Trio ← − Trio*   {*Specify which* Pred *child.*
      InsertNode(bt,TackOn,Pred,Trio)
  endif
end {*CutValue*

Exercise E8.8 and program PG8.4 are appropriate at this point.

■ 8.5.3 Static Tree Files   (optional)

In a *complete* binary tree of up to *n* = 1,048,575 nodes, BSTT examines no more than 20 nodes. In contrast, a tree of size *n* could have depth *n* and require *n* tests during a search. If a binary tree (or any tree) is a directory to a file that is to be searched or is the file itself, the shape may be either *static* or *dynamic*. The two corresponding classes of files are managed quite differently.

A *dynamic* file is one that grows and shrinks and changes shape. The shape is normally controlled by maintaining balance, the topic of section 8.7. The benefits of controlling the depth of a file directory can be great, when costs are amortized over a sequence of operations, but the price for maintaining balance lies in the complexity of the insertion and deletion routines. More complex management requires more programming and debugging time and generally more overhead: more run-time with each use of the routines.

A *static* file is created with a shape that remains fixed. The shape of a binary tree that is the directory to a static file can then be optimized for efficient searching at the time of its creation. The optimum shape is normally determined by the keys of the file—it is *data-directed*.

Since the inorder traverse of a BST visits the keys in order, the creation of a BST from a collection of keys may be considered a *tree sort*. However, the insertion sequence determines the shape of the tree and hence the efficiency of subsequent searches. In particular, the *worst* that can happen with procedure *InsertNode* is for the input file to be already ordered! (A linear list will result.) Insertion can be designed to produce a well-balanced static BST, and such a procedure is to be found in Part II, section P.

There are static trees that cannot be balanced because their shape itself carries the information. One such static tree is a search tree for the international Morse code for telegraphy in which letters are represented by dots (short pulses) and dashes (long pulses). If dots correspond in interior nodes to "go left" and dashes to "go right" and letters are leaf nodes, Figure 8.15 shows a small portion of the search tree.

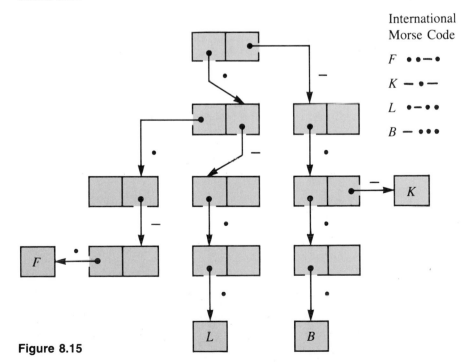

International
Morse Code

F •••—•
K —•—
L •—••
B —•••

Figure 8.15

Program PG8.5 asks for the construction and use of the entire Morse code tree.

The Morse code is a cryptic form of *trie* (pronounced ''try,'' not ''tree''). Most tries use the sequence of letters in a character string to determine which way to branch at a node. Arrival at a leaf node completes the trace of the spelling of a key, and generally uncovers a pointer to an appropriate record. The nodes, however, necessarily have more than two children and so will be reintroduced in Chapter 9.

The Morse code trie has a property present in some search trees but not others: the *links themselves* implicitly encode information. In this book the term *Code-Link Tree* (CLT) is applied to trees with that property. When the links are associated with the digits determined by some number base, a CLT is called a *radix search tree*.

One way to optimize a static binary search tree involves constructing a CLT with these steps:

1. Determine the probability (relative frequency) with which each key is searched.

2. *Encode* the keys as a string of 0's and 1's so that the more frequently searched keys have shorter codes. Such codes are called *Huffman codes*.

3. Construct a CLT from the codes.

A code string of 0's and 1's then leads to a message (a key) at a leaf node.

This approach is used for decoding information that must be transmitted efficiently and for compression of text files in which the keys are characters. It is most effective when the set of search probabilities has a wide range. A discussion of Huffman codes is to be found in Part II, section Q, which uses material introduced in section 8.6.

8.6 Heaps

One balance condition that was introduced in section 8.1.2 can be rephrased as:

■ A binary tree is *complete* if the nodes of every level in it except possibly the last one have two children, and the nodes of the last level are as far to the left as possible.

One specific structural parameter that determines a subset of the set of complete binary trees is stated as:

■ A binary tree is a *heap* if it is complete and if the value of each node is at least as large as the value of its children.

This subset proves to be very efficient and easy to use in many applications.

The natural way to implement a heap is in an array in *heapform* (see section 8.2.1), where the child of a node in $A[i]$ is either $A[2i]$ or $A[2i+1]$. Heaps are not often implemented in linked form because maintaining the balance condition requires additional information in each node.

If a heap is accessed in specified ways, it becomes one support structure for a *priority queue,* discussed in section 8.6.2 and applied in Chapter 10.

The heap formed from a set of values is not unique. Faye's Family can be configured as a heap in several ways; one, shown in Figure 8.16, is formed by adding values to an initially empty heap in the order: Faye, Alia, March, Ralph, Wrye, Jan, Will.

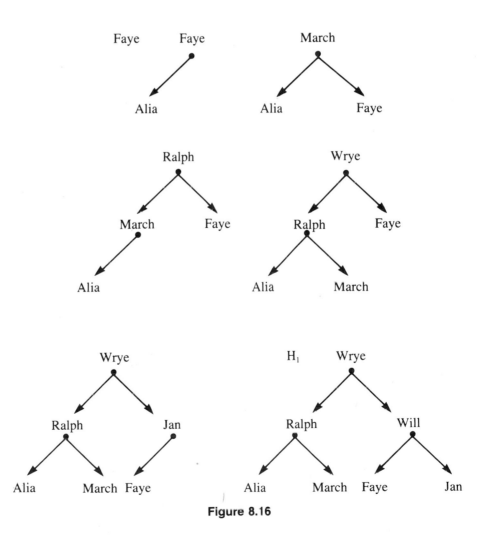

Figure 8.16

In contrast, Figure 8.17 shows the heap when it is constructed by adding names in alphabetical order.

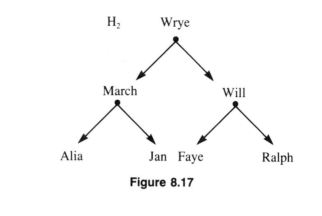

Figure 8.17

Exercise E8.9 and problem P8.7 are appropriate at this point.

The heap structure as explored in the remainder of this section is an endogenous heap implemented in an array $A[1 .. Max]$ in heapform, as shown in Figure 8.18 for Alia's heap.

Figure 8.18

Note: It is either the *heapform-heap* or the *priority queue* that is usually meant by "heap."

Migration

If a heap contains $k - 1$ items in $A[1 . . k-1]$, the value in $A[k]$ may destroy the heap condition if it is included in the structure. If it is allowed to migrate upward, the heap condition can be restored:

```
procedure UpHeap(k)                          {O(ln k)
    while k ≥ 2 do
      p ← INT(k/2)
      if A[k] > A[p]
        then Temp ← A[k]
              A[k] ← A[p]
              A[p] ← Temp
              k ← p
        else exit
        endif
      endwhile
    end {UpHeap
```

(This routine and those in the rest of this section are best understood by tracing an example.)

Exercise E8.10 is appropriate at this point.

Heap Insertion

A value can be inserted into the heap in $A[1 . . n]$ (supported in $A[1 . . Max]$), by inserting it at $A[n + 1]$ and reheaping with *UpHeap:*

```
procedure InsertHeap(v)                      {O(ln n)
    if n ≥ Max
      then {deal with this error
      endif
    n ← n + 1
    A[n] ← v
    UpHeap(n)
    end {InsertHeap
```

The insertion of a value, which may destroy the heap condition, followed by restitution of it, is a common feature of heap operations.

Heap Creation

The level-seeking of *UpHeap* can be used to heap an arbitrary array of values $A[1 . . n]$.

```
procedure MakeHeap                        {O(n ln n)
   for k = 2 to n do
      UpHeap(k)
      next k
   end {MakeHeap
```

The timing function of this procedure is $T(n) = (n - 1) t_k$, where t_k is the time required to execute *UpHeap(k)*. The number of times the **if**-statement of *UpHeap* is executed can be no more than the maximum level in the heap, which is bounded by $INT(\ln n)$. Hence $T(n)$ is $O(n \ln n)$.

One reason that heaps prove to be valuable in practice is the relative efficiency of heap operations.

Priority Retrieval

The largest value (or smallest, or whichever value is heaped to the top) is retrieved and deleted from the heap but not the array by: switch $A[1]$ and $A[n]$, decrement n, and reheap.

Establishment of the heapform after this swap, however, requires that $A[1]$ trickle *down* to its proper level. This downshift can be done with:

```
procedure SwapDown(k)                     {O(ln n)
   while k < n do
      j ← 2 * k
      if j > n then exit endif
      if ( j < n) AND (A[ j] < A[ j+1])
         then j ← j + 1
         endif
      if A[k] < A[ j]
         then Temp ← A[k]
              A[k] ← A[ j]
              A[ j] ← Temp
         endif
      k ← j
   endwhile
end {SwapDown
```

This process can be made somewhat more efficient by shifting values instead of swapping them, as is done in procedure *DownHeap* that follows. The *k*th item is shifted no farther than *n* with:

8.6.2 Priority Queues

In a variety of applications it is desirable to repeatedly insert items into a set from which some optimal value (called the *largest*) can be extracted. (Here "largest" may refer to the item itself or a key field in a record.) An abstraction of such a structure is simply the set of operations that can be applied to it. In this sense, the structure *priority queue* is a set of data to which can be applied:

- *Create* a priority queue from *n* items.

- *Insert* an item.

- *Remove* the largest item.

- *Replace* the largest item *big* by *v* if $v < big$.

It can be useful to apply the following operations that are more difficult to implement efficiently:

- *Change* the priority (size) of an item.

- *Delete* a specified item.

- *Join* two priority queues into one.

There are implementations in which most of these operations are $O(\ln n)$, which is one reason for applying priority queues.

Three implementations of priority queues can be based on structures introduced in previous sections:

1. An array of pointers to priority-class queues, each an instance of QUEUE—a pure queue. This implementation would likely be applied for a fixed number of classes, and most operation procedures would involve a binary search within the sorted array of *k* class headers. With natural algorithms, *Create* is $O(n \ln k)$; *Insert, Remove,* and *Replace* are $O(\ln k)$. *Change* and *Delete* depend on a search of the individual class queues and so are $O(m + \ln k)$, where *m* is the maximum size of a class queue. The operation JOIN is subject to interpretation in this context but is not likely to be as efficient as the other operations.

2. A heapform-heap. *Create* is $O(n \ln n)$; *Insert, Remove,* and *Replace* are all $O(\ln n)$. *Change* and *Delete* are simply linear searches, $O(n)$. *Join* consists of adding the items in heap H_1 to heap H_2, where $n_1 < n_2$ are their sizes. It is then $O(n_1 \ln (n_1 + n_2))$.

   A heapform-heap is the most common implementation for a priority queue.

3. A pointer-linked binary tree heap. *Create* is $O(n \ln n)$. *Insert* and *Replace* are $O(\ln n)$. *Change* and *Delete* involve a binary tree search and so are $O(n)$ at

best. *Delete* and *Remove* would involve rebalancing of the binary tree if the balance condition is not relaxed. If balance is abandoned, the other operations approach $O(n)$ instead of $O(\ln\ n)$. *Join* becomes $O(m\ \ln\ n)$, where $m = Min\{n_1, n_2\}$, $n = n_1 + n_2$, and n_1 and n_2 are the sizes of the heaps to be joined by insertion of the items of one heap into the other.

There are implementations other than the three above, and some can be useful:

4. The degenerate priority-class queue. This implementation has only one item in each class; it is a sorted list of items in an array.

5. A sorted linked list of items. *Create* is in effect *InsertionSort*, $O(n^2)$. *Insert* and *Replace* are $O(n)$ but *Remove* is $O(1)$. *Change* and *Delete* are essentially $O(n)$ linear searches. *Join* is likely to be repeated insertion, $O(m * n)$, where $n = n_1 + n_2$ and $m = Min\{n_1, n_2\}$.

6. An unsorted linked list of items. *Insert* becomes $O(1)$ and hence *Create* is $O(n)$. If the position of a specified item is not known, *Replace* and *Remove* are $O(n)$ linear searches, as are *Change* and *Delete*. *Join* becomes a trivial $O(1)$ operation (as are *Change* and *Delete* if a pointer to the specified item is provided).

7. An unsorted array of items. *Create* is not required, *Insert* is $O(1)$. *Replace*, *Remove*, and *Change* are $O(n)$ linear searches. *Delete* is an $O(n)$ linear search followed by swapping the found item with $A[n]$ and decrementing n. The JOIN operation is ambiguous or simply copies all of the items into some array.

Any priority queue can be used in a sorting algorithm by repeated application of *Remove*, but that does destroy the copy of the structure being used. This process is, of course, *HeapSort* for the heapform heap implementation.

8.6.3 On the Use of Priority Queues

A collection of items that differ in some quality used to select one of them for an application is a natural candidate for retention in a priority queue. The priority queue is the data structure that exemplifies the pair of demands: ''Save this with the others. . . . Find the best one available.''

For specific applications and restrictions, some of the data structures discussed in previous sections and in Chapters 9 and 10 are ideal. For the general situation where items are to be stored and retained in some order determined by their own qualities, the priority queue is the structure of choice. Above all, a priority queue is a structure of *general utility* and *great flexibility*.

Priority queues are applied to the construction of Huffman codes in Part II, section Q, and used in the general traverse of a graph in Chapter 10.

8.7 Balanced Binary Trees

A general binary tree is of the form shown in Figure 8.19, where L and R are subtrees.

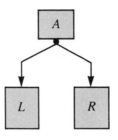

Figure 8.19

The root node may be considered as a *pivot* about which the binary tree it roots can be balanced or unbalanced by some criterion. Since this scheme applies at every node in a binary tree, balance is a *local* effect. It becomes a *global* effect with the restriction that a tree not be unacceptably out of balance at any node. Global balance is important for search trees because it determines the amortized cost of a sequence of searches.

Ways to measure subtrees L and R for comparison with each other that have been applied include:

- height (depth)

- weight (the number of external nodes)

- internal path length (IPL)

Perfect balance is too much to ask because it generally is present only for complete trees, and so balance criteria are designed to *optimize* the balance for arbitrary trees. Insertions and deletions can change the balance at arbitrary points within a binary tree, for better or worse. When an operation changes the balance to the point that it needs to be restored, rebalance is done by *rotation* about a *pivot* node.

Suppose, for example, that the binary tree shown schematically in Figure 8.20 is balanced at n and at p, but an insertion is made into subtree R_2 that causes an inbalance (by the criterion in use).

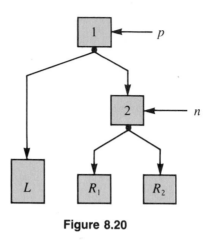

Figure 8.20

Then a single left rotation (SLR) can be used to restore balance and maintain the order condition, as shown in Figure 8.21.

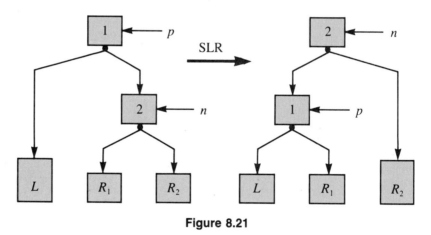

Figure 8.21

As a more specific example, the effect of an SLR on the tree in Figure 8.22 helps its balance (by almost any criterion).

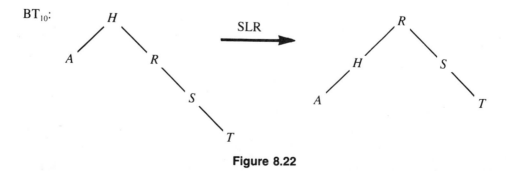

Figure 8.22

Sometimes a single rotation is not sufficient, and a *double rotation* is required, as shown in Figure 8.23.

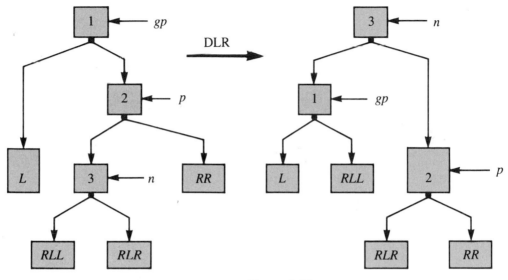

Figure 8.23

For a specific example, a double rotation improves the balance of the tree in Figure 8.24 (by almost any criterion).

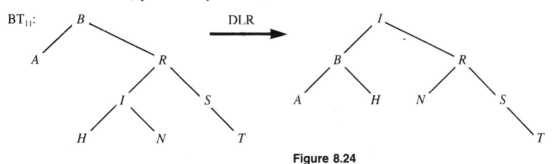

Figure 8.24

The right-rotation forms are symmetric to the left-rotations illustrated. Both single and double rotations are designed to maintain the order of the keys.

Since rotations may take place around any node in the tree, the parent of the pivot node is involved: the pivot node is either its left or its right child, and that pointer is changed. For the sake of clarity, it will be assumed that the pivot node is the *root* in the discussion that follows, and all the subtrees shown are non-*NIL*.

With these simplifying assumptions, SLR becomes:

SLR: $p \uparrow .Right \leftarrow n \uparrow .Left$
 $n \uparrow .Left \leftarrow p$
 {*switch parent-of-*p *pointer to* n

Similarly, DLR is:

DLR: $\quad$ $p \uparrow .Left \leftarrow n \uparrow .Right$
$\qquad$ $gp \uparrow .Right \leftarrow n \uparrow .Left$
$\qquad$ $n \uparrow .Right \leftarrow p$
$\qquad$ $n \uparrow .Left \leftarrow gp$
$\qquad$ {*switch parent-of-*gp *pointer to* n

In practice, a number of special cases must be dealt with.

Several general features of binary tree balancing are of interest. *Insertion* is always made at a leaf node. For height- and weight-balance criteria, insertion requires no more than one rotation (if any) in order to restore balance. With IPL balance, rotations can propagate down the tree.

Deletion can always be of a node with no more than one internal child. If the search for a deletion key locates it at node p, then in the sequence of values that determines the tree, the values adjacent to $p \uparrow .Key$ are

$$Pred \uparrow .Key < p \uparrow .Key < Succ \uparrow .Key$$

where *Pred* is the node in the left subtree of p to which p would be added by an insertion. Similarly, *Succ* is the node in the right subtree of p to which p would be added by an insertion. Insertion always replaces an external node, which has a parent with no more than one internal child. Consequently, the $p \uparrow .Key$ can be swapped with $Pred \uparrow .Key$ (or with $Succ \uparrow .Key$ if $p \uparrow .Left$ is external), and the latter deleted.

Rotations caused by deletion can propagate up along the sequence of nodes in the search path to the deleted node. Reversing this path involves stacking the search path as it is generated, or retracing it, or building the tree with parent links in the nodes, or reversing links as the path is traced (a technique used in Part II, section M) and then restoring them.

The nodes of a balanced tree generally contain information fields that indicate the state of balance at a node. Rotation, insertion, and deletion procedures maintain the fields to reflect altered conditions.

Perhaps the easiest dynamically balanced tree structure to maintain, and one of the most often applied, is the B-tree discussed in section 9.5.

A tree structure that is reformulated as a binary tree and then balanced is the *Red-Black Tree* of section 9.6 and Part II, section U.

Further details about height-balanced trees, commonly called AVL trees, are to be found in section 8.7.1. Details of the management routines for them are to be found in Part II, section R. Weight-balanced trees, commonly called BB(α) trees, are discussed in section 8.7.2.

IPL-balanced trees are treated in [GONNET, 1983]. Their advantage is in management routines that are simpler than for AVL trees, and their disadvantage is in rotations that can propagate *down* the tree.

The analysis of the cost of maintenance procedures for various balance criteria, their amortization, and their relative merits lie outside the aims of this book. As pointed out elsewhere [GONNET, 1983], research is yet to be completed on some questions concerning:

■　the (worst case, average, or amortized worst case)

number of (rotations, node inspections)

to (search, insert, or delete)

a key in (AVL, BB(α), or IPL)

trees.

■ 8.7.1 AVL Trees　　　　　　　　　　　　　　　　　　　　　(optional)

Height-balancing was achieved by G. M. Adel'son-Vel'skii and E. M. Landis in 1962, and hence such trees are called either AVL trees or height-balanced trees.

If *bt* is a binary tree with subtrees *L* and *R*, then *bt* is height-balanced (has the AVL property) iff:

1. $|h(L) - h(R)| \leq 1$, where *h* is the height function.

2. *L* and *R* are themselves height-balanced.

The tree in Figure 8.25 fails to be height-balanced at *E*, and hence *G*, although it would be 1-balanced at *G* on the basis of the relative heights of its subtrees alone.

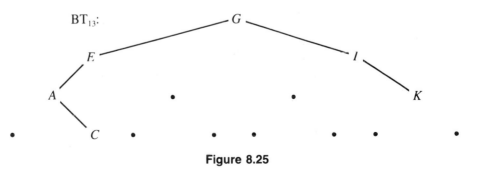

Figure 8.25

A detailed treatment of the management routines for AVL trees is to be found in Part II, section R.

■ 8.7.2 BB(α) Trees (optional)

Suppose that *bt* is an extended binary tree with left and right subtrees *L* and *R*. With the notation: $|T|$ for the number of external nodes in tree T, the weight-balance of *bt* is:

$$\beta(bt) = \tfrac{1}{2} \text{ if } bt \text{ is empty, and}$$
$$= \frac{|L|}{|bt|} \text{ otherwise}$$

Clearly, $\beta(bt) = \tfrac{1}{2}$ implies perfect balance and it must be true that

$$0 < \beta(bt) < 1$$

The parameter that measures how close to $\tfrac{1}{2}$ the balance is to be maintained is α. A tree is of *weight-balance* α or in the set BB(α) if:

1. $\alpha \leq \beta(bt) \leq 1 - \alpha$ and $\alpha \leq \tfrac{1}{2}$

2. if *bt* is not empty, L and R are in BB(α).

Clearly, $\alpha = 0$ is no restriction and $\alpha = \tfrac{1}{2}$ asks for perfect balance. BB(*x*) is a subset of BB(*y*) if $x \leq y$. It happens that if $\tfrac{1}{3} \leq \alpha \leq \tfrac{1}{2}$, then BB($\alpha$) = BB($\tfrac{1}{2}$).

The β values of the nodes of a tree determine its α-class (which it may be desirable to adjust after insertions and deletions). The nodes in Figure 8.26 have their β value as identifier:

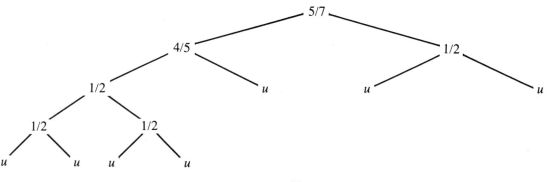

Figure 8.26

The details of managing BB(α) trees are similar to those for AVL trees described in Part II, section R.

Exercise E8.13 and problem P8.8 are appropriate at this point.

■ 8.8 Threaded Binary Trees   (optional)

A binary tree can be traversed without the use of (implicit or explicit) stacks in several ways. One way is with the use of *threads*.

A *thread* is created by replacing *NIL* (external) links. A *NIL* right link is replaced with a pointer to the node that would be processed next in an inorder traverse. A *NIL* left link is replaced by a pointer to the node that was processed last. The leftmost left link and the rightmost right link are set to *NIL*.

A threaded version of BT_8 is shown in Figure 8.27.

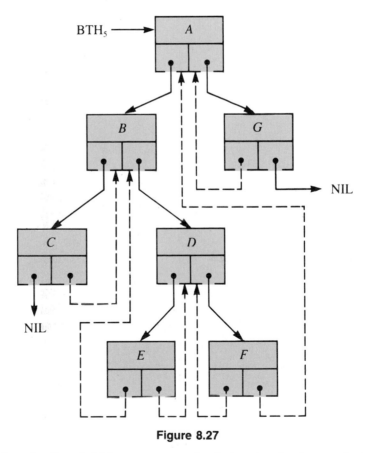

Figure 8.27

The nodes of a threaded binary tree must be designed to implement threads. The links and the threads need to be distinguished. They are distinguished in an array implementation by using negative indices for links and in a pointer implementation by using flags:

ThreadNode = RECORD
       Value : {*ValueType*
       Left   : ↑ *ThreadNode*
       Lflag : BOOLEAN
       Right : ↑ *ThreadNode*
       Rflag : BOOLEAN
       END {*ThreadNode*

It is convenient to initialize the flag fields to *TRUE*, implying that the associated fields are pointers, not threads.

An unthreaded binary tree where the nodes are of type *ThreadNode* can be threaded by calling *Baste*(*bt*,NIL,NIL):

procedure *Baste*(*p,Pred,Next*)   {*O*(*n*)
  if *p* = NIL **then return endif**
  if *p* ↑ .*Left* = NIL
   then *p* ↑ .*Left* ← *Pred*
     p ↑ .*Lflag* ← FALSE
   else *Baste*(*p* ↑ .*Left,Pred,p*)
   endif
  if *p* ↑ .*Right* = NIL
   then *p* ↑ .*Right* ← *Next*
     p ↑ .*Rflag* ← FALSE
   else *Baste*(*p* ↑ .*Right,p,Next*)
   endif
  end {*Baste*

Exercise E8.14 is appropriate at this point.

A traverse of a threaded tree follows the standard pattern of: "step left as far as possible, step right one link, move to the appropriate successor." When a node is reached by following a normal link, its left subtree is to be explored. If it is reached by a thread, its left subtree has *already* been explored. Processing of nodes can be in postorder, preorder, or in the inorder shown on the next page.

```
procedure InThread(bt)                    {O(n)
  GoLeft ← TRUE
  p ← bt
  while p ≠ NIL do
    if GoLeft
      then while p ↑ .Lflag do
             p ← p ↑ .Left
           endwhile
    endif
    PROCESS2( p)
    GoLeft ← p ↑ .Rflag
    p ← p ↑ .Right
  endwhile
end {InThread
```

Insertion of a node into a threaded binary tree raises the question of placement— of where the insertion is to take place. Balancing and order are not related to the choice between external nodes and threads and must depend on applications. Threads have only a minor affect on the emplacement of a new leaf node. To illustrate, consider the insertion of a node q as the right child of a leaf node p in a threaded binary tree:

```
procedure ThreadRight( p,q)
  q ↑ .Lflag ← FALSE
  q ↑ .Left ← p
  q ↑ .Rflag ← p ↑ .Rflag
  q ↑ .Right ← p ↑ .Right
  p ↑ .Right ← q
end {ThreadRight
```

Adding a node as the left child of a leaf node is similar and is left as a problem.

Problem P8.9 is appropriate at this point.

Deletion of nodes from a threaded binary tree (any binary tree) depends upon shape parameters that are heavily application dependent. The crucial issue is: what should be done with the subtrees of the excised node? The possible responses to this question differ only in detail from those applied in unthreaded trees.

Program PG8.7 is appropriate at this point.

Summary

Trees in the mathematical sense of a graph without cycles are a common form, and they can be represented in a program with the structure BINARY TREE. The nodes of a binary tree have two distinguished (left and right) child nodes. Like lists, stacks, and queues, the binary tree is dynamic and may be either endogenous or exogenous.

An important feature of binary trees is that every node is accessible from the root node by following links. There are several ways to traverse a binary tree, either recursively or iteratively. One is the universal iterative binary tree traverse BTT, which allows processing a node at each of three contacts with it during the traverse. Many application algorithms can be based on BTT or on its recursive counterpart RBTT.

Traverses more specialized than BTT process a node on only one of the traverse contacts with it, the standards being: preorder, inorder, and postorder traverses. The recursive forms of these traverses are especially handy for quick application. The iterative forms of the standard traverses require explicit stacks that are less extensive than those in the corresponding recursive forms.

A breadth-first traverse uses a queue to traverse a binary tree level-by-level. When generalized, it becomes the priority-queue traverse of a graph in Chapter 10.

Reaching a sought-for node in the minimum number of steps requires that a decision to traverse either a left subtree or a right subtree be made at each node in the walk. A binary tree with nodes ordered so that node keys direct the walk efficiently is a BST (Binary Search Tree).

An array support system for binary trees called *heapform* is efficient and of great utility. When order and completeness are included in a binary tree supported in heapform, it is a *heap*. (A heap may also be supported with pointers, but not conveniently.) Heaps are a preferred support structure for *priority queues,* which in practice replace several of the simplified application models presented in this book. Note the layers of structure: (array and binary tree) $\rightarrow$ heapform $\rightarrow$ heap $\rightarrow$ priority queue.

Heap algorithms can be assembled into *HeapSort,* a sorting method guaranteed to be $O(n \ln n)$ in the worst case. This is the theoretical optimum.

Binary trees are heavily used as directories to (endogenous or exogenous) files and hence repeatedly searched. The cost of searches must be *amortized* over a sequence of operations.

For *static* files, the shape is determined at creation and must be optimized at that point. A general balancing insertion algorithm is to be found in Part II, section P. A highly tuned static file technique, the use of Huffman codes, is applied to file compression and decoding of messages. The algorithms are to be found in Part II, section Q.

Dynamic files change shape with the operations of insertion and deletion, and so those operations are often sophisticated in order to maintain *balance*. Height, weight, and internal path length are all applied to devise balance criteria. Height-balanced trees (AVL trees) are detailed in Part II, section R. A more general structure, the B-tree, is described in Chapter 9.

Binary tree traverses can be directed without stacks by replacing *NIL* pointers with *threads* that point back to appropriate ancestors, at the cost of the initial threading.

Exercises   immediate applications of the text material

E8.1   Suppose that the vowels form a tree with "O" as the root, and its children are "U", "I", "A", left-to-right and "E" is the only child of "I". Restructure this tree as a binary tree by the transformation rule given in the introduction.

E8.2   How many ways are there to arrange the vowels "A", "E", "I", "O", "U" in a binary tree so that if C_1 is in the left subtree of C_2, then $C_1 < C_2$, and if C_3 is in the right subtree of C_2, $C_3 > C_2$.

E8.3   Derive the level of each node for the tree in Figure 8.28, the depth of the tree, the IPL, and the EPL. Modify the tree to find variations with the same set of keys that are full, or complete.

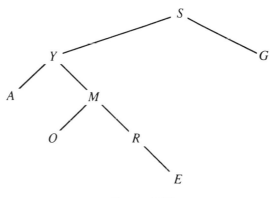

Figure 8.28

E8.4   Show how the vowel binary tree of E8.1 would appear in single-array and three-array form. (In the three-array form, the vowels are to be stored in alphabetical order.)

E8.5   Add parenthesis nodes to BT_9 (section 8.3.2) so that the inorder trace produces the correct infix expression.

E8.6   Trace the action of procedure *PreStack* on BT_8 by indicating the stack contents and p each time they change.

E8.7 There is a **return** on entrance to *PostStack*, but it is not required in *InStack* and *PreStack*. Why is this so?

E8.8 Trace the insertion of T-I-P into the BST of Figure 8.29, followed by deletion of *E* and *O:*

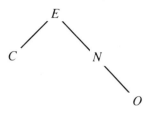

Figure 8.29

E8.9 Construct the heap H_2 of section 8.6 in stages, as was done for heap H_1.

E8.10 Trace procedure *UpHeap* of section 8.5 on the letter sequence T-R-A-S-H-D-U-M-P, applied for $k = 2, 3 \ldots 9$.

E8.11 Trace the action of procedure *DownHeap* (k,n) for $k = 3,2,1$ on Faye's Family, initially stored in alphabetical order.

E8.12 Trace the action of *HeapSort* on an array containing the letter sequence of E8.10.

E8.13 Calculate the weight-balance factors for all nodes of the binary trees BT_1–BT_6.

E8.14 Trace the values of the parameters p, *Pred*, and *Next* in procedure *Baste* of section 8.8 when it is applied to BT_8. Show them as they would appear on top of the stack created by recursive calls and indicate thread assignments.

Problems not immediate, but requiring no major extensions of the text material

---

P8.1 Develop the induction proofs of the two level-count results of section 8.1.2.

P8.2 Suppose that pointers require two bytes of storage and values require four. How much total storage is required for a binary tree of N items? Derive answers for pointers, three-array, and single-array storage.

P8.3 Derive a scheme for adding parentheses to the display of a binary tree in which interior nodes represent binary operators so that the display traverse produces the correct infix expression.

P8.4 Design a procedure that displays node values on all three contacts with a node, then prints an encounter index under the display. (See the discussion of visitation order in section 8.3 for example output.)

P8.5 Design an iterative version of function *TreeCopy* of section 8.3.3.

P8.6 Redesign procedures *NodeSpot* and *InsertNode* of section 8.5.2 so that values may be duplicated in a (partially) ordered binary tree.

P8.7 How many distinct heaps of Faye's Family are there?

P8.8 Design a procedure to calculate weight-balance factors for an arbitrary binary tree.

P8.9 Write the procedure that inserts node q as the left child of a leaf node p in a threaded binary tree.

Programs   for trying it yourself

PG8.1 Write a program that inputs a binary tree (assumed to be correctly linked by the user) and displays the *PreOrder, InOrder,* and *PostOrder* traverses of it. (In a language that fails to support recursion, the results of section 8.4.1 are required.)

PG8.2 Repeat PG8.1 with the iterative procedure BTT and display the stack at an appropriate point if requested by the user.

PG8.3 Write a program that will accept a list of values, treat them as a heapform binary tree, and display them both top-down and sideways.

PG8.4 Write a command-shell program that manages a binary search tree, allowing display, insertion, deletion, and location of values.

PG8.5 Write a program that constructs the International Morse code tree introduced in section 8.5.3 from the table below and allows users to enter a code message of dots, dashes, and separators. The output of the program is the decoded message.

A · −	B − · · ·	C − · − ·	D − · ·	E ·
F · · − ·	G − − ·	H · · · ·	I · ·	J · − − −
K − · −	L · − · ·	M − −	N − ·	O − − −
P · − − ·	Q − − · −	R · − ·	S · · ·	T −
U · · −	V · · · −	W · − −	X − · · −	Y − · − −
Z − − · ·				

PG8.6 Write a program that inputs 10 integers and sorts them with *HeapSort.*

PG8.7 Write a program that creates a threaded tree by accretion (but does not support deletion) and displays the new tree.

Chapter 9

Multiple
Access Paths to Data

ARRAY supplies an individual access path for each of its data cells. STACK and QUEUE supply only one access point for data retrieval and hide data *not* at that point from the user. A linked list provides one general access point (the head) and one limited one (the tail), but it does provide a traverse path to any cell. The traverse path is unique for singly linked lists, and varied for doubly linked and circular lists. BINARY TREE provides only one entry point, but any cell can be reached from it. Without the help of a stack or other external structure, the access path to any cell in a binary tree is unique. This chapter explores some of the ways to enhance the access to structured data.

Multiple access to the cells of a binary tree for backtracking to the parent of a node can be provided with two-way links, in analogy with doubly linked lists. One effect is the removal of stack action in the general traverse, which decreases execution overhead at the expense of extra space in the nodes. Two-way binary trees are discussed in section 9.3, and parent-links are applied in several later sections. Parent links may even replace the child links, as they do in the representation of sets in section 9.7.

Two forms of generalized access should not be overlooked: *indirection* and *external storage*.

Indirection, discussed in section 9.1, is a programming technique that can be applied to any structure. It is important for file directories and sorting because the data in records and the nodes that provide multiple access to them are likely to be bulky. Indirection, like exogeny, provides a *map* to data. The map can act as a surrogate for bulk material that needs to be swapped or shifted or at least needs to *appear* to be moved from the user's point of view. This, of course, is an example of information-hiding like the implementations of data structures in this book that are based on access to structural procedures instead of direct access to data itself.

External storage has been a background theme for all of the structures studied in this book because access to data stored on secondary storage is not done on the same time scale as it is for main storage. Just as important is the massive *size* of the data files that may be stored externally. The choice of data structure to be used for external storage can be profoundly affected by the need to deal with data sets much too large for main memory. An approach to sorting too much data to retain in main memory is outlined in section 9.2, where it leads to merging and merge-sorting in Part II, sections S and T. Some of the structures that provide access to external data are studied in sections 9.4, 9.5, and 9.6.

BINARY TREE provides only two children at each node. An obvious generalization is to structure nodes with more than two children. Having more than two children provides quicker access to the deeper levels of the tree. External files are commonly accessed through a directory with such multichild nodes in order to decrease the number of levels used to reach a given number of nodes.

Applications of multiway tree structures include *m*-way structures in section 9.4, B-trees in section 9.5, 2-3-4 trees in section 9.6 and Part II, section U, and the decision tree of section 9.8 and Part II, section V.

Finally, if a data structure is large, it may be desirable to *limit* access to part of it—to *prune* it. That is the theme of (multiway) game trees, section 9.9 and Part II, section W.

9.1 Access by Indirection

One major activity applied to data is sorting, which generally reduces to the sorting of records by key. It is not uncommon to need access to the data in complex records, such as personnel records, by way of more than one key. Sophisticated ways to access data interrelated in complex ways have been developed under the general heading of data bases. A much simpler approach can be of value: *indirect sorting*.

As a focus, consider an array of student records, $a[1 \ . \ . \ n]$, each containing a name and an identification number. If the records are already sorted physically in ID-number order, the names are surely out of alphabetical order, and locating a name becomes an $O(n)$ operation rather than a binary search of $O(\ln n)$ cost. It is desirable to provide an ordered appearance for a name search without physically moving the records out of ID-number order.

Any sorting algorithm can be implemented indirectly; and, for contrast, both a direct and an indirect sort with the same algorithm are developed here.

A sorting procedure that compares favorably in practice with those of Chapter 1 is the *ShellSort,* developed by D. H. Shell. It is $O(n^2)$ but may be ten or more times as fast as the other methods are for a few hundred items [KERNIGHAN, 1974]. For large data sets, it is less efficient than *HeapSort,* but easier to get right. *ShellSort* acts like *BubbleSort* except that, as it makes a sweep, it compares $a[i]$ with $a[i+Gap]$, where *Gap* is initially $INT(n/2)$ instead of 1. If switches occur on a sweep, it resweeps with the same value of *Gap;* otherwise, it halves *Gap* and repeats.

```
procedure ShellSort(a,n)                              {O(n²)}
   Gap ← n
   while Gap > 1 do
     Gap ← INT(Gap/2)
     Bound ← n − Gap
     repeat
       Exchanges ← 0
       for Lower = 1 to Bound do
         Upper ← Lower + Gap
         if a[Lower].Name > a[Upper].Name
           then  Temp ← a[Lower]
                 a[Lower] ← a[Upper]
                 a[Upper] ← Temp
                 Exchanges ← Exchanges + 1
         endif
       next Lower
     until Exchanges ≤ 0
   endwhile
end {ShellSort
```

To do this procedure by indirection, an array of indices to records in the array must be first created. (Pointers to scattered records would also serve.) The indices are initialized to the initial position of the records:

```
procedure MakeMap
  for i = 1 to n do
    Map[i] ← i
    next i
  end {MakeMap
```

Immediately after execution of *MakeMap*, $a[i]$ and $a[Map[i]]$ are identical. However, the indirect sort compares $a[Map[i]]$ to $a[Map[j]]$; and, if a switch is indicated, it is $Map[i]$ and $Map[i]$ that are switched, *not* the records themselves. (This technique works for the sorts in Chapter 1 as well.)

```
procedure VirtualShell(a,Map,n)                      {O(n²)
   Gap ← n
   while Gap > 1 do
     Gap ← INT(Gap/2)
     Bound ← n − Gap
     repeat
       Exchanges ← 0
       for Lower = 1 to Bound do
         Upper ← Lower + Gap
         if a[Map[Lower]].Name > a[Map[Upper]].Name
           then TempDex ← Map[Lower]
                Map[Lower] ← Map[Upper]
                Map[Upper] ← TempDex
                Exchanges ← Exchanges + 1
         endif
       next Lower
     until Exchanges ≤ 0
   endwhile
end {VirtualShell
```

After execution of *VirtualShell*, the records may be displayed in the order determined by their *Name* fields by:

```
procedure MapOut
   for i = 1 to n do
     NodeOut(Map[i])          {display routine for a node
     next i
   end {MapOut
```

Exercise E9.1 and problem P9.1 are appropriate at this point.

9.1.1 The Indirect Heap

HEAP is a structure that involves a great deal of data movement when it is managed directly. Actually, it is only the address of data that needs to be provided in heap form, just as a data-set is defined to be fully sorted for a user by an appropriate sequence of addresses. The creation of a heap from the data used for *ShellSort* follows the procedures in section 8.6 rather closely:

```
procedure UpHeap(k)
   while k ≥ 2 do
      p = INT(k/2)
      if a[Map[k]].Name > a[Map[p]].Name
         then  TempDex ← Map[k]
               Map[k] ← Map[p]
               Map[p] ← TempDex
               k ← p
         else exit
         endif
   endwhile
   end {UpHeap
```

```
procedure MakeHeap
   for k = 2 to n do
      UpHeap(k)
      next k
   end {MakeHeap
```

The *Name* indexed by *Map*[1] is the top name, whatever its index in $a[1 \ .. \ n]$.

Finally, it is possible to keep an *inverse* map. For example, if *Track*[*i*] is initialized to *i* for *i* = 1,2, . . .,*n*, then the location of $a[j]$ *within the indirect heap, Map,* can be followed by adding a small amount of overhead to the switch:

```
if a[Map[k]].Name > a[Map[p]].Name
   then  Track[Map[k]] ← p
         Track[Map[p]] ← k
         TempDex ← Map[k]
         Map[k] ← Map[p]
         Map[p] ← TempDex
         k ← p
   else exit
   endif
```

After execution of *MakeHeap*, the location of $a[i]$ in the (indirect) heap *Map* is *Track*[*i*]. The parent and child nodes and the level of $a[i]$ can all be derived from *Track*[*i*].

Indirection can be a powerful tool for preserving both storage and time, simply because pointers are relatively small.

Exercise E9.2 is appropriate at this point.

9.2 External Files

Data is stored on disks or tapes in order to preserve it beyond the life of a program execution, but these storage media have been developed with the secondary goal of providing cheap bulk storage. The $2 disk on which this sentence was stored in a portable personal computer holds 195,000 bytes on a side. That is 195,000 characters, or 3,250 sentences like this one. That is enough for a file containing this chapter. The main memory in which such a file would be edited holds an operating system, an editing program, and only a portion of a chapter file. A search through such a file (for misspelled words, perhaps) would require a number of transfers of data between main and secondary storage. Direct access to data in secondary storage may be slower than access to data in the main store of a computing system by a factor of 100 or 1,000 or 10,000. Both their bulk and the time required to access external storage have an impact on the choice of data structures applied to it.

External files with exogenous and/or balanced search-tree directories can combine the speed of main memory with the bulk storage capability of external storage. A common form for such files is that of the *m*-way trees of section 9.4 and the B-trees of section 9.5, and this is supplemented by material on balanced binary trees in section 8.7; Part II, sections P and R, and Red-Black (2-3-4) trees in section 9.7 and Part II, section U.

One approach to organizing large sorted sequential files that has been applied frequently is similar to the use of index tabs in dictionaries and physical files: quick access is provided to a directory of segments of a file. A key can be efficiently placed within a particular segment, and the segment accessed for further search. This organization is called an *indexed-sequential file*.

An indexed-sequential file is sorted as a whole. Sorting such a file, or any large file, may need to be done in manageable pieces much smaller than the file itself. The pieces are then *merged* to form a single file sorted as a whole.

9.2.1 The Merge Operation

Suppose that two arrays, sorted in nondecreasing order, $a[1 .. m]$ and $b[1 .. n]$, are to be written as a single sorted list on a file. (The output file is taken here to be the standard output file.) This merging operation can be done simply by examining the next item in both arrays and writing the smallest of them:

```
procedure StraightMerge                              {O(n + m)
    if a[m] ⩾ b[n]
        then Sentinel ← a[m] + 1
        else Sentinel ← b[n] + 1
    endif
    a[m + 1] ← Sentinel
    b[n + 1] ← Sentinel
    i ← 1
    j ← 1
    for k = 1 to n + m do
        if a[i] < b[ j]
            then Write(a[i])
                    i ← i + 1
            else Write(b[ j])
                    j ← j + 1
        next k
    end {StraightMerge
```

Variations of *StraightMerge* can be designed for linked lists, for more efficient operation when one run is larger than another, and as a sorting procedure. Further discussion is to be found in Part II, section S.

When a large file is to be sorted by merging techniques, the efficiency of the complete operation is affected by the size of the sorted segments, called *runs*. Runs are merged to form larger runs, until there is only one. As the runs increase in size, they cannot be in main memory, and so data is read from two or more files and written onto another in sorted order. The operation of creating runs from sequential files is enhanced by the application of a priority queue. Details are to be found in Part II, section T.

Exercise E9.3 is appropriate at this point.

9.3 Doubly Linked Two-Way Trees

As noted in Chapter 8, trees and binary trees are not the same structure, but the relationships between the nodes of a tree can be retained in a binary tree. Clearly, any binary tree becomes a tree simply by ignoring the distinction between left child and right child. In that sense, a binary tree is a restricted form of tree. The three common restrictions are:

■   A link is directional from parent to child.

- There are no more than two children per node.

- Children of a node are distinguished.

The middle restriction can be restated as:

- The *degree* of each node of a binary tree is no more than 2.

(The degree of a node is the number of links it has to other nodes.) Trees of degree *m* are used in *m-way search trees,* in direct analogy with the binary search trees of section 8.5.

Removal of the first two restrictions together with the assumption that a child has but one parent provides a structure that is commonly used to manage sets (see section 9.7). Removal of the last two restrictions provides a family of structures used in decision making and in the analysis of games (see sections 9.8 and 9.9). Removal of all three restrictions creates a *graph* structure, the subject of Chapter 10.

An increase in the number of children of each node tends to decrease the depth of a tree with a given number of nodes. The depth of a tree determines the maximum number of links that must be traversed in search, insert, or delete operations. Tree depth can be changed by either an insertion or a deletion, which makes it desirable to formulate these operations so that paths from the root to all leaves tend to be the same length. It is possible to balance the root-leaf paths of general tree structures, much like binary trees are balanced in the AVL structure of section 8.7.1. The structures introduced in this chapter provide alternates to AVL trees and randomly formed binary trees, and their balance is a major theme.

Exercise E9.4 and program P9.2 are appropriate at this point.

The mathematical structure of a tree with no more than two children differs in two ways from the computing structure BINARY TREE. One difference is the distinction between left and right subtrees in the binary tree structure. The other difference is that the links in binary trees are directional, and the *edges* connecting nodes in a mathematical tree are two-way connections. When restriction is made to directional links in a mathematical structure it becomes a *directed graph* or *digraph.* A linked list necessarily forms a digraph because links are directional, but when each link is paired with a link in the reverse direction, the pair models an undirected, two-way link.

Figure 9.1 is a valid directed graph. Directed graphs are very general structures, and so general algorithms to traverse them tend to be either more complex or slower than algorithms dealing with structures that have a higher degree of internal structure.

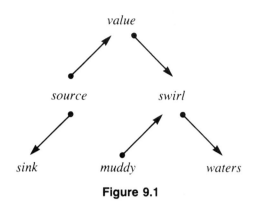

Figure 9.1

Removal of the one-way linkage restriction on binary trees is well worth considering for any application, particularly if the tree is exogenous. In that case, the *Value* field of a node record is a pointer to a storage record, and the storage required for the link does not increase the overall storage requirements a great deal. One additional link in each node can be a great help in the management of a structure:

TwoWayType = RECORD
        Parent : ↑*TwoWayNode*
        Value : {*value type or pointer type*
        Child : ARRAY[*1* . . *2*] OF ↑*TwoWayNode*
        Visit : INTEGER
        END

A *Visit* field is included because it is useful for indicating which subtrees of a node have been explored. A recursive traverse of a tree *twt* built of *TwoWayType* nodes does not differ from the recursive traverse of a binary tree, but the extra link simplifies an iterative traverse. (We assume in the following that the parent field of a root node (only) is *NIL*.) Only minor modification of BTT of section 8.4.1 is needed to walk a tree formed from such nodes.

In the traverse *TwoWayVisit* that follows, *p*↑.*Visit* is set to zero in each node when the traverse is complete. If the tree was initiated that way, *TwoWayVisit* leaves it unchanged. Clearly the *Child* field can be expanded to include more children.

TwoWayVisit includes the cases of preorder, inorder, and postorder processing by applying distinct processes at each of the three encounters with a node.

```
procedure TwoWayVisit(twt)                      {O(n)
  p ← twt
  while p ≠ NIL do
    case of p↑.Visit

        0 : PROCESS1( p)
            p↑.Visit ← 1
            q ← p↑.Child[1]
            if q ≠ NIL
              then p ← q
              endif

        1 : PROCESS2( p)
            p↑.Visit ← 2
            q ← p↑.Child[2]
            if q ≠ NIL
              then p ← q
              endif

        2 : PROCESS3( p)
            p↑.Visit ← 0
            p ← p↑.Parent

    endcase
  endwhile
  end {TwoWayVisit
```

To make a search of a two-way tree for a given value *Wanted,* it is only necessary to let *TwoWayVisit* be a function, let processes 2 and 3 be null processes, and let *PROCESS*1 be:

if $p↑.Value = Wanted$ **then return** p **endif**

Exercises E9.5 and E9.6 and problem P9.3 are appropriate at this point.

An immediate generalization is to assume x children and use *Child*[0] as the parent link:

```
procedure xWayVisit(xwt)                              {O(n)
  p ← xwt
  while p↑ ≠ NIL do
    with p do
      Visit ← (Visit + 1) MOD (x + 1)
      PROCESS(Visit,p)
      q ← Child[Visit]
      if (q ≠ NIL) OR (Visit = 0)
        then p ← q
        endif
      endwith
    endwhile
end {xWayVisit
```

9.4 *m*-Way Search Trees

A very general tree structure, as shown in Figure 9.2, can be built with nodes of the form:

```
mWayNode = RECORD
              Value : ARRAY[1 .. n] OF {value or pointer type
              Key : ARRAY[1 .. n] OF {key type
              ptr  : ARRAY[0 .. n] OF ↑mWayNode
            END {mWayNode
```

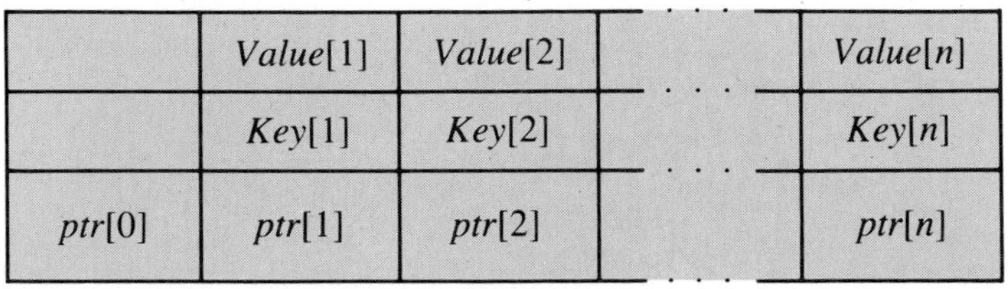

	Value[1]	Value[2]		Value[n]
	Key[1]	Key[2]		Key[n]
ptr[0]	ptr[1]	ptr[2]		ptr[n]

Figure 9.2

A tree with nodes of this kind is an *m-way search tree* (MWT) if no more than *m* of the pointers in *ptr* may be non-*NIL,* and suitable restrictions are placed on the keys.

The nodes of an MWT may be generalized by using *Value[i]* as a pointer to a value record, thereby creating an exogenous search tree. The search tree may then serve as a directory to a file too large to be contained in main (quick-access) memory. Generally, the records themselves reside in auxiliary memory devices, such as disks, as an *external file.* "Disk" is often used as a synonym for all such devices because it is by far the most common one in use. Any detailed timing analysis of a program that deals with access to disk storage must take into account the difference between fetching and storing on disk and in main memory. Generally, reading from and writing on a file that must be opened and closed by the operating system is many times slower than assignment from or to other variables and needs a separate accounting.

In some implementations, *n* may be contained as a field of the record, so that the record size may vary. Essentially, the "key" of a node of this type is multivalued; its value is the set of values in the entire array *Key,* and the search value is found in a node when any of *Key*[1] . . *Key*[*n*] match it. If *n* is large enough, the search through the *n* keys of a node may be a binary search, but the dominant factor in the time required for a search often is the number of disk accesses it uses. The number of disk accesses in a search is affected by several factors, such as the shape of the tree and where the key happens to be found in the tree if it is there. One factor that can be controlled by design is whether the key nodes are stored with the records or in a separate directory. An important parameter that can be controlled simply by programming is *m*, since it determines the minimal depth of the tree.

The formal shape restrictions for the *m*-way search tree structure follow:

- An empty tree is an *m*-way search tree.

- No more than *m* pointers of the array *ptr* point to internal nodes.

- $Key[i] < Key[i+1]$ for $1 \leq i < n$.

- All key values in $ptr[i]$ are less than $Key[i+1]$ for $0 \leq i < n$.

- All key values in $ptr[i]$ are greater than $Key[i]$ for $1 \leq i \leq n$. (There is no $Key[0]$.)

- All subtrees $ptr[i]$ for $0 \leq i \leq n$ are *m*-way search trees.

A 3-way search tree file with integer keys 1–9, 12, 15, 18, 21, and 24 with *n* = 2, *m* = 3 has the form shown in Figure 9.3. This file can readily be extended to a 3-way file with keys 1–26. Note that it is not particularly well balanced; with no restrictions on balance the extension can be done in a number of ways.

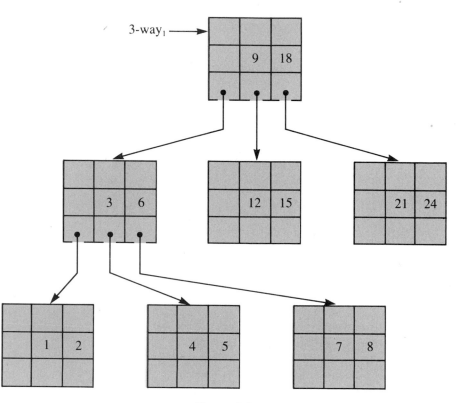

Figure 9.3

The graph of Faye's Family in Chapter 8 may be taken to indicate family relationships. Additional data, such as the ages of family members would be carried in the value field of records or in records that are the target of a pointer used as a value field. An alternate structure is a 4-way search tree where ages are used as keys (but then descendant information may be carried in some other way), as in Figure 9.4.

Exercise E9.7 is appropriate at this point.

Choices need to be made about including information in the nodes themselves to simplify the algorithms that deal with MWTs. Inclusion of less information in the nodes may complicate the algorithms but save node storage. The choice made here is to include quite a bit of information in the nodes, assuming them to be used as a directory to an external file (external to the MWT—the choice of storage location is an independent decision).

Since $m < n$ is allowed, some keys are *inactive* and may be so marked. The management of structures involving m-way search trees is eased if the active keys

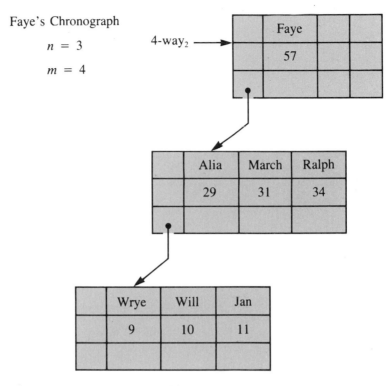

Faye's Chronograph

$n = 3$

$m = 4$

Figure 9.4

are to the left of the inactive keys. If the nodes are maintained in that form, only $m - 1$ key slots (*m* pointers) are needed in the nodes, but one more key slot is usually included because it is very convenient for maintenance of the file. Simplified management routines can be used if three fields are added to the record structure *mWayNode:*

- *Active: INTEGER* (the number of active keys) If this field is present, there is no need to mark active keys individually.

- *Up:* ↑ *mWayNode* (a pointer to the parent of a node, *Node*) If this field is used, *Node* itself is sufficient to locate its parent node.

- *UpKey: INTEGER* (the key in the parent node that points to the node)

As for all tree structures, random insertion and deletion in *m*-way search trees tends to randomize their shape and increase the search time in the worst case. To prevent this, MWTs can be balanced, like the AVL trees of section 8.7, and the *Red-Black Trees* of section 9.6. One form of relatively well-balanced MWT is the *B-tree*, treated in section 9.5. Management of balanced structures requires sophisticated algorithms and an increase in overhead and should be avoided for relatively small files of perhaps 100 nodes or less.

Search, insertion, and deletion in *m*-way search trees generally can be readily extracted from the procedures developed in section 9.5 for B-trees.

Problems P9.4 and P9.5 and program PG9.1 are appropriate at this point.

9.5 B-trees

An *m*-way search tree (MWT) can be balanced by maintaining the number of children of each node to be between limits. Limits of $INT(m/2)$ and *m* determine a *B-tree*. It is convenient to think of external nodes of an MWT as *failure* nodes.

With this terminology, an *m*-way search tree is a B-tree of order *m* if it is empty or:

- The root node has at least two children.

- All nodes except the root and failure nodes have at least $INT(m/2)$ and no more than *m* children.

- All failure nodes are on the same level. (Each path from root to leaf is the same length.)

Both 3-way$_1$ and 4-way$_2$ fail to qualify as B-trees, but a directory to Faye's Family may be stored in a B-tree as shown in Figure 9.5.

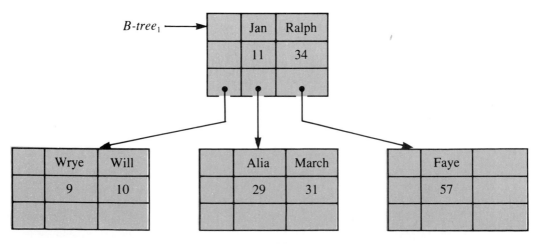

Figure 9.5

An MWT grows by adding to a node at the deepest level. A node to which an addition is made may split because the number of keys it is to contain has reached $m + 1$.

> **Note:** It is convenient to allow a B-tree of order m to have $m + 1$ children temporarily, so that splits can be delayed. If this is not done, a split can propagate up the tree. Delayed splits can be done on the way *down* the tree on any subsequent operation. Over a sequence of operations the effect is much the same, although in a strict sense, B-trees of order m can have nodes that are (temporarily) of order $m + 1$.

A node of order 5 in abbreviated form is shown in Figure 9.6. Here *a–e* may be external, but in general they are subtrees. With the addition of one more key, this node becomes *unstable* (ripe for splitting) if it is in a B-tree of order 5, as shown in Figure 9.7.

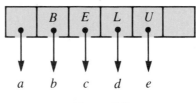

Figure 9.6

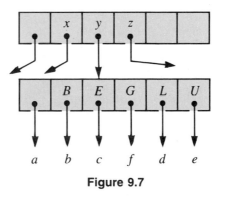

Figure 9.7

(Here f may be a subtree other than an external node if G is lifted from below by a splitting operation of the kind about to be described.)

When this node is encountered on the way down in a subsequent operation, it will be split as shown in Figure 9.8. Details of the management procedures are to be found in the sections that follow.

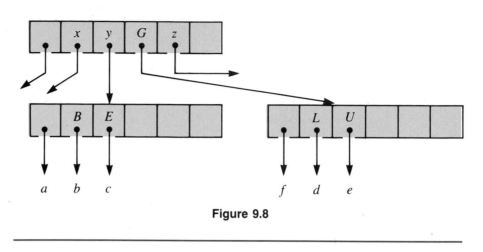

Figure 9.8

Problem P9.6 is appropriate at this point.

9.5.1 Creation and Splitting of B-tree Nodes

When a node splits, a middle key is moved up to the parent node. The growth and splitting can reach the root level of the tree, in which case a new root node may be created. The left child of the new root is the left half of the old root, and its right child the newly split off right half of the old root, as illustrated in Figure 9.9.

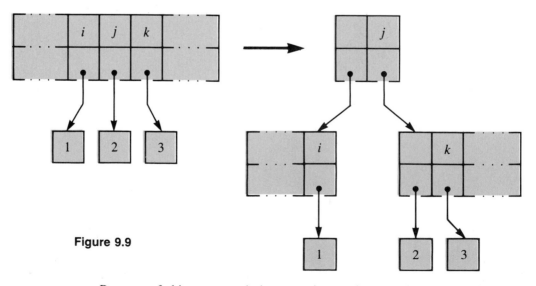

Figure 9.9

Because of this process, it is convenient to have a *Create* operation that attaches a given left child *LefTree* to an (empty) new root node *mwt:*

```
procedure Create(mwt,LefTree)                              {O(m)
  NEW(mwt)
  with mwt do
    ptr[0] ← LefTree
    Active ← 0
    Up ← NIL
    UpKey ← 0
    for i = 1 to m do
      ptr[i] ← NIL
      next i
    endwith
  end {Create
```

The right child may then be included by an operation *NewKeyIn*, which inserts a subtree, along with the key that locates it, into a specified position in a given node:

```
procedure NewKeyIn(Node,Ndex,NewKey,NewValue,SubTree)     {O(m)
  with Node ↑ do
  k ← Ndex
    for i = Active downto k do
      Value[i+1] ← Value[i]
      Key[i+1] ← Key[i]
      ptr[i+1] ← ptr[i]
      if ptr[i] ≠ NIL
        then ptr[i] ↑ .UpKey ← ptr[i] ↑ .UpKey + 1
        endif
      next i
    Value[k] ← NewValue
    Key[k] ← NewKey
    Active ← Active + 1
  endwith
  end {NewKeyIn
```

With these operations, an MWT may be started with a single record by:

```
Create(mwt,NIL)
NewKeyIn(mwt,1,NewKey,NewValue,NIL)
```

A new root node may be constructed with the old tree as its left child, and *SubTree* as its right child by:

```
old ← mwt
Create(mwt,old)
NewKeyIn(mwt,1,NewKey,NewValue,SubTree)
```

Addition and deletion of keys in an MWT depend upon a search for a key or for its appropriate position if it is absent. The core of the tree search is the scan across the keys of a single node to locate either the search key itself or the subtree in which further searching should take place:

```
procedure mWayScan(Node,ScanKey,Ndex,Found)        {O(m)
    Found ← FALSE                          {ScanKey may be larger
    Ndex ← Node ↑ .Active                  {than the keys in Node.
    for i = 1 to Node ↑ .Active do
      if ScanKey = Node ↑ .Key[i]          {The search is complete.
        then Ndex ← i
              Found ← TRUE
              return
      endif
      if ScanKey < Node ↑ .Key[i]          {The subtree to be searched
                                           {next has been located.
        then Ndex ← i − 1
              exit
      endif
    next i
  end {mWayScan
```

The search through the MWT as a whole accepts the location of the search key and follows the lead provided by *mWayScan*. Nodes with *m* active keys are split as encountered with procedure *mWaySplit*, which provides a suitable node, index, key, and subtree for insertion of one key from the split node into the next level up. The search then proceeds from the (altered) parent node:

```
procedure mWaySearch(mwt,SearchKey,Node,Ndex,Found)
    Node ← mwt
    Parent ← mwt                           {O(m · (mwt depth))
    while Node ≠ NIL do
      if Node ↑ .Active = m
        then mWaySplit(Node,Ndex,NewKey,NewValue,SubTree)
              NewKeyIn(Node,Ndex,NewKey,NewValue,SubTree)
      endif
      mWayScan(Node,SearchKey,Ndex,Found)
      if Found then return endif           {SearchKey is found in Node.
      Parent ← Node
      Node ← Node ↑ .ptr[Ndex]
    endwhile
    Node ← Parent                          {SearchKey is not in mwt.
  end {mWaySearch
```

The procedure that remains to be specified is *mWaySplit*. An example will illustrate how a node q is split. Suppose that m is 5, the parent of q is p, and x is the ancestor key of q: $x = p \uparrow .Key[q \uparrow .UpKey]$, as shown in Figure 9.10.

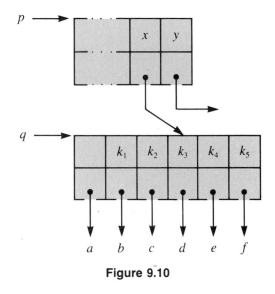

Figure 9.10

Since q has six children, it must be split. The "middle" key, k_3, is moved up to p, inserted into p between keys x and y, and then keys k_4 and k_5 moved to a new subtree, depicted in Figure 9.11.

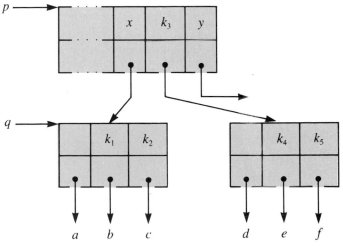

Figure 9.11

The special case that must be considered is when q is the root of the MWT, and so p must be created empty with q as its left child and become the root of the tree. The mechanics are:

```
procedure mWaySplit(Node,Ndex,NewKey,NewValue,SubTree)      {O(m)
    k ← INT(Node↑.Active/2 + 1)              {The index of the key to
    NEW(r)                                    {be moved up one level.
    j ← 1
    for i = k + 1 to Node↑.Active do          {Shift the right
        r↑.Value[ j] ← Node↑.Value[i]         {half of Node to r
        r↑.Key[ j] ← Node↑.Key[i]
        r↑.ptr[ j] ← Node↑.ptr[i]
        j ← j + 1
    next i
    r↑.ptr[0] ← Node↑.ptr[k]
    j ← 0
    for i = k to Node↑.Active do
        if Node↑.ptr[i] ≠ NIL
            then Node↑.ptr[i]↑.Up ← r
                 Node↑.ptr[i]↑.UpKey ← j
        endif
        j ← j + 1
    next i
    NewValue ← Node↑.Value[k]
    NewKey ← Node↑.Key[k]
    SubTree ← r
    Node↑.Active ← k − 1
    r↑.Active ← m − k
    if Node↑.Up ≠ NIL                         {Insert the middle key at the next
        then  Ndex ← Node↑.UpKey + 1          {higher level, at the right of
              Node ← Node↑.Up                 {UpKey, locating the new node.
        else Create(mwt,mwt)                  {A new node is needed. The old
             Node↑.Up ← mwt                   {mwt is the left child of the new.
             Node↑.UpKey ← 0
             Node ← mwt
             Ndex ← 1
    endif
    r↑.Up ← Node
    r↑.UpKey ← Ndex
end {mWaySplit
```

Problem P9.7 is appropriate at this point.

9.5.2 Insertion into a B-tree

Insertions of (key) values into an MWT include two special cases: the MWT may be empty, or the value may be already present. In the absence of either special case, a search provides the location for the insertion. After the initial insertion, it may be necessary to repeatedly split a node into a pair of nodes, which calls for the insertion of a key one level higher to distinguish between them. The process stops when an expanded node has no more than $m - 1$ keys. (In particular, a newly created root node has only one.) With the assumption that the splitting process *mWaySplit* provides a suitable node, index, key, and subtree for insertion at the next level up by *NewKeyIn,* the insertion procedure is:

```
procedure mWayIn(mwt,SearchKey,NewValue)      {O(m · depth)
  if mwt = NIL
    then Create(mwt,NIL)
          NewKeyIn(mwt,1,SearchKey,NewValue,NIL)
            return
    endif
  mWaySearch(mwt,SearchKey,Node,Ndex,Found )
  if Found                                     {SearchKey is not really new.
    then return
    else NewKeyIn(Node,Ndex + 1,SearchKey,NewValue,NIL)
    endif
  end {mWayIn
```

The depth of an MWT containing n keys is restricted by the need for each node to have at least $b = \text{INT}(m/2)$ children and the restriction of failure nodes to the deepest level. If the effect of deletions upon the root node is ignored, there will be at least $(b + b^2)$ keys in an MWT of depth 2, $(b + b^2 + b^3)$ for one of depth 3, and so on. The depth is no more than $\text{INT}(\log_b n) + 1$, where $\log_b$ is the logarithm of base b.

Exercises E9.8 and E9.9 and problem P9.8 are appropriate at this point.

9.5.3 Deletion from a B-tree

Deletion from an interior node of a B-tree can be transformed to deletion that begins at a leaf node by simply exchanging the key to be deleted with the leftmost key in the subtree it locates. Location of the starting point is done by:

```
function LeftMost( p )                           {O(depth)}
   while p ↑ .ptr[0] ≠ NIL do
      p ← p ↑ .ptr[0]
      endwhile
   return p
   end {LeftMost
```

Reduction of a general deletion to a process *CutLeaf* that begins at a leaf node then becomes:

```
procedure mWayOut(mwt,OutKey)
   if mwt = NIL then return endif
   mWaySearch(mwt,OutKey,Node,Ndex,Found )
   if NOT Found then return endif              {since OutKey is already gone
   SubTree ← Node ↑ .ptr[Ndex]
   if SubTree ≠ NIL
      then  SmallChild ← LeftMost(Subtree)
            Node ↑ .Value[Ndex] ← SmallChild ↑ .Value[1]
            Node ↑ .Key[Ndex] ← SmallChild ↑ .Key[1]
            Node ← SmallChild
            Ndex ← 1
      endif
   CutLeaf(Node,Ndex)                {Now the key to be deleted is in a leaf node.
   end {mWayOut
```

The order of *mWayOut* is at least O(depth) because of *mWaySearch,* but then depends on *CutLeaf.* Hence it is $O(Max \{depth, O(CutLeaf)\})$.

Deletion of a key from a node can reduce the number of keys in the node below the allowed limit of $INT((m + 1)/2) - 1$. The "hole" that is created may be repairable by shifting a key from the nearest right sibling or, if that is not possible, from the nearest left sibling. If neither of these shifts is possible, a key is moved down from the parent level, and the shifting process may need to be repeated at that level. The shifting of keys from node to node may propagate to the root and possibly reduce the depth of the tree.

The actual compaction required to remove a key no longer needed in a specific node is:

```
procedure Compact(Node,Ndex)                          {O(m)
  with Node ↑ do
    for i ← Ndex to Active − 1 do
      Value[i] ← Value[i + 1]
      Key[i] ← Key[i + 1]
      if prt[i + 1] ≠ NIL
        then prt[i + 1] ↑ .UpKey ← 1
        endif
      ptr[Active] ← NIL
      Active ← Active − 1
      if Active = 0
        then if ptr[0] ≠ NIL
              then Up ↑ .ptr[UpKey] ← ptr[0]
              endif
            if Up ≠ NIL
              then Up ↑ .ptr[UpKey] ← ptr[0]
              else mwt ← ptr[0]
              endif
            DISPOSE(Node)
        endif
  endwith
end {Compact
```

The shift of a key to the left (or right) actually is a rotation involving the key of the parent node of the pair of nodes involved. The depleted example shown in Figure 9.12 is repaired with the rotation shown in Figure 9.13, followed by compaction.

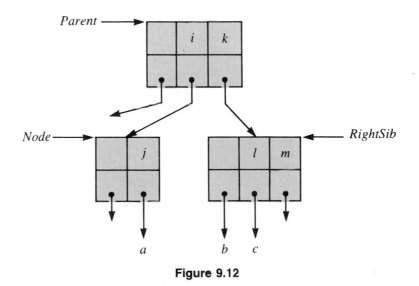

Figure 9.12

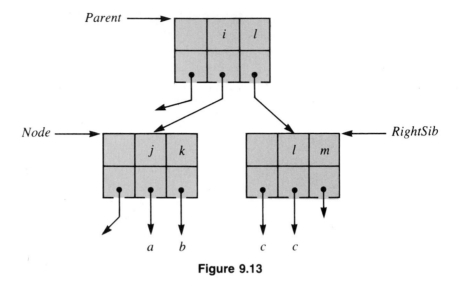

Figure 9.13

The details of the process are:

procedure *ShiftLeft*
    p ← *parent*
    NU ← *Node* ↑ .*UpKey* + *1*
    NA ← *Node* ↑ .*Active* + *1*
    RS ← *RightSib*
    NewKeyIn(Node,NA,p ↑ .*Key[NU],p* ↑ .*Value[NU],RS* ↑ .*ptr[0])*
    p ↑ .*Value[NU]* ← *RS* ↑ .*Value[1]*
    p ↑ .*Key[NU]* ← *RS* ↑ .*Key[1]*
    RS ↑ .*ptr[0]* ← *RS* ↑ .*ptr[1]*
    Compact(RS,1)
    end {*ShiftLeft*

The shift of a key to the right is very similar, as diagrammed in Figure 9.14 and
Figure 9.15, and is left to the problems for detail. It is followed by the removal of
the (redundant) rightmost key in *LeftSib* by compaction.

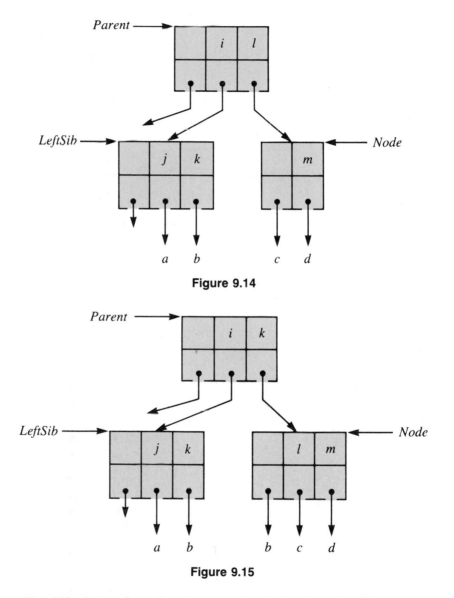

Figure 9.14

Figure 9.15

The shift of a key down from the parent level only takes place if both the right sibling and the left sibling of a node fail to have enough keys to shift. In that case, the node involved can be combined with one of them, since they cannot both be *NIL*. (If both were *NIL*, the parent node would contain no key, which is never allowed to happen.) The keys of the right node of a pair to be combined (Figure 9.16) can be incorporated into the left node of the pair, as shown in Figure 9.17. And this incorporation is followed by the deletion of the (redundant) right-most key from *Parent*.

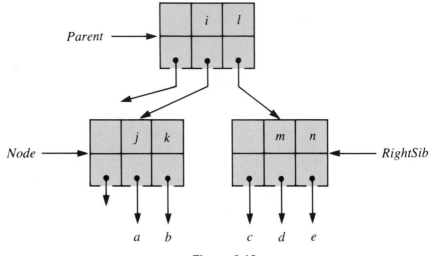

Figure 9.16

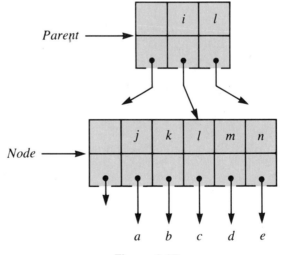

Figure 9.17

The procedure is:

```
procedure ShiftDown(Node,RightSib)            {O(m)
  p ← Parent
  NU ← Node ↑ .UpKey + 1
  NA ← Node ↑ .Active + 1
  RS ← RightSib
  NewKeyIn(Node,p ↑ .Key[NU],NA,p ↑ .Value[NU],RS ↑ .ptr[0])
  for i = 1 to RS ↑ .Active do
    NewKeyIn(Node,NA,RS ↑ .Key[i],RS ↑ .Value[i],RS ↑ .ptr[i])
    next i
  Ndex ← NU
  Node ← Parent
  DISPOSE(RS)
  Compact( p,NU)
  end {ShiftDown
```

Finally, with these tools, we can form *CutLeaf:*

```
procedure CutLeaf (Node,Ndex)
  Limit ← INT((m + 1)/2 − 1)                  {O(m · depth)
  while Node ≠ mwt do
    Compact(Node,Ndex)                        {Remove key from Node
    Size ← Node ↑ .Active
    if Size ≥ Limit then return endif         {since no reshaping is required.
    Parent ← Node ↑ .Up
    NU ← Node ↑ .UpKey + 1
    RightSib ← Parent ↑ .ptr[NU]
    LeftSib ← NIL
    if NU > 1 then LeftSib ← Parent ↑ .ptr[NU − 2] endif
    if RightSib ≠ NIL                         {Try to fill the hole at this level.
      then if RightSib ↑ .Active > Limit
            then ShiftLeft
                  return
            endif
      else if LeftSib ↑ .Active > Limit       {LeftSib cannot be NIL.
            then ShiftRight
                  return
            endif
      endif
    if RightSib ≠ NIL                         {A key is moved down.
      then ShiftDown(Node,RightSib)
      else ShiftDown(LeftSib,Node)
      endif
    endwhile                                  {The root node has been reached,
  Compact(Node,Ndex)                          {and a key shifted down from it.
  end {CutLeaf
```

Problem P9.9 and program PG9.2 are appropriate at this point, and problems P9.4 and P9.5 should be reconsidered.

■ 9.6 2–3–4 Trees   (optional)

The depth of binary search trees can be reduced by using nodes with more than two children and by maintaining balance defined by criteria that tend to keep all paths from root to leaf close to the same length, hence proportional to the logarithm of the number of nodes in the tree. The AVL trees of section 8.7 use balancing to reduce the tree depth, and the m-way search trees of section 9.3 use multichild nodes as a reduction technique. A third approach is to use nodes with 2,3, or 4 children only and keep all but the deepest level full. Such trees are sometimes called *2-3 trees* since the 4-child nodes are considered to be temporary, like the $(m + 1)$-child nodes of the m-way search trees in section 9.4. Like other search trees, 2-3 trees are often exogenous but are illustrated with endogenous examples for the sake of clarity.

Consider a search tree of 2-, 3-, and 4-child nodes formed from the sequence of keys L-O-O-K-I-N-G-W-I-T-H-O-U-T. Figure 9.18 shows what the first three stages might be.

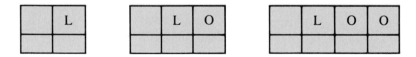

Figure 9.18

To add K it is necessary to split the 4-node before K is added, and it may be done as in Figure 9.19.

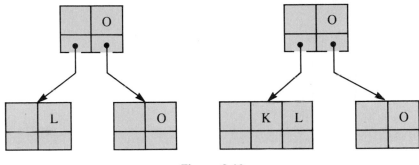

Figure 9.19

Then, in sequence, I and N are added in Figure 9.20. Then, G-W-I-T-H are added in Figure 9.21.

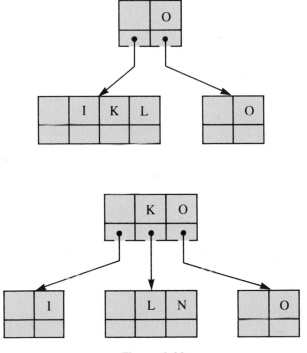

Figure 9.20

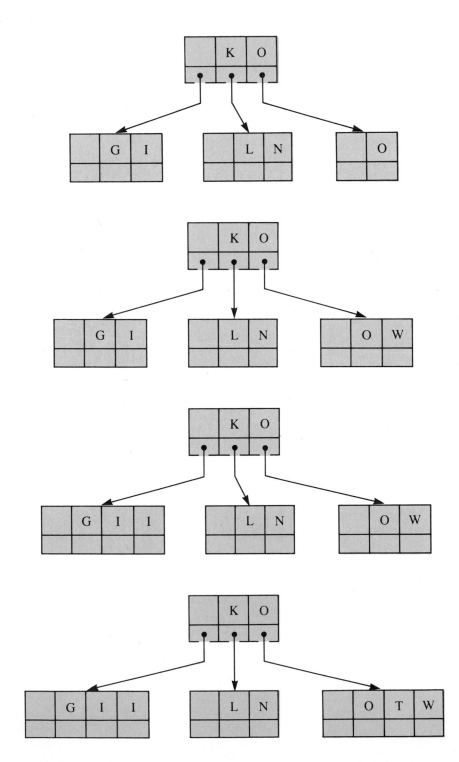

Figure 9.21

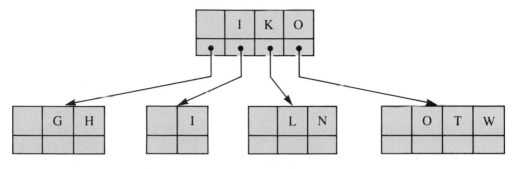

Figure 9.21 (*continued*)

The insertion of the O of O-U-T would cause the 4-node parent of a 4-node to be split. This entails traversing back up the tree, but it can be avoided if 4-nodes are split on the way *down* the tree, during insertion operations. This modification is shown in Figure 9.22.

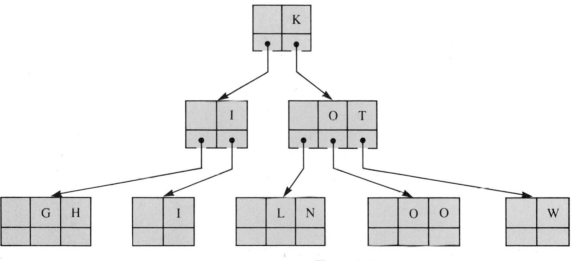

Figure 9.22

If the parent of a 4-node is split before the node itself, there are only two cases to consider, 2-node and 3-node parents, shown in Figures 9.23 and 9.24.

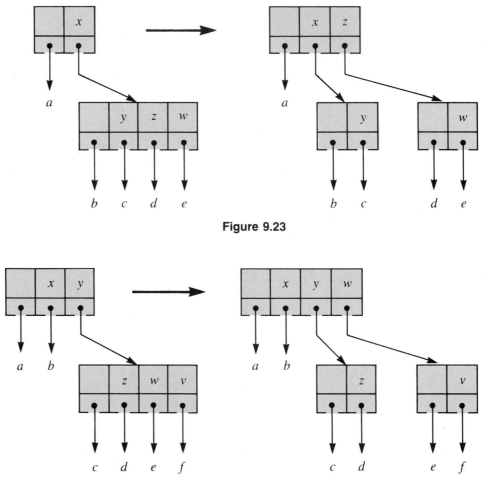

Figure 9.23

Figure 9.24

(The variations of each case provide no surprises.) Note that the depth of the tree is unaltered by these operations. A tree managed in this way begins with a single node; the tree depth is increased only when the root is a 4-node and is then split by an insertion operation, and the terminal nodes all occur at the same level, the deepest one. Such trees are nicely balanced.

The examples given here do not address deletion and they assume that keys may be duplicated. A complete management system needs to allow deletion and deal with duplicate keys, perhaps by representing them as lists or counts, or extending their keys to distinguish them, or simply disallowing them.

It is possible to manage 2-3-4-trees very much like *m*-way search trees, but there is an alternate way: they may be restructured as binary trees, called *Red-Black Trees*. This is the approach explored in Part II, section U.

Exercise E9.10 is appropriate at this point.

■ 9.7 Sets and Their Trees   (optional)

A *set* is a collection of items without order or duplication or internal structure. Sets are useful because they are simple in principle—they represent categories to which items belong or not. Direct management of sets is available in some languages, but not all. For example, in Pascal

```
IF Token IN CodeSymbols THEN Accept(Token)
```

tests to see if the value of variable *Token* is an element of the set *CodeSymbols*.

As a structure, sets must be implemented with other structures at some level. One common support for sets is a tree-like structure that links the elements of a set to the set identifier. For example, if the set *Even* is {16,2,4} and the set *Odd* is {3,1} then they may be indicated as shown in Figure 9.25.

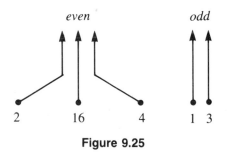

Figure 9.25

Because of the directions of the links, an item needs to be located before its relationship to a set can be determined. In practice the "items" are often indices to an array of pointers that determine a "set" (or several sets) by the relationships between them. The structure of the indices is commonly exogenous and associated with values that may be pointers to records. For convenience, we assume that the locating structure is an array A of records, each of which contains a pointer field p used to link the records together into a tree-like structure. The abbreviation $x \uparrow .p$ is used for $A[x] \uparrow .p$.

The links of a set tree point from child to parent, and one element of a set, sometimes called the *canonical element*, is used as the root of the tree representing the set. The canonical element is simply called the *root* (of the set) in what follows. Figure 9.26 shows the even-odd example of Figure 9.25 when these design decisions are made.

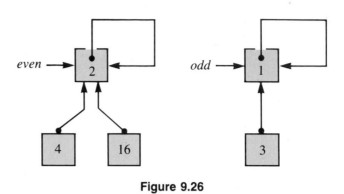

Figure 9.26

Finally, a collection of sets is often mananged so that the sets remain *disjoint:* they have no element in common. The entire collection of sets is then implemented with a *forest*—a collection of trees.

A minimal set of management operations is CREATE, UNION, and FIND. The operation UNION(x,y) forms and returns one set, called the *union* of the sets x and y, containing all of the elements of both. The operation FIND(x) returns the root and hence the set membership of element x. It is convenient to write both of these as functions with side effects. In the most straightforward form they are:

procedure *NewSet*(x)
$x \uparrow .p \leftarrow x$
end {*NewSet*

function *QuickUnion*(x,y)   {$O(1)$
$x \uparrow .p \leftarrow y$
return y
end {*QuickUnion*

function *QuickFind*(x)   {$O(depth)$
  while $x \uparrow .p \neq x$ **do**
  $x \leftarrow x \uparrow .p$
  endwhile
return x
end {*QuickFind*

Figure 9.27 shows the value of *QuickUnion* (2,1) applied to the even-odd example.

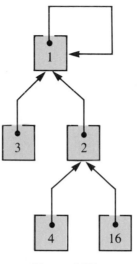

Figure 9.27

A set formed by an arbitrary sequence of UNIONS can be a tree of depth up to $d = n$, where n is the number of nodes in the set. *QuickFind* is $O(d)$, which is $O(n)$. Several ways that are used to reduce the average depth of set trees by modifying both the UNION and FIND operations will be treated here.

One way to reduce the depth of the tree returned by the UNION operation involves storing the count of the number of elements of a set in its root node. The UNION operation then chooses a root with maximal count as the root of the new tree. If the entire forest is stored in arrays, so that pointers are integer indices, the parent field and count field can be combined: the "parent" pointer is set to the negative value of the count for a root node. In a more general setting, separate fields are needed, and the UNION operation becomes:

procedure *CountUnion(x,y)* $\{O(1)\}$
   Total $\leftarrow x \uparrow .c + y \uparrow .c$
   if $x \uparrow .c > y \uparrow .c$
      then $y \uparrow .p \leftarrow x$
           $x \uparrow .c \leftarrow Total$
      else $x \uparrow .p \leftarrow y$
          $y \uparrow .c \leftarrow Total$
      endif
   end {*CountUnion*

CountUnion reduces set tree depths to some extent in a statistical sense but still allows a depth to reach n in the worst case. The cost of using UNION-FIND operations can be averaged over a *sequence* of operations, rather than simply noting the worst-case or average-case cost of individual operations. Such a cost is said to be *amortized* over the sequence, in either a worst-case or an average-case way. Accounting by amortization encourages *path compression*. Path compression uses information gathered during FIND operations to shorten the paths from leaf to root so that subsequent FIND operations will be faster. The price paid for this extended operation is regained later and lowers the amortized average for a sequence of operations.

The most drastic form of path compression is:

■   *The Collapsing Rule*. If y is a node on the path from x to its root node *Root*, then set $y \uparrow .p$ to *Root*.

With this modification:

```
function Find(x)                              {O(depth)
    Root ← x
    while Root ↑ .p ≠ Root do
        Root ← Root ↑ .p
    endwhile
    while x ≠ Root do                         {collapsing
        y ← x ↑ .p
        x ↑ .p ← Root
        x ← y
    endwhile
    return Root
end {Find
```

When applied to the even-odd example union, *Find*(16) returns 1 and has the side effect shown in Figure 9.28.

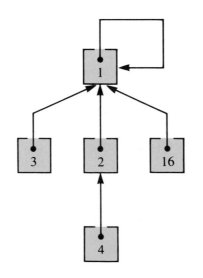

Figure 9.28

Various ways to apply path compression without making two passes over the path have been devised. One of them is *path halving*—a node on the path from leaf to root is repointed to its grandparent:

```
function HalFind(x)                              {O(depth)
    while x ≠ x↑.p do
        y ← x↑.p
        x↑.p ← y↑.p
        x ← y
    endwhile
    return x
end {HalFind
```

Finally, we may combine path compression with a more sophisticated UNION operation that uses a *rank* to decide which root shall be chosen as the root of the union. Ranks of singleton sets are initialized to zero and changed only during UNION operations. If $x↑.Rank > y↑.Rank$, then x becomes the new root. If $x↑.Rank = y↑.Rank$, then y is the new root, and its rank is incremented (by one). The operation is:

```
function Union(x,y)                              {O(1)
    if x↑.Rank > y↑.Rank
        then y↑.p ← x
            return x
        else if x↑.Rank = y↑.Rank
            then y↑.Rank ← y↑.Rank + 1
            endif
    endif
    x↑.p ← y
    return y
end {Union
```

The amortized behavior of sequences of path-compressed FIND and ranked UNION operations have been studied by Tarjan, and found to be very effective. (See [TARJAN, 1983].)

Problem P9.10 and program PG9.3 are appropriate at this point.

■ 9.8 Trees as Decision Tools   (optional)

A node of a tree can contain (or point to) information to be used to make a decision: a decision to carry out a process, to discontinue a traverse of the tree, or to describe the result of processing a subtree rooted at the node. Examination of the node value by a decision-making process results in an *action*. A tree built and used to aid in the making of decisions is a *decision tree*. A binary search tree is a simple example of a decision tree.

A decision tree can be specifically constructed to develop the structure of a program that solves a problem, as illustrated with the Eight Coins problem in Part II, section V.

One common application of trees as decision tools is their use in the calculation of probabilities: value fields at a node contain a set of probabilities that events will occur, and each event is associated with a child of the node. A node roots a (sub)tree if the event it represents is itself divided into events, in which case those events are associated with probabilities that sum to the node probability.

To illustrate, Irish folklore includes an interesting probability problem with possible historical significance. The story is that in olden times, on the twelfth birthday of an Irish maiden she was to choose six long grass stems and hold them in one hand. A friend tied the tops in three pairs, and the bottoms in three pairs. If, when the maiden opened her hand the stems formed a single loop, she would be married within the year. The probability question is: what is the chance of a single loop resulting from random pair selection? A probability tree can help to answer that question.

The three initial top ties form three linear pairs of stems (2-strands). Each bottom tie after that selects an event that either allows the possibility of a single ring or does not. The (probability) decision tree that supplies the answer is shown in Figure 9.29. This tree has three levels below the root, one for the result of each tie, and it has been *pruned*. The nodes 2, 3, and 5 are associated with short loops, and so the subtrees they head are of no interest in the search for the single loop.

Probabilities for the nodes are determined as follows:

- The first (bottom) tie chooses two stems from six, and there are 15 equally likely ways to do that. Of these 15 ways, 3 will form a 2-loop, and 12 a 4-strand. Hence the probability of node 2 is 1/5 and that of node 3 is $4/5 = p_1$.

- For tie 2, there are six equally likely pairs to be chosen from the four loose ends represented by node 3. One of these pairs forms a 2-loop, another forms a 4-loop, and the other four form 4-strands. Hence the probability of node 6 is $4/6 = p_2$.

- Tie 3 will form a 6-loop from node 6 with probability $1 = p_3$.

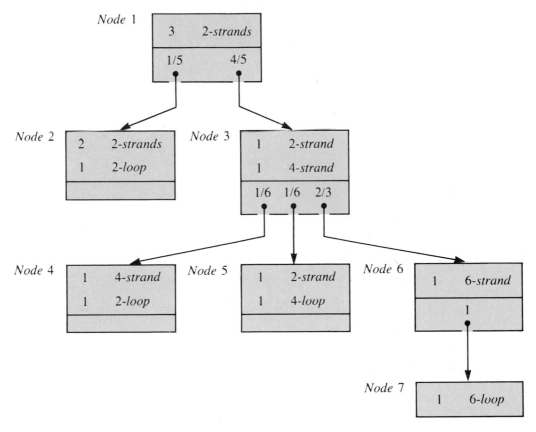

Figure 9.29

The probability that a single loop will result is $p_1 \times p_2 \times p_3 = 8/15$, intuitively quite high, and possibly a bit of a culture shock.

Clearly, it is better to approach such a problem with pencil and paper than to design a program to build and traverse the tree. With more complex problems, however, the tree becomes too large to deal with except by programming. An intermediate situation arises when a tree is used as a design guide for a program that does not actually form the tree involved in its conception. The Eight-Coins problem of Part II, section V, is such a problem.

■ 9.9 Game Trees   (optional)

Many games are played by making decisions based on the current state of the game, described perhaps by a board configuration or by several sets of cards. A game often has the *Markov property*—the effect of moves in the game depends only on its current state and not in any way on how that state was reached. A data structure can be formed with nodes that represent game positions (states), linked to nodes reachable in one move by a player. Such a structure is a tree, specifically a *game tree*.

The term *game tree* is most often applied to trees that represent two-person games where the players alternate. One player, player *Odd*, may be associated with levels 1,3,5, . . ., and the other, player *Even*, with levels 2,4,6, . . . of the game tree.

If moves are not made at random (as they are in the probability decision tree of section 9.8), a player needs to assign values to subtrees rooted at the current node in order to *evaluate* the choices of moves.

There is an astronomical number of nodes in the tree of most games complex enough to be interesting. The restriction to games with finite trees does not resolve this problem (there are believed to be about 10^{100} nodes in a game tree for chess), and so a variety of ways to limit a search for the "best next move" are needed. Limiting is a matter of pruning the tree—removing subtrees or at least removing them from consideration. Some pruning is based on hard (explicit) information and some is *heuristic*—based on the application of a "rule of thumb that usually works."

Discussions of node evaluation and pruning are to be found in Part II, section W.

Summary

Access paths to data are restricted by most of the structures studied in previous chapters. Such paths can be enhanced by general techniques of exogeny and *indirection*. Indirection is applied to *ShellSort* and to heaps in section 9.1, but it can be applied to all data structures. The major benefit of indirection is that pointers (or indices) are moved, rather than bulky records. Exogeny gains its greatest power from application to *external files* because of the difference in time scale between access to main memory and to secondary memory.

Even though any tree can be modeled with a binary tree, in some applications a natural organization uses nodes with more than two children. Given the same number of nodes, the minimal depth of a tree decreases with the number of allowed children, an advantage for directories of external files.

To take advantage of the minimal possible depth requires approaching it, which implies that balance will be maintained over a *sequence* of deletion and insertion operations. The cost of maintenance for a single operation is increased in order to decrease the cost *amortized* over the long term. One common technique applied to multiway search trees is to allow nodes to grow a bit larger than desired and split them on the way down in a later operation. Another is to rotate nodes around a *pivot* to move a structure in the direction of balance. Rotations propagate through the tree during deletions to restore balance.

Two tree structures in common use for (endogenous or exogenous) directories for large files are introduced here, (joining the AVL trees of section 8.7 in that role). One is *m*-way search trees (section 9.4) and their balanced form, B-trees (section 9.5). The other is the binary tree emulation of 2-3-4 trees (section 9.6), Red-Black trees (treated in Part II, section U). Maintenance of B-trees is probably easier than for any other form, and they are popular in practice.

Trees are used as a crutch to the intelligent sifting of information in a number of ways, as indicated in section 9.7. One use of trees is simply as an aid in the design of a program, and the Eight-Coins problem of Part II, Section V, serves as an example. Another is the use of trees within the large, complex, and increasingly important area of artificial intelligence. A brief touch of that role is exhibited in section 9.9 and Part II, section W, in the form of game trees and their pruning.

Exercises   immediate applications of the text material

E9.1   Trace the action of *ShellSort* on the letter sequence: S-H-E-L-L-E-Y-B-E-A-N-S.

E9.2   Trace the action of *MakeHeap* as an inverse-enhanced indirect heap on the letter sequence: T-R-A-S-H-B-I-N-J-O-E.

E9.3   Separately sort the sequences S-H-U-F-F-L-E and B-U-C-K-A-N-D-W-I-N-G and merge them by tracing the action of *StraightMerge* on them.

E9.4   What is the maximum number of nodes in a tree with six levels if the interior nodes have (**a**) 2 children, (**b**) 5 children, or (**c**) 10 children?

E9.5   Rewrite *TwoWayVisit* assuming that the leaf nodes are their own children.

E9.6   Rewrite *TwoWayVisit* assuming that the parent of the root node and the children of leaf nodes are the universal sentinel node *u*.

E9.7   Redraw Faye's Chronograph of section 9.4 as a 3-way search tree.

E9.8   Draw the sequence of 4-way B-trees created from keys that are names of months, entered in calendar order with *mWayIn* and kept in alphabetical order.

E9.9   Draw the sequence of 4-way B-trees created from keys that are the names of months, entered in alphabetical order with *mWayIn* and kept in calendar order.

E9.10   Trace the construction of a 2-3-4 tree from the letter sequence: S-T-R-A-N-G-E-D-U-M-B-O-W-L.

Problems not immediate, but requiring no major extensions of the text material

P9.1 Rewrite *BubbleSort* (Chapter 1) as an indirect procedure.

P9.2 What is the maximum number of nodes in a tree with L levels if the interior nodes have m children?

P9.3 Rewrite *TwoWayVisit* of section 9.3 specifically to be a traverse of each of the types inorder, preorder, postorder, displaying the node values in the appropriate order.

P9.4 (Difficult.) Write a procedure that inserts nodes into m-way search trees, without regard for balance.

P9.5 (Difficult.) Write a procedure that deletes nodes from m-way search trees, without regard for balance.

P9.6 Trace the creation of a 3-way B-tree by adding the letters: O-P-T-I-M-A-L-S-C-U-D-E-R-Y one at a time.

P9.7 Rewrite procedure *mWayScan* of section 9.5 so that it uses a binary search.

P9.8 Trace the behavior of *mWaySearch,* looking for your birthday month in the final structures created in E9.8 and E9.9.

P9.9 Show the result of applying *mWayOut* to the removal of the summer months June, July, and August from the structures created in E9.8 and E9.9.

P9.10 Calendar months are to be placed in the same set if they are in the same pair of seasons: Spring–Summer and Fall–Winter. For each of the set-management techniques from section 9.7, what is the final configuration (set-trees) of the months entered in alphabetical order? Assume that a month record has a tag field that contains one of the values SS or FW. A month is attached to the most recently entered node if it is in the same season pair; otherwise the new month starts a new tree. The months are to be entered in the order: April, Dec, Aug, July, June, Feb, May, Sept, Jan, March, Nov, Oct. After entry of Oct, union each tree through the nearest node of the same season pair on its left.

(a) No compaction (*QuickUnion,QuickFind*)

(b) Root-count (*CountUnion*)

(c) Collapsing rule (*Find*)

(d) Path halving (*HalFind*)

(e) Ranking (*Union*)

Programs   for trying it yourself

PG9.1 Write a program to manage a 3-way search-tree for alphabetic keys with numerical values. Use it to build a search tree of the calendar months 1–12 with keys January–December, inserted in that order. Display the resulting tree, delete the summer months June–August, and display again. (Balance is *not* required.)

PG9.2 Write a program that manages a B-tree as described for the *m*-way search tree in PG9.1.

PG9.3 Write a program that manages ranked sets of calendar months as described in P9.10, option (**e**). The forest created by each addition of a month should be displayed. If the program is written in a language with built-in set manipulation, it is *not* to be used.

Graph
Algorithms

> **Note:** The terminology applied to graphs and to digraphs is distinct in the mathematical literature. The sequence of terms (chain, simple chain, closed chain, circuit) applied to graphs corresponds directly to terms (path, simple path, closed path, cycle) applied to directed graphs. The distinction lies in whether or not edges are directional. In a program, links are directional. If all links in a structure are double links, it models a graph rather than a digraph. However, the algorithms that search for simple chains in a graph, for example, actually locate simple paths. Such algorithms take a simpler form when working within a graph than they do if starting with a digraph. Nevertheless, the terminology (path, simple path, closed path, and cycle) are firmly entrenched in the literature in descriptions of graph algorithms. The standard terminology will be followed here without further apology.

A *graph* is a collection of *V* vertices and *E* (directed or undirected) edges that join the vertices into pairs (see section 6.3). This abstraction reflects a very common pattern; the number of systems and relationships that can be modeled by a graph is huge. An example of a graph that will be called G_1 in this chapter is shown in Figure 10.1.

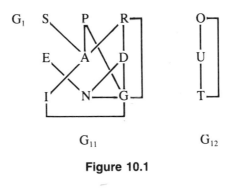

G_{11} G_{12}

Figure 10.1

G_1 has two *components:* subgraphs G_{11} with vertices {S-P-R-E-A-D-I-N-G} and G_{12} with vertices {O-U-T}. A component is a maximal subgraph having a sequence of edges connecting any two vertices in it.

A sequence of edges connecting two vertices is a *path,* but the sequence of vertices encountered as endpoints of the edges defines the same path. A *simple path* is one that repeats no vertex. For example, (S,A,P) specifies a simple path from S to P but (S,A,I,G,D,R,A,P) is not simple.

A *cycle* is a path that is simple except that the first and last vertices are the same. For example, (R,D,G,R) is a cycle.

A graph with no cycles is a *tree.* A collection of trees is a *forest.* Every connected component of a graph contains *spanning trees,* trees that contain every vertex in the graph. One spanning forest of G_1 is shown in Figure 10.2.

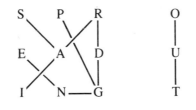

ST$_{11}$ ST$_{12}$

Figure 10.2

Edges may have a cost (distance, weight) associated with them, as in a model of an airline-route system. A *minimal spanning tree* is one with the minimal total cost of the included edges. With weighted edges, pairs of edges joined by paths have a *shortest path*— of minimal total weight. Neither minimal spanning trees nor shortest paths are unique, and the latter may not lie in the former.

Exercise E10.1 is appropriate at this point.

If two vertices are joined by an edge, they are *adjacent*. Graphs in which every pair of vertices is adjacent are *complete*. Graphs that approach completeness are *dense*. Those with few edges are *sparse*. As a working definition, graphs for which E is much closer to V than to V^2 are *sparse*.

A subgraph of a graph is *biconnected* if the removal of any one vertex leaves it connected.

Exercise E10.2 is appropriate at this point.

Given a representation of a graph, some of the processes that are of common interest are:

- Traverse it in one of a variety of ways, visiting every node.
- Determine its components.
- Determine whether there is a path between vertex v_1 and vertex v_2.
- Find a spanning tree in it.
- Find out if the graph contains a cycle.
- Determine its biconnected components.

Also of interest for weighted graphs:

- Find a minimal spanning tree in it.
- Find the shortest path between two vertices.

The efficiency of these operations depends on the data structure used to represent a graph as well as the algorithm used to traverse it.

10.1 Graph Representation

A graph can be represented by itself in the sense that every vertex can be represented as a node linked to all adjacent vertices. For an arbitrary graph of N vertices, $N - 1$ link-fields would be needed in the nodes. The vertices of a graph may have a limited *degree* (number of edges to adjacent vertices). A graph of degree 2 or 3 or 4 could reasonably be represented as itself and a general visitation algorithm such as those of section 7.7 or Part II, section M, applied to traverse its components. Determination of some of its attributes would be difficult, however.

As usual with data structures, a graph representation may be either endogenous or exogenous. Processing is simplified if it is assumed that the structure is exogenous, and access to the information that would appear in a vertex is reduced to an index, $1 \ldots N$. The index can be used as the argument of a function that maps it to the corresponding information, including a node identifier. In this chapter, $Tag(k)$ is taken to be the identifier of vertex k. In the other direction, if id is the identifier of a vertex, $Index(id)$ is the corresponding index. Hence $Index(Tag(k)) = k$ and $Tag(Index(id)) = id$.

We assume here that the raw data concerning vertices and the edges connecting them are available from a file, perhaps the system input file, and that the maps $Index$ and Tag can be created as the data is read. We assume that the number of vertices V and the number of edges E are also known. In practice, sentinel values or End-of-File flags may be used during input, and the entries counted. The function $Index$ in practice may be a search for an index field in a node, just the application of a Pascal ORD function, a search through a sorted table of identifiers, or several other possibilities.

The timing estimates applied to the algorithms of this chapter assume that $Index$ and Tag are $O(1)$.

The efficiency of the representation of a graph depends on whether it is sparse or dense and which algorithms are applied to that representation.

One common representation (introduced in section 6.3) is the *adjacency matrix*. In simple form, it is a Boolean matrix with $TRUE$ entries in row i and column j iff vertices i and j are adjacent. (Variations are a binary matrix using 1's and 0's or a $REAL$ matrix with values representing weights.) For some applications, it is convenient to set the main diagonal entries (at $(1,1),(2,2), \ldots$) to $TRUE$, and that is assumed in this chapter for unweighted graphs. The results for G_1 are shown in Table 10.1, where T is used for $TRUE$ and $FALSE$ entries are blank.

Table 10.1

	S	P	R	E	A	D	I	N	G	O	U	T
S	T				T							
P		T			T				T			
R			T	T	T				T			
E			T	T				T				
A	T	T	T		T		T					
D						T		T	T			
I					T		T	T	T			
N				T		T	T	T	T			
G		T	T			T	T	T	T			
O										T	T	T
U										T	T	T
T										T	T	T

If a graph is dense, an adjacency matrix representation is viable. Almost any algorithm applied to the structure will examine the V^2 entries in the matrix, but a dense graph has that order of edges to examine anyway.

Given V, E, and *Index*, the *Create* procedure for an adjacency-matrix representation is:

```
procedure CreateAM                        {O(V² + E)
    for i = 1 to V do
        for j = 1 to V do
            a[i,j] ← FALSE
        next j
    next i
    for i = 1 to V do a[i,i] ← TRUE next i
    for e = 1 to E do
        Read(id1,id2)
        i ← Index(id1)
        j ← Index(id2)
        a[i,j] ← TRUE
        a[j,i] ← TRUE
    next e
    end {CreateAM
```

For sparse graphs, a common representation of a graph is the *adjacency-list*, not to be confused with the circular-list structure applied to sparse matrices in section 6.3. In its abstract form, the adjacency listing for G_1 is:

```
S : A
P : A G
R : A D G
E : N
A : S P R I
D : R N G
I : A G
N : E D G
G : P R D I N
O : U T
U : O T
T : U O
```

Exercise E10.3 is appropriate at this point.

The adjacency-list structure used here is an array of pointers to linear lists, one pointer per vertex. The list associated with a vertex pointer contains nodes that represent edges. The nodes of such a list contain the index of the vertex that the edge connects to its header vertex. For example, the (partial) list

```
S : A
P : A G
  •
  •
  •
A : S P R I
  •
  •
  •
```

is actually represented by Figure 10.3 if S,P,R, . . .,T are nodes 1,2, . . .,12.

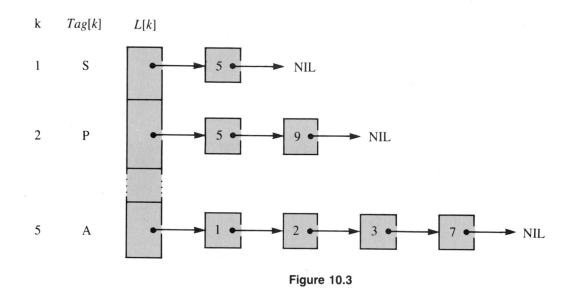

Figure 10.3

> **Note:** The link structure L can also be a linked list of header nodes, and the adjacency node values are then pointers to the headers.

Creation of the adjacency list with the simple structure illustrated above is done by:

procedure *CreateAL* $\{O(V + E)$
  for $k = 1$ **to** V **do**
    $L[k] \leftarrow$ NIL
    next k
  for $e = 1$ **to** E **do**
    Read($id1, id2$)
    $i \leftarrow Index(id1)$
    $j \leftarrow Index(id2)$
    NEW(p)
    $p \uparrow .Value \leftarrow j$
    $p \uparrow .Link \leftarrow L[i]$
    $L[i] \leftarrow p$
    NEW(p)
    $p \uparrow .Value \leftarrow i$
    $p \uparrow .Link \leftarrow L[j]$
    $L[j] \leftarrow p$
    next e
  end $\{CreateAL$

10.2 The Priority-Queue Traverse of a Graph

One way to traverse a graph is:

PQT: **repeat**

1. Process some vertex, *k*.

2. Put all vertices adjacent to *k* "on hold"; that is, place them in a holding structure and mark them to be in the state HELD, giving them a priority value. The other possible states for vertices are DONE (processed) and UNSEEN (not adjacent to any DONE vertex).

3. Choose a vertex from the holding structure as the new *k*.

until *all vertices are in the state DONE.*

In step 2 of *PQT*, a vertex *m* adjacent to *k* may already be in state HELD, in which case an algorithm based on *PQT* may or may not change the priority of *m*.

A *priority queue*, section 8.6.2, is the natural holding structure for such a traverse. In some algorithms derived from *PQT*, the priority-queue acts as a stack or as a queue, and should be replaced by the simpler and more efficient structure. In some applications of *PQT*, an unordered list may be an efficient representation of the holding structure, but it is used as a priority queue.

When vertices are held in a stack, step 3 of *PQT* chooses the most recently held vertex. However, the priority of vertices adjacent to it are (re)determined, even if they are already in the priority queue. In effect, they are moved to the top of the stack when reencountered. (The priority of vertices in state HELD are updated during the traverse.) The result of using a stack in this sense is *depth-first-search* (dfs). Starting at S in G_1:

DONE	HELD	UNSEEN
1. S	—	PREADINGOUT
2. S	A	PRE DINGOUT
1. SA		PRE DINGOUT
2. SA	PRI	E D NGOUT
1. SAI	PR	E D NGOUT
2. SAI	PRG	E D N OUT
1. SAIG	PR	E D N OUT
2. SAIG	PRDN	E OUT
1. SAIGN	PRD	E OUT
2. SAIGN	PRDE	OUT
1. SAIGNE	PRD	OUT
2. SAIGNE	PRD	OUT
1. SAIGNED	PR	OUT
2. SAIGNED	PR	OUT
1. SAIGNEDR	P	OUT
2. SAIGNEDR	P	OUT
1. SAIGNEDRP		OUT
2. SAIGNEDRP		OUT

At this point, all vertices reachable from S have been processed—a component has been discovered, and a new start must be made:

DONE	HELD	UNSEEN
1. SAIGNEDRPO		UT
2. SAIGNEDRPO	UT	
1. SAIGNEDRPOT	U	
2. SAIGNEDRPOT	U	
1. SAIGNEDRPOTU		
2. SAIGNEDRPOTU		

When vertices are held in a queue, step 3 of *PQT* chooses the longest-held vertex. The result is a *breadth-first-search* (bfs). Starting at S for G_1:

DONE	HELD	UNSEEN
1. S	-	PREADINGOUT
2. S	A	PRE DINGOUT
1. SA		PRE DINGOUT
2. SA	PRI	E D NGOUT
1. SAP	RI	E D NGOUT
2. SAP	RIG	E D N OUT
1. SAPR	IG	E D N OUT
2. SAPR	IGD	E N OUT
1. SAPRI	GD	E N OUT
2. 2SAPRI	GD	E N OUT
1. SAPRIG	D	E N OUT
2. SAPRIG	DN	E OUT
1. SAPRIGD	N	E OUT
2. SAPRIGD	N	E OUT
1. SAPRIGDN	E	OUT
2. SAPRIGDN	E	OUT
1. SAPRIGDNE		OUT
2. SAPRIGDNE		OUT

At this point, all vertices reachable from S have been processed—a component has been discovered, and a new start must be made:

DONE	HELD	UNSEEN
1. SAPRIGDNEO		UT
2. SAPRIGDNEO	UT	
1. SAPRIGDNEOU	T	
2. SAPRIGDNEOU	T	
1. SAPRIGDNEOUT		
2. SAPRIGDNEOUT		

A quite different traverse results when the graph edges are weighted, and the weights are used for priorities. A weighting of the edges of G_1 is shown in Figure 10.4.

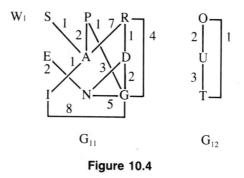

Figure 10.4

Since the weights are of *edges*, not vertices, the "weight" of a HELD vertex is continually updated to be the lowest weight of any edge connecting it to a vertex that is in state DONE. For W_1, starting at S:

DONE	HELD	UNSEEN
1. S	-	PREADINGOUT
2. S	A	PRE DINGOUT
1. SA		PRE DINGOUT
2. SA	PRI	E D NGOUT
1. SAI	PR	E D NGOUT
2. SAI	PRG	E D N OUT
1. SAIP	RG	E D N OUT
2. SAIP	RG	E D N OUT
1. SAIPG	R	E D N OUT
2. SAIPG	RDN	E OUT
1. SAIPGD	RN	E OUT
2. SAIPGD	RN	E OUT
1. SAIPGDR	N	E OUT
2. SAIPGDR	N	E OUT
1. SAIPGDRN		E OUT
2. SAIPGDRN	E	OUT
1. SAIPGDRNE		OUT
2. SAIPGDRNE		OUT

At this point, all vertices reachable from S have been processed—a component has been discovered, and a new start must be made:

DONE	HELD	UNSEEN
1. SAIPGDRNEO		UT
2. SAIPGDRNEO	UT	
1. SAIPGDRNEOT	U	
2. SAIPGDRNEOT	U	
1. SAIPGDRNEOTU		
2. SAIPGDRNEOTU		

> **Note:** The order in which vertices of a graph are processed is affected by their entry order, the vertex at which the search begins, the process of insertion into an adjacency list, and perhaps some details of the implementation of *PQT*. There is not *one* breadth-first or depth-first search, but there is a family of them.

A number of refinements may be made to *PQT* in implementation, and they involve several variables and lists. For sparse graphs supported on an adjacency-list with link-header list L, a traverse uses the following:

- *Unseen* is the state value of a vertex not yet encountered in a traverse. It is treated here as an integer larger than any other priority.

- *Root* is a state value attained only by the first vertex of a component— one that is processed before any vertex to which it is adjacent is processed. Zero is usually used for the value of *Root*.

- T counts the number of vertices removed from state UNSEEN—hence, the number of vertices that have been encountered in the traverse at any point in the traverse.

- $PQ[1 .. V]$ is an indirect priority queue in which low values have a high priority. It contains indices of vertices. It does not appear explicitly in the algorithm but is used by the priority-queue operators. *All* vertices are initially placed in *PQ,* with priority *Unseen.* The value *Unseen* is chosen to be greater than the priority of any HELD or DONE vertex. Vertices are removed one at a time with function *Remove,* as they are processed.

- *Priority* is a variable calculated to sequence the removals from PQ and hence its definition varies from one application to another. It may be set to T for breadth-first search, $V - T$ for depth-first search, or an edge-weight to find a minimum spanning tree.

- $OnPQ[1 .. V]$ is a Boolean list for which $OnPQ[k]$ is *TRUE* if the kth vertex is still in PQ.

- $State[1 .. V]$ contains the priorities of the vertices in PQ. When changed, the values in *State* are set to a *Priority* value.

- $L[1 .. V]$ is the list of adjacency-list headers.

- *Remove* returns and deletes the front value of PQ.

With these tools an adjacency-list traverse is:

```
procedure SparsePQT
  T ← 0
  for k = 1 to V do                      {initialization
    State[k] ← Unseen
    OnPQ[k] ← TRUE
    PROCESS0(k)
  next k
  CreatePQ                               {queue all vertices
  repeat                                 {retrieve them one by one
    k ← Remove
    OnPQ[k] ← FALSE
    PROCESS1(k)
    if State[k] = Unseen                 {a new component starts
      then State[k] ← Root
           T ← T + 1
           PROCESS2(k)
    endif
    p ← L[k]                             {check the adjacency-list
    while p ≠ NIL do
      m ← p↑.Value
      if OnPQ[m]
        then if State[m] = Unseen
               then T ← T + 1
                    PROCESS3(k)
             endif
             if State[m] > Priority
               then State[m] ← Priority
                    PROCESS4(k)
             endif
      endif
      p ← p↑.Link
    endwhile
  until Empty(PQ)
end {SparsePQT
```

Processes 0,1,2,3, and 4 are null or simple or elaborate, depending on the application. If they are all null, then the traverse leaves no trace of its passage and builds no structures suitable for further processing in an application; hence, their use is precisely to build a legacy.

An adjacency matrix form of this procedure, *DensePQT*, can be constructed by simply replacing the **while** loop with:

```
for m = 1 to V do      {check the adjacency-list
  if a[k,m]
    then if OnPQ[m]
              then T ← T + 1
                  PROCESS3(k)
          endif
      if State[m] > Priority
          then State[m] ← Priority
              PROCESS4(k)
      endif
  endif
next m
```

10.3 Applications of Priority-Queue Traverses

This section describes information that is easily extracted during a priority-queue traverse of a graph.

The Process Sequence
The list of vertices in the sequence in which they are processed (in *PROCESS*1) is the *process sequence*. The entry for the root of a component in the process sequence is negated to make component detection easier. The list is kept in $Done[1 .. V]$ and generated by the inclusions:

$$
\begin{array}{ll}
: & c \leftarrow 0 \\
PROCESS1 : & c \leftarrow c + 1 \\
 & Done[c] \leftarrow k \\
PROCESS2 : & Done[c] \leftarrow -Done[c]
\end{array}
$$

The Process Map
The list that specifies at what position in the sequence a vertex is processed is the *process map*. In effect, it is an inverse of (the absolute value of) *Done* and kept in $WhenDone[1 .. V]$. $WhenDone[k] = c$ iff $|Done[c]| = k$. *WhenDone* is generated simply by changing the *PROCESS1* generation of *Done* to:

$$
\begin{array}{ll}
PROCESS1 : & c \leftarrow c + 1 \\
 & Done[c] \leftarrow k \\
 & WhenDone[k] \leftarrow c
\end{array}
$$

The Parent

A vertex k that determines the final priority of a vertex m is its *Parent*, kept in *Parent*[1 .. V]. Parenting data is gathered by:

PROCESS0 : *Parent*[k] ← 0
PROCESS4 : *Parent*[m] ← k

The Ancestor

A vertex that pulls the vertex m into the HELD state from the UNSEEN state is the earliest-processed vertex adjacent to m and is called its *ancestor*. The list *Ancestor*[1 .. V] can be generated with:

PROCESS0 : *Ancestor*[k] ← *Unseen*
PROCESS2 : *Ancestor*[k] ← 0
PROCESS3 : *Ancestor*[m] ← k

The data-collection lists *Done*, *WhenDone*, *Parent*, and *Ancestor* are all generated for essentially no execution-time cost with $O(1)$ operations. However, they do not directly answer the questions about graphs mentioned at the beginning of this chapter and certainly they do not represent the most convenient form for working with components, paths, and spanning trees. Mining the ore they represent is the subject of the subsections that follow.

Note: Almost any application of the preceding data-acquisition lists can be done more succinctly and often more efficiently by incorporating their ultimate use into the traverse itself. The advantage of using them as a standard data-collection format is just that—a system one can come to know and understand and apply quickly.

A trace of the generation of the data-lists by a dfs on G_1, starting at S is:

S = State A = Ancestor D = Done
Pa = Parent P = Priority W = WhenDone

Tag	k	m	T	P	S	W	D	A	Pa
S	1					1	-1	0	0
		5	2	10	10			1	1
A	5					2	5	1	1
		2	3	9	9			5	5
		3	4	8	8			5	5
		7	5	7	7			5	5
I	7					3	7	5	5
		9	6	6	6				
G	9					4	9	7	7
		2	6	6	6			5	9
		3	6	6	6			5	9
		6	7	5	5			9	9
		8	8	4	4			9	9
N	8					5	8	9	9
		6	8	4	4			9	8
		4	9	3	3			8	8
E	4					6	4	8	8
D	6					7	6	9	8
		3	9	3	3			5	6
R	3					8	3	5	6
P	2					9	2	5	6
O	10					10	-10	0	0
		11	11	1	1			10	10
		12	12	0	0			10	10
T	12					11	12	10	10
		11	12	0	0			10	12
U	11					12	11	10	12

The resulting values are summarized in Table 10.2.

Table 10.2

Tag[k]	k	Ancestor[k]	Parent[k]	WhenDone[k]	Done[k]
S	1	0	0	1	-1
P	2	5	8	9	5
R	3	5	6	8	7
E	4	8	8	6	9
A	5	1	1	2	8
D	6	9	8	7	4
I	7	5	5	3	6
N	8	9	9	5	3
G	9	7	7	4	2
O	10	0	0	10	-10
U	11	10	12	12	12
T	12	10	10	11	11

Program PG10.1 is appropriate at this point.

10.3.1 Tracking a Traverse

The progress of a traverse may be printed (or listed on a file) with:

PROCESS*1* : *Write(Tag[k])*

Components may be separated in the listing with a marker (such as an End-of-Linc) by moving the *Write* below the test for *Unseen* and adding:

PROCESS*2* : *Write(EOLN)*

This separation is possible because, if the vertex pulled from *PQ* is in state UNSEEN, it is not reachable from any previously processed vertex and must be in a different component.

Because *Remove* is $O(\ln V)$ when *PQ* is implemented as a heap, and every edge and every vertex is cxamined, traversal time for *SparsePQT* is seen to be $O((E + V) \ln V)$. This can be improved to $O(E + V)$ when *PQ* is replaced by a stack (for dfs) or a queue (for bfs). For *DensePQT* the corresponding times are $O(V^2 \ln V)$ and $O(V^2)$.

10.3.2 Path-Connections and Components

A linear scan of *Done* yields sets of vertices in the same component, separated by root vertices with negative entries. In a computing system that supports set variables and manages them efficiently, the component data may be shifted into sets during a linear scan for further processing.

If *Done* itself is to be used to decide whether two vertices are path-connected (in the same component), it is necessary to scan the component that contains one of them. If $WhenDone[k_1] = c_1$ and $WhenDone[k_2] = c_2$, then k_1 and k_2 are in the same component iff there is no negative entry between c_1 and c_2 in *Done*. This is an $O(V)$ operation for each pair of interest. If it is to be repeated, a scan can be used to build a list of component-completion times, a binary search used to place c_1 between two of them, and a quick check used to see if c_2 lies between the same pair of component-completion times.

The union-find operations of section 9.7 can be applied to *Parent* to build set structures within which the search for a common root node efficiently answers the question of whether two vertices are in the same component.

An approach more efficient than union-find structures uses *Done* as a guide to construct fully collapsed component sets. The procedure *MakeSet* that follows points all of the vertices to the root node of their component, which has an index that is the current value of *SetLink*.

```
procedure MakeSet                              {O(V)
   for c = 1 to V do
      if Done[c] > 0
         then Set[c] ← SetLink
         else SetLink ← −Done[c]
               Set[c] ← SetLink
      endif
   next c
end {MakeSet
```

The Boolean expression for path connection is then:

$$Set[k1] = Set[k2]$$

> **Note:** *MakeSet* works for T and $V - T$ priorities because with their use, root nodes are processed before other nodes in any component. It will not suffice otherwise.
>
> The root nodes in *Set* are self-referencing, as an alternative to root indices of value 0.

The logic of *MakeSet* can be incorporated into *SparsePRT* (or *DensePQT*) by:

$$: c \leftarrow 0$$
PROCESS*1* : $c \leftarrow c + 1$
$$Done[c] \leftarrow k$$
PROCESS*2* : $SetLink \leftarrow Done[c]$
$$Set[c] \leftarrow SetLink$$
$$Done[c] \leftarrow -Done[c]$$
else $Set[c] \leftarrow SetLink$

If *Done* is not needed for any other purpose, it may be dispensed with:

$$: c \leftarrow 0$$
PROCESS*1* : $c \leftarrow c + 1$
PROCESS*2* : $SetLink \leftarrow k$
$$Set[c] \leftarrow SetLink$$
else $Set[c] \leftarrow SetLink$

Exercise E10.4 is appropriate at this point.

10.3.3 Spanning Forests

The data in *Parent* determines a spanning forest, but the links point from child to parent, in the wrong direction for most tree processing. A treeform that can be traversed from root to leaf is an adjacency-list that omits links extraneous to the forest. Figure 10.5 shows the dfs traverse of G_1 beginning at S.

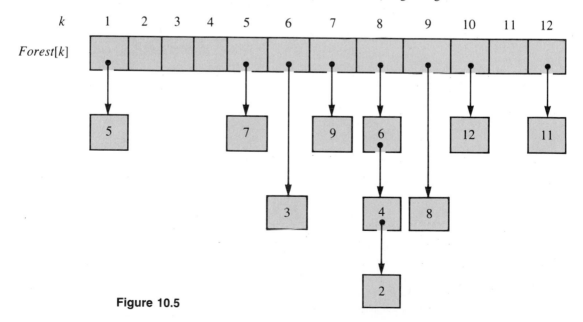

Figure 10.5

Such a forest can be formed from a linear scan of *Parent:*

```
procedure MakeForest                                    {O(V)
   for k = 1 to V do
      Forest[k] ← NIL
   next k
   for k = 1 to V do
      p ← Parent[k]
      if p ≠ 0
         then NEW(q)
            q↑.Value ← k
            q↑.Link ← Forest[p]↑.Link
            Forest[p]↑.Link ← q
      endif
   next k
end {MakeForest
```

This process can be included in *SparsePQT* (or *DensePQT*) by:

```
PROCESS0 : Parent[k] ← 0
              Forest[k] ← NIL
PROCESS2 : else p ← Parent[k]
              NEW(q)
              q↑.Value ← k
              q↑.Link ← Forest[p]↑.Link
              Forest[p]↑.Link ← q
PROCESS4 : Parent[m] ← k
```

The data in *Ancestor* also determine a spanning forest. It may be generated directly in processes 0, 2, and 3 without the use of the list *Ancestor.*

Exercise E10.5, problem P10.1, and program PG10.2 are appropriate at this point.

10.3.4 Cycle Testing

A connected graph G has a cycle iff a spanning tree does not contain all of the edges of G. An extra edge (v_1, v_2) provides a path (not in the tree) between v_1 and v_2; and, together with the connecting path through the tree, it forms a cycle. A graph has no edges that connect trees in its spanning forest, and so any edge not in the forest forms a cycle within a component.

For any edge (k,m) one vertex, say m, is processed later than the other and so is encountered in the adjacency loop of the other. An extra edge can be detected as an adjacency of m to a vertex n where n is processed prior to k. In simplest terms, when this occurs, $OnPQ[m]$ is *TRUE* and $State[m] \neq Unseen$ in the adjacency loop of k. The test for a cycle in dfs is then:

PROCESS0 : *Cycle* ← FALSE
PROCESS3 : **else** *Cycle* ← TRUE

All cycles will be detected (and so could be counted or otherwise noted) because all edges are examined during the traverse.

10.3.5 Biconnectivity

An *articulation point* of a graph is a vertex with the property that, if it is removed, the remaining subgraph has more components than the original. All connecting paths between some parts of the graph and others must pass through it. The articulation points in the graph G_2 of Figure 10.6 are A, B, and C.

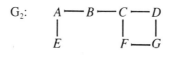

Figure 10.6

A biconnected graph is one where every pair of vertices is connected by at least two disjoint paths, so it has no articulation point through which all of the paths between some pair of vertices must pass. If the edge (E,F) is added to G_2 to form G_3, then G_3 is biconnected.

Biconnected components (maximal biconnected subgraphs) are *not* disjoint, in contrast to (connected) components. For example, G_4 in Figure 10.7 has two biconnected components joined by the articulation point K, which lies in both of them.

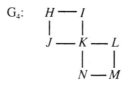

Figure 10.7

As a result, a reasonable goal in the exploration of the biconnectivity of a graph is the determination of its articulation points.

The information needed to detect articulation points is implicit in a search tree generated by dfs when used in conjunction with the edges not in the tree—*ghost links*.

The dfs search forest for G_1 by dfs starting at S has four ghost links, dashed in Figure 10.8. The dfs search tree for G_2 starting at C has one ghost link, as it must, since there are seven vertices and hence precisely six edges in the spanning tree itself. The seventh edge must be a ghost, as shown in Figure 10.9.

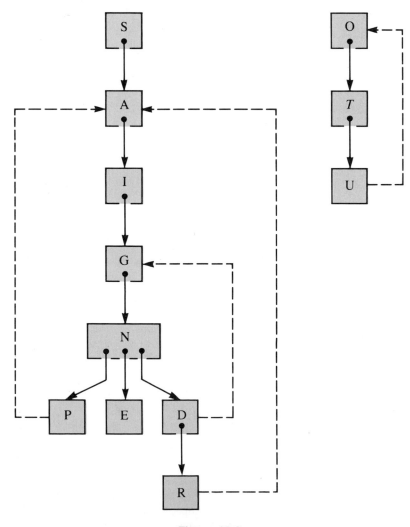

Figure 10.8

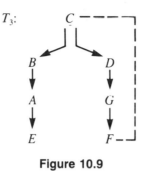

Figure 10.9

Here C is an articulation point because the entire graph cannot be searched from just one of its children—it is the *only* link between the subtrees rooted at its children.

> **Note:** All ghost links (edges left out of the dfs spanning tree) connect vertices to their ancestors. If there had been an edge connecting sibling subtrees, it would have been followed during the search of the first subtree to be processed.

As one consequence of this note:

■ If the root of a dfs search tree for a component has more than one child, it is an articulation point.

This form of articulation point can be detected by a linear pass through either *Done* (for negative entries) or *Parent* (for zero entries) or *Ancestor* (for zero entries) to find component roots. An $O(1)$ check of *Forest* detects multiple children for such vertices.

A ghost link, such as (C,F) in T_3 (Figure 10.9), forms a *cycle*. All of the vertices from the ancestor down through the search tree to the parent to the ghost link vertex and back through the ghost link to the ancestor lie in the cycle and hence form a biconnected subgraph. The possible articulation points in this cycle are vertices with children not on the cycle and the ancestor. (The ancestor may be the only bridge between the cycle to that part of the graph higher in the tree.)

If a vertex k has a child that roots a subtree with no ghost links to vertices higher in the tree than k, then removal of k disconnects this subtree from the parent of k (and higher nodes). In general:

■ A nonroot vertex k is an articulation point iff it has a child that roots a subtree that has no ghost links to vertices higher in the tree than k. (Vertices higher in the tree are necessarily processed earlier.)

We define the *minimum completion time* (mct) of a collection of vertices $\{w_1, \ldots, w_m\}$ to be the minimum completion time of their collective ancestors (to which they are connected by either tree links or ghost links).

Suppose that the completion time of vertex p is c. Then c is an upper bound on the mct of each of the subtrees rooted by its children because there is a link or ghost link from p to each child. If *any* such subtree has an mct of c, p is an articulation point. The union of p and its subtrees has an mct that is the minimum of the subtree mcts and the completion time of the ancestor of p. Children are necessarily completed later than their parents. This suggests a way to search for articulation points:

1. Scan through *Done* backwards, assigning values to lists $UrMin[1 .. V]$ and $UrMax[1 .. V]$. They contain, respectively, the earliest known ancestor completion time and the latest known ancestor completion time of the subtrees rooted by the children of the vertex.

2. Suppose that vertex k is not a component root and its completion time is c. When the scan is complete, if $UrMax[k] = c$, then k is an articulation point.

3. The entries of $Children[0 .. V]$ are initialized to zero. During the scan $Children[k]$ is incremented whenever one of the children of k is processed. Then a component-root r for which $Children[r] > 1$ is true is an articulation point.

The resulting procedure is:

```
procedure Articulation                    {O(V)
    Children[0] ← 0                       {component counter
    for k = 1 to V do
        Children[k] ← 0
        p ← Parent[k]
        if p = 0 then p ← k endif
        UrMin[k] ← WhenDone[p]
        UrMax[k] ← 0
        next k
    for c = V downto 1 do
        k ← |Done[c]|
        p ← Parent[k]
        Children[p] ← Children[p] + 1
        if p ≠ 0
            then a ← Ancestor[k]
                 t ← WhenDone[a]
                 if UrMin[k] > t
                     then Min ← t
                     else Min ← UrMin[k]
                 endif
                 if Min < UrMin[p]
                     then UrMin[p] ← Min
                 endif
                 if Min > UrMax[p]
                     then UrMax[p] ← Min
                 endif
        endif
        next c
end {Articulation
```

Note that $UrMax[k]$ remains 0 for a leaf vertex k. A partial trace of the variables in *Articulation* from the data-acquisition lists of section 10.3 generated by the dfs search of G_1 is shown in Table 10.3.

Table 10.3

c	k	p	a	t	Min
12	11	12	10	10	10
11	12	10	10	10	10
10	10	0	–	–	–
9	2	8	5	2	2
8	3	6	5	2	2
7	6	8	9	4	2
6	4	8	5	5	5
.	.	.	.	.	.
.	.	.	.	.	.
.	.	.	.	.	.

Completion of this trace and determination of *UrMin* and *UrMax* are left for an exercise. However, the last entry shown is sufficient to determine that

$$UrMax[8] = 5$$

and hence vertex 8 is an articulation point.

Exercise E10.6, problem P10.2, and program PG10.3 are appropriate at this point.

10.4 Traverses of Weighted Graphs

The weighted graph W_1 of section 10.2 is reproduced as Figure 10.10 for convenience.

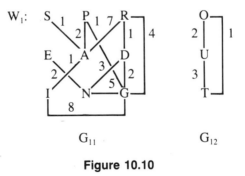

Figure 10.10

Weights are an attribute of edges, but a spanning tree that is to be traversed from vertex to vertex needs to have them attached to the vertices. Vertex weights are determined during the construction of the tree using the following definitions:

DEFINITION: *The weight of a vertex in state* UNSEEN *is Unseen. The weight of a vertex in state* HELD *is the minimum weight of the edges that connect it to vertices in state* DONE. *The weight of a vertex in state* DONE *is the weight with which it exits state* HELD.

The fundamental source of a weight is an adjacency-matrix entry or a field $p \uparrow .w$ in an adjacency-list edge node. During a traverse, weights of vertices are stored in *State,* since they determine priorities. The sum of the final *State* list is the total weight of a spanning forest.

When vertex m is processed in the adjacency loop of vertex k in *SparsePQT,* the value of the variable *Priority* is $p \uparrow .w$. (This is the weight of the edge connecting k and m.) It has already been traced for W_1 in section 10.2, and construction of the tree itself is covered in section 10.3.3.

The spanning tree derived from dfs by using weights as described above is a *minimal spanning tree,* produced by what is known as a *greedy method.* The crux of a greedy method algorithm is that it makes the best available move based on the information available at any stage of the process. In some situations, and forming a minimal spanning tree is one, a global optimum can be derived by repeatedly using a local optimum—the greedy method.

When the greedy method is implemented with *DensePQT,* it follows the scheme known as "Prim's Algorithm." An alternate scheme, known as "Kruskal's Algorithm" is to choose edges one at a time, lowest-weight first, rejecting those that would close a cycle if added to the forest. When complete—all vertices are included—there is one spanning tree for each component.

The traditional approach to Kruskal's Algorithm retrieves edges from a sorted list, say *Edges*[1 .. *E*]. A heap of edges would do as well but would save no processing time: retrieval of all edges is a sorting process of order $(E \ln E)$. An edge in the list is taken to be a record e that contains a weight $e \uparrow .w$, and vertices $e \uparrow .a$ and $e \uparrow .b$.

When an edge e is used to attach vertex m to a vertex k already in the forest, the process of attachment involves lists already familiar from section 10.3:

procedure *Attach(m,k)*
   $c \leftarrow c + 1$
   WhenDone[*m*] $\leftarrow c$
   Done[*c*] $\leftarrow m$
   State[*m*] $\leftarrow e \uparrow .w$
   Parent[*m*] $\leftarrow k$
   Set[*m*] $\leftarrow$ *Set*[*k*]
   end {*Attach*

The resulting lists can be applied as they were in section 10.3, with minor variations. *Parent* entries of component roots need to be changed from self-reference to zero for complete conformity. *WhenDone*[*k*] is the time at which k is added to the forest, but not necessarily when it is joined into its final component tree.

Figure 10.11 shows some snapshots of the process applied to W_1.

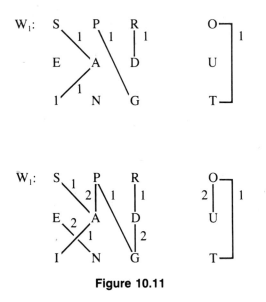

Figure 10.11

At this point, all of the vertices have been chosen; but, as Figure 10.12 shows, the trees of the forest do not represent components of the graph.

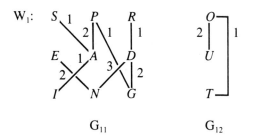

Figure 10.12

Problem P10.3 is appropriate at this point.

The test for cycle generation is a test to see if the two vertices of an edge lie in the same tree. *Set* will not work as it did in section 10.3.3 because component roots are not identifiable until the process is complete and roots are not necessarily added before their children. Some variation of the *Find* operation of section 9.7, acting on *Set*, is needed to test for a common component.

The version of Kruskal's Algorithm presented here examines the vertices of the (greedily) chosen edge. Neither, one, or both are already in the forest: vertex *m* is in the forest if *WhenDone*[*m*] ≠ 0. If precisely one vertex is in the forest, the other is attached to it. If neither is in the forest, one is attached to the other. If both are in the forest in distinct trees, one is attached to the other; but if they are in the same tree, the edge is rejected:

```
procedure Kruskal
    for k = 1 to V do
        Parent[k] ← 0
        Set[k] ← k
        WhenDone[k] ← 0
    next k
    c ← 0
    ec ← 0
    while ec < E do
        ec ← ec + 1
        e ← Edges[ec]
        if WhenDone[e↑.a] = 0                         {e↑.a is not in the forest
            then if WhenDone[e↑.b] = 0                 {and neither is e↑.b
                then Attach(e↑.b,e↑.b)
                endif
                Attach(e↑.a,e↑.b)
            else if WhenDone[e↑.b] = 0                 {only e↑.a is in the forest
                then Attach(e↑.b,e↑.a)
                else if Find(e↑.a) ≠ Find(e↑.b)       {both are in the forest
                    then Parent[e↑.b] ← e↑.a           {and in distinct trees
                        Set[e↑.b] ← Set[e↑.a]
                        State[e↑.b] ← e↑.w
                    endif
                endif
            endif
    endwhile
end {Kruskal
```

Program PG10.4 is appropriate at this point.

10.4.1 The Shortest Path Problem

The *shortest path* problem is to find the path in a weighted graph between two given vertices that has the minimal weight sum of all such paths.

If the weights are all one, bfs will find the shortest path from the starting vertex to *all* vertices in its component. A bfs search attaches to a component tree all vertices reachable from the root with one edge, then all those reachable with two, and so on.

The minimum spanning tree determination with *SparsePQT* repeatedly adds the vertex closest to the *tree*. The shortest path variation is simply to add the vertex closest to the root vertex *r* from which paths are to be formed. (Its state may be initialized to zero instead of UNSEEN so that it is chosen first.)

Suppose that *SparsePQT* is used to derive the shortest path. During the traverse, the vertices in state DONE are connected to *r* by shortest paths. If *m* is moved into state HELD from state UNSEEN in the adjacency loop of *k*, the shortest known path from *m* to *r* is formed by attachment of *m* to the tree at *k*. The total path length to *r* is the path length from *k* to *r* plus the weight of the edge (*k,m*). If *m* is already in state HELD, the path from *m* to *k* to *r* may or may not be shorter than the shortest path known prior to the processing of *k*. The test is simply made by using:

Priority = *State*[*k*] + *p* ↑ *.w*

The final path length from *r* to any *k* is in list *State;* the individual edges in the shortest path tree can be derived from list *Parent*.

A variation for dense graphs, using the adjacency matrix, is to use the list *State* simply as that: an unordered list. The *State* entries of vertices not yet in state DONE are negated to distinguish them. The *Remove* procedure is replaced by a linear scan for the largest negative vertex (closest to zero). When the state of a vertex is changed in the adjacency loop, it is changed to −priority. When a vertex is moved into state DONE, its *State* entry is complemented to make it positive.

The use of *a*[*k,m*] for *Priority* values yields Prim's Algorithm for the minimal spanning forest, and the use of *State*[*k*] + *a*[*k,m*] for *Priority* values yields Dijkstra's Algorithm for the shortest path problem.

Program PG10.5 is appropriate at this point.

Summary

Problems of interest in a wide variety of applications include the mathematical model, *graph*. Graph models have been used for a long time and have accumulated a great deal of nomenclature concerning their paths and cycles. Graphs can be modeled in a program in a number of ways. The two most common structures for representing a graph are the *adjacency matrix,* most suitable for dense graphs, and the *adjacency list* for sparse graphs.

A basic requirement of most algorithms that deal with a graph is a *traverse* of it, generally to make a search for something. The approach taken here is to describe a very general traversal that can be specialized and perhaps made more efficient for particular uses. It is a *priority-queue traverse, PQT. PQT* is shown to be general enough to include dfs (depth-first search) and bfs (breadth-first search).

PQT is used to generate data-acquisition lists *Parent, Ancestor, Done,* and *WhenDone*. These in turn are used to answer questions about a graph—its cycles, components, paths, spanning forest, and biconnection properties.

The use of edge-weights for priorities in *PQT* allows it to be used to find minimal spanning trees and shortest paths.

This chapter is formed around a central algorithm. *PQT* can be specialized, tuned, and expanded as needed. An advantage to this approach is that customizing can be done on familiar grounds, using the programmer's time efficiently.

Further Reading

The reader seeking background material on graphs for this chapter can try any number of finite mathematics texts. They usually include a chapter on graphs and indicate some of the areas of application. A survey of applications at a higher level is [ROBERTS, 1978], which has been supplemented by [ROBERTS, 1984]. Both contain extensive bibliographies.

Numerous books on graph theory are available for the undergraduate level, and the list is growing. The choice is yours. The same is true of books titled *Discrete Mathematics*.

Graph algorithms are being researched extensively. Several books about graph algorithms exist, and again the list is growing. One such is [EVEN, 1979].

A nice treatment of priority-queue traverses, including recursive versions, is given in [SEDGEWICK, 1983].

A number of graph-algorithm topics not covered in this chapter are relatively accessible. They include those for directed graphs, networks, and matching problems. Both [SEDGEWICK, 1983] and [TARJAN, 1983] have good treatments of these topics.

Exercises   immediate applications of the text material

E10.1 Find the smallest graph with more than one minimal spanning tree (mint) and a mint-(shortest-path) pair that have no edges in common.

E10.2 In G_1 of section 10.1, determine:

(a) the longest cycle

(b) a spanning forest different from the one illustrated

(c) the largest biconnected subgraph

E10.3 Form the adjacency listing and adjacency matrix for G_1 if the nodes are in alphabetical order.

E10.4 Trace the operation of *MakeSet* on the summary data for G_1 given in section 10.3.

E10.5 Draw the spanning tree for G_1 that would be produced by *MakeForest* altered to use *Ancestor* rather than *Parent*.

E10.6 Complete the trace of *Articulation* variables started in section 10.3.5 and determine *UrMin* and *UrMax*.

Problems   not immediate, but requiring no major extensions of the text material

P10.1 Incorporate the effect of *MakeForest* (section 10.3.3), using *Ancestor* rather than *Parent*, directly into *SparsePQT* (section 10.2).

P10.2 Design a procedure that uses *UrMax* and *Children* to determine and list of articulation points.

P10.3 Change all of the weights w in W_1 (section 10.4) to $10 - w$ and trace the behavior of Kruskal's Algorithm with snapshots.

Programs   for trying it yourself

PG10.1 Write a program that will read a file of vertices and edges and display a summary of data-acquisition lists like the one for G_1 at the end of section 10.3.

PG10.2 Write a program that determines and displays the spanning forest of a graph. A variation is to use PG10.1 to write files used as input by this program.

PG10.3 Write a program that inputs vertex, edge, and identifier data for graphs and displays components and articulation points. A variation uses the program of PG10.1 to create files used as input for this program.

PG10.4 Write a program that sorts an edge list of a graph and applies *Kruskal* to it and displays the data-acquisition lists that result from it.

PG10.5 Write a program that uses *SparsePQT* to determine the shortest paths from a given vertex to all the vertices reachable from it.

PART TWO

Expansions and Applications

Random Processes

It is not possible to know the future— of a process, of a program, of the behavior of nearly any interesting system. The universe itself, in fact, seems to be indeterminate. To demonstrate the failure of prophecy, give a carefully designed program to ten people to use. They will find errors and want changes—that much is predictable. They will enter, or wish to enter, data sets that the programmer would consider extremely unlikely. One way to prepare for this kind of variation is to generate data sets randomly. The ability to do so is also useful for simulating a large variety of other natural processes.

The simplest way to imitate unpredictable variation is the generation of *pseudorandom numbers*. A random variable x, $0 < x < 1$, has the property that any real number in this range is equally likely. A pseudorandom variable r, $0 < r < 1$, has values that approximate true randomness in two ways:

- The set of values of r is not complete, but there are many of them and no obvious gaps.

- The values in the range of r are of approximately equal likelihood.

A great deal of work has been done on developing programs to produce pseudorandom numbers [KNUTH, 1973], and no programmer should be without access to such programs. In some of the exercises a function *Rand,* available to provide a pseudorandom number on demand, is assumed. Also assumed is a mechanism for reusing the same value or sequence of values produced by it. This assumption is convenient for debugging purposes to isolate the effect of a change in a program, and it provides a way to compare the effect of more than one procedure on the same data. If no other way is available, successive values of *Rand* may be stored in an array or in a file.

In some languages, notably standard Pascal, the programmer might need to provide a pseudorandom number generator. The subject of generating pseudorandom numbers is too large to pursue here, but one popular algorithm is illustrated in Pascal:

```
FUNCTION Random(VAR Seed : INTEGER): REAL;
   CONST  Modulus = {65536};
          Multiplier = {25173};
          Increment = {13849};
   BEGIN
     Seed := ((Multiplier * Seed) + Increment)  MOD  Modulus;
     Random := Seed/Modulus
     END {Random};
```

The values of the constants given here work well on a DEC VAX and other machines, but they will not work well in all cases. For example, for a PDP 11/70, *Seed* is declared externally by

```
VAR Seed : 0 .. 65535;
```

and the constants become:

```
Modulus = 32768;
Multiplier = 13077;
Increment = 6925;
```

The function *Rand* only produces values between 0 and 1. That does not explicitly allow, for example, the random choice of an index for an array declared as $a[-2 \ .. \ 3]$. The requisite mapping can be derived with the following steps:

■ The expression $x = D \cdot Rand$ has values in the range $0 < x < D$ when $0 < Rand < 1$, and $D > 0$.

■ The expression $x = L + D \cdot Rand$ has values in the range $L < x < L + D$.

■ The expression $x = L + (T - L) \cdot Rand$ has values in the range $L < x < T$.

■ The expression $INT(L + (T - L) \cdot Rand)$ takes on integer values $L, L + 1$, ..., $T - 1$ when INT is a function that returns the largest integer less than or equal to its argument.

Consequently, with $T = U + 1$, $INT(L + (U - L + 1) \cdot Rand)$ has possible values L, $L + 1$, ..., U. In particular, $INT(-2 + 6 \cdot Rand)$ will randomly provide in-bounds indices for the array $a[-2 .. 3]$.

A set of 10 values, randomly chosen in the range $[-30 .. 30]$, may be provided in the array e used in the sorting routines in section 1.5 by:

```
procedure ThirtyThirty                              {O(1)
   for  i = 1 to 10 do
      e[i] ← -30 + 61 * Rand
      next i
   end   {ThirtyThirty
```

It is not feasible to explore hypothesis testing, confidence intervals, analysis of variance, and so on in this text. That material belongs in a course in statistics. However, the applicability of *Rand* can be extended enormously by a few additional tools. Some acquaintance with the ideas of probability and statistics is helpful in reading the subsections that follow.

Program PGA.1 is appropriate at this point.

A.1 Mean and Standard Deviation

A sample of values from a population determines a (sample) *mean* that provides an estimate of the mean value of the population, and a (sample) *standard deviation* that is an estimate of the dispersion of the population. For a sample of size n they can be calculated by:

$$\text{mean} = \frac{\Sigma x}{n}$$

$$\text{variance} = \Sigma \frac{(x^2) - (\Sigma x)^2}{n(n - 1)} = (\text{standard deviation})^2$$

These measures provide a convenient and significant way to reduce a collection of measurements to two values, but intelligent interpretation then requires knowledge of statistics.

A.2 Frequency Distributions

A plot of how many minutes 20 people had to wait in line at the check-out counter of a grocery store might look like the histogram of Figure A.1.

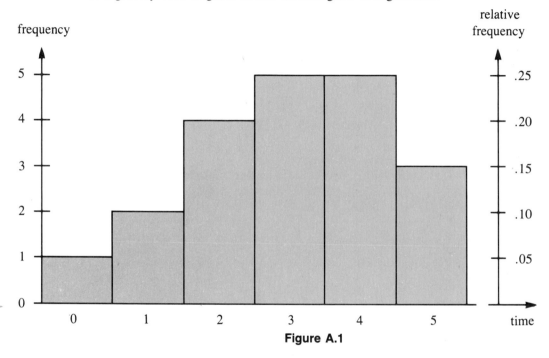

Figure A.1

If this sample of size 20 is the only information about waiting time available, then it must provide the model for the probability, $P[w]$, of waiting w minutes. That model is the *relative frequency,* which is scaled to the right of the histogram. Given that this model is a valid estimate, the relative frequency as a function of time can be accepted as a *pmf* (*probability mass function*). The accumulated (summed) values of a pmf are the *cumulative probability*. The distribution of cumulative probability is called the PDF (*Probability Distribution Function*). For this example, the PDF is plotted in Figure A.2.

Now suppose that we wish to write a program to process data that have the distribution model derived from the sample. We may provide a random variate, *Line,* for test data by the following:

■   Choose a value with *Rand,* uniformly distributed between 0 and 1. If $PDF[w-1] < Rand \leq PDF[w]$, then *Line* $\leftarrow w$.

Geometrically, this amounts to drawing the horizontal line from a point on the vertical PDF axis to where it first strikes the stairstep graph and projecting down to

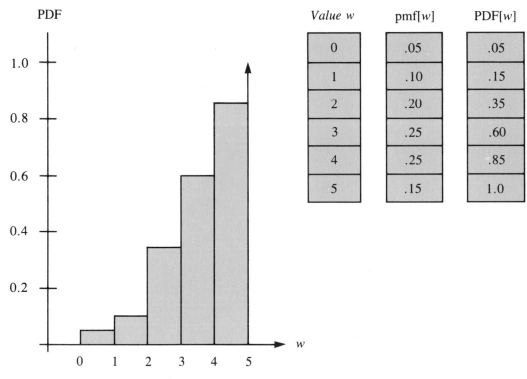

Value w	pmf[w]	PDF[w]
0	.05	.05
1	.10	.15
2	.20	.35
3	.25	.60
4	.25	.85
5	.15	1.0

Figure A.2

a value w. The distribution of *Line* is that of the pmf (from the histogram), and points may be drawn from this distribution as required.

Values that have the pmf of any discrete PDF may be generated from a table like Figure A.2 in this way, which is called *discrete inversion*.

Exercise EA.1 and Problem PA.1 are appropriate at this point.

A.3 Normal Distributions

The most-used probability distribution is not discrete as are those discussed in section A.1 but is the *normal distribution:*

$$P[x] = \exp\left[-\frac{z^2}{2}\right], \quad \text{where } z = \frac{x - \mu}{\sigma}$$

Here μ is the mean value of x, and σ is the standard deviation of its values. The *standard normal distribution* is defined as the one for which $\mu = 0$ and $\sigma = 1$. The relationship given above between z and x defines a map for any normally distributed variable to z-scores, and back again. It is possible to approximate the distribution of z-scores, (the standard normal distribution), by using n values of *Rand:*

$$ z = \frac{\sum_{i=1}^{n} \left(Rand - \frac{n}{2} \right)}{\sqrt{\frac{n}{12}}} \qquad \{Rand \text{ is called } n \text{ times.} $$

In particular, this equation is simplified if n is taken to be 12, in which case:

$$ z = \sum_{i=1}^{n} (Rand - 6) $$

The z-scores generated in this way can be mapped to a value from a normal distribution by:

$$ x = \mu + \sigma z $$

A function that returns a value from a normal distribution is:

```
function Norm(Mu,Sigma)                        {O(Rand)
    z ← 0
    for  i = 1 to 12   do
        z ← z + Rand
        next i
    z ← z − 6
    Norm ← Mu + Sigma * z
    end   {Norm
```

Note: Some caution must be applied to normal distributions because extreme values can occur, whatever μ and σ may be. Sometimes these values are not physically meaningful: the distribution being modeled differs from a normal distribution by not having them. They are "out of bounds" and must be dealt with by checks within the program.

Program PGA.2 is appropriate at this point.

A.4 Exponential Distributions

Arrival times for customers in line at a bank teller's window and for many other arrival and departure processes have neither a uniform distribution like *Rand* nor a normal distribution like *Norm*. The arrival times are more likely to form a *Poisson Distribution* for which the probability that n arrivals have occurred by time t is:

$$P[n,t] = \frac{(\lambda t)^n}{n!} \exp(-\lambda t)$$

In practice, the time interval between arrivals is more useful. This is called the *interarrival time*, and it has an *exponential distribution*. A variate with an exponential distribution may be derived from *Rand* by

$$ia = \frac{-1}{\lambda} \text{LOG}(Rand)$$

where LOG is the logarithm to the base e (2.718 . . .). The distribution of values of *ia* has both mean and standard deviation equal to $1/\lambda$.

Exercises   immediate applications of the text material

EA.1   Develop the function *Line* that will return a value, with the set of such values distributed according to the histogram given in section A.2.

Problems   not immediate, but requiring no major extensions of the text material

---

PA.1   The solutions in a high-school programming contest are timed to the nearest minute. Data from a preliminary contest for the first, "courage-builder," problem came out like this:

time	1	2	3	4	5	6	7	8	9	10
number of solutions	0	0	0	2	1	5	8	9	7	4

Plot the (relative) frequency distribution of this data. Assume that this represents a pmf, and plot the corresponding PDF. What times correspond to the following possible values of *Rand?*

(a) 0.007134   (c) 0.567321   (e) 0.410022

(b) 0.916528   (d) 0.757505

Programs for trying it out yourself. A program, when written for an interactive system, should display instructions that explain to the user what it does and how to use it. It should provide a graceful way for the user to quit.

PGA.1 Write a program that compares the execution times of *SelectionSort*, *BubbleSort*, and *InsertionSort* for 20 sets of 20 values, generated by the uniform variate, *Rand*. Calculate the mean and standard deviation for the three execution times.

In a time-sharing system it may not be possible to determine execution times themselves, but it is possible to count statement executions, including those that result from data-determined, conditional branches.

PGA.2 Do PGA.1, except that a normal distribution is to be used for data values, with mean 10 and standard deviation 10. For contrast, also use data already in order and in reverse order.

Projects for fun; for serious students

PJA.1 Extend PGA.1 and PGA.2 to a serious study of *SelectionSort*, *BubbleSort*, and *InsertionSort* for values of n = 8, 16, 32, 64, 128, 512, and 2048. Use uniform, normal, and exponential variates, in-order and reverse-order data sets, and data sets that are somewhat disarranged from in-order in a variety of ways. For example, choose two indices at random from an in-order sequence and switch the values they point to prior to invoking the sort procedure being studied. Calculate means and standard deviations of execution time. If you have statistics in your background, test the hypothesis that the three sorts have equal execution times (under various circumstances).

Section *B*

Hash Tables

A hash table differs from the array that provides storage for it because store and retrieve operations are specified by a *key* value rather than by an index and the number of legal keys is larger than the number of cells in the array. The operations of interest are STORE(*Key*) and RETRIEVE(*Key*). It is possible to simply store the key and retrieve a Boolean function that indicates the presence or lack of presence of the key in the table. This is the simple way to discuss hash tables, but it is more likely that the key is indeed just a key in a record containing a *Value* field or a pointer (or index) that addresses some bulk of information. In a word, hash tables are apt to be *exogenous*—directories to data stored external to them.

> **Note:** For the sake of simpler exposition in this section, STORE(*Key*) assigns only a key value and RETRIEVE(*Key*) returns only the index of the location of *Key* in a table of keys. These are to be understood as surrogates for more realistic forms of the operations.

The function HF_1 of section 2.5 simply converts letters to integers and sums them. It exhibits two of the properties needed to form a hash table:

- HF_1 transforms keys into integers.

- HF_1 possesses *compression:* the domain space defined by the set of all possible keys is much larger than the range space, the target table.

HF_1 also exhibits an unhappy consequence of compression by hash functions:

$$HF_1(\text{BROTH}) = HF_1(\text{OLIVE})$$

In short:

- Compression causes *collisions*.

The address functions of section 2.3 transform a domain value that is an *n*-tuple of the form

$$[i_1, i_2, \ldots, i_n]$$

into a range value that is a single index in a one-dimensional table. The correspondence is one-to-one, and so there is no compression; but compression can be introduced much as it was for HF_1. For example, a function HF_2 can be defined by

$$HF_2([i_1, i_2, \ldots, i_n]) = (i_1 + \cdots + i_n) \text{ MOD } 25$$

If a key of any kind can be located in an *n*-dimensional table at

$$t = [i_1, i_2, \ldots, i_n]$$

then $HF_2(t)$ provides the same service as for *any n*-dimensional table of keys as HF_1 does for its specific data space.

Both HF_1 and HF_2 fail to define their range as a hash table structure by themselves because compression allows *collisions:* two elements of the domain can have identical range values. In any table structure, RETRIEVE must be the inverse of STORE, and so collisions must be resolved. With this in mind, the desired HASH TABLE structure consists of:

- a domain

- a range

- a hash function *h* that exhibits compression

- a resolution of the collisions caused by *h*

- operations CREATE, STORE, and RETRIEVE

The domain is normally a given in a general sense and may be enormous. For example, it might be identifiers of up to 30 characters in length. The subset of the domain encountered in a specific application tends to be smaller but not well defined, and that makes a compressive system very attractive. CREATE requires no special attention. The range is a design decision that takes into account much of this section.

Suppose that a hash function is available that distributes the domain keys over the indices 0, 1, . . . ,24 in a table *HT* with *uniform probability*. The first entry will not collide with any other. The probability that the second entry will not collide with a previous entry is 24/25. The probability that the third, fourth, . . . entries will not collide when entered is 23/25, 22/25, . . . (directly proportional to the number of free spaces). The probability that there will be no collisions for seven entries in a table of 25 cells is:

$$1 \cdot \frac{24}{25} \cdot \frac{23}{25} \cdot \frac{22}{25} \cdot \frac{21}{25} \cdot \frac{20}{25} \cdot \frac{19}{25} = 0.3969$$

Hence the probability that there *will* be a collision is near 60 percent even though the table is less than one-third full. The cause is not really the small size of the table. (Figure out how likely a birthday collision is in a room containing 25 people.)

The ratio of n/m for n items in a table of size m is called the *load factor,* λ. In this example, $\lambda = 7/25 = 0.28$. Clearly, the probability of a collision increases with λ.

The likelihood of collisions is increased if regularities in the domain keys affect the hash value. For example, a hash function based simply on the last letter of an identifier will map a lot of keys into wherever e, s, and n happen to go. (Try it on the words of the first two sentences of this paragraph.) Every part of a key should be involved—else, for example, the set {THEMES, THEME, THYME, TIME, CHIME, CHINA} will tend to collide. A hash function should tend to scatter natural clusters of the domain over the range.

The probability that a table location will be accessed is affected by two things:

- the selection of elements from the potential set (the domain)

- the transformation of the selected elements by the hash function into range indices

If this probability is not uniform, then there is said to be *primary clustering*. HF_1 and HF_2 are *not* particularly good hash functions. For one thing, all permutations of the same letters (or of the same indices) collide.

B.1 A Choice of Hash Functions

Although no hash function serves well in *all* circumstances, there are theoretical results that provide guidelines. One approach that can be recommended for integer values of z is

$$h(z) = INT(m(z\theta \ MOD \ 1))$$

which satisfies $0 \leq h(z) < m$ when $0 < \theta < 1$. The table indices addressed by h are $0 \ldots m - 1$. Suggested values of θ are:

$$\theta = \frac{\sqrt{5} - 1}{2} \approx 0.6180339 \quad \text{and} \quad (1 - \theta)$$

The size of the range table is chosen to be a prime number that is not close to a power of 2 (admittedly difficult for small tables).

To use the function h as a hash function first requires that the keys be turned into an integer in some efficient way. Keys are stored as binary strings in memory, and a binary string can be decoded as an integer (or sequence of integers) or converted with a utility function (such as *ORD* in Pascal). For the sake of illustration, consider the following simple approach applied to the ingredients of the recipe in section 2.5:

1. Ingredients are considered to be 12 characters in length, left-adjusted and padded with blank spaces.

2. Letters have as their index a two-digit value: $A = 01, B = 02, \ldots, Z = 26$. Blanks have value 00. These values are found by a table lookup, which is much faster than calculation of them.

3. An ingredient is six four-digit integers. For example, BELLPEPPER is 0205, 1212, 1605, 1616, 0518, 0000.

4. The six integers for an ingredient are summed to form z. In functional terms, $q(\text{BELLPEPPER}) = 5156 = z$.

The calculation of q is much faster than it might appear to be. Let $s[1 \,.\,.\, 12]$ be the string of characters of an ingredient. Then a calculation of z requires only one multiplication:

$$z \leftarrow s[1] + s[3] + s[5] + s[7] + s[9] + s[11]$$

$$z \leftarrow z \times 100 + s[2] + s[4] + s[6] + s[8] + s[10] + s[12]$$

It is possible for z to be as large as $6 \times 2626 = 15,756$, but taking the sum *MOD* 10,000 restricts it to four digits (and more than that are unlikely anyway). Now $h(z)$ for BELLPEPPER, with $m = 17$ is:

$$\begin{aligned}
h(z) &= INT(m(z\theta \; MOD \; 1)) \\
&= INT(17(5156 \cdot \theta \; MOD \; 1)) \\
&= INT(17(3186.5827 \; MOD \; 1)) \\
&= INT(17(0.5827)) \\
&= INT(9.9059) \\
&= 9
\end{aligned}$$

For contrast, a second stage of multiplication by the prime base m can be introduced:

$$\begin{aligned}
h_2(z) &= INT(m(m(z\theta \; MOD \; 1) \; MOD \; 1)) \\
&= INT(17(9.9059 \; MOD \; 1)) \\
&= 15
\end{aligned}$$

Both h and h_2 can be easily determined with a hand calculator or a small program as a check on how well they work on a particular data set. Multiplication by 100 can be replaced with multiplication by a power of 2 and hence—in assembly languages—by shifts. There are a large number of possible variations of this scheme.

The results, for the 13 ingredients (including BROTH) and prime bases 17, 31, and 47, are shown in Table B.1.

Table B.1

		$m = 17$		$m = 31$		$m = 47$	
	z	h	h_2	h	h_2	h	h_2
BEEF	0711	7	8	13	2	19	39
BELLPEPPER	5156	9	15	18	1	27	18
BLACKPEPPER	5342	9	2	16	20	25	11
BROTH	2538	9	11	17	20	26	37
CARROT	3639	0	7	0	24	1	8
CUMIN	3030	10	15	19	28	30	9
DILLWEED	2330	0	5	0	18	0	41
MUSHROOM	6557	7	10	13	27	21	3
OLIVE	2934	5	4	9	20	14	29
ONION	2443	14	9	26	17	40	12
POTATO	5631	2	9	4	18	6	46
SALT	3121	15	0	27	12	41	25
TOMATOPASTE	9352	14	8	26	13	40	4

Collisions are produced by all of these functions, except h_2 for the base of 47. In fact, that is a lucky accident. The loading factor for 13 items in a table of 47 items is $13/47 = 0.28$. More importantly, the probability of *no* collisions with 13 items, no matter how randomly h_2 scatters its key, is:

$$1 \cdot \frac{46}{47} \cdot \frac{45}{47} \cdots \frac{35}{47} = 0.1848$$

There is less than a 50/50 chance that *ten* pigeons can be placed at random in 47 pigeon holes without having two pigeons in one hole.

As the size of the table increases, the minimal loading factor with a chance of collision less than 50 percent shrinks. For $m = 997$ it is less than 4 percent.

Problem PB.1 is appropriate at this point.

The unavoidable conclusion is that any practical use of hash tables produces collisions. One way to implement collision resolution is a technique called *linear probing*.

B.2 Linear Probing

Suppose a procedure *Hash* calculates an index k in a hash table $HT[0 \ . \ . \ m-1]$ for *Key*. If the table is empty, STORE(*Key*) would simply be $HT[k] \leftarrow Key$. If it is not, $HT[k]$ may already contain a key, and a collision occurs. The first task of a STORE operation is thus to determine if $HT[k]$ is empty. For that purpose *HT* might be initialized with a value that cannot be a key or associated with a flag array. For the recipe example and most identifiers, *HT* may be initialized to null, blank, or empty strings.

If $HT[k]$ is not empty, then another location must be chosen for *Key,* and it must be found again by RETRIEVE(*Key*). One simple strategy is to start looking at index $k + 1$, then $k + 2$, and so on until a free cell is located, or the table is exhausted without finding one. This is called *linear probing*.

A general probe function for a hash table begins with a starting index and the key value and returns an index. The return value is the index of the actual location of the key if it is found in *HT,* or the negative of that index if the table was searched to exhaustion. An appropriate empty slot for a STORE operation can then be located by probing with the null string *Blank*.

```
function Probe(Start,s)                    {O(m)
  i ← Start
  repeat
    if  HT[i] = s
      then return i endif
    i ← (i + 1) MOD m
    until   i = Start
  return −i
  end   {Probe

procedure StoreHT(Key)                     {O(m)
  k ← Hash(Key)
  dex ← Probe(k,Blank)
  if  dex < 0
    then {deal with a full table
    else HT[dex] ← Key
    endif
  end   {StoreHT
```

function *RetrieveHT(Key)* $\{O(m)$

   $k \leftarrow Hash(Key)$

   $dex \leftarrow Probe(k,Key)$

   if *dex* < *0*

      then {*report not there*

      else return *dex*

      endif

   end {*RetrieveHT*

If the user of *RetrieveHT(Key)* is designed to interpret negative returns as "not there," then *RetrieveHT* may be replaced by *Probe(Hash(Key), Key)*.

The effect of *StoreHT* can be illustrated with the use of $m = 17$, h, and the 13 ingredients in the example, entered in alphabetical order:

					$m = 17$
HT[7]	←	BEEF	0		CARROT
HT[9]	←	BELLPEPPER	1		DILLWEED
HT[9]	*collision*		2		POTATO
HT[10]	←	BLACKPEPPER			
HT[9]	*collision*				
HT[10]	*collision*		5		OLIVE
HT[11]	←	BROTH			
HT[0]	←	CARROT	7		BEEF
HT[10]	*collision*		8		MUSHROOM
HT[11]	*collision*		9		BELLPEPPER
HT[12]	CUMIN		10		BLACKPEPPER
HT[0]	*collision*		11		BROTH
HT[1]	←	DILLWEED	12		CUMIN
HT[7]	*collision*				
HT[8]	←	MUSHROOM	14		ONION
HT[5]	←	OLIVE	15		SALT
HT[14]	←	ONION	16		TOMATOPASTE
HT[2]	←	POTATO			
HT[15]	←	SALT			
HT[14]	*collision*				
HT[15]	*collision*				
HT[16]	←	TOMATOPASTE			

Problem PB.2 is appropriate at this point.

B.3 Secondary Clustering and Double Hashing

Two things about the sequence of *HT* entries are worth noting:

- A different entry order stores some of the keys in different places. For the example, entry in reverse alphabetic order would place CUMIN in *HT*[10] and BELLPEPPER in *HT*[12].

- Entries into *HT*[*k*] can increase the number of comparisons needed to store (or retrieve) items that hash to nearby indices, both smaller and larger. This is called *secondary clustering* as opposed to *primary clustering* in which distinct keys hash to the same index.

Secondary clustering can be alleviated to a certain extent (in tables with more room to maneuver than this example) by *double hashing*. This consists of skipping through the table from a collision in steps of δ, where δ depends on the key. In *Probe*, δ was 1 for all keys, and a workable change is: $\delta \leftarrow HashAgain(Key)$ followed within the search loop by: $i \leftarrow (i + \delta)$ MOD m.

It is necessary for δ to be relatively prime to m (else the search will be compromised). One way to guarantee that is to use *Hash* and *HashAgain* that satisfy:

$0 \leqslant Hash(z) < m$

$0 \leqslant HashAgain(z) < m$

$Hash(z) \neq HashAgain(z)$

A slight variation applicable to the example is to shift the four-digit values over one, and derive a new z, say z_2. For example, z_2 for BELLPEPPER would be

$$2051 + 2121 + 6051 + 6160 + 5180 + 0000 = 21,563$$

Or simply use $1 - \theta$ in place of θ, or use h_2.

With q, $Hash = h$, $HashAgain = h_2$, $m = 31$, and alphabetical entry order:

```
HT[13]  ←  BEEF                                      m = 31
HT[18]  ←  BELLPEPPER                         0   | CARROT       |
HT[16]  ←  BLACKPEPPER                            |             |
HT[17]  ←  BROTH                                  |             |
HT[0]   ←  CARROT                                 |             |
HT[19]  ←  CUMIN                              4   | POTATO      |
HT[0]      collision                         5   | DILLWEED    |
HT[18]     collision                             |             |
HT[5]   ←  DILLWEED (δ = 18)                      |             |
HT[13]     collision                         8   | TOMATOPASTE |
HT[9]   ←  MUSHROOM (δ = 27)                  9   | MUSHROOM    |
HT[9]      collision                              |             |
HT[29]  ←  OLIVE (δ = 20)                         |             |
HT[26]  ←  ONION                                  |             |
HT[4]   ←  POTATO                             13  | BEEF        |
HT[27]  ←  SALT                                   |             |
HT[26]     collision                              |             |
HT[8]   ←  TOMATOPASTE (δ = 13)              16  | BLACKPEPPER |
                                             17  | BROTH       |
                                             18  | BELLPEPPER  |
                                             19  | CUMIN       |
                                                 |             |
                                                 |             |
                                                 |             |
                                                 |             |
                                                 |             |
                                             26  | ONION       |
                                             27  | SALT        |
                                                 |             |
                                             29  | OLIVE       |
                                                 |             |
```

Actually there is one more collision than for $\delta = 1$, but additional entries mapped into the range 16–19 by *Hash* are less likely to interfere with each other when their δs differ, because there is a good chance of skipping over the cluster.

The number of collisions increases rapidly after the loading factor n/m reaches about 3/4, as can be seen by applying double hashing with h_2 and $m = 17$. There is nowhere to go in a small table to escape collisions.

Problem PB.3 is appropriate at this point.

B.4 Deletion and Rehashing

Deletion from a hash table is not merely a matter of replacing a key with the empty key, because a subsequent search may need to keep stepping past its cell into the sequence of stored entries with the same hash value. A deletion cell can be marked as available with some special value and used on a subsequent store that reaches it. (Since retrieval must continue past this point, separate *Probe* procedures are needed for store and retrieve operations.)

It is possible to devise an algorithm that *rehashes* a table. The number of deletions and the loading factor probably both affect the optimal point to do rehashing, which is not particularly efficient. It is probably just as well to make a linear sweep through the table and hash active keys into a new copy of the table, as long as there is room for two copies of the table in memory.

An alternate implementation of hash tables that permits deletion is based on the linked lists described in Chapter 3, and it is to be found in section L.

Problems   not immediate, but requiring no major extensions of the text material

PB.1   Construct a table of hashed indices like the one of section B.1 for the calendar months.

PB.2   Construct the hash table for the calendar months entered in calendar order, into a hash table of prime base $m = 17$.

PB.3   Construct the double-hashing table for the calendar months in calendar order with $Hash = h$, $HashAgain = h_2$, and $m = 31$.

Programs   for trying it yourself

PGB.1 Write a program that accepts identifiers of up to 12 characters in length, converts them to an integer with q, and stores them in a hash table *HT* with the use of $Hash = h$, $HashAgain = h_2$, and $m = 47$. The program should report the number of collisions, the average number of tests by *Probe*, and the loading factor.

Circular
List Operations

A display routine for a circular list differs from that of a linear list because the end of an unsuccessful search is signaled by a return to the starting point instead of by a *NIL* pointer:

```
procedure RoundOut(cList)                          {O(n)
  if  Empty(cList)
    then {deal with this error
    else Display(cList)                            {PROCESS0
         p ← cList ↑ .Link                         {PROCESS0
         while  p ≠ cList  do
         Display(p)                                {PROCESS2
         p ← p ↑ .Link
         endwhile
  endif
end   {RoundOut
```

Additions to a circular list, *cList*, can take place most easily if the new node is to follow immediately after the node distinguished by the pointer *cList*, as shown in Figure C.1.

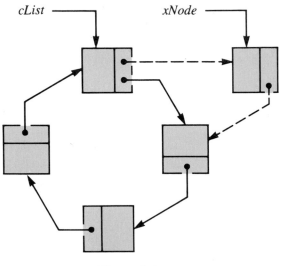

Figure C.1

The insertion routine is straightforward:

procedure *InsertAfter(cList,xNode)*   {*O(1)*
   if *Empty(cList)*
     then *xNode ↑ .Link ← xNode*
        cList ← xNode
     else *xNode ↑ .Link ← cList ↑ .Link*
        cList ↑ .Link ← xNode
     endif
   end   {*InsertAfter*

    When a single list identifier, *cList,* is used, and a node is to be added prior to it, then it is necessary to locate the node that points to *cList,* say *Prior,* and then apply *InsertAfter(Prior,xNode),* as shown in Figure C.2.

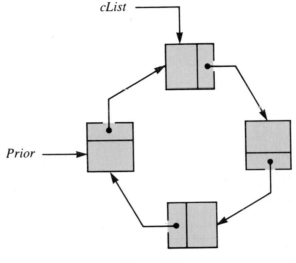

Figure C.2

The location logic is a simple version of *LT* (section 3.3.2):

Prior ← *cList*
if   NOT *Empty(cList)*
   then *p* ← *cList* ↑ *.Link*
        while   *p* ≠ *cList*   **do**
         Prior ← *p*
         p ← *p* ↑ *.Link*
        endwhile
   endif

Deletion in the vicinity of *cList* can take several forms. In particular, the node *cList* ↑ *.Link* (if it exists) can be readily deleted. So can *cList;* in Figure C.3 the *cList* pointer value can move forward or backward relative to the link directions.

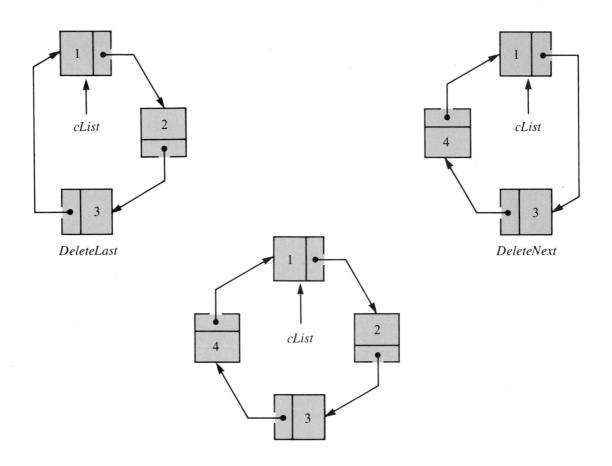

DeleteLast

DeleteNext

DeleteBack

DeleteOn

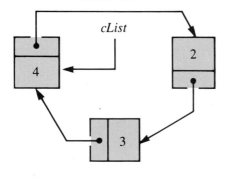

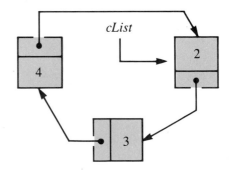

Figure C.3

Some combinations of insertion and deletion operations define formal structures in common use. Of particular interest is the circular queue, discussed in Chapter 5:

A circular queue: *InsertAfter(cList,xNode)*
                        DeleteBack(cList)

The form taken by *DeleteNext* is simply:

procedure *DeleteNext(cList)*   {*O(1)*
  if *Empty(cList)*
    then {*deal with this error*
        return
    endif
  if *cList ↑ .Link = cList*
    then *cList ←* NIL
        return
    else *Next ← cList ↑ .Link*
        cList ↑ .Link ← Next ↑ .Link
    endif
  end {*DeleteNext*

A deletion procedure such as *DeleteBack* is awkward unless the pointer *Prior* is available. Such a pointer can be made available by a change to a two-window system, as shown in Figure C.4.

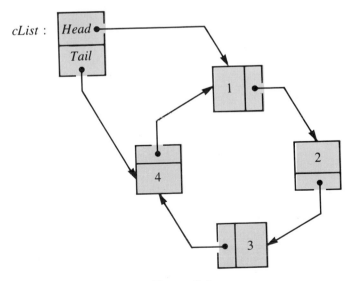

Figure C.4

With the window-pair system, circularity appears to be specious. Nevertheless, circular lists defined with a pair of pointers turn out to be useful when they are maintained in a single array. Routines designed to maintain the single array, specialized to the structure QUEUE, are treated in section 5.3.

Details of the other deletion procedures are left to the exercises.

Exercises   immediate applications of the text material

EC.1   When insertion prior to *cList* is made to an empty list something must be done after the search logic and *InsertAfter(cList,xNode)* of section 3.7 to properly prepare for later insertions. What is it?

Problems   not immediate, but requiring no major extensions of the text material

PC.1   Develop the procedure *DeleteOn.*

PC.2   Develop the procedure *DeleteBack.*

PC.3   Develop the procedure *DeleteLast.*

Section D

Integer Arithmetic of Unbounded Precision

The phrase "unbounded precision" means that the program providing the calculation itself places no limitation on the number of digits in a value. There are limitations to the storage capacity of any computing system; but they are generally very large relative to values that are likely to be used, and the program simply ignores that bound.

The program *Unbound* presented in this section is a simulation of a calculator used in infix mode: a value, an operator, and then a value are entered and the result display is prompted by the entry of a character " = " or one that represents another operator. The functions provided are addition (" + "), subtraction (" − "), multiplication ("*"), division ("/"), display (" = "), clear the accumulator ("C"), and quit ("Q"). The inclusion of M + (add to memory), M − (subtract from memory), MRC (recover from memory), and MCL (memory clear) are left as a challenge.

The program *Unbound* is developed in this section, rather than simply described or listed, in order to document the series of design decisions implemented by the program. The logic of *Unbound* is clarified by developing it in pseudocode and then translating that logic into Pascal.

D.1 The Entry Sequence

A crucial feature of a calculator is that it is fairly *robust:* mistaken entries do little harm, and that feature should be retained in a simulating program. The possibilities for ambiguous entries are much increased with the use of a terminal keyboard in place of the more restricted calculator keypad. In that spirit, extraneous characters are ignored. The accepted characters are digits 0–9 and operators "+", "−", "*", "/", "=", "C", "Q". All others are ignored. For example, A17B3 is accepted as 173. For the sake of robustness, division by 0 simply results in 0.

The basic response of the program is designed to deal with entry sequences such as: 24 + 9 =, which results in a display of 33 and the retention of that value in an accumulator (represented by the variable AC). A string of digits that designates a number is terminated by an operator, and so it is (value,operator)-pairs that are accepted by the program. Although an operator terminates the entry of a number, it is the *previous* operator that usually determines the action. (Operators such as "C" and "Q" are exceptions.) In more detail, if the entering value is X and the result of arithmetic is held in AC, the action of this sequence can be traced as shown in Table D.1.

Table D.1

Entries	X	NewOp	Op	AC
			C	0
24+	24	+	C	24
9=	9	=	+	33

The operation of most calculators is more complex than this example seems to imply. What, for example, is the result of the following entry sequences?

$$- \; 24 \; + \; 9 \; =$$
$$- \; 24 \; + \; 9 \; +$$
$$24 \; + \; +$$
$$24 \; + \; + \; =$$
$$24 \; + \; + \; + \; =$$

The results generated by the program developed here are − 15, − 15, 24, 48, and 72, respectively. The last of these is not standard, but it is convenient to have each new operator invoke the response of the previous one. If no new X is entered, the AC value is used as X.

D.2 Utility Routines

A procedure *Preface* is used to initialize variables and provide instructions to the user; *Clear* is used to set registers such as AC to zero; and *Display* writes out the value in the accumulator AC. These utility routines are supplemented by arithmetic procedures that act on AC.

The procedure *ValueIn* that extracts the tokens X and *NextOp* also returns a Boolean flag *NoX* to indicate the presence of a numeric value between operators.

The command-shell executes the previous operator, *Op*, in response to the next operator, *NextOp*. If no *X*-value is entered with *NextOp*, then the current value of *AC* is copied into *X*. Operators "Q" and "C" require immediate response. When "Q" is *NextOp*, it causes immediate termination of the program. When *NextOp* is "C" both *AC* and *X* are cleared, and *Op* is set to "C" also. When *Op* is either "C" or "=", and an *X*-value is entered with *NextOp*, the *X*-value becomes the new *AC* value.

The command-shell program that results is:

```
program UnBound
    Preface
    Done ← FALSE
    Op ← 'C'
    repeat
        ValueIn(X,NoX,NextOp)
        if   NextOp = 'Q'
            then Done ← TRUE
            else if   NextOp = 'C'
                    then Clear(AC)
                         Clear(X)
                         Op ← 'C'
                 endif
                 if   NoX   then X ← AC endif
                 case of Op
                    '=', 'C' : Swap                    {AC with X
                    '+'      : Add(AC,X)
                    {'-', '*', '/' are similar to '+'}
                 endcase
        endif
        Op ← NextOp
        Display
    until   Done
    end   {UnBound
```

The next level of detail is dependent on the implementation of values, and that implementation must allow assignments $X \leftarrow AC$ and $AC \leftarrow X$ for unbounded strings of digits. Values need to carry a sign, have leading zeroes suppressed for the sake of efficiency and display, be compared in magnitude (left-to-right for corresponding digits), and be used right-to-left in arithmetic operations. The chosen implementation for *AC* and *X* is a pointer to a header of a doubly linked list. Such a list plays the role of a *register*—a storage location directly associated with computation. For reasons that only become apparent when operations are examined in detail, it is convenient to carry one leading zero and link it to itself. When $AC \leftarrow 743$, the resulting register structure is shown in Figure D.1.

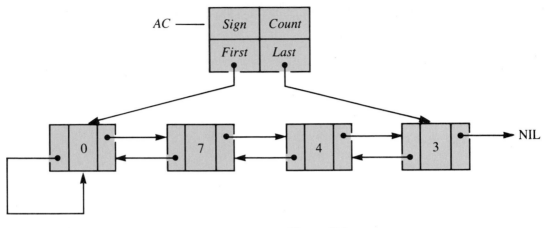

Figure D.1

The *Sign* field is Boolean, with *TRUE* corresponding to positive values—making tests involving signs more convenient.

A header such as *AC* or *X* can then be initialized by:

procedure *NewRegister(R)*
  NEW(*d*)
  d ↑ .*Left* ← *d*
  d ↑ .*Value* ← *0*
  d ↑ .*Right* ← NIL
  NEW(*R*)
  R ↑ .*First* ← *d*
  R ↑ .*Last* ← *d*
  R ↑ .*Sign* ← TRUE
  R ↑ .*Count* ← *0*
  end {*NewRegister*

Setting an initialized register back to zero can be even simpler:

procedure *Clear(R)*
  R ↑ .*Last* ← *R* ↑ .*First*
  R ↑ .*Count* ← *0*
  R ↑ .*Sign* ← TRUE
  end {*Clear*

This procedure, however, does not recover the (possibly many) digit nodes that were in the register *R*. A more practical version of *Clear* is:

procedure *Clear(R)*
  $p \leftarrow R \uparrow .Last$
  $q \leftarrow p \uparrow .Left$
  while $p \neq R \uparrow .First$ **do**
    DISPOSE(p)
    $p \leftarrow q$
    $q \leftarrow p \uparrow .Left$
    endwhile
  $p \uparrow .Right \leftarrow$ NIL
  $R \uparrow .Last \leftarrow p$
  $R \uparrow .Count \leftarrow 0$
  $R \uparrow .Sign \leftarrow$ TRUE
  end   {*Clear*

The speed of arithmetic operations is directly dependent on the number of digits involved, and so removal of duplicate leading zeroes is an essential part of housekeeping:

procedure *Compact(R)*
  $p \leftarrow R \uparrow .First$
  $q \leftarrow p \uparrow .Right$
  while $q \neq$ NIL   **do**
    if $q \uparrow .Value \neq 0$
      then *exit*
      else $t \leftarrow q \uparrow .Right$
          DISPOSE(q)
          $R \uparrow .Count \leftarrow R \uparrow .Count - 1$
          $p \uparrow .Right \leftarrow t$
          $q \leftarrow t$
          if $t \neq$ NIL
            then $t \uparrow .Left \leftarrow p$ **endif**
      endif
    endwhile
  if $R \uparrow .Count = 0$ **then** $R \uparrow .Last \leftarrow R \uparrow .First$ **endif**
  end   {*Compact*

Note: The pair of tests at the top of this loop require a fair amount of modification when implemented in Pascal because the condition:

$$(q \neq \text{NIL}) \text{ AND } (q \uparrow .Value \neq 0)$$

is risky. A more direct translation results from the use of GOTO to implement **exit**.

On the principle of "never trust the user," compaction is included as the last action in *ValueIn*.

The input-token generator *ValueIn* is:

procedure *ValueIn(X,NoX,NextOp)*
  NoX ← TRUE
  Clear(X)
  Read(ch)
  while NOT (*ch* IN *OperatorSet*) **do**
    if *ch* IN [0 . . 9]
      then *NoX* ← FALSE
        NEW(*d*)
        d ↑ .*Right* ← NIL
        d ↑ .*Value* ← ORD(*ch*) − ORD(*'0'*)
        d ↑ .*Left* ← *X* ↑ .*Last*
        X ↑ .*Last* ↑ .*Right* ← *d*
        X ↑ .*Last* ← *d*
        X ↑ .*Count* ← *X* ↑ .*Count* + *1*
    endif
    Read(ch)
  endwhile
  NextOp ← *ch*
  Compact(X)
end {*ValueIn*}

D.3 Arithmetic Operations

The fundamental operation of arithmetic is addition, but it becomes subtraction when the signs of the operands differ. When done by hand, the value of smaller *magnitude* is subtracted from the other. One simple approach to addition is based on two steps:

1. Compare *AC* and *X* and switch them if necessary to insure that $|AC| \geqslant |X|$.

2. If the signs agree, then add magnitudes with procedure *Carry;* otherwise, subtract the magnitudes with procedure *Borrow*.

The resulting logic is:

procedure *Add(X)*
  R ← *LargerOf(AC,X)*
  if *R* = *X*
    then *X* ← *AC*
        AC ← *R*
    endif
  if *X*↑*.Count* = *0* **then return endif**
  if *AC*↑*.Sign* = *X*↑*.Sign*
    then *Carry(AC,X)*
    else *Borrow(AC,X)*
    endif
  end {*Add*

function *LargerOf(AC,X)*   {*O(n)* *Assumes compacted operands*
  if *AC*↑*.Count* > *X*↑*.Count* **then return** *AC* **endif**
  if *X*↑*.Count* > *AC*↑*.Count* **then return** *X* **endif**
  k ← *AC*↑*.Count*
  pAC ← *AC*↑*.First*↑*.Right*
  pX ← *X*↑*.First*↑*.Right*
  while *k* > *0* **do**
    if *pAC*↑*.Value* > *pX*↑*.Value* **then return** *AC* **endif**
    if *pAC*↑*.Value* < *pX*↑*.Value* **then return** *X* **endif**
    pAC ← *pAC*↑*.Right*
    pX ← *pX*↑*.Right*
    k ← *k* − *1*
    endwhile
  return *AC*   {*X* = *AC*
  end {*LargerOf*

Note: The **returns** are replaced by a nest of IF-statements in Pascal. *Add, Subtract, Multiply,* and *Divide* all may switch *X* and *AC* to avoid copying a long list of digits, and so *X* is a VAR parameter in the Pascal implementation.

The last carry operation can create a new digit (as in 997 + 18), which is signaled by a carry after the last *X*-digit has been added to *AC*. The last borrow can propagate to the left (as in 10003 − 4), but that can be handled by continuing to subtract the leading zero node, *X*↑*.First*. With these problems recognized:

```
procedure Carry(X)
  pAC ← AC ↑ .Last
  pX ← X ↑ .Last
  Over ← 0
  for  k = 1 to AC ↑ .Count  do
    Sum ← pAC ↑ .Value + pX ↑ .Value + Over
    if  Sum > 9
      then Over ← 1
           pAC ↑ .Value ← Sum − 10
      else Over ← 0
           pAC ↑ .Value ← Sum
      endif
    pAC ← pAC ↑ .Left
    pX ← pX ↑ .Left
    next k
  if  Over > 0
    then NEW(d)
         d ↑ .Right ← pAC ↑ .Right
         d ↑ .Left ← pAC
         pAC ↑ .Right ↑ .Left ← d
         pAC ↑ .Right ← d
         d ↑ .Value ← Over
         AC ↑ .Count ← AC ↑ .Count + 1
    endif
  end  {Carry


procedure Borrow
  pAC ← AC ↑ .Last
  pX ← X ↑ .Last
  Loan ← 0
  for  k = 1 to AC ↑ .Count  do
    Difference ← pAC ↑ .Value − pX ↑ .Value − Loan
    if  Difference < 0
      then Loan ← 1
           pAC ↑ .Value ← Difference + 10
      else Loan ← 0
           pAC ↑ .Value ← Difference
      endif
    pAC ← pAC ↑ .Left
    pX ← pX ↑ .Left
    next k
  Compact(AC)
  end  {Borrow
```

With *Add* complete, subtraction becomes very simple:

procedure *Subtract(X)*
  $X \uparrow .Sign \leftarrow$ NOT $X \uparrow .Sign$
  $Add(X)$
  end *{Subtract*

Multiplication can be done by repeated addition in two ways: $47 \times 31 =$ $(47 + 47 + \cdots + 47,$ 31 times$)$ and $47 \times 31 = (47 + 3 \times 470)$. The latter approach is used here. It will square 2 raised to the 96th power in a few seconds on an inexpensive microcomputer (after compilation by a \$30 Pascal compiler). This operation would take years by repeated addition.

Several values are involved in multiplication: the original operands X and AC, the shifting values Y (such as 47, 470, . . .), the product of a digit of X with a Y, say M, and the running sum of these products. AC supplies the original Y and then may contain the running sum. The product sign must be determined but not affect the use of *Add* to multiply magnitudes, and a value with a minimal number of digits should be used to control the multiplication loop. This housekeeping is done by:

procedure *SetUp*
  $Y \leftarrow AC$
  $NewRegister(AC)$
  $New\ Register(M)$
  $R \leftarrow LargerOf(Y,X)$
  if $R = X$
    then $X \leftarrow Y$
        $Y \leftarrow R$
  endif
  $NewSign \leftarrow (Y \uparrow .Sign = X \uparrow .Sign)$
  $X \uparrow .Sign \leftarrow$ TRUE
  $Y \uparrow .Sign \leftarrow$ TRUE
  $Clear(AC)$
  end *{SetUp*

A routine is needed to shift successive products one digit to the left. One approach is to shift Y:

procedure *ShiftLeft(Y)*
  NEW(d)
  $d \uparrow .Value \leftarrow 0$
  $d \uparrow .Right \leftarrow$ NIL
  $d \uparrow .Left \leftarrow Y \uparrow .Last$
  $Y \uparrow .Count \leftarrow Y \uparrow .Count + 1$
  $Y \uparrow .Last \uparrow .Right \leftarrow d$
  $Y \uparrow .Last \leftarrow d$
  end *{ShiftLeft*

Multiplication then can be done with:

```
procedure Multiply(X)
   SetUp
   if   X↑.Count = 0   then return endif
   pX ← X↑.Last
   for   j = 1 to X↑.Count   do
      Over ← 0
      MakeCopy(M,Y)
      pM ← M↑.Last
      pX ← X↑.Last
      v ← pX↑.Value
      for   k = 1 to M↑.Count   do
         Product ← pM↑.Value * v + Over
         pM↑.Value ← Product MOD 10
         Over ← Product DIV 10
         pM ← pM↑.Left
         next k
      if   Over > 0
         then NEW(d)
                 d↑.Right ← pM↑.Right
                 d↑.Left ← pM
                 pM↑.Right↑.Left ← d
                 pM↑.Right ← d
                 M↑.Count ← M↑.Count + 1
                 d↑.Value ← Over
         endif
      Add(AC,M)
      ShiftLeft(Y)
      pX ← pX↑.Left
      next j
   AC↑.Sign ← NewSign
   Clear(Y)
   Clear(M)
   end   {Multiply
```

Division by repeated subtraction is as slow as multiplication by repeated addition, but the alternative algorithm used by fifth graders is much more complex than repeated subtraction. For contrast with multiplication, a version of repeated subtraction is applied here: the divisor is added to itself until it is larger than the dividend. Each such addition is paired with an increment of the result.

Auxiliary registers are used as they are for multiplication and destroyed on exit from *Divide*. The initialization is:

procedure *Prolog*
　NewSign ← (*AC* ↑ .*Sign* = *X* ↑ .*Sign*)
　AC ↑ .*Sign* ← TRUE
　X ↑ .*Sign* ← TRUE
　D ← *AC*
　NewRegister(AC)
　NewRegister(R)
　NewRegister(S)
　end {*Prolog*

The resulting divide logic is:

procedure *Divide(X)*
　if *X* ↑ .*Count* = *0*
　　then *Clear(AC)*
　　　　return
　　endif
　Prolog
　MakeCopy(S,X)
　MakeCopy(AC,One)
　R ← *LargerOf(D,S)*
　while *R* = *D* **do**
　　Carry(AC,One)
　　Carry(S,X)
　　R ← *LargerOf(D,S)*
　　endwhile
　Borrow(AC,One)
　AC ↑ .*Sign* ← *NewSign*
　Clear(D)
　Clear(S)
　end {*Divide*

A listing of a Pascal program that results from this design follows:

```
PROGRAM UnBound(Input,Output);
   TYPE   Digit = ↑DigitNode;
          Register = ↑RegisterNode;
          DigitNode = RECORD
                            Value : 0 .. 9;
                            Left : Digit;
                            Right : Digit
                            END;
          RegisterNode = RECORD
                            Sign : BOOLEAN;
                            Count : INTEGER;
                            First : Digit;
                            Last : Digit
                            END;
   VAR   Op,NextOp : CHAR;
         NoX,Done : BOOLEAN;
         One,X,AC : Register;
      OperatorSet : SET OF CHAR;
         Numeric : SET OF CHAR;
{   }
   PROCEDURE Display(AC : Register);
      VAR pAC : Digit;
            k : INTEGER;
      BEGIN
        Writeln;
        pAC := AC↑.First;
        IF  NOT (AC↑.Sign)  THEN Write('-');
        FOR  k := 1 TO (AC↑.Count + 1)  DO BEGIN
          Write(pAC↑.Value);
          pAC := pAC↑.Right
          END;
        Writeln
        END  {Display};
```

```
{   }
PROCEDURE NewRegister(VAR R : Register);
  VAR   d : Digit;
  BEGIN
    NEW(d);
    d↑.Left := d;
    d↑.Value := 0;
    d↑.Right := NIL;
    NEW(R);
    R↑.First := d;
    R↑.Last := d;
    R↑.Sign := TRUE;
    R↑.Count := 0
    END  {NewRegister};
{   }
PROCEDURE Clear(VAR R : Register);
  VAR   p,q : Digit;
  BEGIN
    p := R↑.Last;
    q := p↑.Left;
    WHILE  (p <> R↑.First)  DO BEGIN
      DISPOSE(p);
      p := q;
      q := p↑.Left
      END;
    R↑.Last := p;
    R↑.Count := 0;
    p↑.Right := NIL;
    R↑.Sign := TRUE
    END  {Clear};
{   }
PROCEDURE MakeOne(VAR One : Register);
  VAR   d : Digit;
  BEGIN
    NewRegister(One);
    NEW(d);
    d↑.Value := 1;
    d↑.Left := One↑.First;
    d↑.Right := NIL;
    One↑.First↑.Right := d;
    One↑.Last := d;
    One↑.Count := 1
    END  {MakeOne};
```

```
{   }
PROCEDURE Preface;
    BEGIN
      Writeln('This program simulates a calculator that');
      Writeln('allows unbounded integers. Enter values');
      Writeln('followed by operators. The accepted operators');
      Writeln('are: +,-,*,/,=,C (for clear),Q (for quit),');
      NewRegister(AC);
      NewRegister(X);
      MakeOne(One);
      Numeric := ['0',,'9'];
      OperatorSet := ['+','-','*','/','=','C','Q']
      END  {Preface};
{   }
  PROCEDURE Compact(VAR R : Register);
    VAR  p,q,t : Digit;
    BEGIN
      p := R↑.First;
      q := p↑.Right;
      IF  (q <> NIL)  THEN IF  (q↑.Value <> 0)  THEN q := NIL;
        WHILE  (q <> NIL)   DO BEGIN
          t := q↑.Right;
          DISPOSE(q);
          R↑.Count := R↑.Count - 1;
          p↑.Right := t;
          q := t;
          IF (t <> NIL)
            THEN BEGIN
              t↑.Left := p;
              IF  (t↑.Value <> 0)  THEN q := NIL
              END
          END;
      IF  (R↑.Count = 0)  THEN R↑.Last := R↑.First
      END  {Compact};
```

```
{  }
  PROCEDURE ValueIn(VAR X : Register; VAR NoX : BOOLEAN;
                    VAR NextOp : CHAR);
    VAR  ch : CHAR;
         d : Digit;
    BEGIN
      NoX := TRUE;
      Clear(X);
      Read(ch);
      WHILE  NOT (ch IN OperatorSet)
        DO BEGIN
          IF  (ch IN Numeric)
            THEN BEGIN
              NoX := FALSE;
              NEW(d);
              d↑.Right := NIL;
              d↑.Value := ORD(ch) - ORD('0');
              d↑.Left := X↑.Last;
              X↑.Last↑.Right := d;
              X↑.Last := d;
              X↑.Count := X↑.Count + 1
              END;
          Read(ch)
          END;
      NextOp := ch;
      Compact(X)
    END  {ValueIn};
```

```
{   }
  FUNCTION LargerOf(AC,X : Register) : Register;
    VAR  k : INTEGER;
         pAC,pX : Digit;
    BEGIN
      LargerOf := AC;
      IF  (AC↑.Count <= X↑.Count)  THEN
          IF   (AC↑.Count < X↑.Count)
        THEN LargerOf := X
        ELSE BEGIN
          k := AC↑.Count;
          pAC := AC↑.First↑.Right;
          pX := X↑.First↑.Right;
          WHILE  (k > 0)  DO
              IF  (pAC↑.Value <= pX↑.Value)
                THEN IF  (pAC↑.Value < pX↑.Value)
                        THEN BEGIN
                          LargerOf := X;
                          K := 0
                          END
                        ELSE BEGIN
                          pAC := pAC↑.Right;
                          pX := pX↑.Right;
                          k := k - 1
                          END
                ELSE k := 0
          END;
      END  {LargerOf};
```

```
{    }
  PROCEDURE MakeCopy(VAR M : Register; Y : Register);
    VAR   d,pY : Digit;
             k : INTEGER;
    BEGIN
     Clear(M);
     IF   (Y↑.Count > 0)   THEN BEGIN
         pY := Y↑.First↑.Right;
         FOR   k := 1 TO Y↑.Count   DO BEGIN
           NEW(d);
           d↑.Right := NIL;
           d↑.Value := pY↑.Value;
           pY := pY↑.Right;
           d↑.Left := M↑.Last;
           M↑.Last↑.Right := d;
           M↑.Last := d
           END;
         M↑.Count := Y↑.Count;
         END
    END   {MakeCopy};
```

```
{    }
  PROCEDURE Carry(VAR AC : Register; X : Register);
    VAR   pAC,pX,d : Digit;
        k,Sum,Over : INTEGER;
    BEGIN
      pAC := AC↑.Last;
      pX := X↑.Last;
      Over := 0;
      FOR  k := 1  TO AC↑.Count  DO BEGIN
        Sum := pAC↑.Value + pX↑.Value + Over;
        IF  (Sum > 9)
          THEN BEGIN
            Over := 1;
            pAC↑.Value := Sum - 10
            END
          ELSE BEGIN
            Over := 0;
            pAC↑.Value := Sum
            END;
        pAC := pAC↑.Left;
        pX := pX↑.Left
        END;
      IF  (Over > 0)
        THEN BEGIN
          NEW(d);
          d↑.Right := pAC↑.Right;
          d↑.Left := pAC;
          pAC↑.Right↑.Left := d;
          pAC↑.Right := d;
          d↑.Value := Over;
          AC↑.Count := AC↑.Count + 1
          END
    END  {Carry};
```

```
{   }
  PROCEDURE Borrow(VAR AC : Register; X : Register);
    VAR   pAC,pX : Digit;
          K,Loan,Difference : INTEGER;
    BEGIN
      pAC := AC↑.Last;
      pX := X↑.Last;
      Loan := 0;
      FOR  K := 1 TO  AC↑.Count   DO BEGIN
        Difference := pAC↑.Value - pX↑.Value - Loan;
        IF  (Difference < 0)
          THEN BEGIN
            Loan := 1;
            pAC↑.Value := Difference + 10
            END
          ELSE BEGIN
            Loan := 0;
            pAC↑.Value := Difference
            END;
        pAC := pAC↑.Left;
        pX := pX↑.Left
        END;
      Compact(AC)
      END  {Borrow};
{   }
  PROCEDURE Add(VAR AC : Register; VAR X : Register);
    VAR  R : Register;
    BEGIN                       {X is VAR as AC may swap with it.}
      R := LargerOf(AC,X);
      IF  (R = X)
        THEN BEGIN
          X := AC;
          AC := R
          END;
      IF  (X↑.Count <> 0)
        THEN IF  (AC↑.Sign = X↑.Sign)
                THEN Carry(AC,X)
                ELSE Borrow(AC,X)
      END  {Add};
```

```
{  }
  PROCEDURE Subtract(VAR AC : Register; VAR X : Register);
    BEGIN
      X↑.Sign := NOT X↑.Sign;
      Add(AC,X)
      END  {Subtract};
{  }
  PROCEDURE Multiply (VAR AC : Register; VAR X : Register);
    VAR  pM,pX,d : Digit;
         M,Y : Register;
         v,k,j,Over,Product : INTEGER;
         NewSign : BOOLEAN;
{  }
  PROCEDURE SetUp;
    VAR  R : Register;
    BEGIN
      Y := AC;
      NewRegister(AC);
      NewRegister(M);
      R := LargerOf(Y,X);
      IF  (R = X)
        THEN BEGIN
          X := Y;
          Y := R
          END;
      NewSign := (Y↑.Sign = X↑.Sign);
      X↑.Sign := TRUE;
      Y↑.Sign := TRUE;
      Clear(AC)
      END  {SetUp};
{  }
  PROCEDURE ShiftLeft(VAR Y : Register);
    VAR  d : Digit;
    BEGIN
      NEW(d);
      d↑.Value := 0;
      d↑.Right := NIL;
      d↑.Left := Y↑.Last;
      Y↑.Count := Y↑.Count + 1;
      Y↑.Last↑.Right := d;
      Y↑.Last := d
      END  {ShiftLeft};
```

```
{   }
  BEGIN  {Multiply}
    SetUp;
    IF  (X↑.Count <> 0)
      THEN BEGIN
        pX := X↑.Last;
        FOR  j := 1 TO X↑.Count  DO BEGIN
          Over := 0;
          MakeCopy(M,Y);
          pM := M↑.Last;
          v := pX↑.Value;
          FOR  k := 1 TO M↑.Count  DO BEGIN
            Product := pM↑.Value * v + Over;
            pM↑.Value := Product MOD 10;
            Over := Product DIV 10;
            pM := pM↑.Left
            END;
          IF  (Over > 0)
            THEN BEGIN
              NEW(d);
              d↑.Right := pM↑.Right;
              d↑.Left := pM;
              pM↑.Right↑.Left := d;
              pM↑.Right := d;
              M↑.Count := M↑.Count + 1;
              d↑.Value := Over
              END;
          Add(AC,M);
          ShiftLeft(Y);
          pX := pX↑.Left
          END;
        AC↑.Sign := NewSign;
        Clear(Y);
        Clear(M)
        END
    END  {Multiply};
{   }
  PROCEDURE Divide(VAR AC : Register; VAR X : Register);
    VAR  NewSign : BOOLEAN;
         D,R,S : Register;
```

```
{   }
  PROCEDURE Prolog;
    BEGIN
      NewSign := (AC↑.Sign = X↑.Sign);
      AC↑.Sign := TRUE;
      X↑.Sign := TRUE;
      D := AC;
      NewRegister(AC);
      NewRegister(R);
      NewRegister(S)
      END  {Prolog};
{   }
  BEGIN                      {Divide}
    IF  (X↑.Count = 0)
      THEN Clear(AC)
      ELSE BEGIN
        Prolog;
        MakeCopy(S,X);
        MakeCopy(AC,One);
        R := LargerOf(D,S);
        WHILE  (R = D)  DO BEGIN
          Carry(AC,One);
          Carry(S,X);
          R := LargerOf(D,S)
          END;
        Borrow(AC,One);
        AC↑.Sign := NewSign;
        Clear(D); Clear(S)
      END
    END  {Divide};
{   }
  PROCEDURE Swap;
    VAR  R : Register;
    BEGIN
      R := AC;
      AC := X;
      X := R
      END  {Swap};
```

```
{**

                                                              **}

BEGIN  {UnBound}
  Preface;
  Done := FALSE;
  Op := 'C';
  REPEAT
    ValueIn(X,NoX,NextOp);
    IF  (NextOp = 'Q')
      THEN Done := TRUE
      ELSE BEGIN
        IF  (NextOp = 'C')
          THEN BEGIN
            Clear(X); Clear(AC);
            Op := 'C'
            END;
        IF  NoX  THEN MakeCopy(X,AC);
        CASE  Op  OF
          'C' : Swap;      {AC with X}
          '=' : Swap;
          '+' : Add(AC,X);
          '-' : Subtract(AC,X);
          '*' : Multiply(AC,X);
          '/' : Divide(AC,X)
          END
        END;
    Op := NextOp;
    Display(AC)
    UNTIL  Done
  END  {UnBound}.
```

Section *E*

The Stack Machine

A Pascal program that provides command-shell access to a stack is a straightforward application of the procedures of Chapter 4, as long as some of the realities of Pascal as a working language are respected. In particular, care must be taken with the distinction between value and variable parameters in procedures.

Input and output from a terminal must deal with end-of-line codes, and the dual use of the screen (or print paper) can affect program details. Standard programming techniques suffice, applied within a token-entry procedure that can acquire values for the insert and bound commands.

The command repertoire of section 4.1.1 can be extended somewhat, but a complete set seems to be:

- I   insert

- D   delete the top value

- T   display the top value

- B   set a bound for the number of items on the stack

- C   clear (empty) the stack

- E   exit (quit)

For the sake of robustness, miskeying of input is ignored if possible. For the sake of simplicity, errors of deletion from an empty stack and insertion into a full one only invoke mild reproof. Simplicity also dictates the replacement of function *TopValue* with procedure *Display* that writes an ''empty stack'' message when necessary:

```
PROGRAM StackMachine(Input,Output);
   TYPE  ValueType = 0..99;
         StackType = ARRAY [1..99] OF INTEGER;
   VAR  Stack : StackType;
        Value : ValueType;
        Bound : ValueType;
          Top : ValueType;
           Op : CHAR;
{  }
   PROCEDURE Preface;
     BEGIN
       Write('This program operates a stack with the');
       Writeln(' single-letter commands:');
       Writeln('I - insert a value into the stack');
       Writeln('D - delete the top value from the stack');
       Writeln('T - display the top value of the stack');
       Writeln('B - set the stack bound between 1 and 99');
       Writeln('C - clear (empty) the stack');
       Writeln('E - exit (quit)'); Writeln;
       Writeln('Commands should be separated by spaces.');
       Write('B and I are to be followed by an integer');
       Writeln(' in the range 0 to 99.'); Writeln;
       END  {Preface};
{  }
   PROCEDURE WhatNow(VAR Op : CHAR; VAR Value : ValueType);
     BEGIN
       Value := 0;
       Read(Op);
       WHILE NOT (Op IN ['I','D','T','B','C','E']) DO Read(Op);
         IF  (Op = 'I')  THEN Readln(Value);
       IF  (Op = 'B')  THEN Readln(Value)
       END  {WhatNow};
```

```
{  }
   PROCEDURE Push(Value : ValueType);
     BEGIN
       IF  (Top >= Bound)
         THEN Writeln('Stack full. Try another command.')
         ELSE BEGIN
                 Top := Top + 1;
                 Stack[Top] := Value
                 END  {ELSE}
     END  {Push};
{  }
FUNCTION Empty(Stack : StackType) : BOOLEAN;
   BEGIN
     IF  (Top = 0)
       THEN Empty := TRUE
       ELSE Empty := FALSE
     END  {Empty};
{  }
   PROCEDURE DeleteTop(Stack : StackType);
     BEGIN
       IF  Empty(Stack)
         THEN Writeln('Stack empty. Try another command.')
         ELSE Top := Top - 1
       END  {DeleteTop};
{  }
   PROCEDURE Display(Top : ValueType);
     VAR k : ValueType;
     BEGIN
       Writeln;
       IF  Empty(Stack)
         THEN Writeln('The Stack is Empty.')
         ELSE Writeln('The top value is',Stack[Top] : 3);
       Writeln
       END  {Display};
```

```
{**
                                                        **}

  BEGIN  {StackMachine}
    Preface;
    Top := 0;
    Bound := 10;
    WhatNow(Op,Value);
    WHILE  (Op <> 'E')  DO BEGIN
      CASE  Op  OF
        'I' : Push(Value);
        'D' : DeleteTop(Stack);
        'T' : Display(Top);
        'B' : Bound := Value;
        'C' : Top := 0
        END {CASE};
      WhatNow(Op,Value)
      END {WHILE}
    END  {StackMachine}.
```

Section *F*

Stacks in the Language FORTH

FORTH modules are normally built "bottom up" by defining an operation, called a *word,* that acts on the system stack, then extending that word to a more general or more powerful one, and so on, until the entire program is, in a word, a *word.* FORTH is *extendable,* because the language can be enlarged by the use of defining statements that enter words into a list called the *dictionary.* The words entered into the dictionary are then recognized as operations from which more words may be built.

FORTH is a *threaded language* as it is usually implemented, meaning that execution proceeds from the call of a routine (the execution of a *word*), which consists of calls to other routines, which in turn call others, and so on. At the lowest level the calls request use of the primitive operations known as machine instructions.

FORTH is an *interpretative language* as it is usually implemented, translating and then executing each word as it is encountered. Interpretation is perhaps a more natural partner of stack-oriented languages than of others, because each word performs some operation on the stack, immediately. The interpretative scheme in turn combines readily with an *interactive* system.

A FORTH statement, and the resulting interaction, is:

```
3 4 + . 7 OK
```

The user types 3 4 + . @ (@ means "hit the RETURN key"), and FORTH responds 7 OK. (The underlining of the FORTH response is included for visual clarity in the text; it does not appear in actual output.) Table F.1 shows the execution of this statement in terms of formal stack operations and SUE.

Table F.1

Token	Response	Stack S
3	INSERT(S,3)	$V1\ V2\ \cdots\ Vt\ 3$
4	INSERT(S,4)	$V1\ V2\ \cdots\ Vt\ 3\ 4$
+	**begin**	
	$Sum \leftarrow$ TOP(S)	
	DELETE(S)	$V1\ V2\ \cdots\ Vt\ 3$
	$Sum \leftarrow Sum +$ TOP(S)	
	DELETE(S)	$V1\ V2\ \cdots\ Vt$
	INSERT(S,sum)	$V1\ V2\ \cdots\ Vt\ 7$
	end	
	$Write$(TOP(S))	

Similarly

$$2\quad 3\quad 4\quad +\quad *\quad ,\quad \underline{14}\quad \underline{OK}$$

has the effect on an initially empty stack that is shown in Figure F.1.

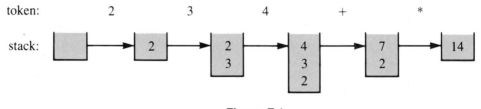

Figure F.1

In general, FORTH reads tokens (separated by blank spaces) left to right, stacks operands, and executes words. In this context, arithmetic operators like "*" and "+" are built-in dictionary words. The definition of a word, say *neword,* is added to the dictionary by simply executing a statement of the form:

```
: neword {details of what to do} ;  OK
```

Here the OK response indicates that a new entry has been put into the dictionary.

Conversion of a length measured in inches to the corresponding length in centimeters can be defined by:

```
: intocm 2.54 * ;  OK
```

This defines *intocm* to be the sequence of operations:

- Push 2.54 onto *S*.

- Multiply the top two values, delete them, and push the product onto *S;* that is, execute the word "*".

The word *intocm* may then be used as any other word:

8 intocm . 20.32 OK

If the top value of the stack is 5 (however it got there):

intocm . 12.7 OK

Values may be stored in variables as well as on the stack. A variable identifier is *bound to* a memory cell (declared) when the connection between the two is established. For example

VARIABLE x OK

declares *x* as a variable, and *x* can then be assigned the value 10 by:

10 x ! OK

(The command "!" is read "store".) Retrieval of a variable value (to the stack) is done with "@", read "fetch". With the assignment above:

x @ . 10 OK
x @ intocm . 25.4 OK

A redefinition of *neword* does not delete the old definition. When the word *neword* is encountered in the scan of a statement being interpreted, the *latest* definition is retrieved. It is possible to back up one definition of *neword* by execution of:

FORGET neword OK

All dictionary entries made since *neword* are lost. In effect, the dictionary itself is treated as a stack with respect to the occurrences of a given word within it, as shown in Figure F.2. It is convenient to assume that a word, ".S", is available to display the stack contents, nondestructively.

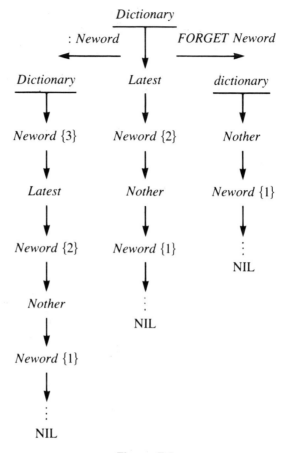

Figure F.2

If the stack contains 5 7 2, bottom to top, then:

```
,S  5  7  2  OK
```

A quirk (or astute design choice, if you like) is that access to the top of the FORTH stack is not just a TOP(S) operation but is essentially the operation pair [TOP(S), DELETE(S)], a *pop*. The use of the top value deletes it. Hence, to square the top value, for example, it is necessary first to duplicate it. A built-in word "DUP" is provided for this purpose. For example, if the stack contains: 5 7 −2 then:

```
,S    5  7  −2  OK
DUP  ,S  5  7   −2  −2  OK
DUP  *  ,S  5  7  −2  4
```

In terms of formal stack operations, DUP is INSERT(S,TOP(S)).

A number of stack manipulation words are contained in the basic dictionary of a FORTH compiler. The action of some of them is displayed here; their expression in terms of formal stack operations is left to the exercises and problems:

```
.S 5 7 2 OK
```

```
/MOD .S 5 1 3 OK                {remainder then quotient, of top
                                {value division of next-to-top
```

```
.S  5 7 2 OK
MOD .S 5 1 OK                   {remainder of top value division
                                {of next-to-top
```

```
.S   5 7 2 OK
SWAP .S 5 2 7 OK
```

```
.S  5 7 2 OK
DUP .S 5 7 2 2
```

```
.S   5 7 2 OK
OVER .S 5 7 2 7 OK              {copy next-to-top and push it
```

```
.S  5 7 2 3 OK
ROT .S 5 2 3 7 OK              {cyclic rotation of the
                               {top 3 values
```

```
.S   5 7 2 OK
DROP .S 5 7 OK
```

```
.S    1 5 7 2 OK
2SWAP .S 7 2 1 5 OK            {swaps top *pairs*
```

```
.S   5 7 2 OK
2DUP .S 5 7 2 7 2 OK          {duplicates top *pair*
```

```
.S    5 7 2 3 4 OK
2OVER .S 5 7 2 3 4 7 2 OK     {copies second pair
                              {and pushes it
```

```
.S    5 7 2 OK
2DROP .S 5 OK                 {discards the top pair
```

Exercise EF.1 and problem PF.1 are appropriate at this point.

F.1 FORTH Control Structures

The discussion of FORTH control structures in this section is very brief, but excellent treatments of FORTH are available for the reader interested in pursuing this topic further, including [BRODIE, 1981] and [BYTE, 1980].

The heart of any procedural language is the set of control structures it provides. It is necessary to have conditional branch statements in a language, and it is very awkward to do without explicit loops. Some peculiarities of control statements in FORTH are created by the way in which words are dealt with sequentially, in conjunction with an operation on the stack.

Everything in FORTH is postfix and stack-related, but the necessary structures *are* provided. For example

```
: Checkten 10 = IF Powwow THEN ; OK
```

adds a word to the dictionary, which—when executed—plays the same *role* in program logic as the SUE statement

if *TOP(S) = 10*
   then *Powwow*
   endif

but it differs because it also manipulates the stack. A partial trace of its action is shown in Table F.2.

Table F.2

token	operation
10	INSERT(S, 10)
=	**begin**
	t1 ← $TOP(S)$
	DELETE(S)
	t2 ← $TOP(S)$
	DELETE(S)
	if $t1 = t2$
	then INSERT(S,1) {*any value but 0 is*
	else INSERT(S,0) {*considered to be* TRUE
	endif
	end
IF	bool ← $TOP(S)$
	DELETE(S)
	{*The decision to execute or not to execute* Powwow
	{*is then, in effect,*
	{**if** bool **then** *Powwow* **endif**

Similarly

```
: Spliten 10 = IF Powwow ELSE Wait THEN ; OK
```

adds a word to the dictionary, which—when executed—plays the role of the SUF statement:

if $TOP(S) = 10$
  then *Powwow*
  else *Wait*
  endif

Problem PF.2 and program PGF.1 are appropriate at this point.

Loop structures in FORTH are only slightly more complex. A *DO-loop* is specified in FORTH by:

```
: DEF {limit} {index} DO {what you will} LOOP;
```

One such loop definition is:

```
:echo 5 to 1 DO ."shout " LOOP ; OK
```

When executed:

```
echo shout shout shout shout shout OK
```

The index of the *DO*-loop is accessed within the loop by the FORTH word "I". With the help of the FORTH word "CR" that prints a carriage return:

```
: echo2 3 to 1 DO CR ."shout " I LOOP ; OK

echo2
shout 1
shout 2
shout 3 OK
```

Exercise EF.2 and Problem PF.3 are appropriate at this point.

Additional features of FORTH are described in [BRODIE, 1981] and [BYTE, 1980].

Exercises immediate applications of the text material

EF.1 Write procedures for *stack* operations to emulate the following FORTH words:

```
MOD, /MOD, SWAP, DUP, DROP, OVER, 2DROP
```

(PF.1 asks for others.)

EF.2 What is the output of the following loop:

```
:mystery 10 1 DO I * . LOOP;
```

Problems not immediate, but requiring no major extensions of the text

PF.1 Write procedures, in terms of *stack* operations, that emulate the following FORTH words:

```
ROT, 2SWAP, 2DUP, 2OVER
```

PF.2 Write a procedure for stack operations, to emulate the **if** . . . **then** . . . **else** construct in FORTH.

PF.3 Choose one of the example problems EP2.1–EP2.5 of Chapter 2.1. Write a sequence of variable definitions and FORTH dictionary words with the property that the final word in the sequence solves the problem.

Programs for trying it yourself

PGF.1 Write a program that manages a stack on demand from an input file with FORTH commands. "`.`", "`.S`", and the commands of EF.1 are a minimum viable set. If convenient, a special symbol may be used in place of *linefeed*. The "FORTH" response should be identical to that of the FORTH interpreter discussed in this section.

Section G

The p-Machine

The information required to execute p-code instructions is contained in Figure G.1.

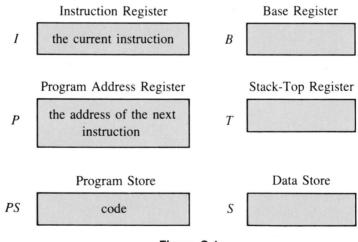

Figure G.1

A p-code program is created and loaded into the program store PS by a p-code compiler (and loader, if that operation is separate). The PS is treated as a ROM (Read Only Memory) by the p-Machine. That is, no program ever alters it, but its contents are accessible. At the initiation of program execution, the program address register P is set to the address of the first (p-code) instruction in PS; and the machine automatically cycles through the following loop until the execution of an instruction (HALT or STOP, in effect) shuts off execution:

repeat {*Execution cycle*

1. Fetch the instruction at the address in P, and place it in I. (It will have a PS address.)

2. Increment P to point to the presumed next instruction.

3. Execute the instruction, *i,* in I.

if *i* is *HALT* then **exit.**

if *i* is an unconditional branch, or a conditional branch with a *TRUE* condition, then update P to the branch address.

forever

The instruction set is chosen with regard to the properties of the hardware that can be built to carry out the cycle, but there are many options. Because the p-Machine is a general-purpose computer, the chosen instruction-set embodies several standard functions:

1. I/O (Input/Output)

2. Copy, to transfer data from one location to another

3. Arithmetic and logic

4. Branch

5. Conditional Branch

These functions help to define the instruction set, and so does the way instructions interact with the stack S. The stack interactions fundamentally determine the ability of p-code to support language features that supplement the actions listed above. The most crucial of such features are those associated with procedures. Procedures affect the p-Machine instructions to such an extent that they need to be discussed before the instruction set itself.

A data set is pushed onto S and popped from S in two ways—in many-valued segments and as individual values—in order to manage the data relevant to the execution of procedures. Such data can vary from one invocation to another of the same procedure. Data, and information about the location of data, can be passed to invoked procedures in a number of ways.

From the view of p-code, it is only necessary to know that a data set local to a particular invocation of a procedure is to be found in the data segment that represents that invocation. A value in a procedure invocation M is located by using the base address (which is in the base register B when M is being executed) and an offset, A, within the segment, that is specific to the variable. This process is illustrated in Figure G.2.

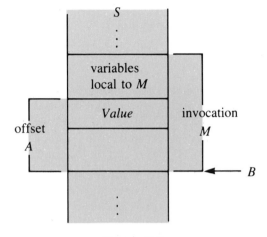

Figure G.2

All data are local to one, and only one, procedure invocation. Consider, for example, the nested procedures below:

```
procedure Alpha
   declare aVar
   procedure Beta
      declare b
      procedure Gamma
         declare c

            .
            .
            .

         aVar ← 3 * b
            .
            .
            .

         end {Gamma
      end {Beta
   end {Alpha
```

During execution of procedure *Gamma*, the stack S might appear as shown in Figure G.3.

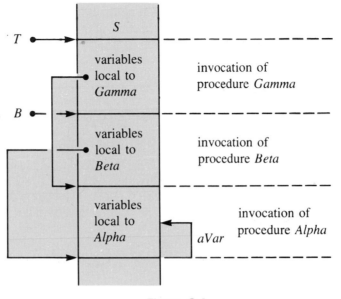

Figure G.3

The dashed arrows imply that the segment to which the variable *aVar* belongs can be traced back through a sequence of base addresses—a linked list, in effect. Then *aVar* is located within its procedure invocation (of *Alpha* in this case). Clearly, some linking mechanism needs to be provided within the instruction format and the segments as they are stacked. The mechanism provided will even allow procedures to call themselves, directly or indirectly. For example, *Gamma* may refer to *Gamma* (directly) or to *Beta* (which may invoke *Gamma* again).

Because of the need for nested invocations of procedures, *two* links are provided in each segment. The segment scheme is shown in Figure G.4.

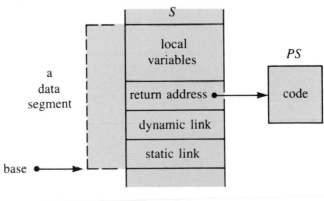

Figure G.4

- The *static link* points to the data segment of the immediately *containing* procedure (in the source code block structure). It is used to resolve variable references. In the example, the static link in an invocation of *Gamma* points to the base of an invocation of *Beta*.

- The *dynamic link* is the address of the data segment of the *calling* (invoking) procedure. It is used to pop the segment off the stack at **return** time. In the most straightforward use of procedures, the dynamic link has the same value as the static link.

To determine the static link, the compiler keeps track of a *level* of declarations in the source code. Essentially this is the nesting level of the defining procedure. In the example, variables *aVar, b,* and *c* might be at levels 1, 2, and 3, respectively. The *difference* in levels between a variable and a segment that *refers* to it is precisely the number of times that the static link must be used to reach the segment in which the variable is *declared*. For example, to find the variable *aVar* at level 1 from procedure *Gamma* at level 3, the static links must be followed twice: to *Beta,* then to *Alpha*. Consequently, the address of a value in S consists of a *level difference* and an *offset* within a segment.

The behavior of the p-Machine does not entirely determine the syntax of p-code statements, but it certainly limits the options. In a simple, suitable format instructions contain three fields:

INST	L	A

```
INST ← instruction code   {opcode
   L ← level difference
   A ← displacement        {offset
```

An instruction is written: INST L,A

The implication is that the pair (L,A) determines an address; but, for some instructions, the pair of fields has other uses. The *syntax* remains the same; the *semantics* varies.

A workable instruction set is the following:

LIT   0,A   {Load the constant (literal) A onto the
                            {top of the stack S: $S[T] \leftarrow A$

OPR   0,A   {Execute operation A. The possible
                            {operations include I/O and arithmetic.

LOD   L,A   {Push the value at address (L,A) onto
                            {S. The address (L,A) is level difference
                            {L, offset A.

STO   L,A   {Pop the value of S and store it in (L,A).

CAL   L,A   {Invoke a procedure, with first executable
                            {statement at A in PS; start a new segment
                            {with dynamic link set to the old B value,
                            {and static link determined from L.

INT   0,A   {Increment T by A: $T \leftarrow T + A$

JMP   0,A   {Jump (transfer control) unconditionally
                            {to the instruction at A in PS.

JPC   0,A   {If the top stack value, $S[T]$, is zero,
                            {then jump to A in PS; otherwise, don't.

This instruction set uses the stack S for transfers of control and data in sophisticated ways, but computation is confined to rather simple stack manipulations. For example, for operation code $A = 2$, execution of OPR is:

begin   {*addition*
    $T \leftarrow T - 1$
    $S[T] \leftarrow S[T] + S[T+1]$
end

For $A = 16$, the execution is:

begin   {*input*
    $T \leftarrow T + 1$
    $Readln(S[T])$
end

The OPR statement has seventeen variations:

```
OPR   0,0      {the last line of a program
OPR   0,1      {unary minus
OPR   0,2      {addition
OPR   0,3      {subtraction
OPR   0,4      {multiplication
OPR   0,5      {integer division
OPR   0,6      {logical odd function—if S[T] is
               {odd, then replace it with TRUE(1),
               {else with FALSE(0)
OPR   0,7      {no operator—used to debug programs
OPR   0,8      {test for S[T−1] = S[T] and replace the
               {pair with TRUE(1) or FALSE(0)
OPR   0,9      {test for ≠
OPR   0,10     {test for < i.e. S[T−1] < S[T]
OPR   0,11     {test for ≥
OPR   0,12     {test for >
OPR   0,13     {test for ≤
OPR   0,14     {print S[T]
OPR   0,15     {carriage return
OPR   0,16     {read into S[T]
```

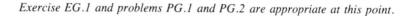

Exercise EG.1 and problems PG.1 and PG.2 are appropriate at this point.

It may surprise you to discover how little of the complexity of this computing machine is generated by reading, writing, and arithmetic and how much by the flow of information and the flow of control. That is, however, true to the nature of computing.

The definitive exposition of p-code and the p-Machine is by the inventor [WIRTH, 1974], who includes a compiler of (limited) Pascal, PL/0, into p-code. The p-code concept has been extended to form the basis of compilers of full Pascal, notably at the University of California at San Diego. A further extension has brought forth machines that execute p-code directly in hardware.

Both FORTH (see section F) and the p-Machine are founded on stack management, but they are quite distinct. For example, only a few of the FORTH *words* come into play in p-code, and they are the familiar operations of arithmetic and logic. FORTH does not need a program store. Commands are interpreted and executed immediately. FORTH makes its stack the center of attention: the p-Machine uses its stack as a scaffold hidden behind the scenes of the high-level languages it supports.

Exercises   immediate applications of the text material

EG.1   Convert the SUE segments that follow into p-code:

```
i ← 1
while  i ≤ 10  do
  j ← 1
  while  j ≤ 3  do
    Write(i,j)
    j ← j + 1
    endwhile
  i ← i + 1
  endwhile
```

```
Read(a,b)
if  a > b
  then a ← a + b
     Write(a,b)
  else a ← a − b
     Write(a,b)
  endif
```

```
i ← 1
while  i ≤ 10  do
  Write(i)
  i ← i + 1
  endwhile
```

```
i ← 1
repeat
    Write(i)
    i ← 1
    until  i > 10
```

```
i ← 1
j ← 2
k ← 4
while  i ≤ k  do
  if  j < k
    then j ← j + 1
       Write(i,j,k)
    else k ← k − 1
       Write(i,j,k)
    endif
  i ← i − 1
  endwhile
Write(i,j,k)
```

```
Read(a)
if  a − 1
  then b ← 10
     Write(a,b)
  endif
if  a = 2
  then b ← 20
     Write(a,b)
  endif
if  a = 3
  then b ← 20
     Write(a,b)
  endif
```

Problems   not immediate, but requiring no major extensions of the text

PG.1   Write a p-code program that will input 10 numbers and print their sum.

PG.2   Choose one of the example problems EP2.1–EP2.5 of section 2.1 and solve it with a p-code program.

Section *H*

Following a Maze

A maze of passages is (topologically) equivalent to a rectangular array of block positions, some occupied and some forming passages because they are not occupied. A very simple example is shown in Figure H.1.

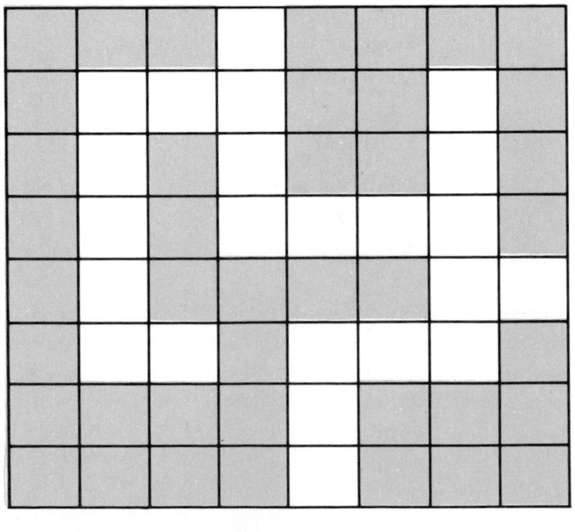

Figure H.1

Such an array of blocks corresponds to an array of values. For example,

$$M[I,J] = 1$$

may correspond to an open (unoccupied) block and $M[I,J] = 0$ to a closed (occupied) block. The maze of Figure H.1 is then represented by:

```
M  1 2 3 4 5 6 7 8
1  0 0 0 1 0 0 0 0
2  0 1 1 1 0 0 1 0
3  0 1 0 1 0 0 1 0
4  0 1 0 1 1 1 1 0
5  0 1 0 0 0 0 1 1
6  0 1 1 0 1 1 1 0
7  0 0 0 0 1 0 0 0
8  0 0 0 0 1 0 0 0
```

While searching such a table for a passageway from an entrance position (R,C) to an exit position, it is convenient to mark positions (I,J) already visited by the assignment $M[I,J] \leftarrow 2$. An algorithm that searches the table form of the maze for passageways from an entrance to another exit can be designed around a stack of positions:

Push (R,C) and set $M[R,C]$ to 2. The pair (R,C) is the *current position*.

repeat

1. Test the four positions adjacent to (R,C) (on the North, East, South, and West). For a position (I,J) for which $M[I,J] = 1$, push (I,J) and set $M[I,J]$ to 2. If no adjacent position is open, then delete (I,J) and set $M[R,C]$ to 0 to indicate that the current position leads nowhere.

2. $(R,C) \leftarrow$ TopValue

until (R,C) is a border position.

If the final (R,C) is the initial entrance pair, then the maze has no other exit because all branch-paths from all blocks accessible from the start block have been tried. The contents of the stack define a path from entrance to exit. If adjacent positions are tested in clockwise order, a trace of the first few loop iterations for the example maze are:

```
(R,C)     STACK
(1,4)     (1,4)
(1,4)     (1,4) (2,4)
(2,4)     (1,4) (2,4) (3,4) (2,3)
(2,3)     (1,4) (2,4) (3,4) (2,3) (2,2)
(2,2)     (1,4) (2,4) (3,4) (2,3) (2,2) (3,2)
(3,2)     (1,4) (2,4) (3,4) (2,3) (2,2) (3,2) (4,2)
(4,2)     (1,4) (2,4) (3,4) (2,3) (2,2) (3,2) (4,2) (5,2)
(5,2)     (1,4) (2,4) (3,4) (2,3) (2,2) (3,2) (4,2) (5,2) (6,2)
(4,2)     (1,4) (2,4) (3,4) (2,3) (2,2) (3,2) (4,2) (5,2) (6,2) (6,3)
(4,2)     (1,4) (2,4) (3,4) (2,3) (2,2) (3,2) (4,2) (5,2) (6,2)
          .
          .
          .
```

Exercise EH.1 is appropriate at this point.

From this point, the algorithm will backtrack, erasing false passages as it goes.

An appropriate data structure for the stack is an array of records, each containing a pair of indices. The entrance pair, for instance, may be entered as integers $I0$ and $J0$ and placed in a position record *Start* by: *Start.Row* ← $I0$, *Start.Column* ← $J0$.

The remaining technical problem is the search of positions adjacent to the current one. The positions adjacent to pair (R,C) are:

$$(I - 1,J), (I,J + 1), (I + 1,J), \text{ and } (I,J - 1)$$

These can be derived by adding pairs $(-1,0)$, $(0,1)$, $(1,0)$, and $(0,-1)$ to (R,C). For convenience in looping through the four possibilities, they can be stored in an array of pairs, shown in Figure H.2.

Delta

Figure H.2

An implementation of this scheme requires that (I,J) + $Delta(k)$ fall within the table for any (I,J) in the maze. Consequently, extra rows of zeros should be provided at each edge of the maze table (in rows 0 and $RowMax$ + 1, columns 0 and $ColumnMax$ + 1).

The algorithm, configured as a procedure to which the maze-table and entrance data are passed is:

```
procedure Mouse(Start,M,RowMax,ColumnMax)
  Push(Start)
  R ← Start.Row
  C ← Start.Column
  M[R,C] ← 2
  repeat
    DeadEnd ← TRUE
    for  k ← 1 to 4  do
      I ← R + Delta[k].Row
      J ← C + Delta[k].Column
      if  M[I,J] = 1
        then Test.Row ← I
             Test.Column ← J
             Push(Test)
             M[I,J] ← 2
             DeadEnd ← FALSE
      endif
    next k
    if  DeadEnd
      then Delete
           M[I,J] ← 0
    endif
    Position ← TopValue
    R ← Position.Row
    C ← Position.Column
    if        R = 0  OR  R = RowMax
       OR   C = 0  OR  C = ColumnMax
      then Done ← TRUE
      else Done ← FALSE
    endif
  until  Done
end  {Mouse
```

Exercises   immediate applications of the text material

EH.1   Complete the trace of the example maze.

Problems   not immediate, but requiring no major extensions of the text

PH.1   *Mouse* can maintain a second stack of *branch points*—blocks with two or more adjacent open blocks. This stack can be used to find *all* the paths from entrance to other exits. How?

Programs   for trying it yourself

PGH.1 Implement *Mouse* within a program.

Section *I*

The Queue Machine

A Pascal program that provides command-shell access to a queue is a straightforward application of the procedures of Chapter 5, as long as some of the realities of Pascal as a working language are respected. In particular, care must be taken with the distinction between value and variable parameters in procedures.

Input and output from a terminal must deal with end-of-line codes, and the dual use of the screen (or print paper) can affect program details. Standard programming techniques suffice, applied with a token-entry procedure that can acquire values for the insert and bound commands.

The command repertoire for a queue machine is:

- I   insert
- D   delete the front value
- F   display the front value
- B   set a bound for the number of items on the queue
- C   clear (empty) the queue
- E   exit (quit)

For the sake of robustness, miskeying of input is ignored if possible. For the sake of simplicity, errors of deletion from an empty queue and insertion into a full one only invoke mild reproof. Simplicity also dictates the replacement of function

Front with procedure *Display* that writes an ''empty queue'' message when necessary.

```
PROGRAM QueueMachine(Input,Output);
   TYPE ValueType = 0..99;
        QueueType = ARRAY [1..99] OF INTEGER;
   VAR ValueIn : ValueType;
         Queue : QueueType;
         Bound : ValueType;
         Front : ValueType;
          Rear : ValueType;
            Op : CHAR;
{   }
   PROCEDURE Preface;
     BEGIN
        Write('This program operates a queue with the');
        Writeln(' single-letter commands:');
        Writeln('I - insert a value into the queue');
        Writeln('D - delete the front value from the queue');
        Writeln('F - display the front value of the queue');
        Writeln('B - set the queue bound between 1 and 99');
        Writeln('C - clear (empty) the queue');
        Writeln('E - exit (quit)'); Writeln;
        Writeln('Commands should be separated by spaces, B and I');
        Write('are to be followed by an integer in the range 0');
        Writeln(' to 99,'); Writeln;
        END  {Preface};
{   }
   PROCEDURE WhatNow(VAR Op : CHAR; VAR ValueIn : ValueType);
     BEGIN
        ValueIn := 0;
        Read(Op);
        WHILE  NOT (Op IN ['I','D','F','B','C','E'])   DO
          Read(Op);
        IF  (Op = 'I')  THEN Readln(ValueIn);
        IF  (Op = 'B')  THEN Readln(ValueIn)
        END  {WhatNow};
```

```
{   }
   PROCEDURE InsertRear(ValueIn : ValueType);
{   }
      PROCEDURE ShiftQ(Queue : QueueType);
         VAR   k : INTEGER;
         BEGIN
           IF   (Front > 0)
             THEN BEGIN
               FOR k := 1 TO (Rear - Front)   DO
                  Queue[k] := Queue[Front+k];
               Rear := Rear - Front;
               Front := 0
               END
           END   {ShiftQ};
{   }
      BEGIN
        IF   (Rear >= Bound)
          THEN ShiftQ(Queue)
          END;
        IF   (Rear >= Bound)
          THEN Writeln('The Queue is full. Try another command.')
          ELSE BEGIN
            Rear := Rear + 1;
            Queue[Rear] := ValueIn
            END
        END   {InsertRear};
{   }
   FUNCTION Empty(Queue : QueueType) : BOOLEAN;
      BEGIN
        IF   (Rear = 0)
          THEN Empty := TRUE
          ELSE Empty := FALSE
        END   {Empty};
```

```
{  }
  PROCEDURE DeleteFront(Queue : QueueType);
    BEGIN
      IF  Empty(Queue)
        THEN Writeln('The queue is empty. Try another command.')
        ELSE BEGIN
          Front := Front + 1;
          IF  (Front = Rear)
            THEN BEGIN
              Front := 0;
              Rear := 0
              END
          END
    END  {DeleteFront};
{  }
  PROCEDURE Display(Front : ValueType);
    VAR K : ValueType;
    BEGIN
      Writeln;
      IF  Empty(Queue)
        THEN Writeln('The queue is empty.')
        ELSE Writeln('The front value is',Queue[Front+1] : 3);
      Writeln
    END  {Display};
```

```
{**

                                                        **}

  BEGIN  {QueueMachine}
    Preface;
    Front := 0;
    Rear  := 0;
    Bound := 10;
    WhatNow(Op,ValueIn);
    WHILE  (Op <> 'E')  DO BEGIN
      CASE  Op  OF
        'I' : InsertRear(ValueIn);
        'D' : DeleteFront(Queue);
        'F' : Display(Front);
        'B' : Bound := ValueIn;
        'C' : BEGIN
                Front := 0;
                Rear  := 0
                END
      END {CASE};
    WhatNow(Op,ValueIn)
    END {WHILE}
  END  {StackMachine}.
```

Section *J*

Queues in Hardware

Some microprocessors, such as the Intel 8086, have an *instruction queue* built into the CPU [INTEL, 1979]. The motivation is that the CPU execution cycle contains essentially four phases: *execution, fetch, read,* and *write*. Here *read, write,* and *fetch* refer to sending and receiving information from the *CPU itself*. In particular, *write* refers to the sending of information to some address that may be associated with a display, but may just be an update of a memory location. The effect of the *write* depends on the instruction that commands it, and the address. The *read* phase involves acquiring data from some address, which may be in memory or may be associated with a terminal. Instructions may or may not read and write in this general sense when they are executed, depending upon their function. The term *fetch* specifically refers to acquiring an *instruction* from memory. The crucial fact is that the CPU is otherwise idle during the fetch operation, unless it is possible to overlap the phases. With overlap, some of the phases can be done simultaneously by the hardware. The instruction queue that makes this possible is a set of 6 *registers,* which are storage locations, like memory cells, except that they are in the CPU itself, not in memory. (*Register* is the more general term; memory cells are registers used in a particular way.) The scheme is a queue, as illustrated in Figure J.1.

The IQ (Instruction Queue) is used to store the next few instructions that are expected to be executed in order. Execution of a branch operation (conditional or not) will cause the next instruction to be taken out of sequence, and so the next instruction may need to be fetched immediately and the instruction queue reloaded from the new point. Without concern for branches, however, fetches into the IQ may take place during execution of the current instruction.

A schematic trace of the overlap can be given using *exec, wr, f,* and *rd* as abbreviations for execute, write, fetch, and read, respectively. A simplified example of instructions 1,2,3,4, and 5 during eight units of time might look like Figure J.2.

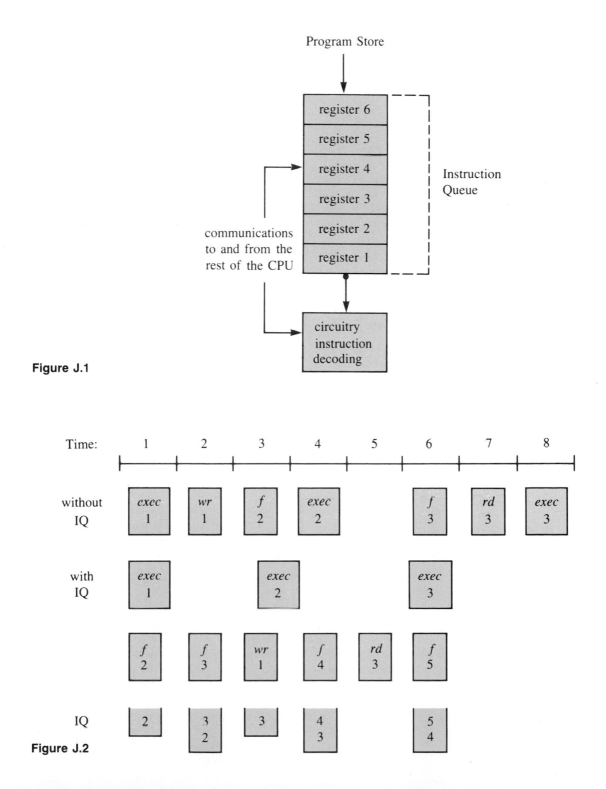

Figure J.1

Figure J.2

The amount of time saved by the IQ mechanism depends upon a variety of factors:

- The speed at which instructions can be moved from the IQ to the decoder, relative to the time required for a fetch from memory. It might be faster by a factor of 1000; and, if so, the IQ-to-decoder move is negligible.

- The amount of time spent in the fetch phase, compared to time spent during execute, read, and write phases. A rough estimate is that fetches can use 10 – 40 percent of the CPU time if there is no overlap.

- The frequency of branch operations. A rough estimate is that 1 instruction in 16 is a branch.

The actual time saved in execution depends so heavily on the particulars of the instruction stream that it needs to be determined or at least verified experimentally. A speedup of 15 percent or so due to the IQ would be a modest expectation.

Program PGJ.1 is appropriate at this point.

The use of an instruction queue is a simple form of a more extensive overlap of instruction execution called *pipelining*. Execution of an instruction in a processor is actually the execution of a sequence of more primitive operations, called *microcode*. *Microcode* is designed to be neatly done with electronic circuitry. The instruction decoder, in effect, invokes a procedure in which the statements are microcode operations. Such procedures may include subprocedures and calls on standard (microcode) utility subprocedures, and so on, just like *any* computer coding. (Some people program in microcode for a living. It may be a relief to know that the buck stops there—the substrate that supports microcode is engineering, not programming.) The meaning of an instruction is determined by a microcode program. Some machines are even designed to allow users to redesign the instruction set by re(micro)programming them.

The circuits controlled by microcode instructions do not have to be idle while other circuits are at work. Pipelining allows parts of several instructions to be moving through the execution system at the same time. The ultimate set of divisions of an instruction that permits pipelining is not (*execute, read, write,* and *fetch*), but the set of available microcode operations.

The fetch of instructions from the program store is an execution bottleneck, and so is the fetch of data, which can be relieved with the use of a *cache memory*. (Data, from the viewpoint of the CPU, include instructions—whatever comes from memory.) A cache memory is memory that can be accessed much more rapidly than the main store because of the way it is constructed. It costs more, else it would simply replace the main store, and so it is relatively small.

Effective use of a buffer, such as a cache memory, is made when it is full of precisely those values that will be needed next. This can be done with high success in several ways, some involving queueing.

Typically, a cache memory ranges from 1K (1024 bytes) to 64K and is 5 to 10 times as fast as main memory, having perhaps 100 nsec (nanoseconds, 10^{-9} seconds) for an access time. Circuitry is designed into the machine to keep track of what is in the cache; it is a "cache directory," such as Figure J.3 shows.

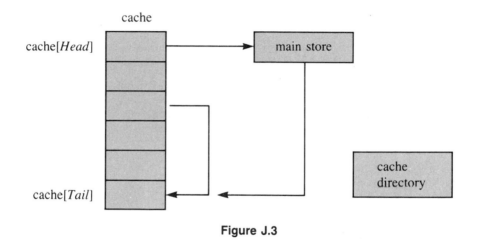

Figure J.3

When a memory-reference is made, if the information is in the cache, the cache is used for the *read* or *store*. An 85–95 percent "hit rate" is typical, but it depends on some strategy for keeping those data most likely to be used soon in the cache. The hit rate depends upon how local the memory references tend to be.

One way to enhance the hit rate involves dividing the cache into areas that will be called *segments* here. Data are fetched from the main store in chunks of segment size, and the collection of segments is treated as a queue (or perhaps a priority queue). A directory of segments that are currently in the cache is maintained. Whenever a segment is accessed, whether or not it is already in the cache, it can be moved to the tail of the queue. The head of the queue is then a segment that has been idle longer than any other segment and may be bumped by addition of a new segment.

A generalization of a cache queue is a cache priority queue, which allows the use of a variety of strategies for determining which segments to retain in the cache and which to swap for a currently needed value.

Programs   for trying it yourself

PGJ.1 Write a program that explores the effect of an IQ. Instructions are to be chosen at random, with:

- 100 percent requiring an *execute* phase and a *fetch* phase, of 6 and 10 units of time, respectively

- 25 percent requiring an additional *read* phase of 8 units of time

- 50 percent requiring an additional *write* phase of 8 units of time

- 20 percent are branch operations that empty an IQ if it is being used

  Determine the time required for each of five runs of 40 instructions each, both with and without an IQ of six registers. Run again with the times for *execute* and *fetch* switched to 10 and 6, respectively.

PGJ.2 Write a program that explores the effect of a cache memory. A sequence of memory references are chosen to randomly call on segments in the cache memory 85 percent of the time. Two units of time are required for retrieval from the cache and 10 for direct retrieval from memory (which brings a new segment to the cache). The tail segment is twice as likely as the next to be hit; it in turn is twice as likely as the next, and so on. The overhead cost of moving a segment to the tail is one unit of time. There are six segments in the cache. Choose five sequences of 40 memory requests each, and determine the total retrieval time needed for them.

PGJ.3 Combine PGJ.1 and PGJ.2 to determine the effect of an IQ and a cache acting in concert.

Section *K*

A Simulation of an Airport Customs Station

A simulation, as the term is used here, is a program that imitates the behavior of a system well enough to be used as an experimental surrogate for the system itself.

Pursuit of the terms "well enough" and "experimental" in the definition given lead to a vast but amorphous literature and practice. The practice is an art of importance that increases with the power of computing, yet the literature contains no decisive entry point. The intent of this section is to provide a program that is a framework for the study of a simple system and hence a window onto one part of the practice of simulation.

A professionally developed simulation program is designed for a real system on the basis of carefully collected and analyzed data. The worth of a thoughtfully determined goal is balanced against the (sometimes considerable) cost of writing and using it. The assumptions built into the system as a program model are checked for validity against the real world, and the behavior of the program is verified to be that of the assumed system. Many systems that are simulated involve random behavior, imitated by a program model, and so experiments are run on the simulation program. These experiments and the analysis of their results are both developed with statistical care.

This section is only intended to provide an example of the possibilities and a minimal framework for experiment. It is only the program portion of a simulation process that appears here.

K.1 The Customs Station

An airport customs station receives arriving passengers at a check-in counter. Passengers wait until one of several clerks is available to serve them. They are served in a time that has an (essentially) normal distribution about a mean. (The distribution cannot actually be normal, since negative service times are not possible, and they are discarded when drawn from it. Such a distribution is called *truncated normal*.) If the passengers have prepaid their customs tax, they depart the counter. If they have not, they are sent to a tax station, where they wait in a tax queue until served by one of several tax agents. They are served at the tax counter in time that has an exponential distribution. On exit from the tax counter, a passenger rejoins the customs-clerk queue but, when reaching a clerk a second time, is serviced in a constant time. A schematic of this system is shown in Figure K.1.

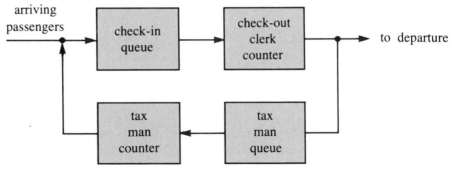

Figure K.1

This system looks deceptively simple, but the events that occur in it are several:

- Arrival: A passenger arrives at the station from outside the station "universe." If there is a free clerk, the passenger is scheduled for check-in immediately; otherwise, the passenger waits in the clerk queue.

- Check-in: A passenger is simply scheduled for checkout at a time that is "now" plus a check-out service time. This becomes the *DoTime* of the passenger—the time at which his or her event is to be done.

- Check-out: A passenger completes service by a clerk and either departs the station or is sent to the tax counter. If there is a free tax agent, the passenger is scheduled for Tax-in immediately and otherwise waits in the tax queue.

- Tax-in: A passenger is scheduled for Tax-out, at a *DoTime* value determined by "now" plus the tax service-time distribution.

- Tax-out: A passenger completes service by a tax agent and, if there is an available clerk, is sent to the clerk counter again, to Check-in, in effect. If no clerk is available, the passenger waits in the clerk queue.

These are processes, represented by procedures in a simulation program written in a language such as Pascal. These processes occur at times determined by random distributions and so occur in a random sequence. At any time, the next process to be executed may be any one of them; and several can occur at the same time. A procedural simulation program moves from event to event, each a process acting on a passenger. The program must be able to schedule the next event and handle events one at a time. Simulation time is tracked by a "clock" that is advanced to the scheduled time of the current event, the *DoTime* of the customer being processed. The clock is not advanced when a completed event is followed by a "simultaneous" event, scheduled at the current clock time.

A common simulation technique is to have one event in a distribution stream (such as the arrival stream) schedule the next one. The process that manages the arrival of passenger *I* fetches the next random interarrival time from the arrival stream, say *ia*. If the system clock is *Clock,* then the arrival of the next passenger, say *J,* occurs at time: *Clock* + *ia*. The arrival of the passenger after *J* is determined at the time of arrival of *J,* when process *Arrival* acts on *J*. Scheduling of processes can be done by a generalization of this kind of scheduling of events in a distribution stream, as indicated by the process descriptions.

Passengers spend most of their time outside of processes. A passenger who has just been checked in at one time will be processed again at his (or her) scheduled check-out time. A number of processes may be active between these times, and several events may occur at the check-out time. The program representation of a passenger (normally a record) waits somewhere when not being processed. This somewhere is an *event queue*—a priority queue of passenger records not currently in process. The priority involved is the time of the next event that is to happen to the passenger. Hence a passenger (record) is scheduled for one event after another until it departs the system, and it waits its turn on the event queue. The priorities may be determined by simply keeping the records of the event queue sorted by the *DoTime* (next-event time) of the passenger records in it.

The scheme outlined above for managing processes (events) and entities (passengers) advances the simulation clock from one scheduled event to the next in an unpredictable but very organized manner. (The next event being the *DoTime* of the record at the front of the priority queue.) This is called *discrete-event simulation,* although it applies strictly only to the program portion of a simulation. It is the technique chosen for the simulation program *Airport* developed for the airport customs station in the remainder of this section.

K.2 The Event-Cycle Level of *Airport*

The program level that corresponds to a command-shell in the management of a simple discrete-event simulation is an *event-cycle level*. At this level, control passes from one process to another, driven by the scheduling of events for entities (passenger records in this case).

The number of passenger entities in the station at any (simulation) time is ultimately determined by the interaction of four distributions: arrival, check-out service, tax service, and the uniform distribution used to decide if a passenger has prepaid the customs tax. The interaction of these is complex for the system as a whole, but for an individual passenger it is relatively simple: a passenger progresses in stages. The stages are each associated with a particular procedure:

- Stage 1. Birth: The passenger arrives, an event managed by procedure *Arrival*. *Arrival* marks the record of passenger P as stage 2 so that its next stage will be recognized by any process that handles it. *Arrival* assigns P to an idle clerk if there is one, and schedules *CheckIn* at the current time. "Scheduled" means placement in the sorted list *EventQueue*. If no clerk is available, P is placed in a waiting line, *ClerkQueue,* and no event is scheduled by *Arrival* for P. *Arrival* also schedules the next arrival, drawing from the interarrival distribution to do so.

- Stage 2. Initial check-in: An idle clerk is put to work on passenger P by procedure *Check-in*. In effect, P is scheduled for check-out at the current time *Clock* plus an increment drawn from a truncated normal distribution that represents clerk service times.

- Stage 3. Initial check-out: The initial check-out service by a clerk is complete. The managing procedure, *CheckOut,* draws a uniform variate to decide whether to send P to *Depart* (where the passenger record will die—leave the system) or to the tax counter. If P is to go to the tax counter, the record is marked stage 4 and scheduled for processing by *TaxIn* at the current time *Clock* if there is a tax agent available. If no tax agent is available, P is placed in the waiting line *TaxQueue*. Since check-out frees a clerk, if *ClerkQueue* is not empty a passenger is removed from it with the queueing discipline FIFO (first-in-first-out): it is a pure queue. *CheckOut* does not make the decision to process this newly freed passenger, however, but simply schedules the processing.

- Stage 4. Tax-counter check-in: Procedure *TaxIn* draws a service time for P from a (truncated) exponential distribution and schedules completion of tax service for P at that increment plus *Clock*. The correct routing of P is insured by marking the record stage 5.

■   Stage 5. Tax-counter check-out: Procedure *TaxOut* schedules *P* for *CheckIn* at the current *Clock* if there are idle clerks; otherwise, *P* is placed in *ClerkQueue*. Routing is insured by marking *P* as stage 6. Since *TaxOut* frees a tax agent, if *TaxQueue* is not empty, a passenger is retrieved from it—with the FIFO queueing discipline—and scheduled.

■   Stage 6. After-tax check-in: This is managed by *CheckIn* and differs from stage 2 in that a constant increment *PaidTime* is added to *Clock* to form the *DoTime* of the check-out event for *P*. Stage 7 marking routes *P* back to *CheckOut*.

■   Stage 7. After-tax check-out: This is managed by *CheckOut* and leads automatically to death— departure from the system.

Passengers are placed in *EventQueue* by procedure *Schedule* and removed from it by procedure *NextEvent*. Procedure *NextEvent* deals with a subtlety that is typical of simulation programming: more than one passenger can be scheduled for check-in with the same idle clerk or tax agent. This is a (deliberate) artifact of the program design; but alternate designs tend to lead to other timing problems, and some can create bugs that are not easy to detect. As given here, *NextEvent* simply reschedules a passenger for whom there is no idle server and chooses another passenger.

EventQueue can never be empty because the last arrival always schedules the next, and that (unborn) passenger cannot be scheduled for any process except *Arrival*, which then schedules another arrival. . . .

The division of labor among the procedures is somewhat arbitrary. In particular, the decision to schedule *P* or place the record in a waiting line *ClerkQueue* (and *TaxQueue*) can be moved to *CheckIn* (and *TaxIn*). With that change, *CheckIn*, *CheckOut*, and *ClerkQueue* form a unit that communicates with the other processes principally by way of the action of *Schedule* and *NextEvent* on *EventQueue*. Procedures *TaxIn*, *TaxOut*, and waiting line *TaxQueue* form a similar tax unit. The program presented in this section leaves them as described, and the alternative design is suggested as a programming project in P.JK.5. (The change simplifies *NextEvent*.)

In various forms, the ability to package procedures, data structures, and persistent variables confined within a unit, and to spawn copies of a unit as a type has been incorporated into languages such as *Simula, Ada,* and specifically simulation languages. Such languages would be an improvement on Pascal for writing simulation programs if they were not so complex themselves. A principle of the conservation of complexity seems to be at work for simulations.

With the procedures roughed out, the event-cycle level of *Airport* becomes:

```
program AirPort
    Clock ← 0
    Preface
    RunAgain(HowLong)
    while  HowLong  do
        OverTime ← Now + HowLong
        while  Now < OverTime  do
            p ← NextEvent(EventQueue)
            case of  p↑.WhatStage
                1 : Arrival(p)
               2,6 : CheckIn(p)
               3,7 : CheckOut(p)
                4 : TaxIn(p)
                5 : TaxOut(p)
            endcase
        endwhile
        RunAgain(HowLong)
    endwhile
end  {Airport
```

K.3 The Gathering of Data

The last and most-abused stage of a simulation is the gathering and interpretation of data generated by it. Statistical techniques of all levels may be brought to bear on simulation data, as long as it is recognized that the data derives from a model and not the actual system.

The generation of pseudorandom numbers and choice of distributions has attracted a great deal of study but perhaps not always enough in practice. It is common to make repeated runs of a simulation program and determine the mean and standard deviation of both single-run results and results from a sequence of runs. Those results are the measurement of the interaction of a model with approximations of random number sequences.

Even elementary statistics lies outside the scope of this book, and so the goal of *Airport* is simply to provide data on the mean *response time* of the model. The amount of (simulation) time spent in the system by a departing passenger is the difference between *Clock* values at arrival and departure. These times, and the times of occurrence for other stages, are kept in an array *Stage*[1 . . 7] in the passenger record. They are updated by the procedures that process a passenger at each stage. The only additional information that is gathered by *Airport* is the state of the system: the queue lengths and the number of idle servers. The intent here is to provide a framework that may be extended in programming projects as desired.

The data provided by *Airport* is enough to experimentally explore the relationship between the mean times of the distributions, the numbers of clerks and tax agents, and the response time. The experimental space for exploring response time has eight dimensions if the standard deviation of the normal distribution for clerk service is taken into account.

When making short runs, the initial conditions of the queues and the initially all-idle servers bias the results. Suggested solutions are long runs, program modification to allow a "warm start," or a limiting process. This is a universal problem in the interpretation of simulation results, with no single general solution.

Projects   for fun; for serious students

PJK.1 With the choices *MeanA* = 1.0, *Mu* = 3.0, *Sigma* = 1.0, *MeanT* = 2.0, *PaidTime* = 1.0, and *NotPaid* = 0.5, determine an optimal balance of clerks and tax agents. The trade-off is to be that two minutes of additional mean response time is as costly in customer-relations as a clerk or tax agent is in money.

PJK.2 Modify *Airport* so that it allows an initial run to reach equilibrium (perhaps) before data-gathering begins. The warm start is to be followed by a run in segments, as before.

PJK.3 Modify *Airport* so that it reports the mean queue-lengths of *EventQueue*, *ClerkQueue*, and *TaxQueue*.

PJK.4 Modify *Airport* so that it reports the *utilization* of its resources: what fraction of the time are how many clerks and tax agents busy? The output should be a plot of time against number busy (a histogram) for each type of server.

PJK.5 Modify *Airport* so that the decision to schedule a passenger or to place the record in a waiting line is included in *CheckIn* and *TaxIn*.

K.4 The Program *Airport*

```
PROGRAM Airport(Input,Output);
   TYPE   Person = ↑Entity;
          Entity = RECORD
                        WhatStage : 0..7;
                            Stage : ARRAY[1..7] OF INTEGER;
                           DoTime : INTEGER;
                             Link : Person;
                               id : INTEGER
                   END;
          WaitingLine = RECORD
                           Front : Person;
                            Rear : Person
                        END;
   VAR   Passenger : Person;
        EventQueue : Person;
                 P : Person;
        ClerkQueue : WaitingLine;
          TaxQueue : WaitingLine;
     EQL,CQL,TQL : INTEGER;
       ResponseSum : INTEGER;
        IdleTaxMen : INTEGER;
        IdleClerks : INTEGER;
        Departures : INTEGER;
          Arrivals : INTEGER;
          OverTime : INTEGER;
          PaidTime : INTEGER;
           HowLong : INTEGER;
              Seed : INTEGER;
             Clock : INTEGER;
        Sigma,Mu : REAL;
           NotPaid : REAL;
             MeanA : REAL;
             MeanT : REAL;
```

```
{   }
  FUNCTION Random(VAR Seed : INTEGER) : REAL;
    CONST  Multiplier = 13077;
              Increment = 6925;
                Modulus = 32767;
    BEGIN       {A version that works well on a KayPro when
                   compiled with JRT Pascal.}
      Seed := (Multiplier * Seed + Increment) MOD Modulus;
      Random := (Seed/Modulus + 1.0)/2.0
      END  {Random};
{   }
  FUNCTION Normal : INTEGER;
    VAR z : REAL;
        k,N : INTEGER;
    BEGIN
      REPEAT
        z := 0;
        FOR  k := 1 TO 12  DO z := z + Random(Seed);
        z := z - 6.0;
        N := TRUNC(0.5 + Sigma * z + Mu)
        UNTIL  (N > 0);
      Normal := N
      END  {Normal};
{   }
  FUNCTION LN(X : REAL) : REAL; EXTERN;
{   }
  FUNCTION Expon(OneOver : REAL) : INTEGER;
    VAR  k,ia : INTEGER;
    BEGIN
      REPEAT
        ia := TRUNC(0.5 - LN(Random(Seed)) * OneOver)
        UNTIL  (ia > 0);
      Expon := ia
      END  {Expon};
```

```
{   }
  PROCEDURE Report(p : Person);
    VAR  k : INTEGER;
    BEGIN                          {Used for debugging}
      Writeln;                     {of modifications}
      Writeln(EQL,CQL,TQL);
      Writeln('Passenger',p↑.id);
      Writeln('Stage ',p↑.WhatStage);
      Write('Stage history : ');
      FOR  k := 1 TO 7  DO Write(p↑.Stage[k]/60.0 : 7 : 2);
      Writeln;  Writeln
      END  {Report};
{   }
  FUNCTION NewPassenger : Person;
    VAR  p : Person;
         k : INTEGER;
    BEGIN
      NEW(p);
      p↑.WhatStage := 1;
      p↑.DoTime := Clock + Expon(MeanA);
      FOR  k := 1 TO 7  DO p↑.Stage[k] := 0;
      p↑.id := Arrivals + 1;
      NewPassenger := p
      END  {NewPassenger};
{   }
  PROCEDURE Schedule(VAR p : Person);
    VAR  q,r : Person;
    BEGIN
      r := EventQueue;
      IF  (r = NIL)
        THEN BEGIN
          p↑.Link := NIL;
          EventQueue := p
          END
```

```
            ELSE IF  (p↑.DoTime < r↑.DoTime)
                 THEN BEGIN
                   p↑.Link := r;
                   EventQueue := p
                   END
                 ELSE BEGIN
                   q := r↑.Link;
                   WHILE  (q <> NIL)  DO
                     IF  (p↑.DoTime <> q↑.DoTime)
                       THEN BEGIN
                         r := q;
                         q := q↑.Link
                         END
                       ELSE q := NIL;
                   p↑.Link := r↑.Link;
                   r↑.Link := p
                   END;
          EQL := EQL + 1
          END  {Schedule};
   {  }
   PROCEDURE Preface;
     VAR   p : Person;
           PT : REAL;
     PROCEDURE Setup;
       BEGIN
         EventQueue := NIL;
         ClerkQueue.Front := NIL;
         ClerkQueue.Rear := NIL;
         TaxQueue.Front := NIL;
         TaxQueue.Rear := NIL;
         EQL := 0; CQL := 0; TQL := 0;
         Seed := 1;
         Arrivals := 0;
         Departures := 0;
         ResponseSum := 0;
         MeanA := MeanA * 60;
         MeanT := MeanT * 60;
         Sigma := Sigma * 60;
         Mu := Mu * 60;
         p := NewPassenger;
         PaidTime := TRUNC(0.5 + PT * 60)
         END  {Setup};
```

```
{   }
  BEGIN
    Writeln('This is a simulation of an airport customs');
    Writeln('station. Passengers enter the station with');
    Writeln('exponentially distributed interarrival times.');
    Writeln('What mean time (in minutes) would you prefer?');
    Write('MeanA = '); READLN(MeanA);
    Writeln('Clerks deal with a new passenger in a normally');
    Writeln('distributed time. What mean service time would');
    Writeln('you prefer?');
    Write('Mu = '); READLN(Mu);
    Writeln('What standard deviation for this distribution');
    Writeln('would you prefer?');
    Write('Sigma = '); READLN(Sigma);
    Writeln('How many clerks do you prefer at the counter?');
    Write('IdleClerks = '); READLN(IdleClerks);
    Writeln('A fraction of the passengers have not paid entry');
    Writeln('tax and are shuttled to a tax counter. What');
    Writeln('fraction would you prefer?');
    Write('NotPaid = '); READLN(NotPaid);
    Writeln('Tax service requires an exponentially dis-');
    Writeln('tributed time. What mean time would you prefer?');
    Write('MeanT = '); READLN(MeanT);
    Writeln('How many tax men do you prefer at the counter?');
    Write('IdleTaxMen = '); READLN(IdleTaxMen);
    Writeln('Passengers re-enter the clerk queue after');
    Writeln('taxes and are re-serviced in constant time.');
    Writeln('What time would you prefer?');
    Write('PaidTime = '); READLN(PT);
    Writeln('You may run the simulation in segments: and the');
    Write('state of the system passes on to the next seg');
    Writeln('ment.');
    Setup;
    Schedule(P)
  END  {Preface};
```

```
{  }
  FUNCTION Empty(VAR Q : WaitingLine) : BOOLEAN;
    BEGIN
      IF  (Q.Front = NIL)
        THEN Empty := TRUE
        ELSE Empty := FALSE
      END  {Empty};
{  }
  PROCEDURE InsertRear(VAR Q : WaitingLine; VAR P : Person);
    BEGIN
      P↑.Link := NIL:
      IF   Empty(Q)
        THEN Q.Front := P
        ELSE Q.Rear↑.Link := P;
      Q.Rear := P
      END  {InsertRear};
{  }
  PROCEDURE RemoveFront(VAR Q : WaitingLine; VAR P : Person);
    BEGIN
      IF  Not Empty(Q)
        THEN BEGIN
          P := Q.Front;
          Q.Front := Q.Front↑.Link;
          P↑.DoTime := Clock
          END
      END  {RemoveFront};
{  }
  PROCEDURE RunAgain(VAR HowLong : INTEGER);
    BEGIN
      Writeln('The current time is ',Clock);
      Writeln('How long do you want this run to be?');
      Write('HowLong = '); READLN(HowLong);
      HowLong := HowLong * 60
      END  {RunAgain};
```

```
{   }
  FUNCTION NextEvent(VAR EventQueue : Person) : Person;
    VAR   NoRoom : BOOLEAN;
             P : Person;
             s : INTEGER;
  BEGIN
    NoRoom := TRUE;
    WHILE  NoRoom  DO BEGIN
      NoRoom := FALSE;
      P := EventQueue;
      EventQueue := EventQueue↑.Link;
      EQL := EQL - 1;
      s := P↑.WhatStage;
      IF  ((s=2) OR (s=6))  AND  (IdleClerks <> 0)
        THEN BEGIN
          InsertRear(ClerkQueue,P);
          CQL := CQL + 1;
          NoRoom := TRUE
          END;
      IF  ((s=4) AND (IdleTaxMen <= 0))
        THEN BEGIN
          InsertRear(TaxQueue,P);
          TQL := TQL + 1;
          NoRoom := TRUE
          END
        END;
      NextEvent := P;
    END  {NextEvent};
```

```
{  }
  PROCEDURE Arrival(VAR p : Person);
    VAR q : Person;
    BEGIN
      Arrivals := Arrivals + 1;
      Clock := p↑.DoTime;
      p↑.Stage[1] := Clock;
      q := NewPassenger;
      Schedule(q);
      p↑.WhatStage := 2;
      IF  (IdleClerks > 0)
        THEN Schedule(p)
        ELSE BEGIN
          InsertRear(ClerkQueue,p);
          CQL := CQL + 1
          END
      END  {Arrival}
{  }
  PROCEDURE Depart(p : Person);
    VAR  s : INTEGER;
    BEGIN
      Departures := Departures + 1;
      s := p↑.WhatStage;
      ResponseSum := ResponseSum + p↑.Stage[s] - p↑.Stage[1];
      DISPOSE(p)
      END  {Depart};
{  }
  PROCEDURE CheckIn(VAR p : Person);
    VAR  s,DeltaC : INTEGER;
    BEGIN
      IdleClerks := IdleClerks - 1;
      Clock := p↑.DoTime;
      s := p↑.WhatStage;
      p↑.Stage[s] := Clock;
      IF  (s = 6)
        THEN DeltaC := PaidTime
        ELSE DeltaC := Normal;
      p↑.DoTime := Clock + DeltaC;
      p↑.WhatStage := s + 1;
      Schedule(p)
      END  {CheckIn};
```

```
{   }
   PROCEDURE CheckOut(VAR p : Person);
     VAR   s : INTEGER;
           TaxPaid : BOOLEAN;
     BEGIN
       IdleClerks := IdleClerks + 1;
       Clock := p↑.DoTime;
       s := p↑.WhatStage;
       ↑.Stage[s] := Clock;
WRITE('CKO ');REPORT(p);        {MODEL TRACE}
       TaxPaid := (s = 7)  OR  (Random(Seed) > NotPaid);
       IF  TaxPaid
         THEN Depart(p)
         ELSE BEGIN
           p↑.WhatStage := 4;
           IF  IdleTaxMen > 0
             THEN Schedule(p)
             ELSE BEGIN
               InsertRear(TaxQueue,p);
               TQL := TQL + 1
               END
           END;
       IF  NOT Empty(ClerkQueue)
         THEN BEGIN
           RemoveFront(ClerkQueue,p);
           Schedule(p);
           CQL := CQL - 1
           END
       END  {CheckOut};
{   }
   PROCEDURE TaxIn(VAR p : Person);
     VAR s : INTEGER;
     BEGIN
       IdleTaxMen := IdleTaxMen - 1;
       Clock := p↑.DoTime;
       s := p↑.WhatStage;
       p↑.Stage[s] := Clock;
       p↑.DoTime := Clock + Expon(MeanT);
       p↑.WhatStage := s + 1;
       Schedule(p)
       END  {TaxIn};
```

```
{    }
   PROCEDURE TaxOut(VAR P : Person);
     VAR s : INTEGER;
     BEGIN
       IdleTaxMen := IdleTaxMen + 1;
       Clock := P↑.DoTime;
       s := P↑.WhatStage;
       P↑.Stage[s] := Clock;
       P↑.WhatStage := 6;
       IF  (IdleClerks > 0)
         THEN Schedule(P)
         ELSE BEGIN
           InsertRear(ClerkQueue,P);
           CQL := CQL + 1
           END;
       IF  NOT Empty(TaxQueue)
         THEN BEGIN
           RemoveFront(TaxQueue,P);
           Schedule(P);
           TQL := TQL - 1
           END
       END  {TaxOut};
{    }
   PROCEDURE Summary;
     VAR ResponseTime : REAL;
     BEGIN
       Write('There were ',Arrivals,' arrivals, and ');
       Writeln(Departures,' departures.');
       ResponseTime := ResponseSum/Departures;
       Writeln('The mean amount of time spent in the system');
       Write('by departing passengers was:', ResponseTime/60);
       Writeln(' minutes.');
       Writeln('Number of idle clerks: ', IdleClerks);
       Writeln('Clerk queue length: ',CQL);
       Writeln('Number of idle tax men: ',IdleTaxMen);
       Writeln('Tax queue length: ',TQL);
       Writeln('Event queue length: ',EQL)
       END  {Summary};
```

```
{   }
BEGIN                                {AIRPORT}
  Clock := 0;
  Preface;
  RunAgain(HowLong);
  WHILE  (HowLong > 0)  DO BEGIN
    OverTime := Clock + HowLong;
    WHILE  (Clock < OverTime)  DO BEGIN
      P := NextEvent(EventQueue);
      CASE  P↑.WhatStage  OF
          1 : Arrival(P);
        2,6 : CheckIn(P);
        3,7 : CheckOut(P);
          4 : TaxIn(P);
          5 : TaxOut(P)
      END
    END;
    RunAgain(HowLong)
  END;
  Summary
END  {Airport}.
```

Section *L*

Chaining in Scatter Storage

In section B, the collision of keys mapped to the the same range index in a hash table was resolved by hunting through the table for an empty cell during the STORE operation and for the key during a RETRIEVE operation. The hash table was a static structure, and the actual location of a hashed key in the table was not always the direct result of the hashing function.

An alternate method is to use a table cell as the header of a linked list that contains all of the keys that hash to the index of that cell. Reaching the head of the list is an immediate result of hashing the key, although the list must be searched for retrieval. (The STORE operation may probe the list to detect duplicate entries.)

With the definitions of section B and the use of q, $m = 17$, $Hash = h$, and alphabetical entry order, a list-header hash table for the list of ingredients of section 2.5 is shown in Figure L.1.

431

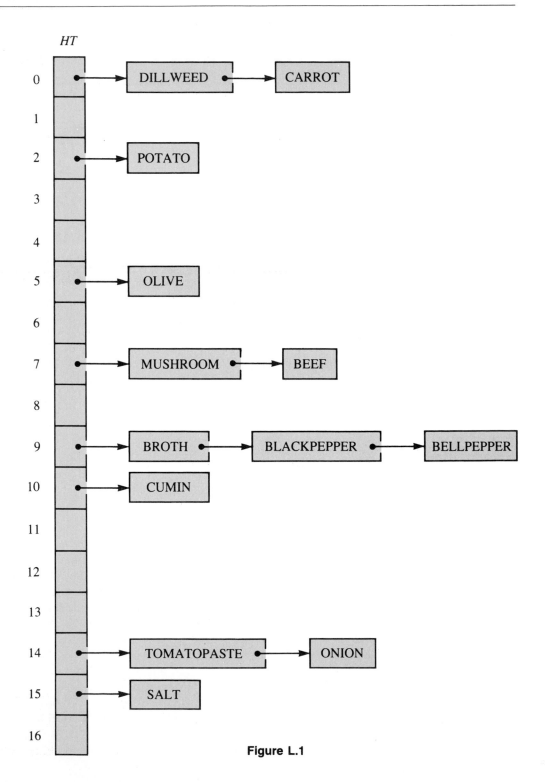

Figure L.1

The major change introduced by chaining lies in the search for a key in the linear list of a header. The function *Probe* used by both *StoreHT* and *RetrieveHT* is a list-walk:

```
function Probe(Start,s)                          {O(m)
   p ← H[Start]
   while  p ≠ NIL  do
      if  p↑.Key = s  then exit endif
      p ← p↑.Link
   endwhile
   return p
   end   {Probe
```

```
procedure StoreHT(Key)                           {O(Probe)
   k ← Hash(Key)
   p ← Probe(k,Key)
   if  p = NIL
      then NEW(q)
              q↑.Value ← Key
              q↑.Link ← HT[k]↑.Link
              HT[k]↑.Link ← q
      else {deal with a duplicate entry
      endif
   end   {StoreHT
```

```
function RetrieveHT(Key)                          {O(Probe)
   k ← Hash(Key)
   p ← Probe(k,Key)
   if  p = NIL
      then {report not there
      else return p
      endif
   end   {RetrieveHT
```

This logic retrieves the location or presence of a key in the table, enough for many applications. In other applications it must be expanded somewhat to allow *deletion* of keys from the table—something difficult to manage with a static hash table. A chained table can be an excellent choice for a hash table from which deletion is to occur.

The chained hash table has a slight advantage over the static table in the easy detection or inclusion of duplicate entries. If the keys are 20-character (20-byte) strings and if pointers require 2 bytes, the static table occupies $m \times 20$ bytes. For n entries, the chained table requires $2 \times m + n \times (20 + 1)$ bytes. As $n/m \to 0$, this approaches $2 \times m$. For keys that are themselves pointers, chaining uses *more* space. A deeper analysis is beyond the scope of this book, but double-hashing of unchained tables is a common professional choice.

Problem not immediate, but requiring no major extensions of the text

PL.1 Design the procedures and functions that would allow deletion from a chained hash table.

Program for trying it yourself

PGL.1 Write a program that accepts identifiers of up to 12 characters in length, converts them to an integer with q, and stores them in a chained hash table *HT* with the use of *Hash* = h and $m = 47$. The program should report the number of collisions, the average number of links followed by *Probe*, and the loading factor.

■

Section *M*

Walking a General List

One technique that is helpful for working through the maze of links of a general list is to mark processed nodes, as done in *Rvisit* (section 7.7). It is convenient to cycle through the paths generated by *Link*[1] . . . *Link*[*n*] by making *Mark* an integer: *Mark* = 0 for an unprocessed node and *Mark* = *i* when the *Link*[*i*] path is being traced.

Marking the nodes prevents redundant wandering through the structure but does not provide the retracing of a path needed to return to a branchpoint in the traverse. The retracing can be done by *reversing* the links and using two pointers, *Son* and *Father* to bridge positions that temporarily lack a link between them.

The operation of the pointers is most easily seen when it is applied to a linear list, as shown in Figure M.1, (where *NIL* links have been left blank for clarity). This scheme can be carried out with the help of a temporary pointer *Base:*

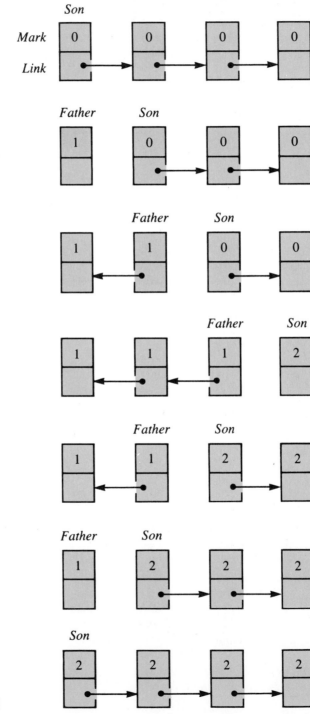

Figure M.1

- If *Son* ↑ *.Mark* = 0 then process *Son* and increment *Son* ↑ *.Mark* to indicate that the link is being followed.

- If *Son* ↑ *.Mark* = 1 then examine *Son* ↑ *.Link*. If it is *NIL* then this route cannot be processed further; increment *Son* ↑ *.Mark* to indicate that *Son* is completely processed. If *Son* ↑ *.Link* is not *NIL* then shift pointers to follow *Son* ↑ *.Link,* as shown in Figure M.2.

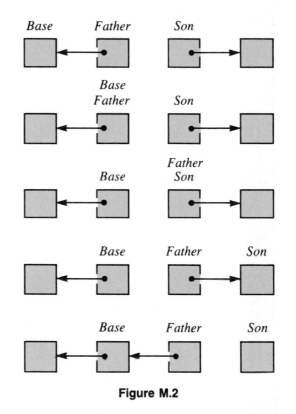

Figure M.2

- If *Son* ↑ *.Mark* = 2 then the path leaving from *Son* is completely processed. The pointers are then shifted to retrace the path that led to *Son,* as illustrated in Figure M.3.

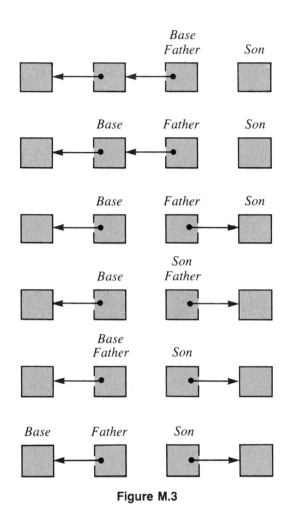

Figure M.3

This schematic process can be generalized to nodes with n link fields by incrementing the *Mark* field each time one of the links leading from a node is followed. The retracing path is followed when $Mark = n + 1$. An abbreviated trace applied to the example of a general list given at the beginning of section 7.7 is shown in Figure M.4.

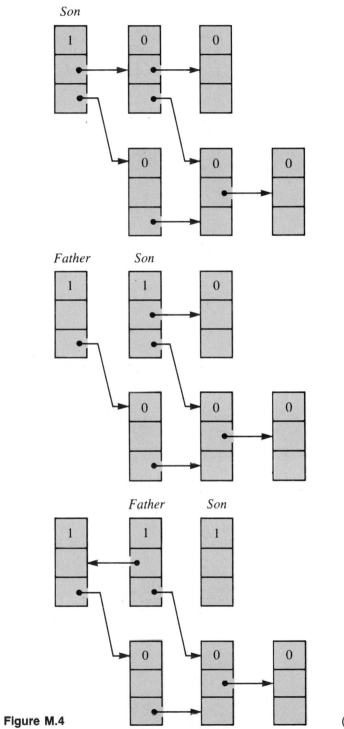

Figure M.4

(*continued*)

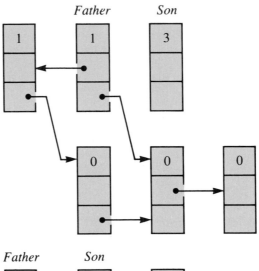

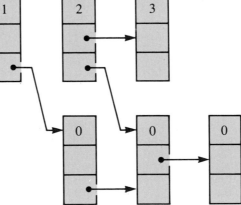

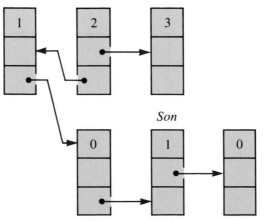

(*continued*)

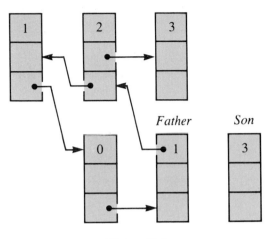

Figure M.4

The SUE version of this scheme is:

procedure *Visit(p)*
  Father ← NIL
  Son ← *p*
  repeat
    k ← *Son* ↑ *.Mark*
    case of *k*
        0 : PROCESS(*Son*)
           Son ↑ *.Mark* ← *Son* ↑ *.Mark* + *1*
      1 .. n : **if** *Son* ↑ *.Mark[k]* = NIL
          then *Son* ↑ *.Mark* ← *Son* ↑ *.Mark* + *1*
          else *Base* ← *Father*
             Father ← *Son*
             Son ← *Father* ↑ *.Link[k]*
             Father ↑ *.Link[k]* ← *Base*
          endif
      n + 1 : *k* ← *Father* ↑ *.Mark*
          Base ← *Father* ↑ *.Link[k]*
          Father ↑ *.Link[k]* ← *Son*
          Son ← *Father*
          Father ← *Base*
          Son ↑ *.Mark* ← *Son* ↑ *.Mark* + *1*
    endcase
  until *Father* = NIL
end {*Visit*

Projects   for fun; for serious students

PJM.1 Implement and test the general visitation algorithm of this section. One way to create a general list for testing is to first place a sparse number of 1's in an N by N table T, with none on the main diagonal $T[k,k]$. Create an array of N nodes, each of which has N Link fields. If $T[i,j] = 1$, then for pointer p to node i, set $p \uparrow .Link[i]$ to node $[j]$.

PJM.2 A fundamental limitation of this algorithm is that the final value of $p \uparrow .Mark$ is $n + 1$, not 0. A change to modular arithmetic for the *Mark* field causes infinite loops. (Why?) One solution is to add a switch that causes the counting process to work with an initial mark of either 0 or $n + 2$. If the switch is global, it can be reset on exit from *Visit* so that it alternates between two values. Incorporate the necessary changes into *Visit* and run it. Hint: Let $k \leftarrow |p \uparrow .Mark - Switch|$ and update $p \uparrow .Mark$ with a displacement that may be ± 1 depending on *Switch*.

The Main Diagonal Circulation Sparse Matrix

An example of a very small but relatively sparse matrix is:

M	1	2	3	4
1	1	0	0	0
2	1	1	0	1
3	0	1	0	0
4	1	0	0	0

n by n for $n = 4$

This matrix is represented as an OL (Orthogonal List) structure in section 6.5. Its cells can also be represented by an interwoven collection of circular lists where there is one value node for each nonempty cell, one braid for each row, one braid for each column, and a header node for each possible index. The value nodes can be represented in the form:

```
CellType = RECORD
              Braid[1] : ↑ .CellType      {row
              Braid[2] : ↑ .CellType      {column
              Dim[1] : INTEGER            {row index
              Dim[2] : INTEGER            {column index
           END
```

The header node for index *k* contains a subnode of *CellType* that is on both the *k*th row braid and the *k*th column braid. As shown in Figure N.1, the header nodes themselves are linked into a double linear list:

HeadType = RECORD
$\qquad$ *Junction : Cell Type*
$\qquad\qquad$ *Forth :* ↑ *HeadType* $\qquad$ {*row*
$\qquad\qquad$ *Back :* ↑ *HeadType* $\qquad$ {*column*
$\qquad$ END {*HeadType*

When the links for the first column and the third row are added to this picture, the result is as shown in Figure N.2. Figure N.3 shows the result when all of the links for the example are in place. (See pages 446 and 447.) The value nodes are linked into the header structure, as shown in Figure N.4 on page 448. This structure is an MDC, for *Main Diagonal Circulation Sparse Matrix.*

In an MDC, header nodes can account for roughly half of the nodes in the structure. For example, a 100×100 matrix with 117 value nodes out of 10,000 possible nodes will also use 100 header nodes. For comparison, if the data field is a pointer, OL of section 6.5 would require space for 317 nodes of *CellType* and MDC would require the equivalent of 257.

The list of headers can also be treated as sparse, with headers only for nonempty rows and columns; but deletion and insertion become somewhat more complex. The basic treatment given here can be modified as needed.

Both STORE and RETRIEVE involve finding the current header, then the predecessor of the node to be accessed. Header location for row or column *dex* is an adaptation of *LT* (section 3.3.2):

function *FindIndex(dex)*
$\quad$ *p* ← *M.Head*
$\quad$ **while** $\quad$ *p* ↑ *.Junction.Dim[1]* < *dex* $\quad$ **do**
$\quad\quad$ *p* ← *p* ↑ *.Forth*
$\quad\quad$ **endwhile**
$\quad$ **return** *p*
$\quad$ **end** $\quad$ {*FindIndex*

The appropriate row and column can then be located by:

Row ← *FindIndex(dex)*
Col ← *Row*

With this minor change for determining *Row* and *Col*, the procedures *FindPred, Retrieve,* and *Store* of section 6.5 for structure OL apply to MDC as well.

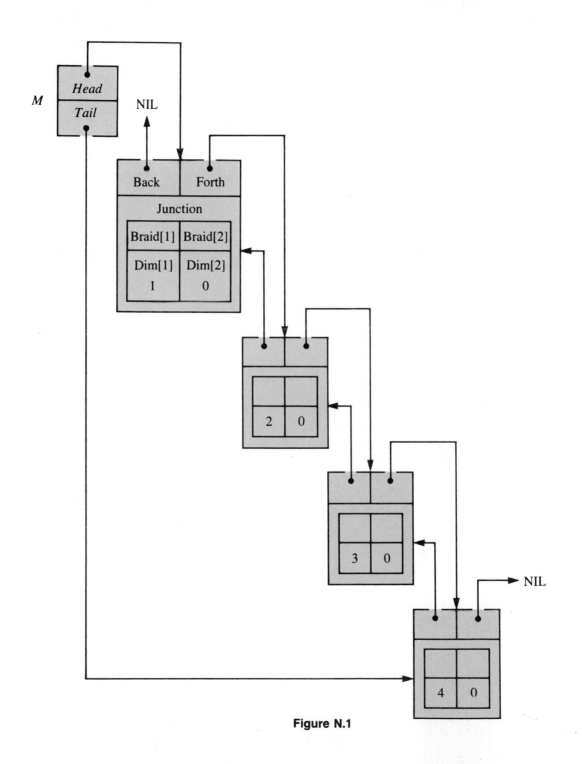

Figure N.1

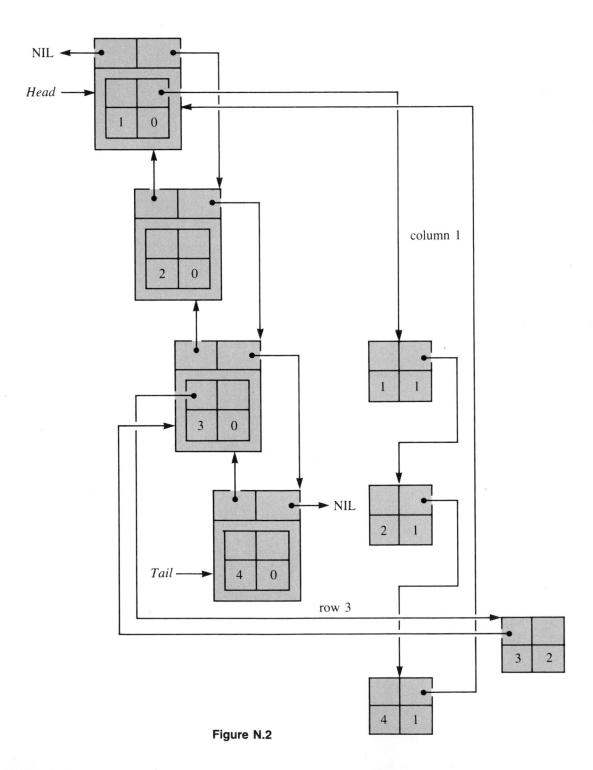

Figure N.2

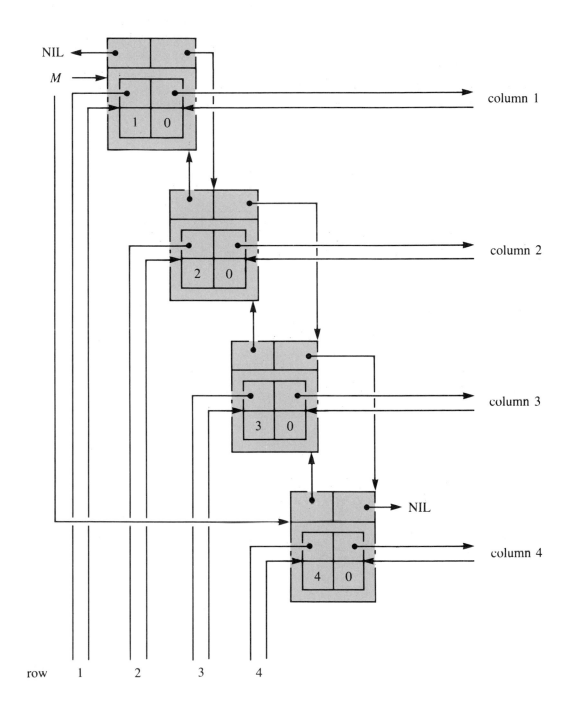

Figure N.3

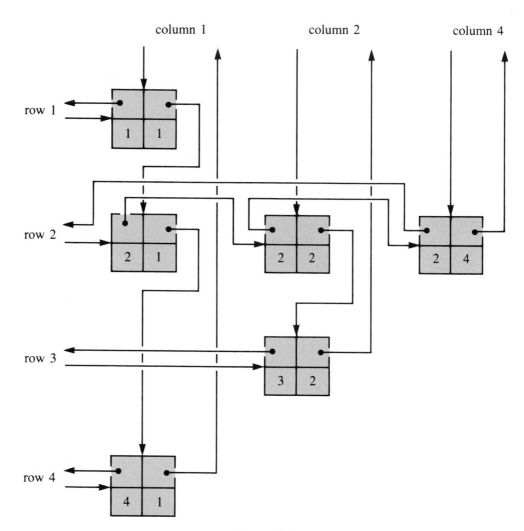

Figure N.4

Section *O*

A QuickSort Program

The procedure *QuickSort* acts on a sequence of keys, assumed to be in array *Key*[*Low* . . *High*]. It repeatedly establishes *Property P(k)*

■   *Key*[*i*] ≤ *Key*[*k*] for *Low* ≤ *i* ≤ *k*

■   *Key*[*k*] ≤ *Key*[*j*] for *k* ≤ *j* ≤ *High*

for some *k*, until the set of keys *Key*[*Low*] ≤ *Key*[*k*] ≤ *Key*[*High*] is sorted.

The value of *Key*[*k*] is called the *pivot,* and its *initial* position within the subrange *Key*[*Low*] . . . *Key*[*High*] is called the *PivotIndex*. When *P(k)* has been established, *k* is the index of the (new) position of the pivot in the range *Low* ≤ *k* ≤ *High*. *QuickSort* then calls upon itself to further arrange *Key*[*Low*] . . . *Key*[*k* − 1] and also *Key*[*k* + 1] . . . *Key*[*High*].

Two auxiliary routines are needed by *QuickSort*. Function *FindPivot* determines the pivot index (and returns 0 if all of the keys in the index subrange [*Low* . . *High*] are identical—hence, if *Low* = *High*). Procedure *Partition* establishes *P(Last)* in the index subrange [*Low . . High*]. (*Last* is the last candidate for *k* in the action of *Partition*.) With these routines:

```
procedure QuickSort(Low,High)
   PivotIndex ← FindPivot(Low,High)
   if   PivotIndex ≠ 0
      then Pivot ← Key[PivotIndex]
           Partition(Last,Low,High,Pivot)
           QuickSort(Low,Last − 1)
           QuickSort(Last + 1,High)
      endif
   end   {QuickSort
```

It is tempting to look for clever pivot-selection strategies, but a simple one is fairly serviceable: choose the larger of the first two values within the subrange [*Low . . High*] that differ. The logic of this strategy is:

```
function FindPivot(Low,High)
   Value ← Key[Low]
   for   m = Low + 1 to High   do
      case
         Key[m] > Value : return m
         Key[m] < Value : return Low
      endcase
   next m
   return 0
   end   {FindPivot
```

Another is: take the first one, *Key[Low]*.

These strategies are helpful in a set with duplicate values, but are inefficient in a set that is already sorted. A better strategy is to choose a pivot at random from *Key[Low . . High]*, but the machinery for choosing a random index is almost as complex as *QuickSort* itself unless it is available as a utility routine. The interested reader may consult section A and the program in section K.

When the pivot value has been determined, *P(Last)* may be developed within the subrange [*Low . . High*] by swapping values that are larger than *pivot* and have a smaller index, with values that are no larger than *pivot* and have a larger index. There are a number of ways to do the testing and swapping operations, but all involve a fundamental asymmetry because one test of values relative to *Pivot* is a strict inequality and the other is not.

The strategy used here is relatively simple to debug. The strategy starts with *Last* = *Low* + 1, and sweeps from *Low* + 1 to *High*, testing *Key[dex]* against

Pivot. When *Key*[*dex*] < *Pivot,* it is swapped with *Key*[*Last*], and *Last* is incremented. Now *Key*[*Last*] (the new *Last*) may not be less than *Pivot,* but it will be swapped with the next such value encountered. This process creates a segment of values from *Key*[*Low* + 1] to *Key*[*Last* − 1] that are all smaller than *Pivot.* Finally, *Key*[*Low*] and *Key*[*Last*] (the *very last*) are swapped. In short:

```
procedure Partition(Last,Low,High,Pivot)
    Last ← Low
    for   dex   = Low + 1 to High   do
      if   Key[dex] < Pivot
        then Last ← Last + 1
             Swap(Last,dex)
        endif
      next dex
    if   Low ≠ Last   then Swap(Low,Last) endif
    end   {Partition
```

QuickSort is faster on the average than the sorting techniques *SelectionSort, BubbleSort,* and *InsertionSort* discussed in Chapter 1, but not for very small or nearly sorted sets. A rough analysis is:

- The operation likely to consume the most time is the exchange of records in *Swap.*

- No element in *Key*[*Low*] . . . *Key*[*High*] is exchanged more than once during a call *Partition*(*Last,Low,High,Pivot*). Hence in terms of *Swap* units of time, *Partition* is $O(High - Low + 1)$.

- It is possible that *Last* = *Low* or *Last* = *High,* in which case one of the subranges at the next call contains *High* − *Low* elements. Hence in the worst case, *Partition* is called *n* times for a file of size *n.* *QuickSort* is thus $O(n^2)$.

- *Partition* tends to produce two new subranges, each with roughly half as many elements as are in [*Low* . . *High*]. Hence *QuickSort* tends to execute ln *n* levels, each acting on subranges of no more than *n* elements. Hence the average growth behavior of *QuickSort* is $O(n \ln n)$.

It is common to supplement *QuickSort* with a switch to *InsertionSort* for small subranges, a practice derived from experience.

Sorting algorithms with worst-case behavior $O(n \ln n)$ are possible, and one such algorithm is discussed in section 8.6.1.

O.1 The QuickSort Demonstration Program

```
PROGRAM QuickSortDemo(Input,Output);
   CONST  Max = 50;
   TYPE  KeyType = ARRAY[1..Max] OF INTEGER;
   VAR   Key : KeyType;
      Swaps : INTEGER;
      Tests : INTEGER;
       Tail : INTEGER;
       Done : BOOLEAN;
{  }
   PROCEDURE Preface;
     BEGIN
       Writeln('This program demonstrates the action of a');
       Writeln('QuickSort procedure. It accepts a sequence');
       Writeln('of up to ',Max,' non-negative integers, sorts');
       Writeln('them, and reports the number of comparisons');
       Writeln('and swaps needed to sort them.')
       END  {Preface};
{  }
   PROCEDURE Display(Low,High : INTEGER);
     VAR  m : INTEGER;
     BEGIN
       Writeln;
       FOR  m := Low TO High  DO Write(Key[m] : 4);
       Writeln;
       Writeln(Swaps,' Swaps, ', Tests,' Comparisons')
       END  {Display};
```

```
{  }
   PROCEDURE Setup(VAR Key : KeyType; VAR Tail : INTEGER);
     VAR  NonNeg : INTEGER;
     BEGIN
       Writeln('Enter values separated by blank spaces,');
       Writeln('terminating the sequence with a negative');
       Writeln('value.');
       Tail := 0;
       Read(NonNeg);
       WHILE  (NonNeg >= 0)  DO BEGIN
         Tail := Tail + 1;
         Key[Tail] := NonNeg;
         Read(NonNeg)
         END;  Readln;
         Swaps := 0;  Tests := 0
       END  {Setup};
{  }
   PROCEDURE RunAgain(VAR Done : BOOLEAN);
     VAR  ch : CHAR;
     BEGIN
       Write('If you wish to run again then enter Y, else N.');
       Readln(ch);
       IF  (ch = 'Y')
         THEN Done := FALSE
         ELSE Done := TRUE
       END  {RunAgain};
{  }
   PROCEDURE QuickSort(Low,High : INTEGER);
     VAR  PivotIndex : INTEGER;
               Pivot : INTEGER;
                Last : INTEGER;
     {  }
     FUNCTION FindPivot(Low,High : INTEGER) : INTEGER;
       BEGIN
         IF  (Low < High)                  {subject to modification}
           THEN FindPivot := Low
           ELSE FindPivot := 0
         END  {FindPivot};
```

```
{   }
PROCEDURE Partition(VAR Last : INTEGER;
                          Low,High,Pivot : INTEGER);
  VAR  dex : INTEGER;
{   }
  PROCEDURE Swap(One,Two : INTEGER);
    VAR  Temp : INTEGER;
    BEGIN
      Temp := Key[One];
      Key[One] := Key[Two];
      Key[Two] := Temp;
      Swaps := Swaps + 1
      END  {Swap};
    {   }
    BEGIN            {Partition}
      Last := Low;
      FOR  dex := Low + 1 TO High  DO
        IF  Key[dex] < Pivot
          THEN BEGIN
            Last := Last + 1;
            Swap(Last,dex)
            END;
      IF  (Low <> Last)  THEN Swap(Low,Last);
      IF  (High > Low)  THEN Tests := Tests + High - Low
      END  {Partition};
{   }
  BEGIN            {QuickSort}
    PivotIndex := FindPivot(Low,High);
    IF  PivotIndex <> 0
      THEN BEGIN
        Pivot := Key[PivotIndex];
        Partition(Last,Low,High,Pivot);
        QuickSort(Low,Last - 1);
        QuickSort(Last + 1,High)
        END
    END  {QuickSort};
```

```
{   }
  BEGIN                {QuickSortDemo}
    Preface;
    REPEAT
      Setup(Key,Tail);
      Display(1,Tail);
      QuickSort(1,Tail);
      Display(1,Tail);
      RunAgain(Done)
      UNTIL  Done
    END  {QuickSortDemo}.
```

A Balanced
Static BST

A static BST that is quite well balanced can be formed from a set of nodes by first sorting them and then arranging them in a tree according to their sorted order. The first 11 nodes can be placed in trees like those of Figure P.1 as they arrive.

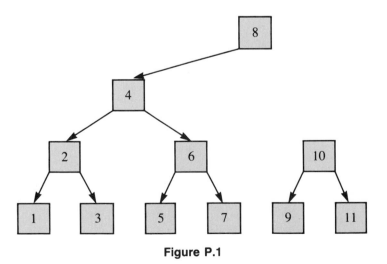

Figure P.1

If node 10 is made the right child of node 8, the result is a BST. If node 12 had arrived before the final connection, node 10 would be its left child and node 12 would be the right child of node 8. After arrival of node 13 and after final connection, the tree would look like the one in Figure P.2.

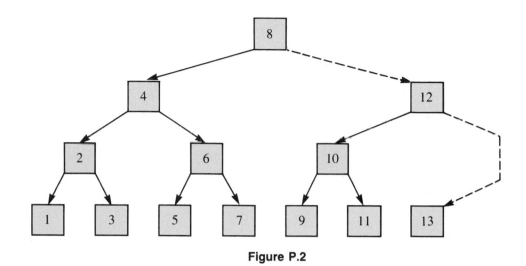

Figure P.2

The general idea is to place each node at the position where it would be in a complete binary tree. This creates a forest of binary trees, and the trees of the forest are connected together into one tree after the last node has been acquired. (The dashed links in the example are created at that time.) Note that the twelfth node cannot arrive until after the eighth. In general there is only one node on each level that is not the child of a higher node. There is never more than one unattached subtree per level.

An incoming kth node is a leaf if k is odd, on the next level up if it is twice an odd number, another level up if it is divisible by 4 but not 8, and so on. (Note that 4, 12, and 20 all contain factors of 4, multiplied by an odd number.) In general, the height of the kth node, counting from the leaves, is determined by the power of the multiples of 2 that k contains. The height determination is:

```
function FinalHeight(k)
    FH ← 0
    while   NOT ODD(k)   do
        k ← k   DIV 2
        FH ← FH + 1
    endwhile
    return FH
    end   {FinalHeight
```

Nodes are accessed by function *NextNode*, which is assumed to take them from a sorted file of nodes or create them from a sorted file of keys (of records perhaps). The node acquired by *NextNode* is inserted into a subtree. For example, the eleventh node is inserted into the subtree rooted at the tenth node and already containing the ninth node, but not yet connected as the right child of the eighth node (if the final node count is less than 12) or the left child of the twelfth node. After the last node is received, the root of the final tree is located as *OneRoot,* and all the subtrees are connected together by *OneTree.* The logic of this scheme is:

procedure *StaticBalance(OneRoot)*
  Setup
  InCount ← *0*
  p ← *NextNode*
  while *p* ≠ NIL **do**
    InCount ← *InCount* + *1*
    Insert(p)
    p ← *NextNode*
    endwhile
  OneTree(OneRoot)
  end {*StaticBalance*

The crucial piece of the puzzle is the linking of *p* into some subtree. Building a complete tree one node at a time quickly shows that the *k*th node is not only a child of a node at the next higher level: it is a child of the last node entered at that next level that is not yet linked to both of its children. If there is no such node, the entry node becomes the root of a new tree of the forest; otherwise, it becomes the root of a subtree of a tree that is already in the forest. A structure is needed to keep track of the one subtree root per level; and an array of pointers, *Root,* is chosen to provide fast access to them. A maximum height of 20 allows up to 1,048,576 nodes in the forest. The initialization of *Setup* is then:

for *k* = −*1* **to** *MaxHeight* **do**
  Root[k] ← NIL
  next *k*

The insertion procedure is:

procedure *Insert(p)*
  Height ← *FinalHeight(InCount)*
  p ↑ *.Right* ← NIL
  p ↑ *.Left* ← *Root[Height − 1]*
  Root[Height] ← *p*
  r ← *Root[Height + 1]*
  if *r* ≠ NIL
    then if *r* ↑ *.Right* = NIL
      then *r* ↑ *.Right* ← *p*
      endif
    endif
  end {*Insert*

To find the final root of the combined tree, it suffices to search through *Root* for the node of greatest height that is not *NIL:*

OneRoot ← *MaxHeight*
while   *Root*[*OneRoot*] = NIL   AND   *OneRoot* > *1*   **do**
  OneRoot ← *OneRoot* − *1*
  endwhile

From the height of *OneRoot,* the subtrees can be systematically connected together:

procedure *OneTree*(*OneRoot*)
  OneRoot ← *MaxHeight*
  while   *Root*[*OneRoot*] = NIL   AND   *OneRoot* > *1*   **do**
    OneRoot ← *OneRoot* − *1*
    endwhile
  Height ← *OneRoot*
  while   *Height* > *0*   **do**
    r ← *Root*[*Height*]
    if   *r* ↑ .*Right* ≠ NIL
      then *Height* ← *Height* − *1*
      else *p* ← *r* ↑ .*Left*
          Hunt ← *Height* − *1*
          repeat
            p ← *p* ↑ .*Right*
            Hunt ← *Hunt* − *1*
            until   *p* = NIL   OR   *p* ≠ *Root*[*Hunt*]
          r ↑ .*Right* ← *Root*[*Hunt*]
          Height ← *Hunt*
      endif
    endwhile
  end   {*OneTree*

Problem   not immediate, but requiring no major extensions of the text

PP.1   Trace the action on *OneTree* when a total of *k* nodes are entered into *StaticBalance* for *k* values 11, 12, and 13.

Program   for trying it yourself

PGP.1 Incorporate the algorithm *StaticBalance* into a program (with a tree display) and experiment with it.

Huffman Code Trees

Messages are frequently decoded one character at a time or one bit (binary digit) at a time. A variety of coding and decoding structures is available for this task, including a search tree (or a search *trie*, described in section 8.5.3). The decoding can be done efficiently if the encoding is done so that the most frequently used messages have the shortest paths in the decoding tree. Since files are messages, application of this approach provides *file compression*.

One extremely short file is:

```
ABBREVIATE_THIS_SHORT_MESSAGE_AS_MUCH_AS_POSSIBLE_
```

When sorted and counted, the character frequency of it is:

A 5	F 0	K 0	P 1	U 1	Z 0
B 3	G 1	L 1	Q 0	V 1	_ 8
C 1	H 3	M 2	R 2	W 0	
D 0	I 3	N 0	S 8	X 0	
E 5	J 0	O 2	T 3	Y 0	

The relative frequencies of the letters that actually occur are:

```
0.16   S   _
0.10   A   E
0.06   B   H   I   T
0.04   M   O   R
0.02   C   G   L   P   U   V
0.00   D   F   J   K   N   Q   W   X   Y   Z
```

The letters with zero frequency may be ignored, and the symbol SP used for the underscore _. The characters in the file can then be used to form a tree in stages. The characters are first considered to be one-node trees with a value that is their frequency of occurrence. At each stage, the lowest available pair of frequencies is taken as the children of a new node. The new node has an effective frequency that is the sum of the frequencies of its children, since it represents their combination. The process is iterated on the roots of the forest of trees that results from the previous stage. The results of the first three stages of this process are shown in Figure Q.1 and the next three in Figure Q.2. Figure Q.3 illustrates the next two combinations.

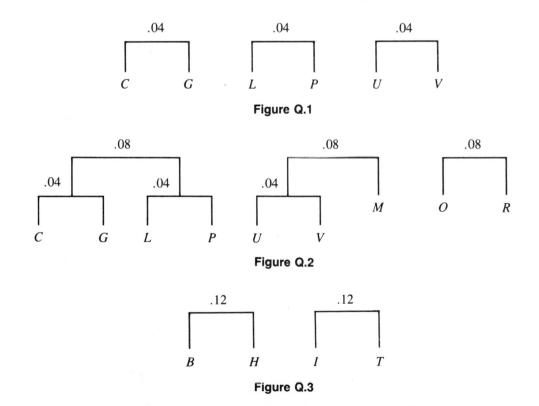

Figure Q.1

Figure Q.2

Figure Q.3

The next two stages join trees of value (0.08 and 0.08) and (0.08 and 0.10). The final result is shown in Figure Q.4.

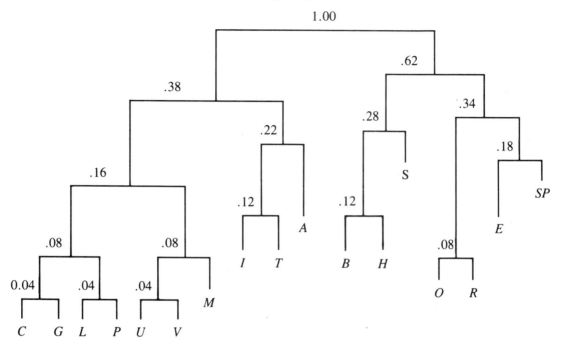

Figure Q.4

Now assign 0 to left links and 1 to right links and let the sequence of links used to reach a leaf directly from the root be its binary code.

The resulting codes are:

A	011	M	0011	C	00000
S	101	I	0100	G	00001
		T	0101	L	00010
		B	1000	P	00011
		O	1100	U	00100
		R	1101	V	00101
		H	1001		
		E	1110		
		SP	1111		

These codes are unique, since the path to any leaf is unique. They also can be separated from each other during decoding, even though they vary in length. Suppose, for example, the following message, encoded by *HT,* is received:

```
101010111001101 1001
```

It can be uniquely decoded by simply following the tree links from root to leaves:

- The first digit, 1, means: take the right link.

- The second digit, 0, means: take the left link.

- The third digit, 1, means: take the right link. This, however, reaches a leaf node, ''S''. Hence this character code is complete and the next digit begins a new search from the root.

Exercises EQ.1 and EQ.2 are appropriate at this point.

Even for so short a file, there is some compression. If characters are encoded in a standard 8-bit code, this file is $50 \times 8 = 400$ bits long. Encoded with the tree above, it is $5 \times 3 + 3 \times 4 + \cdots + 8 \times 4 = 193$ bits in length. In statistical terms, the length of a file encoded with this tree tends to be the expected code length times the number of characters in the file. The expected code length of this tree is $\frac{13}{50} \cdot 3 + \frac{31}{50} \cdot 4 + \frac{6}{50} \cdot 5 = 3.86$ bits.

The general algorithm that joins subtrees of highest priority (frequency, probability, and so on) to form a final tree is called the *Huffman Algorithm*. It remains to describe it in detail.

Q.1 Building a Huffman Tree

The entire coding and decoding system must include a way to encode as well as decode. A reasonable structural system is an array *Symbol*[1 .. *N*] of symbol nodes, arranged for easy access for encoding—sorted by field *Key* perhaps. Each node needs to contain the encoding string, *Code,* of binary digits, to be derived from the Huffman tree after it is constructed.

Each node has a left and right link, which are indices of other nodes in the tree to be constructed. Since the tree contains internal nodes, *Symbol* actually contains *Max* = *N* + (*N* − 1) nodes. Each node has a field *Measure* that contains a positive fraction, with the property that the sum of these values from 1 to *N* is 1.00. The nodes thus have the form:

```
SymbolType = RECORD
                 Measure : REAL
                   Right : INTEGER
                    Left : INTEGER
                     Key : {some ordered type
                    Code : {digit string
             END
```

The heap initially occupies an integer array *Map*[1 .. *N*], the values of its cells being pointers to (indices of) nodes in *Symbol*. (With little change in what follows, the cells of *Map* could contain pointers into a collection of independent records.) The nodes of *Symbol* can be heaped indirectly by using *Measure* values for comparisons, but shifting pointers within *Map*. For example, *UpHeap* (section 8.6) becomes:

```
procedure UpHeap(k)
   while  k ≥ 2  do
      p ← INT(k/2)
      mk ← Symbol[Map[k]].Measure
      mp ← Symbol[Map[p]].Measure
      if  mk < mp
         then TempDex ← Map[k]
              Map[k] ← Map[p]
              Map[p] ← TempDex
              k ← p
      else exit
      endif
   endwhile
end   {UpHeap
```

Note that the inequality is reversed, because *small measures have high priority*.

The required alteration to *DownHeap* (section 8.6) is similar. The next level of heap management is unaffected:

```
procedure MakeHeap
   for  k = 2 to N  do
      UpHeap(k)
   next k
end   {MakeHeap
```

The task of tree-building is accomplished by using the top two items of the heap with an initial directory *Map*[1 .. *N*] and adding one combined item derived from them by summing their *Measure* fields. Eventually there are $2N - 1$ items in the heap; the original *N* values and their combinations pointed to by *Map*[1 .. $2N-1$].

A modification of *DeHeap* (section 8.6) is needed. It assumes the symbols are sorted so that the measure of *Map*[*k*] is no larger than that of *Map*[*k* + 1]:

procedure *MakePair*(*SN*)   {*O*(ln *SN*)
    TopLeft ← *Map*[*1*]
    Lm ← *Symbol*[*TopLeft*].*Measure*
    m2 ← *Symbol*[*Map*[*2*]].*Measure*
    m3 ← *Symbol*[*Map*[*3*]].*Measure*
    if *m2* < *m3*
        then *Rm* ← *m2*
            TopRight ← *Map*[*2*]
        else *Rm* ← *m3*
            TopRight ← *Map*[*3*]
    endif
    SN ← *SN* + *1*
    Symbol[*SN*].*Left* ← *TopLeft*
    Symbol[*SN*].*Right* ← *TopRight*
    Symbol[*SN*].*Measure* ← *Lm* + *Rm*
    UpHeap(*SN*)
    end {*MakePair*

Once the arrays and *Symbol* have been initialized for *N* nodes, the tree is constructed and located by:

function *HuffTree*   {*O*(*N* · ln *N*)
    SN ← *N*
    for *k* = *1* **to** *N* − *1* **do** *MakePair*(*SN*) **next** *k*
    return *Map*[*1*]
    end {*HuffTree*

Finally, the codes are determined for encoding by a traverse of the tree:

■   If $d_1 d_2 \ldots d_k$ is the code string for a parent, then $d_1 d_2 \ldots d_k 0$ is the code for the left child, and $d_1 d_2 \ldots d_k 1$ is the code for the right child. Every node is reached from its parent.

■   The position of a given symbol can be tracked by initializing *Track*[*k*] to *k* and incorporating two statements into the **then** condition of *UpHeap* just before the switch of *Map* values:

    Track[*Map*[*k*]] ← *p*

    Track[*Map*[*p*]] ← *k*

The final value of *Track*[*k*] is the index *m* such that *Map*[*m*] = *k*—the heap position of *Symbol*[*k*].

Exercises   immediate application of text materials

EQ.1   Decode the rest of the message used as an example in this section.

EQ.2   Form a Huffman tree from the file:

THIS_STUFF_IS_OLD_HAT

Problem   not immediate, but requiring no major extensions of the text

PQ.1   Put together the entire Huffman code construction for a set of N frequency counts.

Program   for trying it yourself

PGQ.1 Write a program that reads a sequence of characters and displays the corresponding Huffman tree.

Project   for fun; for serious students

PJQ.1 Write a program that uses one text file to generate a Huffman tree, then will accept other files and encode a text file or decode a binary string that has been encoded with the same tree.

AVL Trees

The time required to locate a value or discover that it is not present in a binary search tree is dependent on the depth of the tree. It is customary to refer to the depth as *height* and talk about *height-balanced binary trees,* a denotation due to the developers of efficient management techniques that control the shape of ordered binary trees. Such trees are called AVL trees after Adelson-Velskii and Landis [ADELSON, 1962].

- The height of tree T is $h(T)$. For node p, $h(p)$ is the height of the subtree rooted at p.

- The *balance factor* of binary tree T with subtrees L rooted at its left child and R rooted at its right child is $Factor(T) = h(L) - h(R)$. This definition extends to any node of a binary tree. If T is an empty tree, $Factor(T) = 0$.

- If $|Factor(T)| \le 1$, then T is *height-balanced.*

467

The nodes of BT_8 in Figure R.1 are tagged with their balance factors:

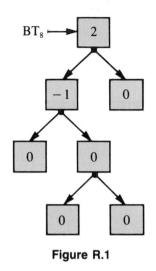

Figure R.1

Exercise ER.1 and Problem PR.1 are appropriate at this point.

Given a binary tree *bt* and a value *v*, one position at which *v* may be inserted to retain the order property is determined by *NodeSpot* and inserted by *InsertNode* (section 8.5.2). The result is not the only BST with the values it contains. The goal of AVL management is to rearrange *bt* after the addition of each value so that it is both height-balanced and a BST. There are a number of cases to consider.

A general binary tree *T* is of the form shown in Figure R.2.

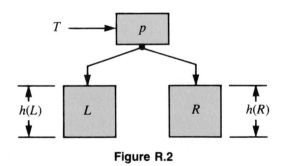

Figure R.2

If $h(L) = h(R)$, then $Factor(T) = 0$ and the addition of one node to form a new binary tree T' may (or may not) change the balance factor of the root node *p* to ± 1, whence T' is still balanced at the node *p*. Balancing within *L* or *R* may be necessary. Note, for example, that a child added to the leftmost leaf node of BT_8 would not change the balance of the root node, but an addition to other leaves would do so. Two rightmost additions will leave the root node balanced but the balance factor of the rightmost node of BT_8 would change to $+2$.

Exercise ER.2 is appropriate at this point.

If $h(L) - h(R) = 1$, then the addition of a node to R will leave the resulting *Factor*(p) either 0 or 1 for the root node p, still balanced. If, however, the new tree T' is formed by adding a node to L, the result can be that *Factor*(p) = 2 unless an adjustment is made. A suitable adjustment switches some of the nodes of L to the right subtree without violating the order property. In that case, p is said to act as a *pivot*.

Suppose an addition is made to the subtree L, rooted at node *Lroot*. If the left and right subtrees of *Lroot* are *LL* and *LR*, respectively, then no unbalance is created by an addition unless the height of one of these subtrees is $h(R)$ and the addition is to that subtree and increases its height. Figure R.3 is a model of T.

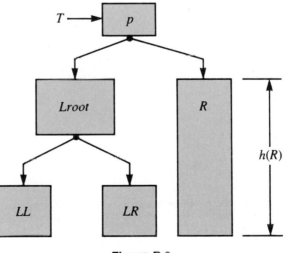

Figure R.3

If the addition increases $h(LL)$ to $h(R) + 1$, T can be restructured without violating the BST property by using p as a pivot, as shown in Figure R.4. If $h(L) - h(R) = -1$ and the addition is at the right in the subtree *RR* (the analog of *LL*), the pivot in the opposite direction that may be necessary is symmetric.

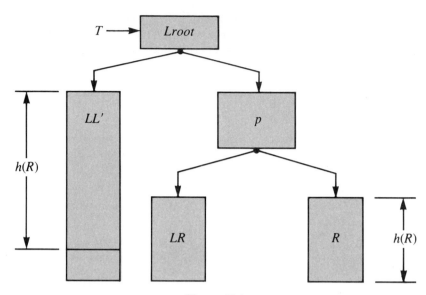

Figure R.4

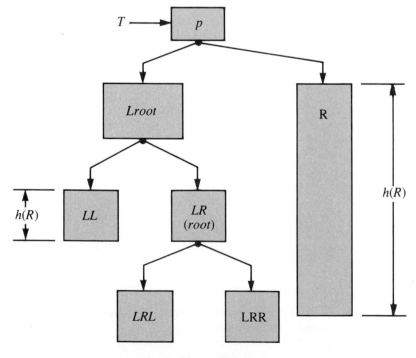

Figure R.5

A second case occurs when $h(LR) = h(R)$ and an addition is made to LR that causes $h(LR)$ to become $h(R) + 1$, whence $h(Lroot)$ becomes $h(R) + 2$. The pivot above will not balance the tree and so one level deeper is involved, as Figure R.5 illustrates. This can be rearranged without violating the BST property by using p as a pivot, as in Figure R.6. The new T' will be balanced if either $h(LRR)$ or $h(LRL)$ is increased by the added node. The symmetric right subtree case for which $Factor(T) = -1$ may also occur and be dealt with by a symmetric pivot.

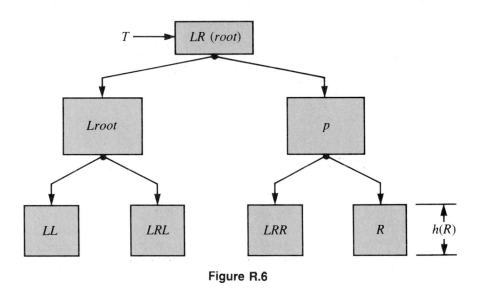

Figure R.6

A special case is required for the addition of a node nn to the non-null child of a two-node binary tree. Figure R.7 shows how the left version of this pivot is modeled.

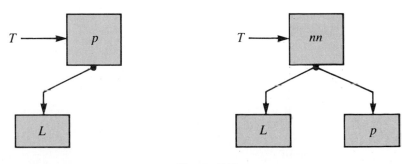

Figure R.7

It is important to realize that "root node" generally refers to the root of a subtree, and that pivoting is carried out as deep in the tree as possible.

Exercises ER.3 and ER.4 are appropriate at this point.

R.1 The Insertion Algorithm for AVL Trees

It is convenient to include a field for the balance factor in the nodes of an AVL tree:

AVLnode = RECORD
          Value : {*value type*
          Left : ↑ *AVLnode*
          Right : ↑ *AVLnode*
          Factor : INTEGER
          END

As a node is inserted, the location of the parent of the inserted node and the closest ancestor with *Factor* > 0, are retained in *Parent* and *Pivot,* respectively.

   An AVL tree is a BST, and so *InsertNode* (section 8.5.2) can be used to insert a node *p* in the tree *T*. However, it is necessary to modify *NodeSpot* (section 8.5.2) in order to retain a pointer, *Pivot,* to the closest ancestor of the new node with nonzero balance factor and its immediate ancestor *Parent*. This can be done by initializing *Pivot* to *T* and *Parent* to *NIL* and adding the statement

if $p \uparrow$.*Factor* ≠ *0*
   then *Pivot* ← *p*
        Parent ← *Pred*
   endif

as the first statement within the **while** loop in *NodeSpot*.

   The insertion algorithm becomes:

procedure *AVLinsert(nn,T)*
   if   *Empty(T)*
      then *T* ← *nn*
           $nn \uparrow$.*Factor* ← *0*
           return
      endif
   NodeSpot(T,nn $\uparrow$.*Value,Trio,p,Pred,Pivot,Parent)*
   InsertNode(T,nn,Pred,Trio)

```
        if  T↑.Right = NIL                  {small-tree cases are
        then PairLeft                       {treated separately
             return
        endif
        if  T↑.Left — NIL
        then PairRight
             return
        endif

        NewFactors                          {change factors between Pivot and
                                            {nn, and determine the apparent
                                            {change to Pivot↑.Factor, PF
        if  Pivot↑.Factor = 0
        then Pivot↑.Factor ← PF
             return
        endif
        if  Pivot↑.Factor + PF = 0
        then Pivot↑.Factor ← 0
             return
        endif
        if  PF < 0
        then LeftPivot
        else RightPivot
        endif
        end  {AVLinsert

        procedure NewFactors
         p ← Pivot
         v ← nn↑.Value
         if  p↑.Value < v
            then p ← p↑.Right
                 PF ← −1
            else p ← p↑.Left
                 PF ← +1
            endif
         Hub ← p                            {the first node between Pivot and nn
         while  p ≠ nn  do
           if  p↑.Factor < v
             then p↑.Factor ← −1
                  p ← p↑.Right
             else p↑.Factor ← +1
                  p ← p↑.Left
           endif
         endwhile
         end  {NewFactors
```

```
procedure LeftPivot
   if   Hub ↑ .Factor = 1                    {do a simple rotation of Hub
      then Pivot ↑ .Left ← Hub ↑ .Right
           Hub ↑ .Right ← Pivot
           Pivot ↑ .Factor ← Hub ↑ .Factor
           Hub ↑ .Factor ← 0
           if   nn ↑ .Value < Parent ↑ .Value
              then Parent ↑ .Left ← Hub
              else Parent ↑ .Right ← Hub
              endif
           return
      endif
                                             {do a deeper rotation
   Cog ← Hub ↑ .Left
   CogLeft ← Cog ↑ .Left
   CogRight ← Cog ↑ .Right
   Hub ↑ .Right ← CogLeft
   Pivot ↑ .Left ← CogRight
   Cog ↑ .Left ← Hub
   Cog ↑ .Right ← Pivot
   case of   Cog ↑ .Factor
      +1 :  Pivot ↑ .Factor ← −1
            Hub ↑ .Factor ← 0
      −1 :  Pivot ↑ .Factor ← 0
            Hub ↑ .Factor ← +1
      else :  Pivot ↑ .Factor ← 0
            Hub ↑ .Factor ← 0
      endcase
   Cog ↑ .Factor ← 0
   if   nn ↑ .Value < Parent ↑ .Value
      then Parent ↑ .Left ← Cog
      else Parent ↑ .Right ← Cog
      endif
   end   {LeftPivot
```

RightPivot is similar.

A *PairLeft* procedure can be implemented like this:

procedure *PairLeft*
   $T \uparrow .Left \leftarrow$ NIL
   if   Trio $= 1$
     then $Pred \uparrow .Right \leftarrow T$
         $T \leftarrow Pred$
     else $nn \uparrow .Right \leftarrow T$
          $nn \uparrow .Left \leftarrow Pred$
          $Pred \uparrow .Right \leftarrow$ NIL
          $T \leftarrow nn$
   endif
   $T \uparrow .Factor \leftarrow 0$
   end   *{PairLeft*

PairRight is similar.

Deletion from an AVL tree requires modification of *CutValue* (section 8.5.2) to determine *Parent* and *Pivot*, and the rebalance operation must proceed up the tree. It is common to forego deletion entirely; inactive nodes may be so marked or simply ignored.

Exercises   immediate applications of the text material

ER.1   Calculate the balance factors for all of the binary trees in Chapter 8.

ER.2   Trace the effects of adding two nodes to BT_8 at every possible combination of positions.

ER.3   Suppose that the days of the week are used to form an AVL tree by adding them one at a time to an empty tree. Diagram the stages of the tree when they are added in the reverse order: Saturday, Friday, . . ., Sunday.

ER.4   Form an AVL tree from the sequence: 1 3 5 7 9 11 8 6 14 by adding them one at a time. They are to be filed in nondecreasing order. Then repeat for the AVL tree that keeps them in nonincreasing order.

Problem   not immediate, but not a major extension of the text

PR.1   Design a procedure to calculate balance factors for an arbitrary binary tree.

Project   for fun; for serious students

PJR.1   Write a program that creates an AVL tree by insertion and displays it.

File Merging
and MergeSort

The *StraightMerge* procedure of section 9.2.1 has two variations of interest, the merging of linked lists and binary merging. The discussion of these forms of merging in this section is based on the assumption that the number of items to be merged is large, but will fit into memory. (Lists too large to fit into memory are discussed in section T.) For large lists, it is worthwhile to spend some effort on preparation before plunging into the heart of an algorithm. In both cases, it is assumed for the sake of simplicity that key values are numerical and that the lists to be merged are sorted in nondecreasing order.

S.1 A Linked List Merge

The two lists *a* and *b* to be merged are accessed by records containing *Head* and *Tail* pointers. The merging operation is a function that produces a similar list *c*.

The role played by the sentinel value in *StraightMerge* is that of simplifier: it simplifies the test for exit in a much-repeated loop and also precludes the need to run out the tail of one of the lists when the other is exhausted. A similar and extended role can be played by a sentinel value in a distinguished node *Pivot* when linked lists are merged.

Pivot is first created with a sentinel value larger than either of the tail node values of *a* and *b* and then used as the tail node of both, as shown in Figure S.1.

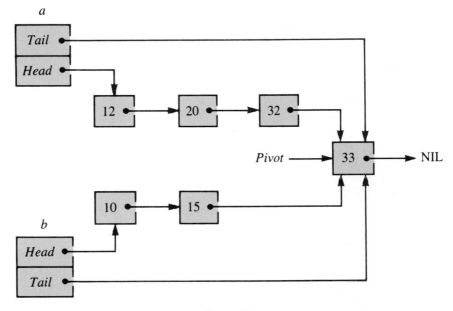

Figure S.1

The merging operation selectively removes nodes from *a* and *b* and adds them to the new list *c*, with head node *Pivot* ↑ *.Link*, as Figure S.2 illustrates.

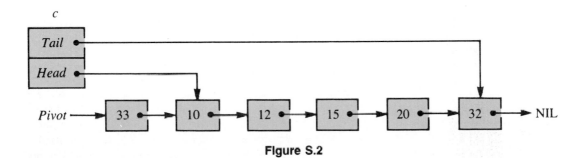

Figure S.2

Preparation for the merge is done by:

procedure *Setup*   {*O(1)*

   if   *a.Tail* ↑ *.Key* ≥ *b.Tail* ↑ *.Key*

      then *Sentinel* ← *a.Tail* ↑ *.Key* + *1*

      else *Sentinel* ← *b.Tail* ↑ *.Key* + *1*

      endif

   NEW(*Pivot*)

   Pivot ↑ *.Link* ← NIL

   Pivot ↑ *.Key* ← *Sentinel*

   c.Tail ← *Pivot*

   a.Tail ↑ *.Link* ← *Pivot*

   a.Tail ← *Pivot*

   b.Tail ↑ *.Link* ← *Pivot*

   b.Tail ← *Pivot*

   end   {*Setup*

After *Setup* has been executed, the leading node of smallest value in either list can be shifted by:

procedure *GetLeader*   {*O(1)*

   if   *a.Head* ↑ *.Key* ≤ *b.Head* ↑ *.Key*

      then *Temp* ← *a.Head*

          a.Head ← *a.Head* ↑ *.Link*

      else *Temp* ← *b.Head*

          b.Head ← *b.Head* ↑ *.Link*

      endif

   Temp ↑ *.Link* ← NIL

   c.Tail ↑ *.Link* ← *Temp*

   c.Tail ← *Temp*

   end   {*GetLeader*

With these tools, the merge is:

function *ListMerge(a,b)*   {*O(n)*

   Setup

   while   *a.Head* ≠ *b.Head*   **do**

     GetLeader

     endwhile

   c.Head ← *Pivot* ↑ *.Link*

   return *c*

   end   {*ListMerge*

In practice, *GetLeader* would not be a called procedure; it is a shorthand reference to code that is incorporated at the point mentioned.

S.2 Binary Merge

Sometimes one list (say *b*) is much smaller than the other (*a*) with which it is to be merged. Suppose the lists are stored in arrays $a[1 .. N]$ and $b[1 .. M]$, sorted in nondecreasing order, and they are to be merged into an array $c[1 .. NM]$, where $NM = N + M$.

The general idea of binary merge is that since *N* is much larger than *M*, entire segments of *a* tend to fall between values of *b*. The search for the possible position of a *b*-value is localized to a small segment of *a* that is searched by the method of binary search to determine an interval of *a* that can be moved to *c*. It is convenient to extend *a* with a sentinel value in $a[0]$ and then to load *c* from right to left.

A value $b[i]$ is compared with a segment of *a* of length $Size: a[Left .. Right]$. If $b[i] < a[Left]$, then the entire segment of *a* can be moved to *c*. If not, the segment is searched with a tailored version of binary search for the largest index *s* such that: $a[s] < b[i]$. The subsequence $b[i], a[s + 1], a[s + 2], ..., a[Right]$ can then be moved into *c*. In either case, a new segment of *a* is chosen for testing against the (possibly) new value $b[i]$.

The move operation is:

```
procedure Move(x,y)                    {O(y − x)
  for  z = y downto x   do
    c[k] ← a[z]
    k ← k − 1
    next z
  end   {Move
```

An effective search segment size is one less than the largest power of 2 less than (N/M). It can be determined by $Size ← Power(N/M) − 1$, using:

```
function Power(x)                      {O(ln x)
  PX ← 1
  while  PX ≤ x  do
    PX ← PX × 2
    endwhile
  return (PX DIV 2)
  end   {Power
```

The initialization procedure is:

procedure *Setup*   {*O(1)*
  if   *a[1] < b[1]*
    then *Sentinel ← a[1] − 1*
    else *Sentinel ← b[1] − 1*
    endif
  a[0] ← Sentinel
  Size ← Power(N / M) − 1
  i ← M
  k ← N × M
  end   {*Setup*

The merge operation is then:

procedure *BinaryMerge*   {*O(n* ln *n)*
  Setup
  while   *i ⩾ 1*   **do**
    if   *b[i] < a[Left]*
      then *Move(Left,Right)*
          Right ← Left − 1
      else *s ← BinSearch(b[i],Left,Right)*
          Move(s + 1,Right)
          Right ← s
          c[k] ← b[i]
          k ← k − 1
          i ← i − 1
    endif
    Left ← Right − Size
    if   *Left < 0*   **then** *Left ← 0* **endif**
    endwhile
  end   {*BinaryMerge*

S.3 Merge Sorting

The simplest form of sorting routine based on merging sorts an array, *a*, with the help of an array, *b*, of the same size. Segments in one array are merged into the other. The segments are initially of length one and are increased in size from one pass of the routine to another until one of them contains the entire file. It is convenient to make passes back and forth between the arrays. The merging procedures of the previous sections do not work unmodified, partly because sentinel records would need to be placed in the middle of a file.

A utility routine used in the merge that copies a segment of one array into another is:

```
procedure Copy(a,x,y,b,z)                    {O( y − x)
  for  dex = x to y  do
    b[z] ← a[dex]
    z ← z + 1
    next dex
  end  {Copy
```

With the help of *Copy*, the basic merge operation is:

```
procedure TailMerge(a,L,M,R,b)               {O(R − L)
  i ← L
  k ← L
  j ← M + 1
  while  i ≤ M  AND  j ≤ R  do
    if  a[i] ≤ a[ j]
      then b[k] ← a[i]
           i ← i + 1
      else b[k] ← a[ j]
           j ← j + 1
    endif
    k ← k + 1
  endwhile
  if  i > M
    then Copy(a,j,R,b,k)
    else Copy(a,i,M,b,k)
  endif
end   {TailMerge
```

Now one phase (pass) is of the form:

```
procedure Phase(a,b,Size)                    {O(N)
  s ← 1
  while  s ≤ (N − 2 * Size − 1)  do
    TailMerge(a,s,s + Size − 1,s + 2 * Size − 1,b)
    s ← s + 2 * Size
  endwhile
  if  (s + Size − 1) < N
    then TailMerge(a,s,s + Size − 1,N,b)
    else Copy(a,s,N,b,s)
  endif
end   {Phase
```

The sort then becomes a repetition of phases:

procedure *MergeSort*   {*O*(*N* ln *N*)
   Size ← *1*
   while *Size* < *N* **do**
     Phase(*a,b,Size*)
     Size ← *2* ∗ *Size*
     Phase(*b,a,Size*)
     Size ← *2* ∗ *Size*
     endwhile
   end {*MergeSort*

Programs for trying it yourself

PGS.1 Write a program that creates two linked lists, sorts them, displays them, merges them with *ListMerge,* and displays the resulting list.

PGS.2 Write a program that initializes two arrays to be sorted— one eight times larger than the other—sorts them, merges them with *BinaryMerge,* and displays the result.

PGS.3 Implement *MergeSort*.

Priority Queue Extension of Merge Runs

The merge operations of section S work within memory, which may not be large enough to hold a file of interest. A common way to handle large files is to write them in segments of sorted values, called *runs*. Pairs of runs are merged to form larger runs—the essential idea of *MergeSort*. The access to external storage is expensive, however, and so larger runs and fewer phases increase efficiency.

One way to form the initial runs for a file is to simply make one pass through the file, writing values found to be in order onto a run file and the others onto a reject file for a second pass. Consider the integer file:

```
2  1  6  3  8  9  4  4  10  5  2  8  ♦  ♦  ♦
```

The first pass would produce the following run and reject:

```
run       2  6  8  9  10  ♦  ♦  ♦
reject    1  3  4  4  5  2  8  ♦  ♦  ♦
```

The straightforward version of this scheme, acting on a source file, whose termination can be recognized by the flag *EOF(Source)*, is:

Read(Source,Cutoff)
while NOT EOF(*Source*) **do**
  Read(Source,x)
  if *x* ⩾ *Cutoff*
    then *Write(RunFile,x)*
        Cutoff ← *x*
    else *Write(Reject,x)*
    endif
  endwhile

483

Unfortunately, if the largest item is first, the run will be only one item long. A second approach is to input M items, sort them internally, and write them out as a run. It is this value M that can be stretched with the help of a priority queue, specifically a heap, although other forms of priority queues would serve.

Suppose the items from *Source* are tagged with a run number R, and placed in a heap, *PQ*, with room for M elements. *PQ* is taken to be an array of records of the form:

```
RECORD
    Run : INTEGER
    Key : {comparable type
END
```

The heap is maintained in lexicographic order:

$PQ[i] < PQ[j]$ iff:

- $PQ[i].Run < PQ[j].Run$, or

- $PQ[i].Run = PQ[j].Run$ and $PQ[i].Key < PQ[j].Key$

For consistency with section S, the highest priority in the heap is the smallest value. The heap is formed with:

```
procedure BuildPQ
    for  i = 1 to M  do
        Read(Source,x)
        PQ[i].Run ← 1
        PQ[i].Key ← x
        UpHeap(i)
        next i
    HN ← m
    end  {BuildPQ
```

The stretched run is then created with:

```
procedure PQruns
  BuildPQ
  R ← 1
  while   NOT Empty(PQ)   do
    Top ← PQ[1]
    if   Top.Run = R
      then Write(RunFile(R),Top.Key)
           Swap(PQ[1],PQ[HN])
           HN ← HN − 1
           DownHeap(1)
      else R ← R + 1
      endif
    if   NOT EOF(Source)
      then Read(Source,x)
              if   x ≥ Top.Key
                then xRun ← R
                else xRun ← R + 1
                endif
              HN ← HN + 1
              PQ[HN].Run ← xRun
              PQ[HN].Key ← x
              UpHeap(HN)
      endif
    endwhile
  end   {PQruns
```

It is possible to derive additional enhancement by replacing $R \leftarrow R + 1$ by a procedure *DumpPQ* that stores the queue on external storage so that the pass through the source file can continue. The dumps are retrieved for the next run.

Program   for trying it yourself

PGT.1 Implement *PQruns*.

Section U

Red-Black Trees

A 3-node or a 4-node can be modeled with a binary subtree, bound together with links that are called *red* links to distinguish them from the links of the 2-3-4 tree in which they occur, called *black* links. With the use of dashed lines to represent red links, the tree is shown in Figure U.1. In a tree represented this way, 4-nodes are characterized by having a subtree root with red links to both children.

The depth of an RBT (Red-Black Tree) binary tree may be twice that of the corresponding 2-3-4 tree, but it is still proportional to the log of the number of keys in it. The links of an RBT need to be flagged with their color; and, if the nodes are entirely supported in arrays, the sign bit of the pointer index may be used. An alternate scheme, used here, is to flag a *node* with the color of the link that leads to it from its parent. It is convenient to include a field in the node that contains a pointer *Up* to the parent of the node.

The creation operation becomes:

```
procedure Create(rbt,LeftChild,RightChild )
    NEW(rbt)
    rbt ↑ .Up ← rbt
    rbt ↑ .Left ← LeftChild
    rbt ↑ .Right ← RightChild
    rbt ↑ .Red ← FALSE
    end   {Create
```

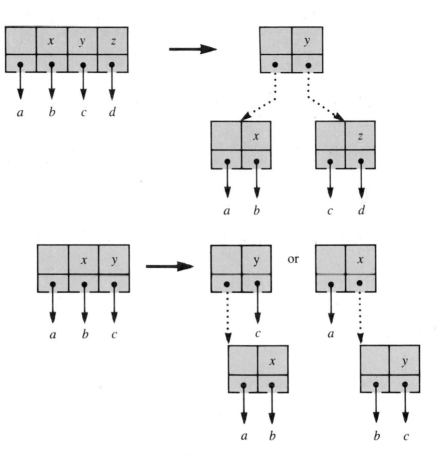

Figure U.1

The search operation, likely to be used more than any other, is then:

procedure *RBSearch(rbt,SearchKey,Node,Found)*
   Node ← *rbt*
   Parent ← *rbt*
   while *Node* ≠ *u*   **do**   {u *is the universal tail.*
     if *SearchKey* = *Node* ↑ *.Key*
       then *Found* ← TRUE
            return
       endif
     Parent ← *Node*
     if *SearchKey* < *Node* ↑ *.Key*
       then *Node* ← *Node* ↑ *.Left*
       else *Node* ← *Node* ↑ *.Right*
       endif
    endwhile
   Found ← FALSE
   Node ← *Parent*
   end   {*RBSearch*

Insertion includes a similar traverse that splits 4-nodes as they are encountered. The splitting operation is applied to the root node, or to a 4-node reached from a 2-node (a 2-4 subtree) or a 4-node reached from a 3-node (a 3-4 subtree).

The root-node split is shown schematically in Figure U.2. The split simply changes two red links to black links. No key value is actually shifted.

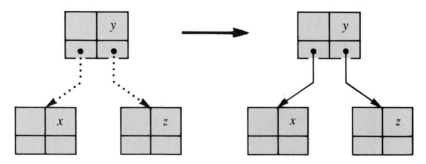

Figure U.2

The 2-4 subtree split schematically changes the (2-node to 4-node subtree) to a (3-node to two 2-nodes) subtree, shown in Figure U.3.

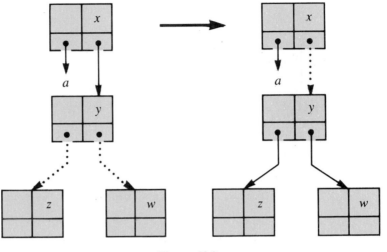

Figure U.3

Once again, no information is altered except the color of the links.

In the case of a 3-4 subtree, the 3-node may have either binary node as the subtree root. For example, Figure U.4 may be represented in either of the ways shown in Figure U.5.

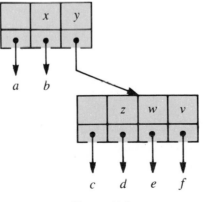

Figure U.4

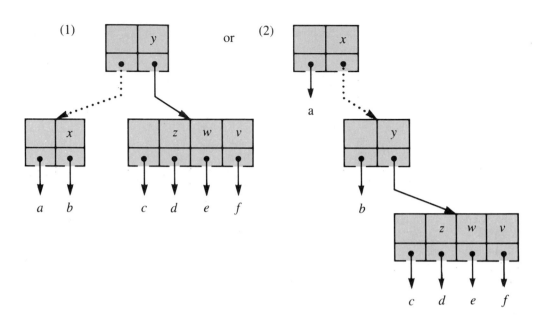

Figure U.5

Similarly, the 3-4 subtree of Figure U.6 has two representations, shown in Figure U.7, both having a red grandparent-parent link relative to the 4-node.

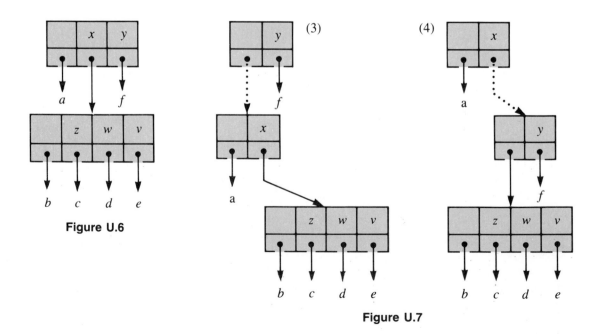

Figure U.6

Figure U.7

When the grandparent-parent link of a 4-node is red, a simple color-shift applied during splitting of the node produces two red links in sequence, as Figure U.8 illustrates for case (2) (from Figure U.5).

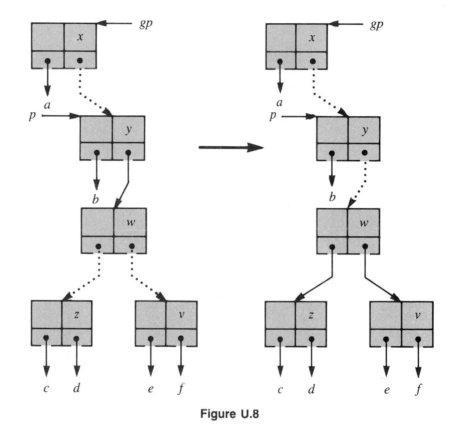

Figure U.8

This is prevented for the case of Figure U.4 by a *rotation,* in which the lexicographic order of the keys is unchanged, but the relative levels of two nodes are switched. A rotation switches the binary-tree levels of the two keys in a 3-node and shifts links to their parent and children to match. A rotation of keys x and y is considered to be the rotation of the child and grandchild of the node n, as depicted in Figure U.9. After this rotation, splitting the right child of gc does not produce two red links in succession.

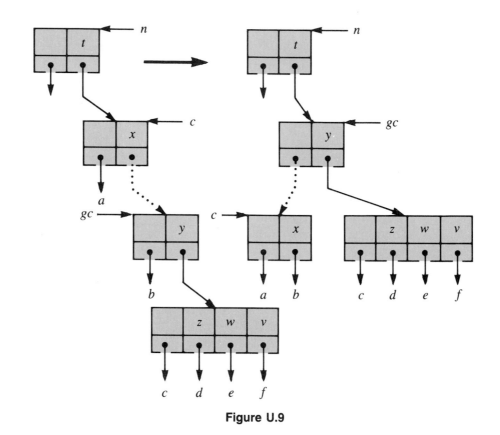

Figure U.9

If a 4-node is the middle child of a 3-node, it remains a middle child after rotation and retains a red grandparent-parent link, as shown in Figure U.10. One approach to resolving this problem is a prior rotation involving the root of the 4-node itself, shown in Figure U.11. Figure U.12 shows the result when this rotation is followed by a rotation at the (original) great-grandparent of *node*.

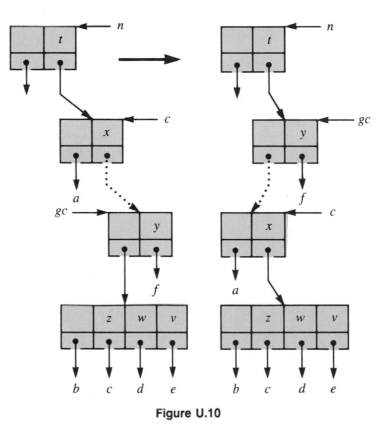

Figure U.10

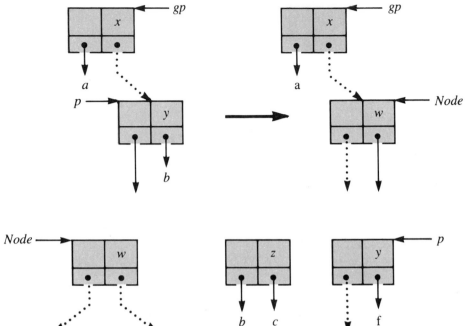

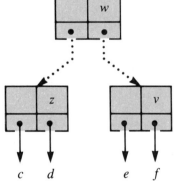

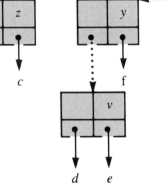

Figure U.11

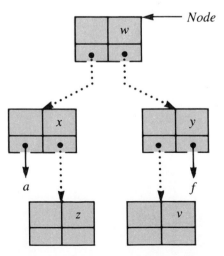

Figure U.12

With color changes at z and f, this double rotation has the effect in the RBT shown in Figure U.13. None of these rotations change the number of levels in the 2-3-4 tree.

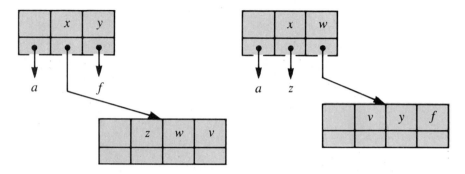

Figure U.13

It is convenient to design a generic rotation that internally traces the path from node to grandchild in order to detect left and right branches:

procedure *Rotate(SKey,n)*

> **if** $SKey > n \uparrow .Key$
> **then** $c \leftarrow n \uparrow .Right$
> **else** $c \leftarrow n \uparrow .Left$
> **endif**
> **if** $SKey > c \uparrow .Key$
> **then** $gc \leftarrow c \uparrow .Right$
> $ggc \leftarrow gc \uparrow .Left$
> $c \uparrow .Right \leftarrow ggc$
> $gc \uparrow .Left \leftarrow c$
> **else** $gc \leftarrow c \uparrow .Left$
> $ggc \leftarrow gc \uparrow .Right$
> $c \uparrow .Left \leftarrow ggc$
> $gc \uparrow .Right \leftarrow c$
> **endif**
> **if** $SKey > n \uparrow .Key$
> **then** $n \uparrow .Right \leftarrow gc$
> **else** $n \uparrow .Left \leftarrow gc$
> **endif**
> $gc \uparrow .Up \leftarrow n$
> $c \uparrow .Up \leftarrow gc$
> $ggc \uparrow .Up \leftarrow c$
> $Color \leftarrow gc \uparrow .Red$
> $gc \uparrow .Red \leftarrow c \uparrow .Red$
> $c \uparrow .Red \leftarrow Color$
> **end** {*Rotate*

The middle-child case is characterized by the alteration in direction of grandparent-parent and parent-node links and requires a rotation to change it into the other case. The splitting operation thus becomes:

```
procedure RBSplit(SKey,Node)
    p ← Node ↑ .Up
    if  p ↑ .Red
        then gp ← p ↑ .Up
             ggp ← gp ↑ .Up
             if  SKey < gp ↑ .Key ≠ SKey < p ↑ .Key
                 then Rotate(SKey,gp)
                          if  SKey < p ↑ .Key
                              then p ↑ .Right ↑ .Red ← TRUE
                                     Node ↑ .Left ↑ .Red ← FALSE
                              else p ↑ .Left ↑ .Red ← TRUE
                                     Node ↑ .Left ↑ .Red ← FALSE
                          endif
             endif
             Rotate(SKey,ggp)
    endif
    if  Node ≠ rbt   then Node ↑ .Red ← TRUE endif
    Node ↑ .Left ↑ .Red ← FALSE
    Node ↑ .Right ↑ .Red ← FALSE
    end   {RBSplit
```

The insertion procedure repeats the search process explicitly, except that it also splits 4-nodes during the traverse. The use of a universal tail node u allows the new node to be treated as the root of a 4-node subtree and immediately split upon entry to properly adjust its relationship to its parent:

procedure *RedBlackIn(rbt,NewKey,NewValue)*
  if   *rbt* = *u*
    then *Create(rbt,u,u)*
        rbt ↑ *.Value* ← *NewValue*
        rbt ↑ *.Key* ← *NewKey*
        return
    endif
  Node ← *rbt*
  while   *Node* ≠ *u*   **do**
    if   *NewKey* = *Node* ↑ *.Key*
      then return   *{or otherwise deal with*
      endif   *{a duplicate key.*
    Parent ← *Node*
    if   *Node* ↑ *.Left* ↑ *.Red* AND   *Node* ↑ *.Right* ↑ *.Red*
      then *RBSplit(NewKey,Node)*
      else if   *NewKey* < *Node* ↑ *.Key*
            then *Node* ← *Node* ↑ *.Left*
            else *Node* ← *Node* ↑ *.Right*
            endif
      endif
    endwhile
  Create(Node,u,u)
  with   *Node*   **do**
    Up ← *Parent*
    Value ← *NewValue*
    Key ← *NewKey*
    Red ← FALSE
    endwith
  if   *NewKey* < *Parent* ↑ *.Key*
    then *Parent* ↑ *.Left* ← *Node*
    else *Parent* ↑ *.Right* ← *Node*
    endif
  RBSplit(NewKey,Node)
  end   *{RedBlackIn*

Problem not immediate, but requiring no major extensions of text

PU.1 Draw the sequence of Red-Black trees that would be created by entering the months in calendar order if they are to be kept in alphabetical order.

Program for trying it yourself

PGU.1 Write a program that will accept strings and place them in a Red-Black tree ordered lexicographically. The program should display the tree after entries. Test it with the months of the year, entered in reverse calendar order.

Section V

The Eight Coins Problem

Some problems are both well enough known and representative enough that every computer science major should work through them at some time. One of these is the Eight Coins Problem, a representative of a class of common weighing puzzles. It is this:

■ One of eight apparently identical coins is known to be counterfeit and hence of different weight from the other seven. An equal-arm balance is to be used to discover in three weighings which coin is different and whether it is heavier or lighter.

There are sixteen possible results: 1–Light, 1–Heavy, 2–light, . . ., 8–Heavy, and a structured approach is likely to be worth developing. A systematic approach to the determination is to form a decision tree where each node describes a weighing to be made, determined by the results discovered so far. An interior node also determines which child to use for the next decision, and a leaf node is the correct answer if reached by proper use of the tree.

Let the coins have weights $w[i]$ for $1 \leq i \leq 8$. A verbal description of the decisions to be made is:

1. Compare the sum of weights 1–3, s_1, and weights 4–6, s_2. There are three possibilities: $s_1 = s_2$, $s_1 < s_2$, and $s_1 > s_2$. If $s_1 = s_2$, then the counterfeit coin is isolated as the pair of coins 7 and 8, and the other six are all of standard weight. When coins 7 and 8 are compared with each other, one of them will be heavier. The other two cases use the second comparison to isolate a similar

pair of coins and provide relative weight information. At the third weighing, one of the isolated pair is compared to a standard coin, and the answer becomes apparent.

1.1 $s_1 = s_2$: The bad coin is isolated in the pair $w[7]$ and $w[8]$, and so they are compared to each other.

    1.1.1 $w[7] > w[8]$: One of them, say $w[7]$, is compared with a standard coin, say $w[1]$.

        1.1.1.1 $w[7] > standard$: Then $w[7]$ is the bad coin, and it is heavy. Otherwise, $w[8]$ is the bad coin, and it is light.

    1.1.2 $w[7] < w[8]$: This is symmetric to 1.1.1 above.

1.2 $s_1 < s_2$: Now $w[7]$ and $w[8]$ are known to be standard. Two of the coins in the triplets forming s_1 and s_2 need to be isolated, and two are switched. For example, the comparison might be between $s_3 = w[1] + w[4]$ and $s_4 = w[2] + w[5]$, isolating $w[3]$ and $w[6]$ from the other four.

    1.2.1 $s_3: < s_4$: Clearly coins 3 and 6 were standard, and either coin 1 is light or coin 5 is heavy because switching coins 2 and 4 left the balance tipped in the same direction. Either coin 1 or coin 5 is to be tested against a standard, because these two are now isolated as the bad pair.

    1.2.2 $s_3 = s_4$: Then coin 3 or coin 6 is counterfeit, and one should be tested against one of the six known standards.

    1.2.3 $s_1 > s_4$: The switching of coins 2 and 4 caused the balance to shift, and so one of them is counterfeit.

1.3 $s_1 > s_2$: This is entirely symmetric to 1.2 above.

Even with the abbreviation of the verbal description, the decisions to be made do not jump out at the reader. A tree diagram is helpful.

In Figure V.1, the notation

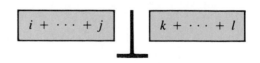

Figure V.1

indicates a comparison of $i, \ldots, j$ with $k, \ldots, l$.

The tree is illustrated in Figure V.2. The design of the tree calls for a comparison of a final pair with a standard weight:

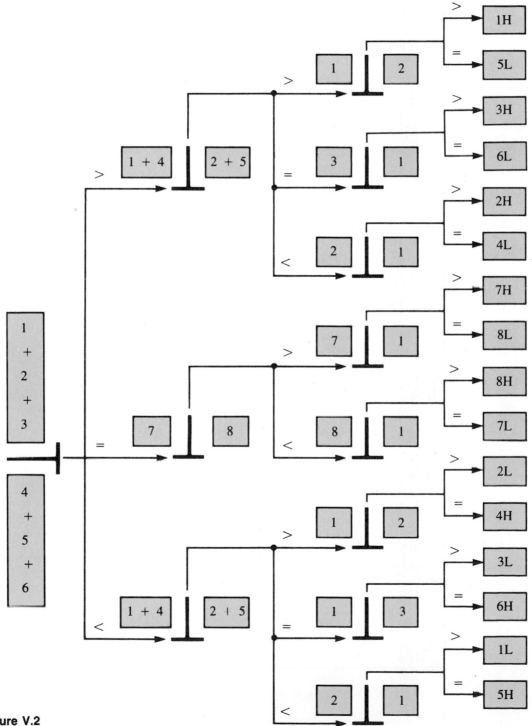

Figure V.2

```
procedure Compare(Coin1,Coin2,Standard,BadCoin,Light)
  if  Coin1 > Standard
    then BadCoin ← Coin1
          Light ← FALSE
    else  BadCoin ← Coin2
          Light ← TRUE
    endif
  end  {Compare
```

The procedure then becomes:

```
procedure EightCoins(w,BadCoin,Light)
  S1 ← 0
  s2 ← 0
  for  i = 1 to 3   do
    s1 ← s1 + w[i]
    s2 ← s2 + w[i+3]
    next i
  if  s1 = s2
    then if  w[7] > s[8]
            then Compare(w[7],w[8],w[1],BadCoin,Light)
            else Compare(w[8],w[7],w[1],BadCoin,Light)
            endif
            return
    endif
  if  s1 > s2
    then case
            s3 = s4 : Compare(w[3],w[6],w[8],BadCoin,Light)
            s3 > s4 : Compare(w[1],w[5],w[8],BadCoin,Light)
            s3 < s4 : Compare(w[2],w[4],w[8],BadCoin,Light)
          endcase
          return
    endif
  { s1 < s2
    case
      s3 = s4 : Compare(w[6],w[3],w[8],BadCoin,Light)
      s3 > s4 : Compare(w[5],w[1],w[8],BadCoin,Light)
      s3 < s4 : Compare(w[5],w[1],w[8],BadCoin,Light)
    endcase
  end  {EightCoins
```

Program   for trying it yourself

PGV.1 Write the Eight Coins program and run it with several of the possible input
sets.

Section **W**

Node Evaluation and Pruning of Game Trees

A game progresses as the odd player makes a move to level 2, the even player moves to level 3, and so on. The *active* player is player *Odd* on odd levels and player *Even* on the others. The value of a node is the value of it to the player who moves *from* that node. A leaf node represents a final configuration of the game and hence a win or loss for some player. The value of a leaf node is the *payoff* for some player, and the convention is:

■   A positive value for a leaf node represents a winning value for the player who moves from it. A negative value represents a winning amount for the other player. Zero represents a tie.

In very few games can the board configuration be described with great brevity and the game tree drawn on a sheet of notebook paper (but see problem PW.1). The game tree in Figure W.1 is arbitrary and greatly pruned. In GT₁ there are wins for *Odd* at nodes 5, 11, and 14 and wins for *Even* at nodes 6, 10, and 12.

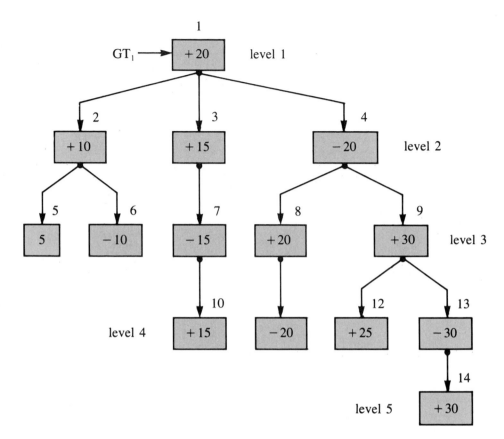

Figure W.1

The tension in a competitive game comes from the opposition in viewpoint of the value of a configuration. Players can evaluate the node they occupy by examining the values of the children of that node. *Odd* wishes to maximize the payoff:

■ The value of node p for *Odd* is the maximum from the view of *Odd* of the values of $p \uparrow .Child[i]$ for all i.

Similarly, *Even* wishes to minimize the payoff (to *Odd*), but minimizing values is equivalent to maximizing their negatives. We can combine these disparate views into a single rule:

■ The value of node p for the player moving from it is:

$$v = Maximum\{-p \uparrow .Child[i] \uparrow .Value \text{ for all } i\}$$

With this convention, the values of the nodes of GT_1 can be derived bottom-up from an assignment of values to the terminal positions represented by the leaf nodes. The value of node 2 for example is:

$$Maximum(-(+5), -(-10)) = +10$$

The value of node 2 for *Odd* is $-(+10) = -10$, and so a move to node 2 would represent a loss of 10 units for *Odd*.

Exercise EW.1 and problem PW.1 are appropriate at this point.

Node evaluation as the maximum of the negative of the values (as determined by the opposition) of the children, is based on a crucial assumption:

■ The player in opposition always makes the move that is optimal for him or her.

The bottom-up determination of node values can be done with either recursion or with a post-order traverse— once the leaf-node values are in place, either calculated or estimated. With the assumption that leaf values are determined by a procedure *LeafValue*, a recursive procedure *NodeValue* can be designed to assign a value v to the given node, choose the next node *Choice,* and return v.

```
function NodeValue(gt,Choice)          {O(n)
    Choice ← NIL
    NoChild ← TRUE
    MaxValue ← TooSmall                 {less than any possible node value
    for  i = 1 to MaxChild  do
      p ← gt ↑ .Child[i]
      if  p ≠ NIL
        then NoChild ← FALSE
             v ← −NodeValue(p,Choice)
             if  v > MaxValue
               then MaxValue ← v
                    Choice ← p ↑ .Child[i]
             endif
        endif
      next i
    if  NoChild
      then v ← LeafValue(gt)
      else v ← MaxValue
    endif
    gt ↑ .Value ← v
    return v
    end   {NodeValue
```

When a game tree is large, a search that reaches to the leaves of the tree is impractical, since *NodeValue* or its equivalent will not execute in a reasonable length of time. Most human players of games "look ahead" only a few moves to make a decision, rather than making an exhaustive search. A procedure can do the same, effectively pruning the tree.

In a look-ahead procedure, some way is needed to assign values to nodes that are not terminal and whose subtree is not traversed. Evaluation of such nodes may be done with a procedure, say *BaseValue,* that plays a role similar to that of *Leaf Value* for terminal nodes. Both procedures are highly dependent upon the game being played.

Given the existence of *BaseValue,* the number of nodes to be searched can be limited by restricting the depth of the search. A node being processed is some number of levels down from a root node, and an index *LevelsDown* can be used to track it. *LevelsDown* is initialized to the maximum depth to be allowed for the search and decremented at each new level. If *LevelsDown* = 0 at some node, then *BaseValue* is applied in lieu of searching the children of the node. When modified to use these tools, *NodeValue* can be used for a limited look-ahead determination of node values.

Problems PW.2 and PW.3 are appropriate at this point.

W.1 Alpha-Beta Pruning of a Game Tree

A procedure like *NodeValue* examines every subtree of a child, but that may not be necessary. Consider the tree fragment in Figure W.2.

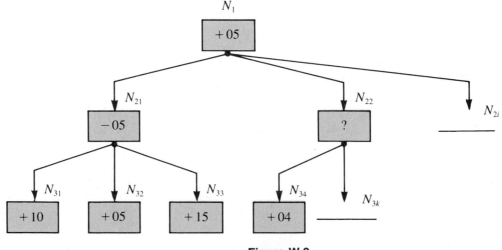

Figure W.2

After (the even) node N_{21} has been processed, its value is known to be -5; hence the value of N_1 is *at least* $+5$. The known minimum for a node at any point in a search of its subtrees is called its *alpha value*. The adversary *Even* controls the moves from N_{2j} for $j = 1, 2, \ldots$; and so, as soon as N_{34} is found to be 4, the value of N_{22} is known to be *at least* -4. Since the value of N_{22} to *Even* is at least -4, it is worth *no more than* 4 to *Odd*, whence *Odd* will prefer N_{21} to N_{22}. There is no need to traverse the other children of N_{22}.

In general, an even node chooses its child with the smallest (odd) value and passes that value up to its (odd) parent. If an even node e has a child with a value smaller than the alpha value of its parent, then the search of the tree rooted at e may be abandoned. It is said to be *pruned* from the search. The children of N_{22} are pruned and not generated in the sense that they will not be used even if they physically exist in the structure.

The equivalent pruning on information given by the grandchildren of an even node is called *beta pruning*. The combination of both kinds of pruning is called *alpha-beta pruning*. Because of the symmetry introduced by the alternation of values in *NodeValue*, alpha-beta pruning is identical for odd nodes.

An additional phase of pruning can be initiated by passing the alpha value of a node p to a grandchild, *gcp*, as a lower bound, *Bound*. As soon as it is known that a grandchild of *gcp* has a value lower than *Bound*, the child *cgcp* in which it is rooted will not allow the value it passes up to *gcp* to be as large as *Bound*, and so the remaining children of *cgcp* can be pruned. Figure W.3 illustrates this phase.

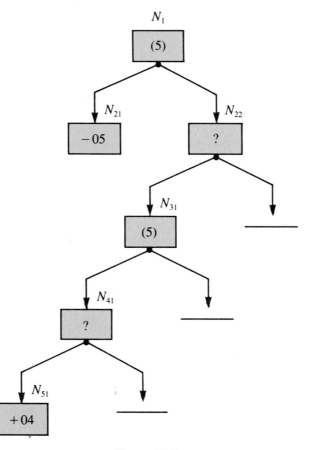

Figure W.3

After N_{21} is valued, *alpha*(N_1) is 5. This puts a lower bound of 5 on N_{31}: as soon as N_{51} has a value of 4 determined for it, the children of N_{41} will only lower its value, and so the other children of N_{41} can be ignored. This form of pruning is called *bounding*.

Alpha-beta pruning, bounding, and level-limiting can all be incorporated into *NodeValue* to form:

function *PruneValue(gt,Choice,Bound,Level)*
  if *Level = 0* **then return endif**
  Choice ← NIL
  NoChild ← TRUE
  MaxValue ← *Bound*
  for *i = 1* **to** *MaxChild* **do**
   p ← *gt* ↑ .*Child*[*i*]
   if *p* ≠ NIL
    then *NoChild* ← FALSE
       v ← − *PruneChild(p,Choice,* − *Bound,Level* − *1)*
       if *v* > *MaxValue*
        then *MaxValue* ← *v*
          Choice ← *p* ↑ .*Child*[*i*]
       endif
    endif
   next *i*
  if *NoChild*
   then *v* ← *Bound*
   else *v* ← *MaxValue*
   endif
  p ↑ .*Value* ← *v*
  return *v*
  end {*PruneValue*

Exercise immediate application of text materials

EW.1 Show how the values of the interior nodes of GT$_1$ are derived from the values of terminal nodes.

Problems

PW.1 Draw the game tree for the game of NIM when $n = 6$. NIM is played by two alternating players, each of whom may pick up 1, 2, or 3 toothpicks from a pile that initially holds *n*. The player who empties the pile loses.

PW.2 Redesign *NodeValue* to be depth-limited.

PW.3 Write a search procedure that calls *NodeValue*.

Program   for trying it yourself

PGW.1   Write a program that creates 32 random leaf-node values in the range
$[-10 \, . \, . \, 10]$, builds a game tree from them, prunes it with *PruneValue*,
and displays the pruned tree.

Project   for fun; for serious students

PJW.1   Make PGW.1 a procedure, n leaf nodes a variable, and study the mean
and standard deviation of the nodes in the pruned trees as a function
of n.

REFERENCES

Adelson-Velskii, G. M. and E. M. Landis. *Soviet Math (Dokl.)* 3 (1962), 1259–1263.

Aho, Alfred V. and Jeffrey D. Ullman, *Principles of Compiler Design*, Addison-Wesley, 1977.

Bentley, Jon L., "Programming Pearls," *ACM Communications*, August, 1983 and thereafter.

Brodie, Leo, *Starting FORTH*, Prentice-Hall, 1981.

BYTE Magazine, August, 1980 (Issue on the FORTH language).

Even, Shimon, *Graph Algorithms*, Computer Science Press, 1979.

Intel, *The 8086 Family User's Manual*, Intel Corp., 1979.

Kernighan, B. W. and P. J. Plauger, *The Elements of Programming Style*, McGraw-Hill, 1974.

Knuth, Donald E., *The Art of Programming*, Vol. 1, Addison-Wesley, 1973.

Ledgard, Henry and Michael Marcotty, *The Programming Language Landscape*, SRA, 1981.

Roberts, Fred S., *Discrete Mathematical Models*, Prentice-Hall, 1976.

Roberts, Fred S., *Applied Combinatorics*, Prentice-Hall, 1984.

Sedgewick, Robert, *Algorithms*, Addison-Wesley, 1983.

STACK, IEEE Computer Society Journal, *Computer*, May 1977 (devoted to stack machines).

Tarjan, Robert E., *Data Structures and Network Algorithms*, SIAM, 1983.

Touretsky, David S., *LISP, A Gentle Introduction to Symbolic Computation,* Harper & Row, 1984.

Wirth, Nicklaus, *Algorithms + Data Structures = Programs,* Prentice-Hall, 1976.

INDEX